D1526124

The ETHICAL FOUNDATIONS *of* CRIMINAL JUSTICE

Richard A. Spurgeon Hall

with the assistance of
Carolyn Brown Dennis
Tere L. Chipman

CRC Press
Boca Raton London New York Washington, D.C.

Library of Congress Cataloging-in-Publication Data

Hall, Richard, 1946–
    The ethical foundations of criminal justice / by Richard Hall,
  with the assistance of Carolyn Brown Dennis, Tere Chipman.
        p.   cm.
    Includes bibliographical references and index.
    ISBN 0-8493-9116-4 (alk. paper)
        1. Criminal justice, Administration of — Moral and ethical aspects.
    2. Social ethics. I. Dennis, Carolyn Brown. II. Chipman, Tere.
    III. Title.
    HV7419.H35 1999
    364—dc21   99-33982
                                                                         CIP

No claim to original U.S. Government works
International Standard Book Number 0-8493-9116-4
Library of Congress Card Number 99-33982
Printed in the United States of America   2 3 4 5 6 7 8 9 0
Printed on acid-free paper

Preface

There is a dearth of textbooks at the undergraduate level that address the ethics of criminal justice. This book is intended to meet that need. Its purpose is to acquaint students with the basic concepts, arguments, and methods of ethics as these relate specifically to the field of criminal justice. The field of criminal justice, as its name suggests, is ripe for treatment from the standpoint of ethics or moral philosophy; it fairly bristles with topics and concepts inviting philosophical inquiry, with issues and problems requiring philosophical resolution. Although this is a book in the ethics of criminal justice — a domain of legal ethics which, in turn, is a branch of applied ethics — it is no less an introduction to theoretical ethics. Ideally, ethical theory would be studied in a separate course as a prerequisite for a second course in the ethics of criminal justice, but this is often not feasible. The only introduction students may have to philosophical ethics is through a course in applied ethics, but "applied" ethics presupposes that students have prior knowledge of some theory which is to be applied. Thus, this text is designed to serve the needs of not only students who have already taken a course in ethics but also those who are coming to the field for the first time. This book seeks to acquaint students with the theory to be applied. It briefly surveys the entire field of theoretical ethics, both normative ethical theories and the fundamentals of meta-ethics. Among other things, it introduces students to the classic theories of normative ethics. Each of these theories is given an impartial exposition, then subjected to a thorough critical evaluation to separate the salvageable ore from the dross. This procedure provides students with a model of critical thinking which, it is hoped, they will emulate in thinking through substantive moral issues for themselves. Moreover, the book contains a distinct unit devoted to those topics in the ethics of criminal justice which help define it as a distinct field within the province of legal ethics. However, a course in the ethics of criminal justice may not only be a student's first, and only, course in ethics, but also their first, and only, course in philosophy. Again, ideally, students would not venture into any course in ethics without first taking an introductory course in philosophy, but this ideal of a system of prerequisites is far from being realized on college campuses. So this book is designed to remedy this need by furnishing students with some of the most basic concepts and methods of philosophy they need for ethical reflection, and to show them how ethics is essentially related to other branches of philosophy, so that they might apply ethics to criminal justice in a philosophically sophisticated way. This book is specifically addressed to the needs of students specializing in criminal justice, criminology, law, and cognate fields. Although the text is designed to be understood by undergraduates, the level of discussion is at a depth and breadth to be of interest and use to graduate students, as well. The text, though it aspires to the maximum of clarity and cogency, does not "talk down" to its readers. It is my belief that students ever need to be increasing their vocabulary, not only by mastering the jargon of a particular field, but also by acquainting themselves with the widest range of nontechnical English vocabulary, one of the richest and most diversified of any language.

My view is that a textbook, however good, being a merely secondary source, is no adequate substitute for primary sources. Students, instead of working their way through the actual writings of philosophers and thereby learning how to read philosophy and to extricate and analyze arguments for themselves, rely on the textbook editor to do the work for them. This not only deprives them of the opportunity of learning how to read and think for themselves, but also limits them to the editor's interpretation of the primary sources which, for all they know, may be mistaken or one-sided. Furthermore, the editor may exclude things from discussion which are important or are of especial interest to a particular student. The typical thinking behind a textbook is that students are incapable of doing the research necessary for finding the important original sources in a field, and then of reading and understanding them. The point of a textbook is to simplify things as much as possible. The effect is rather like that of the mother bird who predigests her fledglings' food, so as to make it more digestible for them, and regurgitates it into their mouths. Textbooks too often are the literary equivalent of pabulum; they all read the same way, being written in a dull, innocuous, and nondescript style. This book does not pretend to escape these defects endemic to textbooks, but it does seek to mitigate them as far as possible. It does so in two ways: by providing quotations from primary sources, enabling students to compare their interpretations with mine and giving them a sense of the variety of literary styles used in philosophy, and by furnishing extensive footnotes, which will, it is hoped, both prompt and facilitate further research in the field, making the book especially useful to advanced students. This book should be taken minimally as a guide to the primary sources in the field. It will equip students with that set of concepts and methods which will enable them to do their own independent research if they so desire. Think of this book as a comprehensive and detailed atlas of the terrain of The Ethics of Criminal Justice. This is a book in applied ethics, and so the emphasis throughout is on practical issues and actual situations that the practitioners of criminal justice may typically encounter. Students will be encouraged to make rational and philosophically informed decisions in the face of some very perplexing choices. However, this book, because of its large section devoted to theoretical ethics, might be better regarded as less a textbook in applied ethics than as a textbook in ethics — with a specific application to moral issues in criminal justice. Not every moral issue in criminal justice is covered; for example, some issues pertaining to the courts and the behavior of attorneys and judges are omitted. It was thought that these issues were more appropriately treated by a book on legal ethics. Instead, this book concentrates largely on those moral issues most likely to be encountered by the police and other agents of law enforcement. As to any moral issue in policing that may have been left out or given short shrift, this book should give its readers sufficient grounding in theoretical ethics to enable them to work through that issue for themselves.

The authors

Richard A. Spurgeon Hall received his Ph.D. in philosophy from the University of Toronto. His specialties, other than ethics, include aesthetics, the philosphy of religion, and the history of American philosphy. Among his publications are a book and articles on the ethics of Jonathan Edwards, the premier 18th-century American philospher and theologian. He is currently an assistant professor of philosophy in the department of philosphy and religion at Methodist College in Fayetteville, NC. Previously, he taught at Clarkson University, S.U.N.Y. at Potsdam, and Kutztown University in Pennsylvania. While at Clarkson, he received an award for excellence in teaching. Hall is also a playwright and actor. He currently tours the country with his own play, *Spurgeon Speaks Again!*, a one-character play about the life and ideas of Charles Haddon Spurgeon, the great Baptist preacher of Victorian England who is Hall's great-great-grandfather.

Carolyn Brown Dennis was born and raised in Fayetteville, NC. After graduating from Meredith College, Raleigh, NC, with a Bachelor of Arts in Sociology and Religion, she returned to graduate school a few years later and received a Master of Criminal Justice from New Mexico State University, Las Cruces, NM. Her work experience includes over 5 years as a probation/parole officer and extensive work with people with a variety of problems. In addition, she has been a fundraiser for a major medical center and has served as a child support enforcement agent. Currently, Ms. Dennis is teaching freshman and sophomore students in the discipline of Criminal Justice at Fayetteville Technical Community College. She resides with her husband and their four dogs.

Tere L. Chipman was born in Louisville, KY, and is a graduate of Eastern Kentucky University and Webster University. She served 8 years in the U.S. Army as a Special Agent with the U.S. Army Criminal

Investigation Command. Subsequent to leaving the Army as a CWII, Ms. Chipman spent 4 years as a Criminal Justice Research Associate at the North Carolina Justice Academy located at Salemburg, NC. She is currently a member of the Criminal Justice faculty at Fayetteville Technical Community College in Fayetteville, NC.

Contents

Part four. Topics in the ethics of criminal justice

Dedication

To Eileen Marion Hall

part one

Preliminaries

chapter one

What is ethics or moral philosophy?

> CRITO: I agree with what you say, Socrates, but I wish you would consider what we ought to *do*.
>
> SOCRATES: Let us look at it together my dear fellow; and if you can challenge any of my arguments, do so and I will listen to you; but if you can't, be a good fellow and stop telling me over and over again that I ought to leave this place without official permission.
>
> —Plato (*Crito*)

Some moral dilemmas

A 1993 U.S. Supreme Court decision in a civil suit which drew wide outrage saw convicted subway mugger Bernard McCummings awarded $4.3 million in a suit he had brought against the City of New York. McCummings was shot twice in the back in 1984 by Transit Authority Officer Manuel Rodriguez as he attempted to flee a subway platform after beating and robbing a 71-year-old man. At the time of the crime, McCummings had just gotten out of prison for robbery. Since the shooting, McCummings, who was 23 years old when he was injured, has remained paralyzed from the chest down. After pleading guilty to the mugging, he was sentenced to prison, where he served 2 years. When McCummings brought suit against the City, however, a jury and appeals court found that the officers had used excessive force. Before paying the award, the City appealed to the Supreme Court. In upholding the cash award to McCummings, the Supreme

Court reiterated earlier rulings that police officers cannot use deadly force against unarmed fleeing suspects who pose no apparent threat to officers or to the public.

McCummings's victim, Jerome Sandusky, who was carrying less than $30 at the time he was attacked, decried the ruling, saying, "[I]t's justice turned upside down ... and it sends a terrible message that crime does pay. ...Ordinarily I would be sorry for anyone that was made a cripple, but he was made a cripple because of his own action." Gerald Arenberg, of the National Association of Chiefs of Police, sided with Sandusky. "The criminal is very well protected by the Supreme Court," Arenberg said in a national interview. Lawyers for the City were disappointed. "The message is," said one, when faced with a fleeing suspect, "it's probably wiser for a police officer to do nothing, in terms of civil liability."

Opinions on the case, however, varied. "It was the right decision," said David Breibart, McCummings' lawyer. "It gives me great faith in the system." A *Washington Post* editorial, in contrast, suggested that police are bound by the rules of fair play when criminals are not. "What if felons knew that cops could shoot them if they fled?" the editorial asked. "More of them would likely freeze and put up their hands. ...[C]riminal behavior should not be treated as if it were some sort of quasi-legitimate enterprise, governed by the laws of negligence. ...McCummings was as much a victim of his own criminality as he was of a violation of the rules regarding the use of deadly force. Once he chose to break the law he wasn't entitled to be compensated by it." McCummings' victim agreed. Recently, Sandusky filed suit against McCummings seeking to get the $4.3 million award. Sandusky brought suit under New York's modified "Son of Sam" law, which is intended to prevent criminals from profiting from their crimes.[1]

We have in the Bernard McCummings case a *bona fide* issue: There are two equally defensible sides, each boasting creditable defenders who gave plausible defenses of their respective positions. It is a classic legal issue which was addressed by three courts representing distinct levels of the judiciary. More fundamentally, it involves several perennial moral issues, a fact indicated by the public outrage elicited by McCummings' winning his suit. What are these specifically moral or ethical issues? One issue concerns whether or not a criminal suspect — who, it must be borne in mind, is nevertheless innocent until found guilty by a court — should lose any or all of his civil rights, among which are his rights to life and physical safety. A second moral issue is whether or not the interests of the state or community should take precedence over the interests of any individual, even if that individual is a suspected felon; in other words, should the personal good or well-being of any individual be sacrificed to promote the public good and welfare of society? A third such issue concerns the nature of justice. Is it just that McCummings won his case? Is it possible that the enactment of civil justice, of the sort McCummings enjoyed, may be in flagrant violation of the canons of a "higher" order of justice? And should the demand of strict justice, as represented by the rules of fair play, ever be compromised in the interest of protecting society? These are some of the moral conundrums raised by the McCummings case.

Let us take another case, that of Mark Fuhrman, the Los Angeles Police Department detective involved in the O.J. Simpson trial. The defense attorneys alleged that Fuhrman had planted a bloody glove at Simpson's estate and tampered with blood stains extracted from the Ford Bronco that Simpson drove in his effort to escape.[2] Now suppose, for the sake of argument, that Fuhrman did indeed plant the glove and tampered with blood stains. And, suppose further, that Fuhrman was privy to information that showed that Simpson was incontrovertibly guilty of the double murder; however, that information had been destroyed and so could never be submitted in court. Frustrated by this, Fuhrman decided to try to clinch Simpson's guilt by planting the glove and tampering with the blood. He might have rationalized his decision as follows: "If I manipulate the evidence, then Simpson's conviction is assured and justice is served. If I don't, then Simpson may go free and both justice and society are betrayed." The moral issues involved in this case are similar to those in the McCummings case. These concern the nature and value of justice and the weight that should be given to considerations of the public good in making a moral decision. But, more particularly, the Fuhrman case raises two related issues: (1) whether or not one should break one's moral obligation (i.e., the duty to be honest in all our dealings in order to meet another no less imperative obligation — the duty to further the cause of justice in all things); and (2) whether or not one should abandon one's duty, trust, or oath for the sake of the public good. In other words, do immoral means justify a higher moral end?

Consider one last case, this time entirely fictional, although disturbingly close to reality. It is the subject of a film, *Magnum Force*, starring Clint Eastwood. In this film, a group of vigilante policemen, led by no one less than the police chief himself, is frustrated by the enormity of crimes being committed with impunity. Known felons are acquitted on technicalities; notorious murderers, gangsters, and pimps escape apprehension and are left free to perpetuate their crimes. These policemen, then, decide to take the law into their own hands. They bypass due process by secretly assassinating criminals who elude the law's net. Harry (the character played by Clint Eastwood), who is investigating the string of assassinations, comes to the startling realization that they are being carried out by members of his own police force. He is invited to join the vigilantes, who seek to persuade him of the merits of their cause by explaining that in a perfectly just society all their victims would have been convicted and punished anyway. They are merely rectifying the failures of the law and its officers in the name of abstract justice and the common good. Harry unambiguously declines their invitation and responds by reminding them that the currently constituted legal system, however inept it may be in the ministrations of justice, is still the best we have. He cautions them, moreover, that the means by which they are attempting to realize their utopian dream of justice may turn that dream into a nightmare. To what lengths are they prepared to go? Are they prepared to execute speeders or owners of dogs which foul the sidewalk, if this is what it takes to usher in the rule of perfect justice? Harry thus echoes the words of Sir Thomas More in Robert Bolt's play, *A Man for All Seasons*. John Roper, More's future son-in-law, urges him, as Lord Chancellor of England, to arrest a man on no definite charge. More protests that he will do no such illegal thing, even if it might benefit him in the short term. His rationale is as follows: "This country's planted thick with laws from coast to coast — man's laws, not God's — and if you cut them down — and you're just the man to do it — d'you really think you could stand upright in the winds that would blow then?"[3]

The above cases vividly illustrate the moral issues raised by the following: (1) conflict between the moral promptings of private conscience and the legal demands of the state; (2) conflict between doing one's duty and pursuing the public good; (3) conflict (particularly onerous) among our duties; (4) the question of whether even the noblest ends ever justify immoral means; (5) the nature of justice, and the tension between the imperfect order of civil justice and the uncompromising standards of absolute justice; and (6) the meaning of a civil or natural right, and the potential conflict between that right and the demands of justice or the need to ensure the common good.

These issues are also prime examples of moral dilemmas. Dilemmas catch us off guard. We do not seek them, and we cannot escape them. Any way out of them will be problematic; any choice we make may be condemned by somebody. Expressed colloquially, dilemmas put us between a rock and a hard place; they are cases of your being damned if you do and damned if you don't. The source of these dilemmas is a conflict between obligations, principles, or values — in brief, it is a conflict between loyalties. In the McCummings case, the conflict is between Rodriguez's obligation to maintain law and order and his obligation to honor the rights and to safeguard the life of a criminal suspect. In the case of Fuhrman, the conflict is between his duty to be honest and his loyalty to the order of justice. Finally, in *Magnum Force*, Harry had to decide between his duty to uphold the principles of law and due process and his commitment to the ideal of moral justice.

How, then, might we resolve these conflicts, how might we extricate ourselves from these dilemmas? The rational way is to engage in the discipline of ethics or moral philosophy. Let us begin describing this discipline by distinguishing it from some allied areas — namely, morality and law — with which it is often confused.

Ethics and morality

Morality has to do, most generally, with the totality of our relationships with others. More specifically, it is the entire system of laws, principles, rules, and values by which we regulate our individual and social lives and conduct. It specifies our duties or obligations to others and to society, establishes standards of right and wrong conduct, and reflects society's understanding of the nature of moral good and evil. Some of these principles and values are enshrined in the moral codes of the world's great religions, such as the Decalogue (Ten Commandments) common to both Judaism and Christianity, or in the codes of civil law found in any civilized society, such as the Constitutional Law of the United States and the Common Law of Great Britain. Some, however, are so fundamental and pervasive in our thinking and living that they hardly need to be formalized in any code. Such is the principle of fairness. The youngest children, as soon as they are able to speak, are quite capable of uttering, "It's not fair." It is almost as if certain moral judgments were innate or imprinted in our minds before birth.

Thus, morality is fundamentally a social system wherein we find ourselves. None can escape its domain, because, as Aristotle long ago observed, "Man is a social animal."[4] We are inextricably bound up in what Joseph Butler, an 18th-century Anglican bishop and moral philosopher, called the "moral institution"[5] of life, which is allied with such other great human institutions as law, religion, science, and art. A Robinson Crusoe, perhaps, is outside this moral/milieu until, of course, he meets his Friday. Jonathan Edwards, America's premier philosopher and theologian, declared, "Moral agents are *social*; affairs of morality are affairs of society."[6] The moral realm is thoroughly social with respect to its origins, functions, and sanctions:

1. Its laws and values originate and abide in a society.
2. One of its principal functions is to promote social cohesion, stability, peace, and prosperity.
3. The infraction or flouting of moral laws and values can bring into play sanctions enforced by public opinion and civil codes.

Morality is a social institution, but it nevertheless allows and even encourages, especially in our Western tradition, individual dissent from and criticism of the governing mores in the name of personal autonomy and responsibility, though just how far depends on the political and legal institutions of that society. Individuals come to have the moral codes they have by internalizing those of their social environment, which includes the institutions of family, religion, and society. But certain exceptional individuals — moral heroes, we might call them — are somehow able to transcend the moral codes long entrenched and hallowed in their social group so as to criticize and improve upon them. Such was Jesus, who declared, "Think not that I have come to abolish the law and the prophets; ...but to fulfill them;"[7] or Jeremiah and other Old Testament prophets who sought to bring the people to a deeper understanding of the Law; or the Abolitionists who routinely committed acts of civil disobedience in response to a higher moral calling.

Ethics, or moral philosophy, though belonging to the moral institution of life, is a step removed. It takes within its purview all the elements of morality (e.g., moral laws, rules, principles, values) with the aim of reflecting on them *critically*. Its function is to establish the criteria for sound moral judgments or to construct rational justifications for our moral principles. According to Melden, "The history of moral philosophy can be summed up as the history of the attempt of philosophers to clarify the conditions and criteria of moral reasonableness, of that reasonableness in conduct and attitudes that distinguishes the moral person, in the best sense of that term, from the nonmoral or immoral person."[8]

Ethics and law

"Law" in this case refers to the body of statutes or rules found in various codes of civil (manmade) law.[9] In the U.S., these include state and federal laws which are designed, among other things, to regulate commerce and the transfer of property, to protect our civil rights, and to promote the public safety. The principles determining and governing these ordinances are enshrined in the traditions of common law and constitutional law. The political agencies entrusted with making, enforcing, and interpreting these laws are the legislative and judiciary branches, respectively, of both the federal and the state governments.

To some degree, the moral code is coextensive with the legal code. Thus, we find laws proscribing murder and theft in both the Decalogue and the Criminal Code. However, there is not necessarily a one-to-one correlation between the moral and the legal codes. Some moral laws (e.g., Christ's commandment that his disciples love their enemies) are not reflected in any of our civil statutes. And, of course, there are many criminal laws (e.g., the rules of the road) that find no correspondence in any moral code. In other words, the moral institution of life is distinct from the legal institution.

This is evident in three ways. First, moral laws are typically thought to be universally binding; civil laws are not. Laws proscribing murder and theft are found everywhere in the world, but the laws (say, controlling speed limits) change from nation to nation, even from state to state.

Second, the moral law may be in conflict with the civil law. For instance, the laws segregating the races in the American South before enactment of the civil rights legislation in the 1960s, the apartheid laws of South Africa before the Mandela regime, and the many laws restricting Jews in Nazi Germany, though all perfectly "legal", were clearly immoral. The potential conflict between the moral and the civil law makes for cases of "liberty of conscience" or "civil disobedience". Henry David Thoreau, Mahatma Gandhi, and Martin Luther King, Jr., for example, all broke civil laws which they thought to be in violation of some moral law. They thought only by breaking immoral civil laws could they obey the moral law; to do otherwise would be to break a higher law and so violate their conscience.

Third, the moral law applies not only to our overt actions, but equally to our inner dispositions and motives. It is not enough merely to refrain from doing a bad thing, but we must not even want or intend to do it. Merely the desire or intention of doing evil, though we are thwarted in our efforts to act on it, is sufficient for us to stand condemned by the moral law. Jesus powerfully expresses the moral law's hold even over our hearts when he warns, "You have heard that it was said, 'You shall not commit adultery.' But I say to you that everyone who looks at a woman lustfully has already committed adultery with her in his heart."[10] The moral law's profound grip is a matter of common experience. All of us have felt the pangs of conscience, even after doing things which are quite legal. By contrast, the law is concerned only with our overt actions, not with the quality of our character. Only if we actually break the law are such things as motives considered either to establish or mitigate guilt. When Dietrich Bonhoeffer, the Protestant pastor, theologian, and martyr, conspired to kill Hitler, it is unlikely that he had any twinge of conscience.

Ethics and social science

Moral philosophy can be easily criticized for failing to come up with any decisive answers to the moral perplexities that confront us. After a period of about two and a half millennia, philosophers are no closer to answers than they were at the start. It has been suggested that others should conduct the inquiry into what we ought to do. And who are better qualified than social scientists — psychologists, sociologists, and anthropologists — whose business it is to study human behavior, both individual and collective? After all, they must be the best qualified for such an undertaking, as they use the scientific method and can get empirically verifiable results. Perhaps they can find answers to the eternal question of what we ought to do and its cognates where moral philosophers have notoriously failed.

Even the much vaunted scientific method, the theories of human nature, and the vast store of evidence that social scientists have at their disposal, however, are inadequate (even irrelevant) for addressing the great questions of ethics and resolving our moral dilemmas. Social science can be of no help in arbitrating conflicts between moral rules and obligations. For example, it could not have helped Rodriguez in the McCummings case to decide between his duty to maintain law and order and his duty to honor the rights of a suspect, or Fuhrman to choose between his obligation to truthfulness and his loyalty to justice. Moreover, social science cannot define ideal justice or specify exactly the proper balance between the individual's rights and freedom and the demands of the state. Nor can it help us much in determining whether a vague moral rule applies in a given case, such as whether abortion is really murder or whether Rodriguez was really guilty of using excessive force against McCummings. Finally, anthropology can fully describe, document, and theorize about the moral practices of different cultures — for example, the practice of female circumcision in the Sudan or bride-burning in India — but it can say nothing about whether or not these practices are morally acceptable.

The reason that the social sciences are powerless to help us resolve these issues is because they, in virtue of their being sciences, are *descriptive* disciplines; they are principally concerned with what *is* the case. The issues in question, however, are all *normative* in character, which means that their resolution depends ultimately upon a method of moral evaluation, not factual description. Now, moral philosophy, whatever its defects and failures, is preeminently a normative or *prescriptive* discipline; it is principally concerned with what *ought* to be the case. It is especially rich in the criteria and methods of evaluation, developed over a very long history, which are appropriate to ethical questions. Moral philosophy is adept in clarifying the nature and criteria of valid moral judgments. Social science, for all its prestige as a science (although its reputation in this regard is far from untarnished), is no adequate substitute for ethics. Anthropology, sociology, and psychology are not qualified methodologically or conceptually to usurp the domain traditionally held by moral philosophy. Nevertheless, the social sciences do have a role to play in moral philosophy. They provide pertinent background (indispensable facts and theories of human behavior) to ethical inquiry; they furnish, as it were, empirical grist for the philosophical mill. The relevance of social science to ethics will be spelled out in more detail in a subsequent chapter.

Ethics and philosophy

What, then, is ethics or moral philosophy? Let us begin with their etymological definitions. The root word of "ethics" is *ethos*, a Greek work meaning "customs", "habitual behavior", or "character". The root word of "moral" is *mores*, the Latin word for "behavior", "character", or "morals". Something of their root meanings is still reflected in the current usage of these words. "Ethics" still connotes character, and "morality" yet suggests morals and character, and both refer to behavior. Incidentally, the expression "moral philosophy" used to have a much wider reference. In the 18th century, for example, it referred to any investigation of the human world — the study of human nature, history, society, law, etc. — in addition to what we now mean by "ethics". In other words, "moral philosophy" referred to what we currently refer to as the social sciences — psychology, sociology, anthropology (and history, if one considers it a science).

But what is the current understanding of ethics as a philosophical discipline? Ethics is a branch of philosophy, so it is appropriate to look first at the meaning of "philosophy" as this is the trunk of the tree of which ethics is a branch. Right away, however, we encounter a problem — namely, the meaning of "philosophy". The definition of philosophy is itself a philosophical problem, which has invited some facetious answers. For example, a philosopher has been compared to a blind man in a dark room looking for a black cat that is not even there. However, as in other cases, the best place to start in coming to understand philosophy is to begin with its etymological definition. "Philosophy" is derived from two Greek words, *philos* ("love") and *sophia* ("wisdom"). In its original sense, then, "philosophy" means "love of wisdom". But then the question arises, "What is wisdom?" For Socrates, it is an awareness of one's own ignorance, of the limits of one's knowledge; for Aristotle, it was understanding the causes of things. This concept of philosophy as the love of wisdom held sway until the end of the Middle Ages.

A traditional task of philosophy has been the attempt to see things in their entirety. Halverson has written, "Philosophy is man's quest for the unity of knowledge: it consists in a perpetual struggle to create the concepts in which the universe can be conceived as a universe and not a multiverse."[11] Today, the field of human knowledge has become fragmented. The reason is that the sheer amount of human knowledge, which is ever increasing, can no longer be comprehended by a single mind. Ever-increasing specialization is now the rule. However, philosophers have long harbored the hope of disclosing the interconnections among the various departments of knowledge, of unifying them according to a few simple principles. Think of a gargantuan jigsaw puzzle made up of numberless pieces. There is no picture — indeed, there may be none at all — on the box to guide you. You must put the puzzle together out of the daunting jumble of jigsaw pieces as best you can. The jigsaw pieces are myriad bits of information we have about the world. The philosopher aspires to put them together to make a coherent picture or pattern of reality. St. Thomas Aquinas and G.F. Hegel are pre-eminent examples of philosophers who have sought to construct a systematic view of the world. They are nicknamed, aptly enough, "system builders". Philosophers today, however, have largely given up on this constructive, synthetic goal of philosophy because, among other things, of the explosion of knowledge that has engulfed us in the last 100 years. A trace of this grandiose task of philosophy is found today in the work of cosmologists who are attempting to reduce all the forces of nature (gravity, magnetism, electricity) to a unified field theory.

Instead of *synthesis*, contemporary philosophers emphasize another traditional task of philosophy, namely, that of critical *analysis* — instead of building things up, analysis breaks them down into their clearest terms. This is the more modest task of philosophy as envisioned by the seminal 17th-century English philosopher, John Locke, who thought the philosopher to be best "employed as an underlaborer in clearing the ground a little, and removing some of the rubbish that lies in the way to knowledge," and so keep the estate of science in good order. This meant clarifying the language of science. Locke complained, "Vague and insignificant forms of speech, and abuse of language, have so long passed for mysteries of science; and hard and misapplied words, with little or no meaning, have by prescription, such a right to be mistaken for deep learning and height of speculation."[12] The analytic task of philosophy is to render our basic concepts, especially those endemic to science, crystal clear and to make sure that the logic of our language is consistent. Bertrand Russell, the distinguished English philosopher of this century, echoing his great predecessor Locke, gave expression to this task of philosophy as fundamentally conceptual analysis: "The most important part (of philosophy) ... consists in criticizing and clarifying notions which are apt to be regarded as fundamental and accepted uncritically. As instances I might mention: mind, matter, consciousness, knowledge, experience, causality, will, time. I believe all these notions to be inexact and approximate, essentially infected with vagueness, incapable of forming part of any exact science."[13] Charles S. Peirce, the great American philosopher at the turn of the century, epitomized this approach to philosophy in the title of a seminal article, "How To Make Our Ideas Clear."

All definitions of "philosophy" are but variations of these two basic conceptions of the task of philosophy — philosophy as synthesis or as analysis; the one is a constructive endeavor, the other a critical one. These two concepts are not mutually exclusive. Constructive philosophers avoid the preliminary task of analysis at their peril, and philosophers concerned principally with the minutiae of analysis can ill afford to ignore the larger picture. Whatever one's conception of the

philosophical enterprise, it can be safely said that philosophy minimally involves our taking stock of all our beliefs — beliefs about the
world, nature, God, good and evil — and then weighing them, one by
one, to determine which ones really do hold water and are worthy of
our assent.

The fields of philosophy

However, any definition of "philosophy" that may be given is going
to be inadequate. The best way to understand what philosophy is, is
to eavesdrop on philosophers at work, to take note of the sort of
questions they address, and to follow their thought processes as they
endeavor to answer them. Philosophy is fundamentally a problem-
solving activity; it attempts to answer systematically certain kinds of
questions. Indeed, "philosophy" is defined by the very questions that
philosophers typically raise. What are these questions? In a small
book entitled *Introduction to Logic*, published in 1800, Immanual Kant,
the great German philosopher, succinctly posed the questions that
drive philosophy as follows: What can I know? What can I hope?
What is man? What ought I to do?

Let's begin with the question of "What can I know?" There is
much that I think I know. I apparently know something about the
world and my fellow human beings. I have knowledge of those things
studied by physics, biology, history, and psychology. There is that
vast store of knowledge that is science. But can I know anything about
God, about whether He exists, and, if He does, about His nature? Can
I know anything about the nature of good and evil? Science is knowledge. But is the converse true — is all knowledge science? Is there
perhaps any such thing as nonscientific knowledge, a knowledge that
is acquired independently of the scientific method through, say, intuition, some mystical apprehension, or revelation? Or, is the whole
concept of nonscientific knowledge an oxymoron? A related question
is "What is the difference between knowledge and opinion?" How
can I tell whether any of my beliefs constitutes genuine knowledge
rather than mere opinion? Again, how do I know what I think I
know? What is the best means for acquiring knowledge? Is it experience, or pure thought, or a combination of both? Finally, are there any
limits to what I can know? Can I, in theory, know everything there is
to know? Or are there certain parts of reality which will always be
shrouded in mystery? Is there any such thing as absolutely certain
knowledge, or does all knowledge just exhibit different degrees of

probability? The various attempts to answer these questions have given rise to a subfield of philosophy known as *epistemology*. This word is derived from the Greek words *episteme* ("knowledge") and *logos* ("word" or "reason"). Epistemology, then, is the theory of knowledge, with respect to its nature, extent, and method of acquisition.

A second great question of philosophy is "What may I hope?" May I hope for life after death? May I hope that there is a purpose or meaning to human existence, or even the existence of the world? Are the courses of human and natural events leading inexorably to the realization of some cosmic end? Questions concerning the purpose or meaning of life belong to the field of *teleology*, the name of which is derived from the Greek root *telos*, which means goal, end, or purpose. Teleology, then, is the study of purposes.

However, answers to the question of what may I hope presuppose an answer to the more fundamental question of what is there in the world. Presumably, there are physical things investigated by the natural science — things such as stars, planets, rocks, minerals, plants, and animals. But, is there another kind of thing which includes entities such as souls and minds? Is there a God and an afterlife? The study of what there is, and the related question of what is truly real as opposed to what is merely apparent and illusory, is called *ontology*. "Ontology" is derived from the Greek root *ontos* ("being"), so ontology is the science of being, or reality, or what there is. The systematic study of the afterlife is called *eschatology*, a term derived from the Greek word *eschatos*, meaning "further". Eschatology, then, is the study of the last things, not only of what comes after death, but also of what comes at the end of history or time. Eschatology is a branch of theology. Whether or not there is a God, who is capable of framing and implementing purposes in the world, or a hereafter, wherein we might experience the final denouement of things, is going to be relevant as grounds of hope. If God exists, and more specifically if there is an afterlife, then we have substantial grounds for hope.

On the other hand, if there is neither God nor an afterlife, then human existence is without purpose and meaning. It is, in Macbeth's terrible words, "a tale Told by an idiot, full of sound and fury, Signifying nothing,"[14] and so affording scant grounds for hope. Teleology, ontology, and eschatology are all branches of the discipline known as *metaphysics*. This word is derived from the Greek expression, *meta ta Physika*, which means "beyond or after physics". This expression was first used by Andronicus of Rhodes about 70 B.C. as an arbitrary title for a collection of Aristotle's miscellaneous writings.

These writings were found outside Aristotle's famous treatise en-titled *Physics* and so were collectively designated by Andronicus as "beyond physics".

The next great question is "What is man?" or, to put it in more contemporary terms, "What is it to be human or a person?" Some say that we are creatures uniquely struck in the image of God, but others claim that we are merely the accidental byproducts of a blind, evolu-tionary process. The psalmist asked, "What is man that thou art mindful of him, and the son of man that thou dost care for him?"[15] Are we fallen angels or risen apes? The study of human nature is under-taken not only by philosophy, but also by the social sciences of psy-chology, sociology, and anthropology.

We come now to the last of the great questions that Kant thought constituted the field of philosophy: "What ought I to do?" Cognate questions are how should I treat my neighbor? What are my duties and obligations? What is the meaning of "good", "evil", "right", and "wrong"? What is the good life? What should be my goal or end in life? What is the good that I should single-mindedly pursue? All these are questions addressed by ethics or moral philosophy.

Socrates thought that the question of how one ought to live was the supreme question of life, not just of philosophy. Certainly it is a question, like the other philosophical questions, that we cannot avoid even if we wished. The specific question of how we ought to act in any given situation, or the more general question of how we ought to conduct our lives, is an example of what the great American philoso-pher and psychologist, William James, called "genuine options".[16] A genuine option is *living, forced*, and *momentous*. First, a living option is a choice between two practically feasible courses of action. A career choice between becoming a lawyer or a physician is a choice between two real possibilities which might be of interest to one. By contrast, a dead option is a choice between two completely implausible courses. Thus, a career choice between becoming an alchemist or a slave trader is purely academic as neither is a real possibility. Second, a forced option is a choice between two courses of action which we must make; indeed, to refuse to make a choice itself constitutes a choice. Hamlet's choice between living or committing suicide, poignantly proposed in his "to be or not to be" soliloquy, is impossible for him to avoid, so much so that if he chooses not to decide — to put off the decision — then he has in fact made a real enough choice to live. On the other hand, an avoidable option is a choice between two courses of action that we do not have to make. Thus, the choice of eating at Hardee's or at Burger King may be avoided altogether by choosing to eat at neither place but opting instead to eat at McDonald's. Finally, a momentous option is one which is unique, where the consequences either way are significant, and where the decision either way is irrevocable. Such an option is the choice between marrying someone or not, or betting all your life's savings on a horse race or not. Robert Frost memorializes a momentous option in his poem "The Road Not Taken": "Two roads diverged in a woods, and I/I took the one less traveled by/And that has made all the difference."[17] In contrast to this is the trivial option of whether or not to choose vanilla or chocolate ice cream for desert. A mother's decision either to have an abortion or to give birth to her child, the jurist's decision either to vote or not to vote for the death penalty in a capital case, and Truman's decision either to bomb or not to bomb Hiroshima are all examples of moral dilemmas which are truly momentous options.

The decision to ignore these questions, as not being worth our time or effort to answer, is itself a morally significant decision. By contrast, ethics urges us to take these questions very seriously and gives us the tools and techniques to answer them rationally. Ethics cannot promise to give us the correct answers, because there are not any. But it can give us ways to substantiate our answers and so help us to live with them. This much we know: The life of reason is superior to the alternative.

There is yet another subfield of philosophy that Kant did not explicitly mention because, perhaps, it is so fundamental. "Logic" is derived from the Greek word, *logos* ("speech", "reason", or "theory"), a root that provides the suffix not only for "epistemo*logy*," but also for many other academic disciplines, as well: bio*logy*, zoo*logy*, geo*logy*, psycho*logy*, anthropo*logy*, etc. This is appropriate because logic is at the root of all other academic disciplines as well as philosophy itself. Josiah Royce, the great American philosopher at the turn of the century, once compared logic to the kitchen in a house. Just as a house is uninhabitable without a kitchen, the mansion of philosophy cannot be lived in intellectually without logic. Logic is the fundamental discipline of philosophy insofar as it provides the field with its method and many of its most basic concepts. To use another analogy, logic is the indispensable toolbox of philosophy. The tasks of logic, then, include the evaluation of arguments as to their validity and the identification of fallacious reasoning. Ethics has recourse to logic, as it is concerned with the evaluation of moral arguments. We shall have more to say about logic in a subsequent chapter.

Epistemology, metaphysics, logic, and ethics are not the only subfields of philosophy, but they are the central ones which determine the nature and methods of the field and inform all its other branches. Thus, philosophy of law is another subfield of philosophy. Its operative questions are what is the nature of law and from whence comes its authority. These questions are related to those of metaphysics and ethics. Philosophy of art, or aesthetics, has to do with the nature, theory, and value of art. Its operative questions are what is art and how ought we to evaluate it. Its question concerning aesthetic value is related to ethics, which is concerned with another kind of value, namely, moral value. Social and political philosophy are concerned with the nature of the good society, the theory of justice, and the ideal polity. These issues, of course, represent the extension of ethics from the private to the public realm.

These various branches of philosophy, then, though distinguishable as independent subfields of the same discipline, are interrelated. Inquiry within any one of them will necessarily impinge upon others. Think of philosophy as a vast mansion and its various subfields as rooms within it. Each room has doors opening into other rooms or to corridors which connect the rooms. In the same way, each subfield of philosophy has doors which lead us into other subfields. And just as one cannot live a full domestic life confined to just a single room of a house, one cannot inhabit exclusively but a single field of philosophy in order to have a full and complete understanding of it. Take, for example, ethics. Ethics has doors opening to other subfields of philosophy. Thus, the ethical issue of whether there is such a thing as natural law which transcends and sanctions all civil laws and to which civil laws, to be valid, must conform is fundamentally a metaphysical issue. It is also related to political philosophy. So, too, does the moral issue of whether any one of us is really responsible for our actions depend for its resolution on whether or not we have free will, an issue again of metaphysics, as well as of philosophical psychology. The issue of the origin of so-called moral laws and the source of their authority is related to the metaphysical issues of whether there is a God and an afterlife. Obviously, whether or not there is a God who holds us accountable is going to have some bearing on our conduct. Feodor Dostoevski made the terrible observation that if God does not exist then anything is permissible, such as the Holocaust. Moreover, whether or not there is a life after death — that is, perhaps, a final judgment, heaven or hell — must have an impact on how we behave. Finally, the question as to what constitutes an authentically good life for human beings depends for its answer on some theory of human nature, an issue of anthropology and psychology. And so it goes.

The branches of ethics

Ethics is a branch of philosophy, but, more immediately, it is a branch of the philosophical discipline called *axiology*, a word derived from the Greek word *axios*, which means "value" or "worthy". Axiology, then, is the general theory of value or good. Its operative questions include: What is the nature of value or goodness? What types of value or good are there? By what criteria is something deemed valuable or good? And is value or goodness an objectively real part of the universe? Now, one type of value or goodness, and the one we shall be principally concerned with defining and understanding, is so-called *moral* or ethical value or good, such as justice, courage, and temperance, but there are other kinds of value. Another kind is so-called *aesthetic* value, such as beauty and sublimity, which is typically exhibited in works of fine art and certain works of nature. Thus, we speak of a beautiful painting or landscape, or of a sublime piece of music or poem. The study of aesthetic value is the province of *aesthetics* (derived from the Greek word *aesthetikos* meaning "perceptive"), which is coordinate with ethics as another branch of axiology. Moral and aesthetic values do not exhaust the domain of value or goodness; there are other kinds of values, such as religious values (holiness) and cognitive values (truth), which also come within the purview of axiology.

Ethics is divided into three subfields: *normative ethics, metaethics,* and *applied ethics*. Normative ethics, as its qualifier suggests, has to do with norms or standards of conduct. More specifically, it has to do with the rational justification or logical defense of those principles or rules of conduct whereby we regulate our behavior. Let us illustrate this with the case of Fuhrman who, as suggested, may have been tempted to tamper with the evidence in order to guarantee the conviction of a man whom he knows with certainty to be a murderer. Suppose that he succumbs to the temptation. His simply deciding to tamper with the evidence is a moral or ethical decision. If he gave it no prior thought, or merely acted on a gut instinct, he did not engage in ethical reflection. However, his decision to tamper may have been the result of a chain of reasoning like this:

> If I tamper with the evidence and secure a conviction,
> a notorious and proven felon will be imprisoned for

life, with society as the beneficiary. However, if I do
not tamper with it, then the felon will go free and the
public will stand to suffer. Now, one of my rules or
principles in acting is always to consider the consequences for society at large. If I determine that a proposed course of action will have the effect of harming
others, then I always refrain from it. However, if I
determine that such a course will result in benefiting
the majority of people, then I am resolved to pursue it.
Now, in the case at hand, clearly the way to benefit
society is to ensure the imprisonment of a public enemy. It is true that in doing so I shall be guilty of
violating my professional code of conduct by perpe-
trating a lie, but this, I think, is justified by consideration of the public good — the end here definitely
justifies the means. Hence, I have no hesitation in tampering with the evidence.

Fuhrman, however, might have engaged in another chain of reasoning
which would result in the opposite conclusion. He may have instead
flatly refused to tamper with the evidence, and reflected as follows:

If I tamper with the evidence and so guarantee the
conviction of this known felon, which undoubtedly
would be for the public good, I would have still done
wrong in three ways: I would have broken my oath to
uphold my professional code of conduct, I would have
lied, and I would have set a bad example and precedent, which, in the long run, could have deleterious
consequences for the whole of society. Although I am
mindful of the consequences of any action and by no
means indifferent to their importance, the ends, however noble and salutary, can never justify the means. I
believe that there are certain moral laws which are
objective, absolute, universally binding on all human
beings, and divinely sanctioned. These rules can never
be violated for the sake of some expediency. Therefore,
I am firmly resolved not to tamper with the evidence,
even at the risk of eventually harming the public.

To act consciously according to some moral principle, either a
principle of promoting the public good or a principle of conforming
to some moral law, is better than just acting on a hunch. However, to
act consciously according to some clearly articulated moral principle

brings us only to the threshold of normative ethical theory. We can be said to engage in normative ethical theory only when we begin to give a rational justification or systematic defense of our rule or principle of conduct, whatever that may be. Thus, when we give our *reasons* for believing that either our actions should always be determined by considerations of the public welfare or there really exists some moral law to which our actions should conform, then we are engaged in normative ethical theory.

Metaethics, as the name suggests, is a discipline that is "beyond" or "after" ethics in the sense that it does not seek to justify any moral principle or rule of conduct, but seeks instead to give a rational critique of the language and logic of normative ethical theory. It attempts to clarify the meaning of ethical discourse and evaluate the logic of its argumentation. It thus represents a "higher" discipline within the domain of ethics. A typical question of metaethics is this: What exactly is the meaning of the term "good"? Is it reducible to "happiness" or "pleasure"? Or, though associated with these qualities, does it perhaps mean something else entirely? Another question is how is it possible to derive an "ought" from an "is"? Suppose a mother tells her son to clean his room. He asks, "Why?" She replies, "Because I am your mother." Her argument boils down to this: (1) I am your mother; (2) therefore, you ought to clean your room. The logical problem with this inference is that the conclusion (2), which is a *prescriptive* statement, is derived from the premise (1), which is a *descriptive* statement. But how can one validly infer a command from a factual description? To do so is to commit the so-called naturalistic fallacy. We shall discuss this problem, and its possible solution, in more detail in a subsequent chapter on metaethics; it is mentioned here simply to serve as an illustration of the kind of questions addressed by this branch of ethics.

Finally, there is applied ethics, which, as the name suggests, is the application of both normative and metaethical theory to the solution of practical moral problems. The major fields of applied ethics are environmental, business (professional), medical, and legal. Environmental ethics, for example, addresses questions concerning the "rights" and moral status of nonhuman species. Business ethics typically treats the moral responsibilities of employers to employees and of corporations to consumers, the state, and the environment. Medical ethics basically has to do with the moral issues pertaining to a woman's right to an abortion, the practice of euthanasia, and genetic engineering. Legal ethics is principally concerned with the responsibilities of the judiciary (e.g., lawyers, judges, courts) to the citizenry and the state. The ethics of criminal justice is a branch of legal ethics.

It should be obvious that these various subfields of ethics — normative ethics, metaethics, and applied ethics — though distinct, cannot be studied in isolation from one another. Normative ethics provides the conceptual grist for the mill of metaethics, and without an application to life theoretical ethics is merely an emasculated and idle academic game. Indeed, to treat the question of how one ought to live as unrelated to life is oxymoronic.

Ethics and other academic disciplines

Ethics bears on virtually every other academic discipline, particularly the theoretical and applied sciences. Every academic field of study, for example, proscribes in no uncertain terms vices such as cheating and plagiarism, the presupposition being that honesty is good and dishonesty is bad. Even the sciences, though apparently normatively neutral, insist on probity on the part of their investigators; falsification of data constitutes nothing less than treason to the very ethos of science. And scientists who must experiment on animals or use human subjects have to adhere to strict guidelines governing these procedures; the assumptions here are that cruelty to animals is wrong and that the lives, health, and dignity of human beings are sacrosanct. The field of criminal justice especially is fraught with moral assumptions concerning the apprehension and interrogation of criminal suspects, the treatment of prisoners, the gathering of evidence, and the relations of law enforcement officers to the general public.

In some cases, the moral values presupposed by and governing a field are made fully explicit, such as in the Hippocratic oath of medicine or the various codes of professional conduct in law enforcement. In other cases, though, the moral values of a field remain unacknowledged; indeed, they are sometimes smuggled in under the ruse of normative neutrality. This is the case with economics. Karl Marx's labor theory of value pretends to be a morally neutral scientific principle.[18] It states that a commodity's value is a function of the quantity of labor required to produce it. The theory then goes on to imply that workers cannot possibly be compensated for the full value of their labor in a capitalist society; hence, capitalism is unjust. Although Marxists are sharp-eyed enough in seeing the moral defect in capitalism, they are surprisingly blind to the defects in the moral value implicit in their own labor theory of value. It is by no means clear that a commodity's value is only a function of the amount of labor required to produce it. There are other factors relevant to the determination of the value of a commodity — for example, the *quality* of labor expended in its production, or the kind of skills needed to produce it, or the value or importance of the product to consumers. Now, an invaluable function of ethics is to ferret out in any field all such hidden moral assumptions and to subject them to a rigorous, critical examination to determine whether there are rational grounds for their acceptance.

The value of ethics

What benefit is there in studying ethics? Unfortunately, the study of ethics will not necessarily make you a more moral person. You may in fact be expert in moral philosophy, able to rattle off normative ethical theories, adept in metaethical analysis, and astute in seeing the applications of moral theory to moral practice, yet be a moral moron in terms of your own personal conduct. Plato fondly believed that if you only knew what was good you could not help but become so; however, our experience is quite otherwise. We typically know what is good, what we ought to do, and where our duty lies, but we perversely ignore or refuse to do it. No one gave more succinct and eloquent expression to this diremption between the intellect and the will, the head and the heart, than Portia in Shakespeare's *The Merchant of Venice*:[19]

> If to do were as easy as to know what were good to do, chapels had been churches, and poor men's cottages princes' palaces. It is a good divine that follows his own instructions. I can easier teach twenty what were good to be done than to be one of the twenty to follow mine own teaching. The brain may devise laws for the blood, but a hot temper leaps o'er a cold decree.

What the study of ethics can do for you is this, which is no small thing:

1. Give you a clearer, richer, and more subtle understanding of the meaning of key ethical concepts such as good, bad, right, wrong, and ought. You will discover that these concepts are by no means clearly and precisely understood, but, because you use them daily and they inform your evaluations of the world, it behooves you to understand them better.

2. Show what reasons might be adduced in support of your moral code, or the rules or principles whereby you guide your conduct. The ability to justify rationally your code or rules of conduct will give you greater confidence in them and may provide an extra incentive for following them.
3. Give you the tools with which to make your moral decisions and evaluations logically. Again, there is not always one correct moral decision or evaluation; however, if your rationale for making a particular decision is coherent and consistent, then you can better live with that decision and explain it to others.
4. Make you more adept at explicating the assumptions and implications implicit in your moral beliefs and values.
5. Make you appreciate just how complex some of the moral issues and dilemmas really are that you might face.
6. Give you the encouragement and the techniques with which to evaluate conventional moral codes.
7. Spare you the dangers of moral naiveté.
8. Enable you to detect and scrutinize the moral assumptions, hardly acknowledged and typically left unexamined, implicit in such institutions of life as science, business, and politics.

Nothing could be more appropriate than to address the supreme question of life — "What ought I to do?" — rationally. We should be no less rational in addressing this question than in addressing the great questions of science. Socrates believed that the most contentious issues of all, the ones that vex us most, that make our blood boil and even bring us to blows, are questions of moral value and judgment:[20]

> What sort of thing, then, is it about which we differ, till, unable to arrive at a decision, we might get angry and be enemies to one another? Perhaps you have no answer ready, but listen to me. See if it is not the following — right and wrong, the noble and the base, and good and bad. Are not these the things about which we differ, till, unable to arrive at a decision, we grow hostile, when we do grow hostile, to each other, you and I and everybody else?

The study of moral philosophy, if we allow it, will enable us to bring some sweetness and light to such disputes and so diminish their rancor.

Thematic continuities

As you read through this book, you should take note of certain recurrent themes.[21] They represent something of a consensus among moral philosophers (a rare enough occurrence) and so may qualify as established truths in the field, though one must be especially careful in making such a claim in ethics.

Reason and ethics

One such theme is the central and indispensable role played by reason in moral reflection. "Well, then, how can we consider the question *most reasonably* [italics added]?"[22] Socrates insists to Crito. The question is whether or not Socrates should allow his friend Crito to help him escape from prison. It was an article of faith with Socrates that to be moral one must be rational. Taking their cue from him, both Plato and Aristotle thought that moral virtue was a kind of knowledge, like physics and mathematics, and that it could be discovered through the application of reason. For Plato, knowledge of the good made for wisdom, and for Aristotle, the cultivation of a good moral character and leading a morally virtuous life depended on the knowledge of virtue and the exercise of reason. Their philosophical successors, the Stoics, such as Marcus Aurelius and Cicero, affirmed that a morally virtuous life is one lived according to nature. And, because they thought nature was inherently a rational system, then by being moral one had to be rational as well.

Continuing this rationalist strain in moral philosophy into the early modern period, Thomas Hobbes took pains to defend the value of justice by the natural light of human reason. Joseph Butler conceived of conscience as a rational faculty and a legitimate means whereby we might know our obligations. And Kant, like Socrates, equates the moral with the rational. Thus, he believed that human beings are naturally endowed with a "rational will" from which he derives the fundamental principles of morality; and he used the logical principle of contradiction to test the validity of moral rules. Finally, in our own century, John Dewey was a stalwart advocate of the application of experimental reason, such as displayed in the social sciences, to solving the problems both of moral theory and practice.

Psychology and ethics

A second noteworthy theme that recurs throughout the history of moral philosophy is the theory of human nature. Moral philosophers invariably hold to some theory of human nature which informs their moral reflections. Determining what human beings *ought* to do depends upon an understanding of what they *can* do. Moreover, it is important to know what it takes to make people do what they ought; it is useful to know what motives or incentives might prompt people to behave well. *Moral psychology*, then, is a vital part of moral education. Thus, Plato and Aristotle had well-developed theories as to the nature and capacities of the human soul to undergird their view of the morally virtuous life as one in which the soul's natural capacities are exercised according to reason and wisdom. Butler provided a close analysis of the psychology of conscience and self-interest in the moral life. Hume gave an account of the logic of moral evaluation in terms of a psychological theory of the moral sentiments of sympathy and benevolence, and Kant's theory of human nature as something capable of free choice and rational voli- tion is the basis of his theory of moral obligation.

However, a word of caution is due here. Though moral philoso- phers typically agree that reason and human nature are central con- cerns of moral philosophy, they disagree widely in their conceptions of reason and human nature. Attempt to understand as clearly as you can what exactly each means by "reason" and what view of human nature he holds.

Perennial problems and issues

You should note certain persistent issues of moral philosophy that crop up in all the ethical theories we shall be considering.[23] One issue concerns the specific nature of that moral reason that is a theme of ethics. Is it *a priori* (independent of experience), like the deductive reasoning typically found in logic and mathematics? Or, is it more *a posteriori* (dependent upon experience), like the inductive reasoning mostly found in the natural and social sciences. Precisely what, if anything, does moral reason discover?

A second issue is about the relationship between a theory of moral obligation and a theory of goodness. What precisely is the relationship between, on the one hand, the concepts of right, wrong, and duty, and, on the other, the concept of goodness? Which comes first? What is the ultimate meaning of "good"? Is it merely a synonym for "pleasure" or "happiness" or does it mean something else entirely? How is a moral value such as justice different from either an aesthetic value such as beauty or a natural value such as health? Are there any such things as "moral" facts? How do they differ from nonmoral facts?

Notes

1. Schmalleger, Frank, *Criminal Justice Today: An Introductory Text for the 21st Century*, 4th ed., Prentice Hall, Upper Saddle River, NJ, 1997, p. 224.

2. Schmalleger, Frank, *Criminal Justice Today: An Introductory Text for the 21st Century*, 4th ed., Prentice Hall, Upper Saddle River, NJ, 1997, p. 149.

3. Bolt, Robert, *A Man for All Seasons: A Play in Two Acts*, Random House, New York, 1962, p. 66.

4. Aristotle, The Nicomachean ethics, in *The Ethics of Aristotle,* Thomson, J.A.K., Ed., Penguin Books, Baltimore, MD, 1956, p. 277.

5. Frankena, William K., *Ethics*, 2nd ed., Prentice-Hall, Englewood Cliffs, NJ, 1973, p. 6.

6. Hickman, II, Edward, Ed., *Miscellaneous Observations on Important Theological Subjects in the Works of Jonathan Edwards*, The Banner of Truth Trust, Edinburgh, 1979, p. 486.

7. Matthew 5:17 (revised standard version).

8. Melden, A.I., Ed., Editor's essay, in *Ethical Theories: A Book of Readings*, 2nd ed., Prentice-Hall, Englewood Cliffs, NJ, 1967, p. 5.

9. I use the expression "civil law" in its general nontechnical sense (unless otherwise noted) to refer to manmade laws, distinct from scientific law and natural law.

10. Matthew 5:27–28 (revised standard version).

11. Quoted in Velasquez, Manuel, *Philosophy: A Text With Readings*, 5th ed., Wadsworth, Belmont, CA, 1994, p. 8.

12. Locke, John, The epistle to the reader, in *An Essay Concerning Human Understanding,* Vol. I, Fraser, A.C., Ed., Dover Publications, New York, 1959, p. 14.

13. Russell, Bertrand, Logical atomism, in *Contemporary British Philosophy,* Muirhead, J.H., Ed., Macmillan, New York, 1924, p. 380.

14. Shakespeare, William, The tragedy of Macbeth, in *The Complete Works,* Wells, S., Taylor, G. et al., Eds., Clarendon Press, Oxford, 1986, p. 1124.

15. Psalm 8:4 (revised standard version).

16. James, William, The will to believe, in *Essays in Pragmatism,* Castell, A., Ed., Hafner Publishing, New York, 1948, pp. 88-90.

17. Frost, Robert, The road not taken, in *The Poetry of Robert Frost,* Lathem, E.C., Ed., Holt, Rinehart & Winston, New York, 1969, p. 105.

18. I am indebted for this example to W.T. Jones et al. See *Approaches to Ethics: Representative Selections from Classical Times to the Present,* 3rd ed., Jones, W.T. et al., Eds., McGraw-Hill, New York, 1977, p. 8.

19. Shakespeare, William, The comical history of the merchant of Venice, or otherwise called the Jew of Venice, in *The Complete Works*, Wells, S., Taylor, G. et al., Eds., Clarendon Press, Oxford, 1986, p. 483.

20. Plato, Euthyphro, in *The Collected Dialogues of Plato*, Hamilton, E. and Cairns, H., Eds., Bollingen Series LXXI, Princeton University Press, 1961, p. 175.

21. I owe the clarification of these themes to Melden. See Melden, A.I., Ed., Editor's essay, in *Ethical Theories: A Book of Readings*, 2nd ed., Prentice Hall, Englewood Cliffs, NJ, 1967, pp. 14–17.

22. Plato, Crito, in *The Collected Dialogues of Plato*, Hamilton, E. and Cairns, H., Eds., Bollingen Series LXXI, Princeton University Press, 1961, p. 31.

23. The formulation of these problems is derived from Melden, A.I., Ed., Editor's essay, in *Ethical Theories: A Book of Readings*, 2nd ed., Prentice Hall, Englewood Cliffs, NJ, 1967, pp. 17–19.

part two

Normative ethical theory

chapter two

Introduction

The nature of ethical theory

The purpose of an ethical theory is twofold: (1) to justify rationally, or give compelling reasons for the acceptance of, those basic moral rules or principles typically expressed in moral judgments; and (2) to re-solve any conflict that might occur between two or more equally binding moral rules or principles. To see how this works, consider the following pair of moral principles:

1. It is right and obligatory for a policeman to use deadly force to stop a dangerous suspect from fleeing the scene of his crime.

But why should Rodriguez adhere to this principle? How might it be rationally justified? Answering these questions is precisely the task of a normative ethical theory; however, another equally binding rule or principle could be evoked in this case, which might read:

2. One should never deliberately harm an innocent person, even if he appears to be a criminal suspect.

Principles 1 and 2 are in conflict, and it is another task of normative ethical theory to resolve this conflict. The way in which it does so is by evoking a *second-order* principle, which prescribes which of two conflicting rules or laws takes precedence over the other. An example of such a second-order principle in this case might be as follows:

3. The sanctity of human life is superior to all other values.

Thus, if there is a conflict between one's duty to preserve human life and any other duty, the duty to preserve human life takes precedence. But now this second-order principle itself requires justification, yet a further task of normative ethical theory.

The anatomy of ethical theory

An ethical theory typically sets up a hierarchy or system of principles, rules, or values. First, it seeks to reduce morality to a basic minimum of the most general principles, or a set of the most comprehensive values. Kant and Mill, for example, reduced it to one such fundamental principle: for Kant, it was the categorical imperative; for Mill, the principle of utility. Such principles as these are evoked to justify moral judgments like 1 and 2 above; alternatively, these judgments are said to be derivative from the more fundamental principle. Furthermore, an ethical theory should have at hand certain second-order principles to arbitrate conflicts between the first-order principles. And, of course, any of these principles in the hierarchy must itself be rationally grounded.

The evaluation of ethical theory

To pass muster, an ethical theory must conform to certain requirements which have to do with its consistency. First, it must be internally consistent. This means that all of its principles or rules (first- and second-order) must fit together logically, with any one of them being either implied or presupposed by others. Any inconsistency here is fatal to a theory, however impressive and complex it may otherwise seem.

Second, it must be consistent with the generally held beliefs about the world, with the prevailing world-view. This means it must not be in conflict with currently accepted scientific theories, and it must be especially conversant with the current theories of human nature formulated by the social sciences. Now, this does not mean that moral philosophy must be uncritical in its acceptance of scientific findings — far from it — but it must at least be informed by the best scientific information and ideas. This is especially true of that branch of legal ethics extending to criminology or criminal justice. Moral issues in criminal justice may require a knowledge of psychology and even biology. Thus, for a person to be held responsible and culpable for his conduct, he must be a free agent, someone who was capable of freely choosing to do what he did. However, some mental illness, genetic deformity, or chemical imbalance in this person's body which compels him to do wrong exempts him from full culpability because of the lack of choice. So a medical knowledge of what mental and physical conditions are really beyond a person's control is critical in the determination of guilt.

Third, a normative ethical theory must not fly in the face of what I shall awkwardly call "moral common sense", which reflects a sort of moral consensus among civilized men and women as to the most basic moral norms of behavior which must never be violated (although the existence of such a sense and of such norms requires justification, which we shall address later). For example, there is, I should think, a broad general agreement — at least among people in the civilized world — that judicially torturing a murderer to death would be wrong, however heinous his crime. Most of us would be appalled by, and would condemn, the spectacle of drawing and quartering, or breaking a felon on the wheel, which were common enough forms of capital punishment until as late as the mid-18th century. The constitutional amendment forbidding cruel and unusual punishment reflects such a moral consensus. Now, any moral theory that permits, much less encourages, such Draconian punishment would be seriously flawed.

Overview of normative ethical theories

Rodriguez shot McCummings twice in the back. Should he have done so? Was he right in doing it? How might Rodriguez have decided whether or not to shoot, and how might we judge whether or not he was right in doing so?

If answering that, under the circumstances, Rodriquez was right to shoot, we might justify our answer by pointing to the beneficial consequences of his action, either for himself alone or for others generally. Thus, we might argue that by shooting a dangerous suspect in the line of duty, Rodriguez guaranteed himself a raise, a commendation, or even a promotion. Indeed, these prospects could have run through Rodriguez's mind beforehand and could have helped to determine his decision to shoot, or they could have been used by him afterwards to rationalize the rightness of his decision. On the other hand, we might disregard any future benefits for Rodriquez personally and point instead to the public benefits of his action. Thus, we might reason that by shooting McCummings, Rodriguez had protected the lives and health of others who may have been in the vicinity. Note, however, that we might just as well have pointed to the probable bad consequences to justify the wrongness of Rodriguez's shooting McCummings. Thus, we might calculate that by shooting as he did Rodriguez risked a civil liability suit (which is, in fact, what happened) or faced disciplinary action from his superiors. Moreover, there could have been bad consequences for others. Innocent bystanders, for instance, could have been accidentally injured or killed had Rodriguez missed his target. Trying to decide on a course of action or judging its rightness or wrongness on the basis of its outcome may involve weighing the good consequences against the bad. The appeal to the beneficial results of an action to determine its rightness (or wrongness) and so justify it is the approach of *consequentialist* or *teleological* theories of ethics. Appealing only to the benefits for ourselves, exclusively of others, is the approach of *moral* or *ethical egoism*, whereas appealing more altruistically to the benefits for others, as well as for ourselves, is *utilitarianism*.

In judging and justifying Rodriguez's conduct, however, we might take an entirely different tack. We might ignore completely its likely consequences, good or bad, and consider only his motives or whether he violated some moral law or standard. If he acted solely from a sense of duty (not from personal interest), his conscience was clear, and no moral law was violated, then he was right to shoot McCummings. On the other hand, if any of these conditions were not met, his action might be deemed wrong. Rodriguez himself, moreover, though he might have had qualms about shooting McCummings, may have decided to shoot him anyway from a sense of duty, however painful. Note, though, that we might just as easily condemn Rodriguez according to the moral law that forbids the killing of innocents — even if they be suspects, especially if they are unarmed. The appeal to anything other than the consequences of an action in order to determine its rightness is the approach of *nonconsequentialist* or *deontological* theories of ethics. The appeal may be to the will of God, as expressed in the laws of the Decalogue or some other religious code of ethics. To declare an action right or wrong only because God either wills or forbids it is to apply the *divine command* theory of ethics. Alternatively, the appeal may be to an abstract moral or natural law thought to be as objective as the laws of physics, absolute insofar as it is unvarying and universally binding on all persons, divinely sanctioned, and discoverable by reason no less than the principles of geometry. The appeal to such a law is made by the various forms of the *natural law* theories of ethics. Or, the appeal may be to an innate sense of duty which Kant called the *categorical imperative*. Kant's ethical theory, incidentally, is the very paradigm of deontological ethics and spawned variants of itself, such as David Ross' theory of *prima facie* duties.

In evaluating Rodriguez's action we might dispense with rules and consequences altogether. We, or he, might just consider his action by itself and "know" intuitively that it was either right or wrong. It was simply something about the action itself that determined our judgment. The appeal to intuition in the evaluation of actions is made by the appropriately named *intuitionist* theories of ethics. On the other hand, we might consider not just Rodriguez's action but also the total context in which it occurred — the crime committed by McCummings, his being armed or unarmed, the presence or absence of others at the scene, etc. On the basis of our grasp of this larger situation, we might then pronounce Rodriguez's action as right or wrong. Any appeal to the entire context of an action as the basis of its evaluation is the approach of so-called *contextualist* or *situationist* theories of ethics.

We might also evaluate Rodriguez's action on the basis of its appropriateness. If the action were appropriate to or warranted by the situation, then we would deem it right. By contrast, if the action were inappropriate or unwarranted by the situation, because it was excessive, then we would deem it wrong. Furthermore, in evaluating Rodriguez's conduct in the case, we might consider his other actions while on duty, or those of his fellow police officers in similar cases. Inquiry may be made into the quality of his character as, for example, reflected in his policing record. Considerations like these as to the propriety or suitableness of conduct in any given situation, and to character, belong to the various forms of *virtue* or *aretaic* theories of ethics.

Finally, in assessing Rodriguez's conduct, we might consider whether or not it was an expression of love to neighbor. Was it perhaps motivated by feelings of respect or esteem for one's fellow human beings, especially McCummings' victim and the innocent bystanders, if any? On the face of it, his shooting McCummings would not qualify as an act of brotherly love. However, had he refrained from shooting McCummings, from the realization that McCummings was a person with dignity who should not be shot like some rabid animal, his action would qualify as benevolent. Judging actions according to whether they are expressions of benevolence or not is the method associated with so-called *agapistic* theories of ethics.

These, then, are the various branches and sub-branches of normative ethical theory. One major branch is composed of teleological theories which, in turn, branches out into different forms of egoism and utilitarianism. Coordinate with them is the branch constituted by deontological theories, which divides into the theories of divine command, natural law, the categorical imperative, and *prima facie* duties. Then there are the varieties of intuitionist, situationist, and virtue-based theories of ethics. Finally, there is the branch represented by variants of agapistic ethics. We can conveniently represent them and their relationships in the form of a tree; however, this taxonomy of normative ethical theory should not be interpreted too rigidly — the branches of the tree are not hermetically sealed. Philosophers do not begin with such a schematization and then try to squeeze their theories into one or another of its compartments. The theories were developed first, and any classificatory scheme is constructed from them for the sake of clarifying them by picturing their larger relationships. However, the finer network of more subtle connections among the theories may not be visible. Thus, virtue-based theories share elements in common with teleological theories. Kant's categorical imperative has much in common with the theory of natural law. And agapistic theories share elements with both teleological and virtue-based ethics. You should be on the lookout for subtle similarities between apparently disparate theories, as well as for their differences.

Obligation and value

In judging that Rodriguez's shooting of McCummings was either right or wrong or declaring that he ought not to have acted as he did, we make *deontic* judgments concerning moral obligation. The objects of these judgments are actions, which we either pronounce right or wrong, or advise that they ought or ought not be done. Normally, persons or traits of character are not the objects of deontic judgments. Thus, we do not speak of a "right" person or a "wrong" character, but of a "good" person or a "bad" character — though there is a sense in which we might say that he is the right person for the job or that an actor was assigned the wrong character to play on stage. But "right" and "wrong" in these cases are used in their nonmoral sense. In their moral sense, "right" and "wrong" refer to actions, not to persons, traits, motives, intentions, etc. Normative ethical theories which have to do principally with actions and why they are right, wrong, or obligatory are specifically theories of moral *obligation*. These include the various forms of teleological, deontological, intuitionist, and situationist ethics.

We might, however, judge Fuhrman's motives and intentions in planting the bloody glove as good but his racist remarks as bad; or judge Rodriguez's character as good and McCummings' as bad. In doing so we make *aretaic* judgments, the objects of which may be things such as persons or traits of character such as courage and temperance, dispositions, motives, and intentions. Thus, the objects of aretaic judgments, in contrast to deontic judgments, are usually things other than actions — though we do speak of good or bad deeds, conduct, and behavior. Normative ethical theories which are concerned chiefly with the justification of aretaic judgments are specifically theories of moral *value;* among such are virtue-based and agapistic theories of ethics.

Now, this is not to say that normative theories of obligation may not consider aretaic judgments, or that normative theories of value may not consider deontic judgments. But, ethical theories emphasize one or the other of the forms of moral judgment and are classified accordingly. Thus, those like deontological theories, which are principally concerned with the rightness, wrongness, or obligatoriness of action, are more theories of moral obligation; whereas, those like virtue-based theories, which are fundamentally about the goodness or badness of character, motives, and intentions, are more theories of moral value. Both of them, in turn, are distinct from but coordinate with theories of nonmoral value such as aesthetic value. Theories of moral and nonmoral value together constitute the field of axiology or the general theory of value.

chapter three

Teleological theories of ethics

"Man does *not* strive for pleasure; only the Englishman
does." —Friedrich Nietzsche (*Twilight of the Idols*)

Suppose that Rodriguez sought to justify his decision to shoot
McCummings, or Fuhrman his decision to plant the bloody glove and
tamper with the blood stains, or Harry Callahan his decision to decline the invitation to join the vigilante police, by appealing to the
consequences of their actions, either for themselves or for others. Any
such appeal is basic to teleological theories of ethics. Teleological
ethics, then, justifies, decides, or evaluates actions or moral precepts
by pointing to the benefits that will likely result from performing or
following them. Now, if Rodriguez, Fuhrman, or Callahan appealed
only to prospective benefits for themselves, they were thinking as
moral egoists. Moral or ethical egoism justifies, decides, or evaluates
actions or moral principles solely by reference to whether doing or
conforming to them furthers one's own self-interest. Thus, Rodriguez
or Fuhrman may have decided to do, or justify what they did, on the
basis of a prospective reward such as a citation, promotion, or some
other advancement of their careers. On the other hand, in deciding
what they ought to do, or subsequently justifying it, they may have
considered not just the possible benefits to themselves, but to others
as well. They may have had in mind the public good, that their actions
would contribute somehow to public safety and the maintenance of a
just social order. If so, they would be thinking like utilitarians. Utilitarianism justifies, decides, or evaluates actions or moral principles

solely on the basis of whether doing or conforming to them promotes
the interests of the majority of people. We shall turn first to various
forms of ethical egoism, beginning with psychological egoism, the
descriptive theory upon which it depends.

Ethical egoism

Psychological egoism

As we mentioned earlier, ethical theories presuppose and take their
character from some theory of human nature. In the case of ethical or
moral egoism, it is *psychological egoism.* Psychological egoism is a
descriptive theory that holds that every one of our actions, even those
which appear unselfish, is motivated by self-interest. Indeed, we cannot but act in our own self-interest; doing otherwise is impossible.
Pure altruism, in other words, is an illusion. How is this so?

Thomas Hobbes (1588–1679), one of the classic exponents of egoism, ruthlessly exposed the selfish motive that lurked behind even
seemingly unselfish acts. Take acts of charity, for example. What
could be more altruistic than they? But, for Hobbes, by serving in soup
kitchens, building houses for Habitat for Humanity, or donating money
and goods to the Salvation Army we delight in showing off our
capacities to serve. We are reminding ourselves, and demonstrating to
the world, that we are fully capable of taking care not only of ourselves but of others, as well. We fairly revel in our strength and
capacities. The hidden motive lurking behind all this, of course, is
nothing other than pride. So, the Princess Dianas and Mother Theresas
of the world, through their so-called good works of charity, are simply
exercising and bringing attention to their proud self-sufficiency. But
what about pity, our feeling sorry for those in distress, which issues
in acts of compassion for those who suffer? What possible selfish
motive could be at work here? According to Hobbes' analysis, we feel
sorry for others because their pain reminds us that we might very well
have been in their shoes, and their pain would then have been ours —
but for the grace of God go I! Thus, pity is nothing other than *self*-pity.[1]

Even beyond those charitable and compassionate acts that have as
their motives pride and self-pity, respectively, any apparently unselfish acts — no less than obviously selfish ones — have as their motive
our personal desire to perform them; we *want* to do them. Hence, even
our altruistic conduct is motivated by nothing more than self-interest.
Moreover, the performance of unselfish acts typically gives us pleasure

and feelings of self-satisfaction which may come from an awareness of the admiration of others (or only ourselves), the gratitude and happiness of those we serve, or simply a clear conscience. Thus, based upon the analysis of Hobbes and other egoists, the fundamental and supreme motive of all our conduct, however much we may deny it, is self-gratification.

Ethical egoism

Ethical egoism is the prescriptive counterpart to the descriptive theory of psychological egoism. It maintains that we ought always to act so as to serve our own best interests, to maximize the benefits to ourselves. Our acts are right, and obligatory no less, if and only if they are likely to produce beneficial results for ourselves; wrong, if they do not. The only consequences ethical egoism is concerned with are those conducive to our own personal well-being or happiness; all else is irrelevant. Now, this does not preclude our helping others (acting altruistically) in some cases, but only if it in some way redounds to our benefit. If not, then we should refrain from doing it. In other words, we should help others only if we thereby help ourselves.

Moral or ethical egoism can take one of three forms: *individual, personal,* or *universal*.[2] The most extreme form is individual egoism, according to which not only I, but everyone else as well with whom I associate, should serve my own personal interest. This view was strenuously advocated by Friedrich Nietzsche (1844–1900) and put into practice by his friend (whom he later renounced), Richard Wagner, the great German composer of music drama. Nietzsche believed that there were certain extraordinary men of genius (what he called "supermen") whom lesser men ought to serve that their genius might flourish and so advance civilization, in the same way that rank-and-file soldiers serve their commanding generals that they might win battles.[3] Interestingly, Nietzsche's own favorite example of a superman was neither Frederick the Great nor Otto von Bismarck, as one might expect, but the great German poet and dramatist Johann Wolfgang von Goethe. Wagner, a megalomaniac of heroic proportions but indisputably a genius, saw himself as a superman who shamelessly used his friends and committed adultery with their wives. The result was some of the greatest operas ever written and a revolution in music.[4] Personal egoism is more moderate in its demands. It states that I, no one else, ought to act in my own self-interest in all things. Universal egoism, however, looks almost saintly in comparison.

It prescribes that not only I, but each one of us, ought single-mindedly to act in our own interest.

Of the three forms, universal egoism is the most defensible, with three different kinds of argument being offered in its defense. One kind of argument maintains that our actively seeking to promote the interest of others through charitable and benevolent deeds runs the risk, paradoxically, of sabotaging it. Hence, we should confine ourselves to the promotion of our own interest. For one thing, says the moral egoist, I know what my own interests are better than I know another's, and so I am more likely to succeed in realizing them. I may make a mistake about what is truly in another's best interest and so diminish rather than promote that person's happiness. An example of one's making a mistake about another's best interest is found in Moliere's comedy, *A Doctor in Spite of Himself.* Mr. Robert happens upon Scanarelle beating Martine, his wife. He valiantly intervenes and tries to stop it. But Martine, instead of being grateful, is furious at him. She slaps Mr. Robert and protests: "Suppose I want him to beat me!"[5] A second reason that may be given in defense of ethical egoism is that by looking out for only our own interests we are not invading the privacy of others, which we would surely do if we looked out for theirs. After all, privacy is a precious thing and the right to it is sacrosanct. And, finally, the moral egoist may point out that charity can backfire. It diminishes the recipient's dignity and weakens his self-reliance by making him dependent upon the generosity of others. The effect of this, far from being gratitude towards the benefactor, may be resentment and even hatred. The hand that feeds is sometimes bitten.

A second line of argument in support of moral egoism, suggested by Ayn Rand, is that egoism, by urging us to pursue our own best interests single-mindedly, fully respects the integrity of the individual; whereas altruism, by urging us to disregard our own interests in the pursuit of others', requires us to sacrifice ourselves to them which does violence to our individual integrity.[6] After all, even Jesus says we ought to love our neighbors *as* ourselves, not more so.[7]

Finally, moral egoists support their position by arguing that it acknowledges the powerful incentive of self-interest for our meeting such obligations as keeping our promises and not harming others. Thus, our failure to keep promises can redound in serious disadvantages to ourselves, such as the loss of others' trust and respect together with their attendant consequences. So, purely out of self-interest, we will be encouraged to perform certain basic duties. Moral egoism, then, provides the best support for the moral life.

Critique

The criticisms of ethical egoism have been directed against (1) the psychological theory which is its foundation, (2) the moral theory itself, and (3) the inference from the descriptive to the prescriptive theory. We shall begin with the first criticism.

Psychological egoism holds that human beings are incapable of acting other than out of self-interest. As a psychological theory, it must pass muster as a scientific theory, which means there must be evidence to support it. Unfortunately, it fails this basic test. Hobbes pretends to have given us a rigorous scientific demonstration that apparently altruistic virtues such as pity and charity are nothing more than expressions of self-interest — and worse — of hypocrisy, as the sordid motives of pride and self-pity hide behind the mask of virtue. Hobbes exposes the worm in the apple, and we his readers take as much glee in his ruthless unmasking as we do in Moliere's triumphant exposing of Tartuffe when he shows the latter's attempted seduction of Orgon's wife.[8] However, the most that Hobbes has done is to show that pride and self-pity *may* be the motives of charity and pity, but he is far from proving that they actually are. Moreover, that selfish motives may very well be at work behind our unselfish acts does not mean that purely altruistic ones may not be at work, as well.

Moral egoists make a big point of the fact that our unselfish acts are no less self-interested than our selfish acts because fundamentally we want to do them; our real motive in either case is personal desire. As the egoist tells it, anything we do we do because we want to, but this is plainly false. There are many things I do that I emphatically do not want to do. I do not want to go to the dentist for my checkup, but I go anyway. The egoist then retorts, "Yes, you did not want to go because of the inconvenience, discomfort, and even pain; but go you did, not because of what you thought awaited you, but because you wanted healthy teeth!" So, even the unpleasant visit to the dentist is motivated by a desire for a long-term gain; however, we might make the following reply: "This is true, but I am able to distinguish between short-term and long-term desires, and to frustrate the former to satisfy the latter. The point is that I am at least capable of doing what I don't want to do *at the moment*, even though I desire the long-term benefit.

Moreover, there are other things we do not want to do, nor do we want — indeed, we may be oblivious to — any long-term benefits that might accrue to us from doing them, but we do them anyway, not from any desire of either a short-term or even long-term gain, but from a sense of duty or obligation. We believe we must do them. Lord Admiral Nelson once exhorted the fleet by reminding his sailors that England expects every man to do his duty. Suppose a sailor believes that he will die in the battle. He does not believe in a Valhalla where his bravery will be rewarded. Suppose, further, that he has no relatives or friends, and so thinks that he will be quickly forgotten in death and that the battle honors will be bestowed not on him individually but on the crew of his ship collectively. Yet, could he not still be relied on to do what he ought, not from any desire even of a hero's wreath, but solely from a sense of obligation? Remember Jesus in Gethsemane. He does not want to die. He fervently prays that he be spared this bitter cup. But, if his Father wills his death, then Jesus is determined to go through with it.[9] At this moment of decision, he is motivated not by his own desire but wholly by God's will. No mention is made in the story of his looking forward to some heavenly reward for his obedience.

Now, the egoist, like the bulldog, may still be difficult to shake off. He could come back with this: "Yes, but in the final analysis doesn't the sailor *want* to do his duty, doesn't Christ *want* to obey his Father? In other words, are not even they doing ultimately what they desire?" Indeed, they are, but to say that they are thereby acting from "selfish" or "self-interested" motives is to stretch the accepted meanings of these terms out of all recognition. Indeed, these terms become meaningless, constituting a further criticism of psychological egoism. If, as the egoist insists, any action is necessarily self-interested at some level, then "self-interestedness" is a vacuous expression. "Self-interestedness" can mean something only if there is such a thing as "disinterestedness"; again, "selfishness" can mean something only if there is such a thing as "unselfishness". Hence if, on the egoist's account, no act or motive can qualify as disinterested or unselfish, neither can any act qualify as self-interested or selfish, but this is patently absurd. We can and do speak of acts as being either self-interested or selfish on the one hand, or disinterested and unselfish on the other. We readily recognize examples of either kind when we see them.

Another objection that may be made to psychological egoism is that it fails to distinguish between motives and the objects or ends desired. It is not just motives that determine whether an action is selfish or not, but also the ends aimed at. Suppose that on my vacation I have a choice between boating and fishing with my best friends or helping build a house for Habitat for Humanity. In both cases, my motive may be the same — namely, personal enjoyment. This would be enough for the egoist to pronounce either of my actions selfish or self-interested, but even though my motives are identical, are not the ends I am pursuing in each case quite different? The object of pleasing just myself is different from that of contributing to the well-being of others less fortunate than I. In the one case, I am aiming to please only one person, myself; in the other, I am aiming to promote the well-being of others. Note, too, that a pleasure such as fishing can hardly weigh equally with the well-being that comes from having a secure home.

Another point advanced by egoists is that we typically enjoy performing unselfish or altruistic acts — they make us feel good. So again, our motives are purely selfish or self-interested. This invites two objections. First, it would seem that to enjoy doing good for others is hardly a symptom of selfishness. Do we really regard people who enjoy helping others as selfish? On the contrary, we regard people who derive no pleasure at all from doing good to others, who even hate doing it and will only do it grudgingly and under duress, as the selfish ones. Second, those who do good to others may do so not because of any satisfaction they get from it, but for the sake of making others happy. Their intention and principal motive is helping others; any pleasure they may get from doing so is merely an incidental byproduct of their action. Even if they anticipated no personal satisfaction from the act, this would not stop them from performing it. Consider this analogy. When I get into my car and drive somewhere, my intention is to arrive at a certain destination. On the way, I may find myself enjoying the scenery and the music on the radio, but listening to music and looking at scenery are not the reasons for my trip; these are simply welcome fringe benefits. And even if I knew that there would be neither music nor scenery on the trip, this would not be sufficient to stop me.

Finally, psychological egoism may be criticized for linguistic confusion and fallacious logic. First of all, egoists confuse self-interest with selfishness; but there is clearly a difference between them. A selfish person necessarily ignores, discounts, or opposes the interest of others; a self-interested person need not. Sitting by myself at home on weekends watching television and getting drunk is selfish, but going out and building houses for Habitat for Humanity is not. In both cases, though, I am enjoying myself and serving what I think is my self-interest. Moreover, we regard the two cases quite differently. Though we may not condemn outright those whose idea of a good time is sitting home amusing themselves, we do reserve our admiration for others who go out and do things for others.

Second, egoists also confuse the pursuit of pleasure or happiness with self-interest. If we like what we do then we must be acting from self-interest; however, many of the pleasures we pursue can be contrary to our self-interest. True, they may gratify our immediate, short-term interest, but they frustrate our real, long-term interest. For example, many people enjoy smoking or overeating or drinking to excess, and these activities are done from self-interest. But these pleasures are hardly in anyone's *genuine* interest; they may give superficial pleasure now, but in the long run they can create havoc with our health and kill us. So, here we have the case of pleasure being in fact at odds with our true happiness or well-being; whereas, things that are immediately painful and inconvenient, such as regular dental checkups or colonic irrigations, contribute to our real good and well-being. Hence, the pursuit of pleasure is not necessarily motivated by self-interest.

Third, egoists often fail to understand that self-interest is wholly compatible with altruism; in fact, our real self-interest may very well lie along the path of unselfishness. Thus, the motives of our actions may indeed be self-interested, but the results may be altruistic. These cases are often referred to as examples of "enlightened" self-interest, a favorite concept of economists and financiers. For example, a company may donate to charity merely for the sake of a tax write-off, not to mention the free advertising and good publicity that may also result. The motive is clearly self-interested and mercenary, but as a consequence many people benefit enormously. Again, Andrew Carnegie's motive for giving away his vast wealth to various philanthropic causes may have been nothing more than quieting an uneasy conscience about the way he had exploited others in clawing his way to success, but the results of his philanthropy — the public libraries, universities, foundations, and museums — are monuments in our cultural landscape.

Psychological egoism has also been criticized on logical grounds. First, it commits the so-called *ad hoc* fallacy. This logical fallacy is committed whenever a person counters any possible criticism of his position with a purely arbitrary argument or explanation. Suppose I tell you that my Mickey Mouse watch is activated not by anything mechanical or electrical, but by Mickey Mouse himself, who is tucked safely inside. But, you protest, a mouse is too large to fit into a wristwatch. I reply that Mickey Mouse is a magical mouse who can make himself as big or small as he likes. So, you then open up the watch to find the mouse, but your search is in vain. My quick response is that, being magical, the mouse can make himself invisible at will. And so it goes. A certain group of psychiatrists are expert in *ad hoc* arguments. If you dare criticize any of their pet theories, they come back at you with the comment that your criticism is itself a symptom of a malady! The same is true of psychological egoists. Mention any obviously altruistic act or public benefactor that might prove him wrong, and the egoist snaps back quickly with some hidden or unconscious motive to explain it away. Theories or explanations that cannot possibly be proven wrong, that can expand like a rubber band to fit round any problematic fact or objection and are immune to criticism, are themselves highly suspect because they turn out to be empty of any real meaning. Moreover, psychological egoism has been criticized not only because it cannot possibly be proved wrong, but also because it cannot be proved right. The theory that all our behavior is motivated solely by self-interest or selfishness has never been shown to be true with hard facts. Indeed, how could such a theory be empirically proven at all? What tests or experiments might be constructed, or what observations might be made, that would show egoism was true and a law of human behavior?

We turn now from our critique of psychological egoism to a critique of moral or ethical egoism, its prescriptive counterpart. As a normative ethical theory, moral egoism boils down this argument:

1. You cannot but act from self-interested or selfish motives, however altruistic or unselfish your actions may seem.
2. Hence, in all your actions, you ought to act solely from motives of self-interest or selfishness.

Apart from the fact that the first premise has not, and perhaps cannot, be proved true, the argument itself is redundant. What point is there in telling us that we ought to do what we want to do, what in fact we cannot help but doing? Unless physically restrained, we are going to do it anyway! Normally, we are advised, told, or commanded not to do what we want but what we *ought*. Furthermore, moral egoists have no recourse but to fall back on nonmoral reasons to justify why we should always act in our own self-interest. Thus, not acting so can be explained as foolish or stupid, but foolishness and stupidity are *natural* vices, not moral ones. People who exemplify these vices may be pitiable or laughable but hardly censurable or punishable. Moreover, what is specifically immoral about *not* acting in our own self-interest? What moral reason might be given for acting self-interestedly? Indeed, in what sense is it morally right at all to act according to self-interest? It just does not seem to make sense to talk that way. It goes against the grain of that moral common sense, which, as we discussed in an earlier chapter, is a criterion that any normative ethical theory must meet in order to be acceptable.

Yet another, more serious logical problem with moral egoism is that it contradicts itself. On the one hand, it insists that we cannot help but act self-interestedly, but then it stipulates that we ought to act so; however, to insist that we ought to act so presupposes that we might act otherwise (i.e., that we might act disinterestedly or not in our own interest). But to presuppose this is to acknowledge tacitly that we *can* act other than self-interestedly!

Moral egoism is inconsistent in another sense. Its basic precept is that each of us ought to pursue our own interests, regardless of others', unless pursuing their interests will advance our own. Universal egoism prescribes that each and every one of us has the obligation to pursue his own interest, but suppose another's interests conflict with mine? I am obliged, according to egoism, to allow him full rein to further his interests, even at the expense of mine; however, I am no less obliged, on the same principle, to promote my interests at the expense of his. Indeed, I have the moral obligation to minimize his interference with my interests. Suppose, for example, that I fall in love with my best friend's wife. It is certainly in my immediate interest to have the opportunity to be with her; however, it is no less in my friend's best interest that I do not see her. Now according to the rule of moral egoism, each of us has not only the right, but the obligation no less, of pursuing what we think is in our own best interest. It is a classic dilemma, which is precisely what a normative ethical theory is supposed to help us escape. One of the hallmarks of a plausible ethical theory is that it be *universalizable*. You will remember that a moral judgment, though it may be a particular judgment about a single case, is in fact a universal judgment about all such cases. If my friend tells me that I ought not to commit adultery with his wife, he is not only making a deontic judgment about me, but he is also making a judgment about anyone in a similar situation. What he is saying, implicity, is that nobody ought to commit adultery.

Thus, apart from advancing nonmoral reasons for acting self-interestedly and being redundant, there are three additional logical flaws in moral egoism: (1) it distorts the meaning of moral discourse,

(2) it cannot be justified on purely moral grounds, and (3) it is inherently inconsistent in two ways. Still further criticisms may be made of moral egoism with respect to the reasons, other than the principle of psychological egoism, that moral egoists give in support of their theory. Let us now consider each of these reasons and the objections that might be made to them.

You will recall that moral egoists attempt to justify their theory by appealing to the interests of others. Thus, moral egoism, unlike altruism, does not invade people's privacy or diminish their self-respect or weaken their self-reliance or run the risk of going against their best interest. By minding our own business, as moral egoism encourages, we do not risk harming others, but is not this concern for the well-being of others a form of altruism, the very thing that egoists claim is impossible? Such an altruistic concern flatly contradicts two basic principles of egoism: First, it contradicts the basic principle of psychological egoism which maintains the impossibility of our ever having a purely altruistic or unselfish motive. Second, it contradicts the precept of moral egoism which asserts that we ought only do what is conducive to the advancement of our own interest. Paradoxically, the very reason here given to support moral egoism turns out to be nothing other than an appeal to the interests of others!

Ayn Rand, you will remember, defends egoism because it respects our individuality. Altruism, she thinks, does not because it requires our sacrificing some personal interest for the sake of another's. Two responses may be made to Rand: First, she is overvaluing individualism at the expense of other values which are not less important. Certainly the freedom to pursue our personal interests is an inalienable and sacrosanct right, but the collective interest of society also counts for something. Justice, a social interest, is no less a value than individualism and may be threatened by individuals in the single-minded pursuit of their own interests. Rand needs to show that individualism is a superior value to justice, and whenever the two conflict the latter should give way. This would be difficult to prove. Rand and other egoists regard *my* interests as being not just equal to but as actually more important than those of others. But what possible justification could there be for such preferential treatment? Given that we are all equal in our moral dignity or worth, to prefer my own interests — simply because they are mine — to others' is at best arbitrary and at worst unjust. Rand needs to show exactly why I should put my interests first. Furthermore, there are some distinguished philosophers and social scientists who have maintained that our very identity as individuals depends on the degree of our socialization.[10] This means that the more we identify with the interests of society as a whole, rather than with our own narrow concerns, then the stronger becomes our individual identity.

A second objection that may be made to Rand's position is that she presents us with a *false dilemma*. We commit this logical fallacy when we insist that there are only two options when there might be more. For example, suppose that I tell you that you will get either an A or an F in my course. You might legitimately reply, "But why not a B or a C?" I have arbitrarily presented you with only two choices when in fact there are more. Rand's false dilemma is that in our moral conduct we have only two choices — either to act selfishly or to sacrifice ourselves completely for another's sake. Well, there is a wide middle-ground between these extremes. A constable helps an old lady to cross the street. He did not have to do this; it might have been slightly inconvenient for him to have done so, and meanwhile he might have missed the chance of catching the eye of an attractive blonde. But it can hardly be said that his altruistic act was heroic, whereby he sacrificed as much of himself as a martyr would have done. To say that he did would be comically hyperbolic.

Then there are the moral egoists who rationalize their theory by claiming that it provides the powerful incentive of self-interest to ensure that we adhere to basic moral principles such as promise-keeping; however, there are cases when adherence to a moral principle can be contrary to our self-interest. For example, I want desperately to go with my girlfriend to the beach this weekend. My ex-wife calls to remind me that I promised to help her move into her boyfriend's house that same weekend. I want to go to the beach; my interest clearly lies there. But, feeling bound by my promise, and contrary to my interest, I go and help my ex-wife. Apart from the fact that we nevertheless discharge many of our obligations even when they are contrary to our self-interest, we may have a good reason for doing our duty other than self-interest. This is a possibility that moral egoists automatically disallow.

Perhaps the most serious criticism that can be made of moral egoism is that it fails to provide the means for resolving conflicts of interest among individuals. This is a serious failure, as a litmus test of the plausibility of any ethical theory is how well it can arbitrate social conflicts. Furthermore, far from resolving them, moral egoism indeed worsens such conflicts. Take the case of my falling in love with my best friend's wife. The more my friend and I pursue our own self-interest, according to the dictate of moral egoism, the greater will be the conflict between us. Moral egoism, then, is an asocial, if not anti-social, theory.

Although moral egoism is a seriously flawed theory, it has been tenacious. The staying power of a philosophical theory and its capacity to invite considerable criticism mean that it is compelling. The first moral egoist of note is the Greek philosopher Epicurus (341–270 B.C.). He understood the goal of life to be the acquisition of pleasures. The word "Epicurean", which is applied to those things which give exquisite pleasure, is derived from his name; however, he did not thereby give us a license to overindulge our fleshly desires. Far from being an apostle of sexual promiscuity and gluttony, as one might think, he espoused instead an abstemious way of life. He knew perfectly well that the overindulgence of our bodily appetites risks sickness and even death. The morning hangover and the distended stomach are painful. He understood that as we get older the minimizing of pain and discomfort becomes more urgent than maximizing pleasure, so he advised us to exercise considerable self-control over our physical desires, to use moderation in their satisfaction, and to prefer the pleasures of the mind (such as reading and thinking) to those of the body, as they are harmless and more enduring. Strangely enough, his ideal of life was perhaps closer to that of a cloistered monk rapt in contemplation than that of a Hugh Hefner holding court in his Playboy mansion.[11]

Hobbes was a prominent egoist of the early modern period. He believed all human beings were driven in all their actions by the motive of pleasure. This led him to a rather grim conclusion about human nature. He rightly saw that our unbridled pursuit of our personal pleasure could bring us into conflict and make us dangerous to one another. His assessment of human existence in the state of nature, which is without the restraints and constraints imposed by social and political institutions such as governments, courts, and police, is that it would be "solitary, poor, nasty, brutish, and, short."[12] This is why we, out of self-interest, opt to give up certain of our freedoms to the government in return for its protection. This arrangement is known as the *social contract*, which is the basis of another ethical theory to be discussed later.

Moral egoists like Epicurus and Hobbes are hedonists. *Hedonism* is the view that the only thing that has intrinsic worth or value (i.e., valuable for its own sake) is pleasure. All other goods, whether moral or natural, boil down to some form of pleasure. Egoism is thus also a *reductionist* theory insofar as it reduces all good and evil to nothing but the psychological states of pleasure and pain, respectively. Something is deemed good only if it is enjoyable, bad if painful. On this account, then, good and evil are purely subjective states of mind, not objective qualities of the world. Were we constituted differently, then the very things that now give us pleasure might cause us pain, and those things which are now painful to us would become pleasurable. Thus, honey might revolt us, while wormwood and gall would gratify our palates.

Moral egoism, like any normative ethical theory, presupposes and is colored by a metaphysical viewpoint, a conception of what is real and what is not. Moral egoists tend to be materialists or naturalists. *Materialism* or *naturalism* is the view that all there is in the world is space, time, matter, and motion. It denies the supernatural and typically an afterlife and God, as well. It conceives of human beings as purely physical beings whose minds are ultimately reducible to matter. Thus, for Epicurus, the mind or soul was nothing more than a collection of very fine atoms, like air, which at death are dissipated in the atmosphere.[13] Hobbes thought that what we call "mind" or "soul" could be adequately explained in terms of physical processes.[14] Now, if you believe that we are nothing more than collections of material atoms which will be dispersed when we die, then it makes sense to think of our own pleasure as the only real goal of life which we ought earnestly to pursue. What else is there to live for? It cannot be to serve a nonexistent God, to adhere to a supernatural moral law, or to realize some spiritual ideal. The only happiness available to us is in the here and now, not in any hereafter.

Note, however, that egoism may be attacked on both anthropological and metaphysical grounds. If human beings are more than just physical organisms, being endowed with something spiritual and supernatural such as minds or souls which will survive death and be held accountable for what was done in life, and if God and the supernatural are realities, then the naturalistic theory of ethical egoism may prove to be inadequate. An effective way of challenging ethical theories is to challenge their metaphysical presuppositions.

So far we have been very critical of moral egoism. Can anything be said in its defense? One of the merits of this theory is that it has made clear just how pervasive a motive of our actions self-interest really is, though we need not be ashamed of acting from self-interest as, no less clearly, it is not the same as selfishness. Furthermore, moral egoism rightfully reminds us of the virtue of self-reliance, of the importance of correctly determining as far as we can what is truly in our *best* interest before we act, and of taking responsibility for our actions.

Utilitarianism

Now let us suppose that Rodriguez, Fuhrman, and Harry Callahan had made their decisions not by considering any benefits they might have realized personally, but by considering the benefits that might redound to the public at large as a result of their decisions. Thus, Rodriguez shot McCummings out of consideration for the safety of nearby passengers, Fuhrman tampered with the evidence because of the social good that he thought would follow upon the conviction of a murderer, and Harry refused to throw his lot in with the vigilante police because of the harm that might be done to society by flouting its laws.

By considering the prospective consequences to society generally rather than to themselves individually, they would be thinking like utilitarians. According to utilitarianism, before we act we should first carefully calculate all the probable social consequences of our contemplated course of action. If we decide that the action will likely benefit more people than not, or will hurt the fewest people than not, then we ought to perform it. That action then is right. If we determine instead, however, that the action will likely harm more people than not, or benefit the fewest people than not, then we ought to refrain from it. That action then is wrong. Utilitarianism can be summed up with its basic precept: "The sole ultimate standard of right, wrong, and obligation is the *principle of utility*, which says quite strictly that the moral end to be sought in all we do is the greatest possible balance of good over evil (or the least possible balance of evil over good) in the world as a whole."[15]

What, though, do utilitarians mean by "benefit"? They disagree somewhat as to its meaning. Some, such as Jeremy Bentham (1748–1832), mean by "benefit" as whatever is conducive to the greatest amount of pleasure for the greatest number of people;[16] others, such as John Stuart Mill (1806–1873), might substitute "happiness" for pleasure.[17] But, so-called *ideal* utilitarians such as G.E. Moore (1873–1958) think in terms neither of pleasure nor happiness but more broadly of public interest. Unlike Bentham, and perhaps Mill, Moore is not a hedonist.[18] As this suggests, utilitarianism takes different forms, some of which are attempts to emend the theory by meeting objections made to its original form. We shall now consider some of these standard objections.

Critique

Objections to utilitarianism are directed either at its hedonism or its consequentialism. Let us begin with the first sort. As we saw in the previous paragraph, there is some ambiguity concerning the exact meaning of "good" or "benefit" that determines the rightness of an action and so makes it obligatory. Bentham and Mill, in some places, say it means pleasure, but in others, happiness. Indeed, they refer to utilitarianism itself as the "greatest happiness principle". They use "pleasure" and "happiness" interchangeably, which suggests that they think these terms are synonyms. If so, then they are overlooking the important distinction between pleasure and happiness.

Aristotle pointed out that pleasure is not the same as happiness. For one thing, happiness lasts longer than any momentary pleasure. Also, although pleasure is related to happiness, a life full of pleasure does not necessarily add up to a happy life. Second, happiness is a quality that pervades our entire person and existence, whereas pleasures are functions of particular appetites or capacities.[19] Thus, food gives pleasure to my palate or warmth to my body or a rainbow to my eye. Third, there is no such thing as an excess of happiness (none of us can be too happy), but there can be an excess of pleasure. The very things that give us pleasure can give us pain — a surfeit of food can give us a stomachache; too much alcohol, a hangover; overexposure to sunlight, a sunburn. Moreover, a continuous run of pleasures can end up just being wearisome and boring. An old Arab proverb has it that "All sunshine makes a desert."[20] George Bernard Shaw in his play, *Man and Superman*, describes hell as a pleasure-seeking state of mind. We find Don Juan, the great voluptuary, where we expect to find him ... in hell. He has grown bored with the lotusland of hell, however, and wishes to escape to heaven, which he may do. According to Shaw's conception, heaven is a state of mind which craves strenuous activity and welcomes obstacles to be overcome. Heaven is a place for heroes and reformers, the heirs of Prometheus.[21]

Now, assuming that both Bentham and Mill are hedonists who define "good" as pleasure, they disagree as to the nature of pleasure. Bentham describes pleasure in purely *quantitative* terms; that is, there can be more or less of it, it can be more or less intense, it can be long or short in duration. Mill, however, thought pleasure could admit of *qualitative* differences as well; that is, pleasures differ not only in degree but also in kind. On his analysis, the mental pleasure derived from listening to classical music or reading good books, though perhaps less intense, is superior in kind to the physical pleasures of eating or sexual inter-course. Thus, Mill thought poetry was superior to bowling.

Furthermore, "pleasure" as used by utilitarians is ambiguous. It can mean the objects themselves that give us pleasure — things such as food, friends, and music. This sense of the word is reflected in the expression, "the simple pleasures of life," or in the bartender's ques-tion, "What is your pleasure?" Or, the word can refer to the qualitative tone or "feel" of the pleasure which we take in objects. The pleasure we take in reading poetry feels different from the pleasure of a fine wine. Both are instances of pleasure, but the one involves the mind, the other the body.

Related to this problem of defining "pleasure" is utilitarianism's insistence on maximizing the pleasures of all people, but what exactly will please everybody? It is a commonplace fact that what may be pleasurable to one may be disagreeable to another. Many times I have gone into stores and complained about the background music. The clerk's response is always the same: "You are the only one who has ever complained. Our customers like it." This is good utilitarian think-ing. If the majority likes something, then the store must provide it. But what about the tastes of the minority, even if it is only one person? This involves the principle of fairness or justice which, as we shall see below, utilitarianism can violate.

However they may disagree as to the nature of pleasure, these classic utilitarians defined "goodness" as "pleasure", both terms be-ing simply synonyms. A further criticism of utilitarianism is that the good is conceptually distinct from pleasure. Not all pleasures are good, and not all goods are pleasurable. Thus, if we accept Aristotle's distinction between pleasure and happiness, happiness is not plea-sure but it is nonetheless good. Furthermore, there are many pleasures which are not good. Smoking is pleasurable for some, but it is bad for their health. And many painful things are good for us. Root-canal work is hardly pleasurable, but it may be necessary for good dental health. Finally, there are many goods we seek, not so much for any pleasure we may take in them, but for their own sake; thus, truth is good in and of itself and something we seek for its own sake. If we are rational, we always want to know the truth and do not rest content with rumors or half-truths, but knowledge of the truth may cause us grief, such as when we know that cancer is the correct diagnosis of a loved one's illness. In other cases, the goods we seek for their own sake give us pleasure, but pleasure is not the reason for our seeking them. We seek friendship and knowledge, not because these things will give us pleasure, but because we deem them valuable in and of themselves. The pleasure that comes from acquiring these goods is an unsought byproduct of their acquisition. Some hedonists do not equate pleasure with goodness, affirming only that it is an essential part; but it is a major concession that the good cannot be dissolved without a trace into pleasure.

Philosophers have held differing conceptions of the good: as intellectual virtues, such as intelligence and theoretical wisdom (Aristotle); as moral virtues, such as temperance and prudence (the Stoics); as God and our fellowship with him (St. Augustine and St. Thomas Aquinas); as power (Nietzsche); as the realization of our higher selves (C.W. Hegel and F.H. Bradley).[22] Yet, in all of these cases, the good is conceived of as something distinct from either pleasure or happiness, though they often accompany and are commonly associated with the good. The pleasure that comes from acquiring these goods is an unsought byproduct of their acquistion.

Frankena has astutely observed that there is a quality, other than the pleasure they give, which makes experiences and activities good in and of themselves. He calls this "excellence".[23] For example, a virtuoso performance on a musical instrument certainly gives us pleasure, but it also fills us with an admiration for its effortless skill and sheer panache, its elusive and subtle quality of excellence. William James (1842–1910) speaks of the fine line that separates an inspired work of artistic genius from a work that is just extremely good — the distinction, say, between a Mozart opera and a Salieri.[24] This distinction is ever so subtle and inexpressible, but it nevertheless represents the difference of a light year. Merely competent works of art can give us much pleasure — in some cases more — than towering masterpieces, but we admire the latter more for their indefinable excellence. Frankena concludes that something is good if we enjoy it; further, we must enjoy it for it to qualify as intrinsically good; however, the presence (or absence) of some excellence can make it more or less good. Frankena, then, does not entirely reduce the good to either pleasure or happiness, though either of these is an essential element of it. There is always some nonhedonic remainder that he calls excellence and which arouses our admiration.

Two further objections may be made to the hedonism of utilitarianism. We perhaps all know from personal experience that the more we seek pleasure for its own sake, the more likely it is to elude us. Consequently, the more we strive to maximize the pleasures of all, as utilitarianism requires, the less likely we shall succeed. This syndrome is called the *hedonic paradox*. The lesson to be learned from this is that pleasure is experienced when we forget about getting it because we are too preoccupied with pursuing something else. Pleasure is typically the byproduct that occurs in the course of some activity. It is like the laborer who whistles while he works; he does not work in order to whistle, but whistles out of enjoyment of the work. And if one equates the good with happiness (as Mill sometimes does), many of the above objections still apply. Again, goodness is a category distinct from that of happiness. Happiness is good, but not all goods are reducible to happiness. Thus, the soldier who unthinkingly and reflexively throws himself upon a handgrenade to protect his comrades does something that is morally good, but certainly not productive of his happiness — at least not in this life. Goodness, then, is reducible to neither mere pleasure nor happiness.

Another set of objections is directed against the "consequentialism" of utilitarianism, the theory's exclusive preoccupation with the consequences of actions as the basis of their moral evaluation. One such objection is the problem of correctly predicting all the probable consequences of an action which are relevant to the public good, and then determining whether they in fact would be good. The course of events can play tricks on us and is fraught with irony. Things we think must happen do not, and things we never foresaw occur. Having each time to calculate accurately the results of a morally significant action, in order to decide whether to perform it, is impractical, time consuming, and liable to error.[25]

Another objection is that utilitarianism assumes that only the consequences of actions are relevant in determining their moral worth, and in so doing overlooks the moral relevance of such things as motives and intentions. Motives seem to count for very little in utilitarian calculations. Consider, for example, this hypothetical case. A street thug pushes an old woman down in order to steal her purse. In doing so, he pushes her our of the way of a heavy slate that is falling from a roof. Had he not pushed her, the woman's head would have been crushed, causing severe injury or death. A policeman who witnessed the thug's "heroic" act believes it deserves public recognition. As a result, the thug is the proud recipient of honors, including a medal bestowed by the mayor in a special ceremony, as well as the heart-felt gratitude of the old lady's friends and relatives. Now according to utilitarianism, the thug fully deserves the community's admiration. The unmistakable consequence of his action was wholly good; however, his motive was wholly bad. Our moral common sense tells us that the thug emphatically does not deserve his accolades; though, happily, the consequence of his action was good, it still does not make his action right. Obviously, motives are relevant factors in the moral evaluation of actions. In some cases, we are prepared to overlook the consequences of an action entirely in our moral evaluation of it. We may excuse the disastrous effects of a person's actions by saying that his heart was in the right place or that he meant well. Indeed, for Christ, a person's inward feelings or dispositions alone, even if they do not issue in actions, are sufficient to bestow moral value. He thus would condemn those who are angry at their neighbor, or men who lust after women only in the privacy of their hearts.[26]

Related to the above is the objection that utilitarianism tempts us to disregard, or even override, the moral force of prior obligations whenever it is convenient. Thus, I may decide after all to keep a promise I made, not because it is obligatory, but because of the benefits I anticipate will redound to others by my keeping it. Yet, I might decide to break my promise to someone upon the later realization that the benefits from my breaking it would far exceed the benefits to the person from my keeping it. Suppose, for example, my grandmother bequeaths to me her estate, which has been in our family for generations. Her only condition is that I never sell it or in some way allow it to leave the family's possession; I, in turn, must bequeath it to one of my children. I solemnly promise her faithfully to keep the house in perpetuity. Now, it turns out that a group home desperately needs larger facilities for its retarded children and adults. My estate is perfectly suited to meet their needs, and the home's administrators ask me if I would be willing to sell the estate to them. I consider that the estate, which is too large for me anyway, would benefit the group home's current residents and future ones, as well. The money from the sale would enable me to buy a smaller house, which could also be bequeathed to one of my children, and the remaining funds could be invested in my children's higher education. Thus, the number of beneficiaries, as well as benefits accruing to them, would be considerably larger by my selling the estate than by keeping it as I promised. Although my transaction would be perfectly right and even obligatory on utilitarian grounds, if I do sell the estate to reap these positive results, it would nevertheless be wrong insofar as I have violated a still-binding obligation.

The criticisms that may be made of utilitarianism do not stop here, however. Perhaps the most serious criticism is that it actually invites injustice. Justice is no less a value than utility or the public good. Consider the case of scapegoats, where innocent people might be punished for the sake of some social benefit. In retaliation for guerrilla attacks from the Resistance, the Nazis would randomly round up a group of innocent people and execute them. This would act as a deterrent against future attacks and thereby ensure public peace and security. Shirley Jackson's short story, *The Lottery*, is about how once a year a community ritualistically kills an innocent person chosen at random. It is an ancient custom, hallowed by age, which, it is super-stitiously believed, ensures a fruitful crop every autumn. The poten-tial conflict between utilitarianism's "greatest happiness principle" and the principle of justice has been memorably illustrated by William James, the distinguished American philosopher and psychologist, in the following hypothetical situation:[27]

> If the hypothesis were offered us of a world in which
> ... millions of us [were] kept permanently happy on
> the one simple condition that a certain lost soul on the
> far-off edge of things should lead a life of lonely tor-
> ture, what except a specific and independent sort of
> emotion can it be which would make us immediately
> feel, even though an impulse arose within us to clutch
> at the happiness so offered, how hideous a thing would
> be its enjoyment when deliberately accepted as the
> fruit of such a bargain?

Related to this is the criticism that utilitarianism may violate our basic human rights. Consider the following situation. Some police officers are searching a suspected voyeur's residence and discover a cache of films and photographs depicting some women of the com-munity in various states of dress and undress and engaging in sexual acts. The officers duly hand over this evidence to the court; however, they secretly conspire to make copies of these films and photographs in order to enjoy them in the privacy of their own homes and to sell them for considerable profit to out-of-state dealers in the pornographic trade. Nobody, including, of course, the compromised women, knows anything of the officers' covert activities nor, let us suppose, will ever know.[28] Now, based upon utilitarianism's "greatest happiness prin-ciple", the officers have done nothing wrong; indeed, they acted rightly! Countless men stand to enjoy these images, and (unless you are a disciple of Mill) you cannot legitimately complain that their pleasure is unseemly or salacious, as you have Bentham's authority for declaring all pleasures equal. But obviously the women depicted in the films and photographs have been wronged, even without their knowledge, and their right to privacy has been egregiously violated. Thus, utilitarianism seems to make little provision for ensuring justice and safeguarding our rights.

Further, utilitarianism may be criticized for making an unwarranted assumption. In its insistence on promoting the greatest good of all, it assumes that all people should be treated as equals. Each one deserves exactly the same proportion of good, no more or less than another, but why? Is it not possible for some to deserve more than others because of their talent or hard work? Consider the following scenario. A public school is doing extremely well. It has a well-stocked library, excellent teachers, well-equipped laboratories, and top-of-the-line technology. The reason is that the parents in the district have chipped in their time and money to provide them. Now the state intervenes and, in the interest of promoting the public good, wants to take some of these things from the school and share them among other schools in the county so that their students may benefit as well. This means that, though the good school now will have slightly less (but not significantly), many more students stand to benefit; however, does not the school whose parents have sacrificed and worked hard to ensure the best for their children deserve more than the other schools whose parents have not? Again, utilitarianism's "greatest happiness principle" comes into sharp conflict with the principle of fairness or justice.

One final criticism of utilitarianism is that it fails to distinguish between our moral duties and so-called supererogatory acts, thereby leaving the definition of "moral obligation" obscure. A *supererogatory* act is one that is above and beyond the call of duty; it is one that we are not obligated to do, though it is good that we do it. In other words, supererogatory acts are morally good but not morally obligatory. Go back to the McCummings case for a moment. Rodriguez had the legal duty to stop McCummings and the moral duty to assist Sandusky, McCummings' victim. But suppose, in addition to performing these duties, Rodriguez took it upon himself to call Sandusky's relatives to inform them personally of what happened and to volunteer to help them out in any way he could. Such an act would have been purely supererogatory. He was under neither a legal nor moral obligation to perform it, nor would he have been blamed had he not; however, it would have been commendable had he performed it. In all three cases — his performing his moral and legal duties as well as his supererogatory deeds — the social consequences would be expected to be good. According to utilitarianism, we are obliged to do those things which

we think will contribute to the public good. Performing a supererogatory act, no less than meeting a moral obligation, will benefit others;
therefore, for utilitarians, a supererogatory act, whenever possible, is
as binding on us as a moral duty.

Emendments to utilitarianism

In their attempts to meet these objections, utilitarians have proposed
various revisions of the theory. Let us now reconsider each of these
objections, and see how the original theory was revised to meet it.

The first group of objections was directed at the theory's hedonism, at its arbitrary reduction of goodness to pleasure or happiness.
There have been utilitarians who, while still insisting that we ought to
maximize the amount of good in the world for the maximum number
of people, do not define the "good" as either pleasure or happiness.
Moore, for example, believes that good is a primitive concept that is
indefinable, like "yellow" or "sweet".[29] He cited goods such as friendship, education, art, and public order, which, though indeed associated with pleasure and happiness, are quite distinct from them. So,
when we act to promote the public good, as we ought, we are looking
to increase these intrinsic goods, not just the stock of human pleasures
and happiness. Other utilitarians have defined the "good" as the
satisfaction of our preferences,[30] so an action is right if it tends to
satisfy the preferences of most people. This revised form of utilitarianism, espoused by such as Moore and which defines "good"
nonhedonistically, is called *ideal utilitarianism*.

A second group of objections was directed at utilitarianism's
consequentialism — the twin difficulties of accurately predicting and
then determining the value of and probable consequences of an action. To meet this objection, some utilitarians have proposed that we
should look at the consequences of applying certain *rules* covering our
actions rather than trying to work out the consequences of each and
every single act in order to decide whether or not it ought to be
performed. Consider the case of Harry Callahan, who is invited to join
a group of vigilante police and take the law into his own hands. Now
suppose that, rather than focusing on the particular act of his joining
the group and the benefits to society that might result, he considers
acts of vigilantism *in general* and the sort of social consequences they
tend to have — a matter of historical record. He realizes, perhaps, that
vigilante acts almost always have disastrous consequences. A principle or rule may then be formulated: Vigilantism in the long run

issues in more misery for more people than the alternative of adhering
to the principles of law and due process; hence, it is wrong. Applying
this rule to his own case, Harry decides to refuse the invitation. This
procedure of consulting general rules or principles of conduct and
their social consequences, instead of considering a particular act and
its social consequences, is called *rule-utilitarianism*, as distinct from
act-utilitarianism. Rule-utilitarianism is the more efficient, insofar as it
spares us the necessity of figuring out all the morally relevant consequences of each of our acts when deciding whether or not to perform
them, and it ensures that we will not make errors in our calculations.
It is also more practical. Moral rules or precepts have the advantage
of being teachable to children and reflect the moral wisdom of generations of human beings. In this respect, unlike act-utilitarianism, rule-
utilitarianism harmonizes better with moral education and bears the
authority of our collective moral experience.

Another advantage that rule-utilitarianism has over act-utilitarianism is that it is more consistent with our common notions of fairness
and justice. Thus, rule-utilitarians would enjoin us to act on just
principles, honor the rights of individuals, and generally meet our
moral obligations because historical experience has shown that doing
so leads to better social results overall than not. What better reasons
or incentives are there for being moral than being so makes for the
happiness of all? Political authorities who flout the canons of justice
and trample on individual rights invite revolutions and civil wars.
Consider the case above of the policemen's gloating over and profit-
ing from the photographs and films they had confiscated from a
voyeur. No immediate harm to the public would likely come from
their activity, but such practices, if commonplace and done with
impunity, would hardly contribute to the common good.

Though having a distinct advantage over act-utilitarianism, rule-
utilitarianism, however, is not without its problems. Rules of conduct
can be vague, or they can be in conflict, or they can admit of exceptions. In such cases, we have no recourse but to consider the consequences of the particular action proposed and to run the attendant
risks, which brings us back to act-utilitarianism.

Merits of utilitarianism

A merit of utilitarianism is its practicality, for it recognizes that actions
have consequences and takes them seriously. Furthermore, through
its "greatest happiness principle" it furnishes us an apparently clear

and effective device by which to resolve moral conflicts, particularly conflicts between equally binding duties. And, because the theory insists that these consequences must raise the stock of human happiness, it has the additional merit of being a humane theory to which it would be difficult to take exception. An effect of applying utilitarian principles is social improvement. Utilitarianism thus links moral philosophy with social and political philosophy. It is no accident that the classic utilitarians, Bentham and Mill, not only did important work in the latter fields, but were politically active in programs of social and legal reform. Another merit of this theory is its impartiality; in the application of its "greatest happiness principle" all people are treated equally. Impartiality, an aspect of justice, is a measure of a moral theory's adequacy. Although utilitarianism has been traditionally criticized for exalting utility and expediency at the expense of justice, at least foundationally it is a just theory.

A third merit of utilitarianism is its radical inclusiveness. As pleasure (or happiness) is the goal of action and the basis of moral worth, there are no logical or just grounds for excluding the pleasures of some, or ranking their pleasures lower than those of others. The point is that, if any being is sentient (i.e., has the capacity for feeling pleasure or pain), then it has moral worth and so its pleasures count. But more than human beings can feel pleasure or pain — so can animals. Thus, on this principle they too have moral worth or dignity and their well-being ought to be promoted as well. Bentham and Mill were early advocates of the moral rights of animals.[31] Utilitarianism, then, is eminently practical, humanitarian, impartial, and inclusive, merits which should be possessed by any normative ethical theory.

Utilitarianism, though not so called, first emerged as a normative ethical theory in Great Britain during the early 18th century. We find elements of it in the moral thought of John Gay (1669–1745), Hume, and William Paley (1743–1805), among others.[32] The impetus for it came from a desire on the part of many philosophers of the Enlightenment to put ethics on a purely secular footing, making it independent of theology and religion. It is a *naturalistic* theory of ethics insofar as it locates the source of moral values and the ultimate authority for moral evaluations not in the will or mind of God, or some supernatural realm, but in the heart and mind of humanity. However, utilitarianism did have its theological exponents, such as Paley and Gay. The theory still has its adherents, one of whom is John Rawls, who has given it a powerful modern form. We shall discuss Rawls in a subsequent chapter on the social contract, a distinct normative ethical theory.

Assessment of teleological theories

Moral egoism, with its "everyone-for-himself" mentality, is the least satisfactory moral theory, especially for those who work professionally with criminals. Probation officers, youth counselors, and prison rehabilitators would perhaps be ill-advised to counsel their charges on the basis of moral egoism. Moral egoism may even lead to, and be used to rationalize, crime. The notorious financier, Ivan Boesky, used to exhort receptive audiences of college students not to be ashamed of greed. "Greed is good" was the message of this apostle of egoism, at least until he was jailed on charges of embezzlement and fraud. Indeed, some philosophers think moral egoism does not even qualify as a normative ethical theory, as it is powerless to resolve conflicts and cannot be universalized. It is nothing more than a grandiose rationalization for selfishness.

Of teleological theories, the various forms of utilitarianism, particularly a combination of ideal and rule-utilitarianism, are the strongest contenders. Utilitarianism is egoistic but insists that we consider the interests of others not only as equal to our own, but perhaps even to sacrifice our own for the sake of the majority's. Consequently, it is also known as *altruistic egoism*. As this expression suggests, moral egoism may be compatible with utilitarianism. Adam Smith (1723–1790), in *The Theory of Moral Sentiments*, his classic treatise on moral philosophy, argued that a multitude of individuals, all pursuing their own personal self-interests, will tend indirectly but inexorably to advance the interests of the entire society.[33] This is the thinking that lay behind the trickle-down theory of "Reaganomics" which was popular among economists such as Milton Friedman during the 1980s. The idea was that if individual entrepreneurs and corporations were unfettered from unnecessary government regulations and restrictions, they would become wealthier and more productive and thereby increase the prosperity of all — a swelling tide will raise all the smallest boats. Smith, however, presupposed the workings of an "invisible hand" (i.e., providence) to ensure that universal egoism would indeed have an altruistic effect. The 17th-century satirist, Bernard Mandeville, in his *The Fable of the Bees*, took Adam Smith one step further by arguing that people's engaging in morally questionable activities such as gambling and prostitution might in the end reap greater social benefits than what might be obtained were these practices banned.[34] Imagine, for example, the impact on our economy and society if pornography in all its various forms were declared illegal, given our previous experience with Prohibition. This begs the question, though, in favor of teleological ethics — we are assuming that, morally speaking, only ends count, not means.

Like moral egoism, utilitarianism in its classic form, is a hedonistic moral theory. This is also the grounds for another objection against it (and against any hedonistic theory, for that matter) which was raised by Albert Schweitzer (1875–1965) in the second volume of his *Philosophy of Civilization*. In this work, preliminary to formulating his own ethical theory, he carefully and appreciatively surveys the variety of normative ethical theories and salvages what he thinks is best from each. His objection to any hedonistic theory of ethics is that the morally good is antithetical to human pleasure or happiness, as illustrated in the case of the soldier who throws himself on a grenade to protect his comrades.[35]

My closing observation on teleological ethics is this: It is probably a safe bet to suppose that many Americans individually are predominantly moral egoists both in theory and practice, but that the American nation as a collective — as represented by its political, social, and legal institutions — is fundamentally utilitarian in its polity.

Notes

1. This is how Hobbes disposes of charity and pity: "There can be no greater argument to a man, of his own power, than to find himself able not only to accomplish his own desires, but also to assist other men in theirs: and this is that conception wherein consisteth *charity*." And: "Pity is imagination or fiction of future calamity to ourselves, proceeding from the sense of another man's calamity." (From Selby-Bigge, L.A., Ed., On human nature, in *British Moralists*, Vol. II, Dover Publications, New York, 1965, pp. 298–299.) Jonathan Edwards was no less severe than Hobbes in his estimate of pity. While a missionary in Stockbridge, MA, Edwards set an Indian student to the exercise of copying the line, "He that pities another thinks on himself" (cited in Winslow, Ola E., *Jonathan Edwards 1703–1758: A Biography*, Macmillan, New York, 1940, p. 275).

2. I am indebted to Jacques P. Theroux for this threefold distinction, which I have not seen made elsewhere; see his *Ethics: Theory and Practice*, 5th ed. (Prentice Hall, Englewood Cliffs, NJ, 1995, p. 42).

3. Nietzsche writes, "What is good? Everything that heightens the feeling of power in man, the will to power, power itself. ...What is happiness? The feeling that power is *growing*, that resistance is overcome. Not contentedness but more power; not peace but war." (From

The Antichrist, in *The Portable Nietesche*, trans. by Walter Kaufmann, Viking Press, New York, 1968, p. 570.) John Hospers comments as follows on Nietzsche's ethics: "He said that in nature there are individuals who are 'naturally superior': through strength or craft they dominate the other members of the species and have no interest in their inferiors except to use them for their own purposes. Working on this assumption, Nietzsche held that the natural state of war and cutthroat competition among organisms is the desirable state and that the character traits to which this state of affairs gives rise — strength, craft, resourcefulness, ruthlessness — should be encouraged in human behavior." (From Hospers, John, *Human Conduct: An Introduction to the Problems of Ethics*, Harcourt, Brace & World, New York, 1961, p. 99.)

4. While writing *Tristan and Isolde*, a music drama with the theme of adultery, Wagner was having an adulterous affair with Mathilde Wesendonk, the wife of his patron who gave him an allowance and the use of his estate so that he might have the leisure to compose (see Osborne, Charles, *The Complete Operas of Richard Wagner*, Dacapo Press, New York, 1990, p. 135).

5. Moliere, A doctor in spite of himself, in *The Misanthrope and Other Plays* (trans. by John Wood), Penguin Books, Baltimore, MD, 1959, p. 169.

6. Ayn Rand writes: "As a basic step of self-esteem, learn to treat as the mark of a cannibal any man's *demand* for your help. To demand it is to claim that your life is *his* property — and loathsome as such claim might be, there is something still more loathsome: your agreement." (From Rand, Ayn, *Atlas Shrugged*, Random House, New York, 1957, p. 1059.)

7. Jesus cites the second great commandment of the law as, "You shall love your neighbor as yourself." Matthew 22:30 (revised standard version)

8. Moliere, Tartuffe, in *The Misanthrope and Other Plays*, trans. by John Wood, Penguin Books, Baltimore, MD, 1959, pp. 148–153.

9. In Gethsemane, just before his arrest, trial, and crucifixion, Jesus utters these words: "My father, if it be possible, let this cup pass from me; nevertheless, not as I will, but as thou wilt." Matthew 26:39 (revised standard version)

10. This view was given classic expression by George Herbert Mead: "His (the human animal) own self is attained only through his taking the attitude of the social group to which he belongs. He must become socialized to become himself." (From his *Movements of Thought in the Nineteenth Century*, Chicago, 1936, p. 168; quoted in Schneider, H.W., *A History of American Philosophy*, Columbia University Press, New York, 1946, p. 392.)

11. "When we say that pleasure is the end, we do not mean the pleasure of the profigate or that which depends on physical enjoyment ... but by pleasure we mean the state wherein the body is free from pain and the mind from anxiety. Neither continual drinking and dancing, nor sexual love, ... brings about the pleasant life; rather, it is produced by the reason which is sober." (From Epicurus, Letter to Menoeceus, in *Letters, Principal Doctrines and Vatican Sayings*, trans. by Russel M. Geer, Bobbs-Merrill, Indianapolis, IN, 1964, p. 57.)

12. Hobbes, Thomas, *Leviathan*, Clarendon Press, Oxford, 1958, p. 97.

13. "The soul is a finely divided, material thing, scattered through the whole aggregation of atoms that make up the body, most similar to breath with a certain admixture of heat ... However, if the whole body is destroyed, the soul is scattered and no longer enjoys the same powers and motions; and as a result, it no longer possesses sensation." (From Epicurus, Letter to Herodotus, in *Letters, Principal Doctrines and Vatican Sayings*, trans. by Russel M. Geer, Bobbs-Merrill, Indianapolis, IN, 1964, p. 23–24.)

14. "For seeing life is but a motion of Limbs, the beginning whereof is some principal part within; why may we not say, that all *Automata* (engines that move themselves by springs and wheeles as doth a watch) have an artificial life? For what is the *Heart*, but a *Spring*; and the *Nerves*, but so many *Strings;* and the *joints*, but so many *wheeles*, giving motion to the whole Body, such as was intended by the artificer?" (From Hobbes, Thomas, *Leviathan*, Clarendon Press, Oxford, 1958, p. 8.)

15. Frankena, William K., *Ethics*, 2nd ed., Prentice-Hall, Englewood Cliffs, NJ, 1973, p. 34.

16. According to Bentham, "Nature has placed mankind under the governance of two sovereign masters, *pain* and *pleasure*. It is for them alone to point out what we ought to do." (From Jeremy Bentham's *An Introduction to the Principles of Morals and Legislation*, Hafner Publishing, Darien, CN, 1970, p. 1.)

17. Mill distinguishes higher pleasures or happiness from mere sensuous pleasures and ranks the former higher on the scale of value: "Human beings have faculties more elevated than the animal appetites, and when once made conscious of them do not regard anything as happiness which does not include their gratification." (From Mill, John S., in *Utilitarianism*, Piest, O., Ed., Bobbs-Merrill, Indianapolis, IN, 1957, p. 11.) In distinction from Bentham's, Mill's utilitarianism is eudaemonistic (based on happiness).

18. "This name [utilitarianism] ... does not naturally suggest that all our actions are to be judged according to the degree in which they are a means to *pleasure*. Its natural meaning is that the standard of right and

wrong in conduct is its tendency to promote the *interest* of everybody. And by *interest* is commonly meant a variety of different goods." (From Moore, George E., *Principia Ethica*, Cambridge University Press, 1959, pp. 105–106.)

19. "There is another condition of happiness; it cannot be achieved in less than a complete lifetime. One swallow does not make a summer; neither does one fine day. And one day, or indeed any brief period of felicity, does not make a man entirely and perfectly happy." (From Thomson, J.A.K., Ed., *The Ethics of Aristotle*, Penguin Books, Harmondsworth, Middlesex, 1953, p.39.)

20. Barclay, William, *The Beatitudes and The Lord's Prayer for Everyman*, Harper & Row, New York, 1964, p. 30.

21. In conversation with the Devil and others in hell, Don Juan muses: "In heaven ... you live and work instead of playing and pretending. You face things as they are; you escape nothing but glamor; and your steadfastness and your peril are your glory. ... Thither I shall go presently, because there I hope to escape at last from lies and from the tedious, vulgar pursuit of happiness." (From Shaw, George B., *Man and Superman: A Comedy and a Philosophy*, Bantam Books, New York, 1963, p. 117.)

22. Frankena, William K., *Ethics*, 2nd ed., Prentice-Hall, Englewood Cliffs, NJ, 1973, pp. 86–87.

23. "In fact, I am inclined to think ... there is something else besides enjoyableness or satisfactoriness that makes activities and experiences good in themselves, and I suggest that this is always the presence of some kind or degree of excellence. Many of our activities and experiences involve or are involved in an endeavor to achieve excellence by some standard appropriate to them, for example, athletic activities, artistic creation, and science or history." (From Frankena, William K., *Ethics*, 2nd ed., Prentice-Hall, Englewood Cliffs, NJ, 1973, p. 91.)

24. "The difference between the first and second best things in art absolutely seems to escape verbal definition — it is a matter of a hair, a shade, an inward quiver of some kind — yet what miles away in point of preciousness!" (From Perry, Ralph B., *The Thought and Character of William James*, *II*, Little, Brown and Co., Boston, MA, 1935, p. 257.)

25. Mill himself makes this very objection to his own theory, but gives a rule-utilitarian reply by saying that actions have many precedents, the consequences of which are well-known enabling us to formulate general rules as to what kind of actions should be done. (See Mill, John Stuart, in *Utilitarianism*, Piest, O., Ed., Bobbs-Merrill, Indianapolis, IN, 1957, pp. 30–32.)

26. "You have heard that it was said, 'You should not commit adultery.' But I say to you that everyone who looks at a woman lustfully has

already committed adultery with her in his heart." Matthew 5:27–28 (revised standard version)

27. James, William, The moral philosopher and the moral life, in *Essays in Pragmatism*, Castell, A., Ed., Hafner Publishing, New York, 1954, p. 68.

28. This hypothetical case was suggested by one used by James Rachels (see his *The Elements of Moral Philosophy*, 2nd. ed., McGraw-Hill, New York, 1993, pp. 107–108).

29. "Or if I am asked 'How is good to be defined?' my answer is that it cannot be defined, and that is all I have to say about it. … My point is that 'good' is a simple notion, just as 'yellow' is a simple notion; that, just as you cannot, by any manner of means, explain to any one who does not already know it, what yellow is, so you cannot explain what good is." (From Moore, George Edward, *Principia Ethica*, Cambridge University Press, 1959, pp. 6–7.)

30. Rachels, James, *The Elements of Moral Philosophy*, 2nd ed., McGraw-Hill, New York, 1993, p. 105.

31. "The day *may* come when the rest of the animal creation may acquire those rights which never could have been withholden from them but by the hand of tyranny. The French have already discovered that the blackness of the skin is no reason why a human being should be abandoned without redress to the caprice of a tormentor. It may come one day to be recognized that the number of the legs, the villosity of the skin, or the termination of the *os sacrum* are reasons equally insufficient for abandoning a sensitive being to the same fate. What else is it that should trace the insuperable line? … the question is not, Can they *reason*? but, Can they *suffer*?" (From Bentham, Jeremy, *Principles of Morals and Legislation*, Hafner Publishing, New York, 1948, p. 311.)

32. A convenient and compact two-volume anthology of selections from the works of these men and their contemporaries is Selby-Bigge, L.A., Ed., *British Moralists*, Dover Publications, New York, 1965.

33. "The rich only select from the heap what is most precious and agreeable. They consume little more than the poor, and in spite of their natural selfishness and rapacity, though they mean only their conveniency, though the sole end which they propose from the labours of all the thousands whom they employ, be the gratification of their own vain and insatiable desires, they divide with the poor the produce of all their improvements. They are led by an invisible hand to make nearly the same distribution of the necessaries of life, which would have been made, had the earth been divided into equal portions among all its inhabitants, and thus without intending it, without knowing it, advance the interest of the society, and afford means to the multiplication of the species." (From Smith, Adam, *The Theory of*

Moral Sentiments, Raphael, D.D. and MacFie, A.L., Eds., Liberty Fund, Indianapolis, IN, 1984, pp. 184–185.)

34. "So they that examine into the Nature of Man, abstract from Art and Education, may observe, that what renders him a Sociable Animal, consists not in his desire of Company, Good-nature, Pity, Affability, and other Graces of a fair Outside; but that his vilest and most hateful Qualities are the most necessary Accomplishments to fit him for the largest, and, according to the World, the happiest and most flourishing Societies." (From Mandeville, Bernard, *The Fable of the Bees: Or, Private Vices, Publick Benefits*, Vol. I, Clarendon Press, Oxford, 1957, pp. 3–4.)

35. "As soon as the notion of pleasure is brought into connection with ethics, it shows disturbances, as does the magnetic needle in the neighborhood of the poles. Pleasure as such shows itself incapable in every respect of being reconciled with the demands of ethics, and it is therefore given up. Reflection upon the ethic which is to produce happiness is compelled at last to give up the positive notion of pleasure in any form. It has to reconcile itself to the negative notion which conceives pleasure as somehow or other a liberation from the need of pleasure. Thus the individualistic, utilitarian ethic, also called Eudaemonism, destroys itself as soon as it ventures to be consistent." (From Schweitzer, Albert, *The Philosophy of Civilization*, Prometheus Books, Buffalo, NY, 1987, p. 118.)

chapter four

Deontological theories of ethics

Stern Daughter of the Voice of God!
O Duty! if that name thou love,
Who art a light to guide, a rod
To check the erring, and reprove;
Thou, who art victory and law
when empty terrors overawe;
From vain temptations dost set free;
And calm'st the weary strife of frail humanity!

—William Wordsworth (*Ode to Duty*)

Suppose now that Manuel Rodriguez had not shot McCummings because he believed that doing so violated God's law against killing; or that Mark Fuhrman, though tempted, had decided not to tamper with the evidence to secure a conviction because he thought to do so contravened some natural law against bearing false witness; or that Harry Callahan, though invited, had refused to join the vigilante police for no other reason than that his intuition told him that doing so was just inherently wrong. The decision in each case was based not on the probable consequences of the proposed action but on something else such as divine law, natural law, or intuition, respectively. Hence, the justifications for their decisions exemplify one form or other of the aptly named *nonconsequentialist* theory of ethics, otherwise known as *formalism* or, most commonly, *deontological* ethics. This normative ethical theory, being nonconsequentialist, affirms that in deciding whether to perform some action, or how to evaluate it morally, its consequences — whether they concern one's own private good or the public good — are utterly irrelevant. The only relevant concern — as the terms "deontologism" and "formalism" suggest — is whether or not the act in question conforms to or violates some moral norm or law, or whether it can be intuited to be inherently right or wrong. If the action violates no moral precept or is felt to be inherently right, then it is permissible; however, if it does violate some moral principle or is felt to be inherently wrong, then it is forbidden. Hence, for the deontologist, the moral worth of an action resides not in its bearing on human happiness or well-being (as it does for the teleologist), but solely in its relation to some moral law or quality inherent in itself. Deontologism could not be further removed from teleological ethics.

Corresponding to the hypothetical justifications of the three policemen above, there are three forms of deontological ethics distinguished according to their different conceptions of the source of moral value. According to the so-called *divine command* theory, that source is the will of God. For *natural law* theory, it is some objective moral law which is as real a part of the universe as the laws of physics and, like them, discoverable through reason. Three variants of natural law theory are represented by the ethics of Aristotle, Kant, and Ross. And according to the theory of *moral intuitionism*, the source of moral worth is a certain quality actually inhering in the action, trait, disposition, or character that is described as being right or wrong, good or bad. The presence of that quality is detectable through a sort of rational intuition or insight that all normally intelligent human beings are capable of having. We shall now consider each of these normative ethical theories, beginning with the divine command theory.

Divine command theory

This is perhaps the earliest normative theory of ethics, though in its oldest forms it was more assumed than formally worked out. Ancient peoples typically believed that their moral laws were the gifts of gods; they found an ultimate sanction for their moral codes in what they believed were divine edicts which were revealed to human beings through the mediumship of specially appointed prophets, seers, and sibyls. The most ancient known code is the *Code of Hammurabi*, named after a king of Babylon (1704–1662 B.C.E.). It is inscribed on a pillar of jet black diorite, eight feet high, together with an engraving of the king receiving the code from the hand of the sun god, Shamas. The next oldest code is the *Decalogue,* or the Ten Commandments, engraved on stone tablets which Moses is said to have received directly from God atop Mt. Sinai, an event recorded in the Old Testament book of Exodus. The Book of Manu, dating from around 250 B.C.E., is the Hindu moral code traditionally thought to have come from their supreme god. And legend has it that the Islamic code was dictated to Mohammed by the angel Gabriel. These peoples — Babylonians, Jews, Hindus, and Muslims — make the same claims for their different codes; each regards their code as being unique, objectively valid, absolute, and universal because of its divine origins.

The divine command theorist, whatever his creed, makes the same central claim, that the source of all moral value is the will of God. If God wills something, then it is morally good or obligatory; if He forbids it, then it is morally evil; if he is indifferent towards it, then it is morally neutral. Thus, murder, theft, and adultery are morally wrong because, and *only* because, God forbids them; whereas, justice and mercy are morally good *only* because God approves of them. According to the Swiss Protestant theologian, Emil Brunner, "There is no 'intrinsic' Good. What God does and wills is good, and all that opposes the will of God is bad. The good has its basis and its existence solely in the will of God."[1] Indeed, it is conceivable that God might change His mind and command murder, as when He commanded Abraham to kill his son Isaac, or forbid acts of clemency. Simply by willing it, God could make vice virtue and virtue vice.

The divine command theory is first broached as a philosophical theory in Plato's dialogue, *Euthyphro.* Socrates and Euthyphro are attempting to define "holiness" or "piety". Euthyphro proposes the definition that holiness is whatever is loved (willed) by the gods. Socrates objects that this definition is ambiguous: Does Euthyphro mean that something is holy precisely because it is loved by the gods (in other words, their loving it at all is the cause of its being holy) — its being holy is the effect of their loving it? Or, does he mean that the gods love something because it is already holy; that is, its being antecedently holy is the cause of the gods loving it — their loving it is the effect of its prior holiness?[2] Generalizing from the case of holiness (a religious value), we can say either that something is morally good or right because God wills or commands it to be, or that God wills or commands it because it is morally good or right to start with. Either moral value depends on God's will or God's will depends on moral value. In *Euthyphro*, Socrates dramatically presents the two options: either the source of value lies in the divine will, or elsewhere. Both Socrates and Euthyphro agree that it lies elsewhere and reject the divine command theory, though without explanation.

The antiquity of the divine command theory and its association with the world's great religions have not spared it from trenchant criticisms. One such criticism is that it makes nonsensical God's moral goodness, His attributes of love and justice. According to the divine command theory, if God acts from good motives, or for any good reasons or purposes, then they are good only because God declares them so. Thus to say that X is good is to say that God willed it. And to say further that God's *willing* X to be good because it was done from good motives or for good reasons is to say that these motives or reasons are good only because He willed them to be. Consequently, God cannot act from good motives or for good reasons, because to suggest that He does is to beg the question or to go around in a circle: "God's will is good" means nothing more than "God's will is willed by Him." Consequently, God cannot act from good motives or for good reasons other than His willing them as such. Now, our moral common sense tells us that anybody who acts, not from good motives or for any good reasons but only from an urge or will to act, can hardly be said to be acting morally at all — that person is acting blindly, mechanically, or irrationally, which is not the way God is conceived of as acting. Furthermore, God is classically defined as being perfectly good, but according to the divine command theory, God's being good means nothing more than that God willed Himself good. Thus, according to this theory, the only intrinsic good in the world, that which is good in and of itself and from which all goodness is derived, is the divine will. We cannot inquire any further into why it is good without begging the question.

The divine command theory may also be criticized because it makes purely arbitrary the qualities of moral goodness, rightness, or obligatoriness. One's character, disposition, or trait is deemed good or bad or one's action is deemed right, wrong, or obligatory only because God wills or declares it as such. God could just as easily have commanded murder and theft as good, and forbidden justice and mercy as bad. The divine command theory's reduction of moral value to arbitrariness, albeit divine, has two paradoxical implications. First, it destroys the foundation for God's own moral goodness, thereby rendering Him unworthy of our praise and honor. This point is made by Leibniz (1646–1716) in his *Discourse on Metaphysics*:

> In saying, therefore, that things are not good according
> to any standard of goodness, but simply by the will of
> God, it seems to me that one destroys, without realiz-
> ing it, all the love of God and all his glory; for why
> praise him for what he has done, if he would be equally
> praiseworthy in doing the contrary?[3]

Second, it destroys the basis for any moral goodness on our part.
Thus, we ought to do what is right or obligatory, or refrain from doing
what is wrong, only because God commands or forbids it, respectively. And if we ought to obey His commands only because He is all-
powerful, then our obedience is exacted by fear. Fear, though, is not
an adequate moral motive; to obey from fear is not to act morally. The
performing lions and tigers in a circus do no less. This reduces moral
value to the squalid principle of might makes right. "But what makes
might right?" we may legitimately reply. And, third, if moral values
are merely arbitrary, then they cannot admit of any rational justification. The only rationale that can be given for doing what is right and
refraining from doing wrong, for being morally good instead of bad,
is God's will. And because we cannot justify that without begging the
question, then all rational argument comes to a screeching halt. Consequently, some critics have declared the divine command theory null
and void as a normative ethical theory. As we have seen, one of the
minimum requirements for an adequate ethical theory is that it provides reasons or logical grounds for moral evaluations.

A third criticism that may be levied against the divine command
theory is that a command, in and of itself, cannot create a moral
obligation to obey it. If a drunkard orders me off the street, I owe him
no obedience. If a member of a gang that has kidnapped me orders me
to do something I may obey, but out of prudence and not a sense of
moral obligation. A command's moral obligatoriness depends on the
character of the commander. If I am under his legitimate authority, or
if he is worthy of obedience because of his superior knowledge, skill,
or wisdom, then I have a duty to obey him. Thus, we ought to obey
God's commands, not because they are commands, but because they
are *God's* commands. If God is perfectly good, being perfectly loving
and perfectly just, together with being all-knowing and all-wise, then
we, as His inferior creatures, are obligated to obey Him. We obey
Him, not from the brute force of His commands, but from His worthiness to be obeyed; however, the divine command theory prevents
us from obeying God for any reason other than the command itself.
If we obey from consideration of God's worthiness or goodness,

being itself the result of a prior divine command, then we are back in our circle.

A fourth objection that may be made to the divine command theory is epistemological: how do we know that a moral law that is said by its adherents to be a divine command is in fact so? This objection takes several distinct forms. To start with, as we mentioned earlier, there is a variety of moral codes, each of which is claimed to be divinely inspired by the culture which produces it, such as those of Hammurabi, Moses, Manu, and Islam. Moreover, these codes contain different laws, and a law in one may contradict a law in another. Suppose that the Islamic code forbids the consumption of alcohol, though not beef; the Code of Manu forbids the consumption of beef, though not alcohol; and the Mosaic Code forbids neither. What are we to do? Each of these codes claims divine authority, and so, on the divine command theory, must be adhered to. But in cases of contra-dictory laws, only one can be right. But which one? We have no recourse than to consider the source of these codes. They cannot all be equally divine in origin. If they are, then either God contradicts Him-self or there are many gods holding different moral opinions. Neither an irrational God nor polytheism is acceptable. Therefore, we have no alternative but to accept one of these codes as being divinely inspired and reject the rest. Now, though, we have the problem of determining which of these codes, all having an equal claim to divinity, is actually of God. The divine command theory provides no criteria or tests for distinguishing the code that originates in God from that which does not — to distinguish the authentic from the fake.

A related epistemological difficulty is this: Assuming that we know which moral code originates with God and so contains His commands, how do we know that all its laws have equal weight and thus are equally binding? The same religion may split into separate factions over a disagreement concerning the status of a law in their common code. For example, in the Old Testament, God clearly com-mands His menfolk to wear hairlocks and hats. Orthodox Jews abide by that law, but Reformed Jews do not. Who is right, and how can we tell? Furthermore, a religion may split into opposed camps over the *interpretation* of the same law. The Decalogue states, "Thou shalt not kill." The Amish, Mennonites, and Quakers believe that this injunc-tion applies even to the enemies of their country, and so they are pacifists; however, most members of other Protestant denominations and Roman Catholics think it excludes foreign enemies and so allow that a "just" war is morally permissible. Again, the divine command theory is powerless to help here.

A fifth objection that may be raised against the divine command theory is that it violates the *law of parsimony*, also known as *Ockham's Razor* after the medieval monk who first formulated it.[4] This law is basically a principle of economy which states that we should not assume more than is necessary in our explanations; in other words, we should keep our assumptions to a minimum when explaining things. Consider this admittedly farfetched example. A small child wants to know why the grandfather clock in the corner ticks. I explain that a mouse lives inside which makes it tick. Now, the ticking of the clock can be explained just as easily, and more convincingly, in terms of the mechanical springs, levers, and pulleys to be found inside it. I do not need to assume the existence of any mechanically minded mouse. To do so is to make a completely unnecessary assumption. By the same token, to explain the origins of moral value by reference to God or to define moral terms such as "good" and "right" in terms of a divine will or to find the authority or sanction for moral laws in God's commands is to assume that God does indeed exist. But this is an assumption, and though plausible reasons may be given for its acceptance, equally plausible reasons may be given for its rejection.

What if, however, one rejects the assumption that God exists? This brings us to a sixth objection to the divine command theory — namely, that either it is impossible for atheists to be morally good or, if they are morally good, they are so by accident and can give no explanation for their being so. According to the divine command theory, I can be morally good and do what is morally right or obligatory only if I know what God wills in the case. But if I do not believe in God, then there can be no question of my consulting His will. An atheist can be moral through adherence to the legal code where it agrees with the moral code, such as where it proscribes murder and theft; however, he cannot be moral for the right reason, which is willing conformity to God's will. And, in conduct that lies beyond the province of the civil law, he can hardly know whether he is acting either morally or immorally because he acts in ignorance of God's commands. The atheist then is morally blind. This implication of the divine command theory is clearly false. There are many men and women who, though atheists or agnostics, live morally exemplary lives. Buddhism, one of the world's great religions whose moral code rivals Christianity's, is an atheistic religion. Does this mean that Buddhists are morally stunted because they typically do not believe in God? Furthermore, many normative ethical theories, particularly utilitarianism and intuitionism, are purely secular in outlook and do not depend on the existence of God or the supernatural in their moral evaluations.

Incidentally, this implication of the divine command theory that atheists must necessarily be immoral, amoral, or, at best, morally blind has had some interesting legal ramifications. At some places and time, even in the United States, people have been disqualified from holding public office or positions of public trust because they are atheists. John Locke, one of the most liberal minds of the 17th century, in his *Letter on Toleration* argued persuasively for religious toleration in England. He contended that the various sects of Protestants, Jews, and even Catholics should be allowed the freedom to practice their beliefs. Yet, he explicitly stipulated that one group under no circumstances should be tolerated by the state, and that was atheists.[5] The rationale behind all these decisions was that atheists are morally suspect, an implication of the divine command theory.

Finally, it can be objected that the divine command theory confuses morality with religion. The fact is the "moral institution" of life (to borrow Bishop Butler's phrase) is fundamentally distinct from religious institutions. Some religions, such as Voodoo and Satanism, are amoral or even immoral. Even in the great religions of Judaism, Christianity, Islam, Hinduism, and Buddhism, being moral, though essential, is only part of being religious. Morality concerns our relationships with our fellow human beings, but religion is concerned chiefly with our relationship to a sacred or transcendent order which is typically represented by gods or God. Thus, in Judaism, there are the "moral" commandments which prescribe our relationships with our neighbor (the proscriptions of murder, theft, and adultery), but then there are the specifically "religious" commandments which prescribe our relationship to God (the forbidding of idolatry and the honoring of the Sabbath). The classic discussion of the fundamental distinction between morality and religion is to be found in Plato's dialogue, *Euthyphro*. Here, Socrates argues that morality has to do with our duties to our neighbor, whereas religion has to do with our duties to God.[6]

The clearest way to understand the distinction between morality and religion, and to see that the moral cannot be reduced to an exercise of the divine will, is that if you seek to justify the rightness of an action or the goodness of a character-trait by reference to God's will, I can still ask whether or not it is *really* good. You declare X good or right because God commanded it. Yet, I can still legitimately ask whether it is good. God commanded Abraham to sacrifice his son, but one can still inquire as to whether Abraham's intention to sacrifice his son was good. Indeed, we can question even God's commands and ask whether any of them is really good. This suggests that moral goodness or rightness is not completely reducible to the divine will, that these qualities are autonomous, and that moral evaluations can be explained and justified without appealing to a deity whose existence is far from established.

Religion, though distinct from it, is not completely irrelevant to morality. It can lend its sanction and authority to our moral beliefs and values — it can, as it were, ratify them. It can provide sometimes needful incentives for being moral, especially in the case of children. Religion can give its imprimatur to the moral life; however, it cannot supplant or totally absorb the moral within itself.

Before we close our discussion of the divine command theory, it behooves us to inquire into its possible merits as a normative ethical theory. One of its merits is that it puts our moral values and beliefs on a firm footing. We can look to the Ten Commandments, for example, and confidently declare that here indeed is an infallible guide to life. We can have confidence in the absolute rightness of a moral code founded upon divine fiat. Our values will be no less destructible than God Himself. They will be like the proverbial rock in the midst of the shifting sands of time and opinion. Second, the divine command theory naturally lends itself to the moral education of the young. It gives strong backing to those moral codes we might endeavor to inculcate in children. Finally, it provides an effective incentive, especially to the immature, for being moral — although it does smack of the carrot and the stick.

Natural law theory

Deontologists such as Plato and St. Thomas Aquinas who reject the divine command theory affirm that moral goodness and rightness are *sui generis*, meaning that they are unique values which cannot be defined or explained in terms of the divine will or any other nonmoral thing. They require no sanction or authority outside of themselves. Moreover, they are objectively real and universal qualities which even God cannot invalidate or change by an arbitrary act of His will. He is bound by reason and wisdom to will only what is good and right and to forbid their opposites. One classic expression of this view, which is a deontological alternative to the divine command theory, is the *natural law theory*.

To understand this normative ethical theory, we need to begin with an excursion into metaphysics. As we mentioned in the first chapter, a discussion of ethics cannot be done in a vacuum. The room of ethics has doors leading to other rooms in the mansion of philosophy. Like any other ethical theory, natural law theory too presupposes a certain metaphysical view of the world. It is to the metaphysical theory undergirding natural law theory that we shall now turn.

As its name suggests, the theory of natural law takes its cue from nature, and the first natural law theorist was Aristotle (384–322 B.C.), who, not coincidentally, was a biologist and wrote the first textbooks in botany and zoology. He had made the commonplace observation that in the natural order there are processes forever going on of birth, growth, maturation, decay, and death. Living organisms are dynamic things which are constantly undergoing some kind of change. Aristotle further observed that all the changes and activities of organisms seemed to be for the realization of a certain end or purpose.[7] Thus, trees alternately produce and shed leaves. The chlorophyll in the leaves interacts chemically with sunlight and through photosynthesis produces oxygen, which makes life possible. Trees have myriad uses other than the production of this gas; they provide essential habitats for a variety of flora and fauna, and for us they are an indispensable source of shade, food, fuel, timber, and even beauty. But the function they perform naturally and best, and for which they are physiologically designed, is the photosynthetic production of oxygen, which is their chief purpose or end. Consider another example. A woman's body, together with the changes and activities specific to it, is made to bear and nurture children. It is physiologically constructed for that task. Her body may have many other uses, such as athletic competition, physical labor, or modeling, but the function it performs naturally and for which it is uniquely designed is the bearing and nurture of offspring, which is its chief purpose or end. (Let me not be misunderstood as saying that a woman's purpose is to bear children, but only the purpose of her *body*.) For Aristotle, then, every organism has something that it does best and that it is naturally equipped to do, and whatever that may be is its unique purpose or function. Consequently, everything in nature has a purpose, which represents a teleological view of nature.[8]

Aristotle believed that every natural process, because it is natural, is good, and its unique function or purpose is also good because this represents its optimal state. On the other hand, whatever interferes with a natural process, preventing it from performing its proper function or realizing its end, is bad. Now, in order for an organism to function optimally and expeditiously attain its purpose, its activity must conform to a pre-established pattern, order, rule, or law; otherwise, it will by dysfunctional and fail in its purpose. This is the law of its nature. Thus, a tree and a woman's body, if free to abide by the innate laws of their natures, will produce oxygen and children, respectively.

Let us now turn to the moral implications of this teleological theory of nature. Human beings, like other organisms, have certain naturally implanted appetites, desires, instincts, dispositions, and capacities. Thus, we have appetites for food, drink, and sexual intercourse; we desire shelter, companionship, and knowledge; we have instincts for pleasure and survival; and we have the capacities for various forms of physical activity and thought represented by the myriad skills human beings have perfected. Each of these appetites and desires represents a certain vital need and has a specific function or purpose, the fulfillment of which is necessary for survival. Thus, the purpose of our appetite for food, or hunger, is to ensure the nourishment of our bodies. If that purpose is met, then health is maintained. The purpose of sexual relations is to produce offspring. If that function is fulfilled, then the survival of our species is promoted. Whatever is conducive to the realization of these several purposes essential to human health and survival Aristotle deems good, but whatever is not he deems bad. However, what we do naturally, uniquely, and best is to reason or engage in logical thought — hence Aristotle's definition of "man" as a rational animal. So, for Aristotle, our highest function and aim in life is the rational contemplation of existence, which issues in philosophical wisdom or theoretical insight into the nature of things.[9] All of our other activities and functions, to be well-ordered and good, must ultimately be directed to the realization of this, our supreme end as human beings. Consequently, the good life is the rational life, the one which is lived strictly according to the regimen of reason, the law of our nature, thereby enabling us to reach the goal of wisdom.

We shall close our exposition of the theory of natural law with a specific application. Christian ethics, particularly that of the Roman Catholic Church, has traditionally condemned homosexual acts. One rationale for this condemnation, based on natural law theory, is that such acts are "unnatural", which means they are contrary to the law of sexual intercourse. The purpose or function of sexual intercourse is procreation, which is good because it is its natural, proper, and useful effect, and whatever interferes with or prevents the realization of this good purpose is bad. Homosexual acts, obviously, thwart that purpose.

They represent a hideous perversion of the intent and integrity of sexual activity. Hence, they must be condemned as evil. Now note that what makes homosexuality wrong according to natural law theory is not the unsavoriness of the act itself, but its dysfunctionality. Again, the Roman Catholic Church's prohibitions against masturbation (what, significantly, it euphemistically calls "self-abuse"), abortion, and artificial means of birth-control — all of which impede procreation — are applications of the theory of natural law. Curiously, St. Thomas Aquinas considered masturbation a worse sin than adultery, as the latter might at least result in conception.

There are several problems with the natural law theory of ethics. We shall begin with the problem of determining whether there are any such things as natural laws. The concept of natural law presupposes that there are purposes that both are and ought to be realized in nature; realizing these purposes, which represents a more perfect state of existence, is good, and thwarting them is bad. However, if there are no objectively real purposes in nature, then any moral evaluation based upon success or failure in their realization is baseless. So are there any such purposes? There may be, but identifying them is difficult. The difficulty is determining whether an effect of something is its actual purpose. Nature produces myriad effects, but how can we tell that any of them qualifies as a *bona fide* purpose or end? What criteria might we apply in determining whether any particular effect is indeed a purpose? All purposes are effects, but not all effects are purposes. Consider our example of trees. Trees have multiple effects in the ecosystem, such as the production of oxygen, habitats, and food, but which of these effects is its purpose? Moreover, any effect we designate as a purpose may in fact be merely a means to some future effect (of which we might be quite ignorant) that is the real purpose of the thing in question. Effects may themselves be but causes or links in a long causal chain that terminates in the realization of a purpose of which we are scarcely aware. But, there again, there may be no purposes at all in the affair, but only a long sequence of causes and effects.

Furthermore, those effects we think of as nature's purposes are invariably effects beneficial to ourselves. An effect of the ozone layer is the blocking out of ultraviolet rays harmful to human beings; hence, that must be its purpose. An effect of rain is replenishment of the earth which makes possible the growth of crops essential to the maintenance of human life; again, that must be its purpose. It seems that our criterion for deciding that a natural effect is an end is that it in some way benefits us, but this is too subjective a criterion. Ozone, rain, and countless other natural phenomena do benefit us, but it does not follow that this is their objective or natural end. Our teleological interpretation of nature smacks too much of *anthropomorphism*, which is understanding the world exclusively from a narrow human perspective, as if everything in the universe revolved around us. As the Greek philosopher Xenophanes of Colophon (c. 570–c. 480 B.C.E.) once quipped, "The gods of the Ethiopians are dark-skinned and snub-nosed; the gods of the Thracians are fair and blue-eyed; if oxen could paint, their gods would be oxen."[10]

Finally, modern science has abandoned a teleological view of nature. Teleology played an indispensable part in both ancient Greek and medieval science. It was then thought that to comprehend fully how something came to be the way it is, to explain completely its structure and how it was made, you had to understand its function or purpose. Thus, just to identify an unfamiliar tool, to explain adequately how and why it was made the way it is, you need to know what it is used for. If I know a hammer is designed specifically to bang in nails, I can better understand how and why it came to have the shape it has. Similarly, to understand the physiology of a tree — its high trunk, its broad crown, and myriad leaves — I need to know its function in the ecosystem, what it is that a tree is uniquely and perfectly equipped to do. However, in the second half of the 17th century, this traditional teleological view of nature was largely given up by natural scientists for the very reasons that we have already cited. The members of the then recently formed Royal Society of London, a still extant scientific body dedicated to the promotion of the natural sciences, stipulated in their charter that they would not be concerned with inquiring into the purposes or ends of things as this lay beyond the competence of science and its method.[11] Such an inquiry was better left to theologians and metaphysicians. So, science became exclusively concerned with *how* things happen, not *why* (in its purposive sense).

Another set of problems with natural law theory clusters around the very concept of law. This theory, either deliberately or inadvertently, confuses as one two distinct conceptions of law. One conception is used in the sciences and is exemplified in Newton's Laws of Motion and Boyle's Laws of Gases. These scientific or physical laws are *descriptive*; their function is to describe certain regularities among natural events which render these events intelligible, predictable, and so perhaps controllable. But another conception of law is used in moral and legal codes and is exemplified in the Decalogue and the statutes legislated by state governments. These moral or civil laws are *prescriptive*; their function is to prescribe and proscribe certain forms of conduct and to sanction the imposition of penalties or public disapproval for their infraction. The difference between these two conceptions of law is basically this: in the one the law informs us as to what is actually the case; in the other conception, the law informs us as to what we may or ought to do. Other differences follow from this. Scientific or physical laws may be verified as true using the canonical procedures of testing, observation, and experimentation enshrined in the scientific method. Moral or civil laws, on the other hand, admit of no such empirical verification. Once we inform ourselves of the law, there is no further question as to whether or not the law is "true" and no need or provision to test for its truth. If it is the law, then it is binding, and that is the end of it. Moreover, physical laws are discovered; they have an objective and unchanging existence "out there" and need only to be formulated. Moral and civil laws, by contrast, are manmade and may be changed. Finally, scientific laws are inexorable and cannot be broken with impunity. If I jump out of a window on the tenth floor, I must suffer the consequences, unless some kind of human intervention occurs, but I may exceed the speed limit on the highway and get away with it; indeed, I may even be apprehended but talk my way out of a ticket.

Now, natural law conflates into one both of these distinct conceptions of law — the law as description and the law as prescription. Natural law purports to describe what is actually the case — for example, that the purpose of trees is to produce oxygen. But then it presumes to tell us what ought to be the case; namely, that trees ought to realize their purpose by producing oxygen, and so they are good if they do but bad if they do not. Even if we can establish a thing's purpose (which, as we have already seen, is difficult enough), it by no means follows that the thing *ought* to realize that purpose. To infer that it does is to commit the *naturalistic fallacy*. A form of the naturalistic fallacy is to infer what ought to be (an "ought" statement) from what is (an "is" statement). Incidentally, we shall return to the issue of this fallacy, and how it might be avoided, in a subsequent chapter in metaethics.

Related to this is that the theory of natural law confuses moral goodness with natural goodness, two quite distinct senses of good. It may be naturally good for the tree to produce oxygen, as this is a beneficial result and is the hallmark of a healthy tree. By the same token, it is naturally good for a married couple to have many children;

it is a legitimate function of marriage and may be an unending source of profound happiness to the parents and other relatives. But is it morally good as well? And is it morally wrong for a couple not to produce children when they are able? These are particularly significant questions in light of the fact that our planet, with its limited and strained resources, is already vastly overpopulated. Again, to derive a moral value or obligation from a naturally good state of affairs is to commit the naturalistic fallacy.

Further, it would seem that, on the principle of natural law theory which regards as evil any interference with natural processes that thwarts the realization of their ends, many technological interferences in the course of natural events must be regarded as evil as well, despite the fact that they improve the human condition. This would include such things as the genetic altering of wheat and corn in order to produce a more viable crop, medical interventions such as drugs and surgery to cure and prevent disease, and the damming and diversion of rivers from their natural courses for the sake of hydro-electric power. If artificial means of birth control are to be condemned on the principle of natural law because they thwart the realization of the true end of sexual intercourse, then should not these other interventions be condemned on similar grounds? In the 18th century, debate raged over the propriety of inoculating against smallpox. Those opposed to it contended that this was to interfere with the natural course of nature and so a willful violation of God's laws.[12] More recently, opponents of cloning and other forms of genetic engineering for eugenic purposes who cite the "unnaturalness" of such procedures are echoing the theory of natural law. Indeed, there are many sexual practices which are either legally or morally proscribed simply because they are deemed "unnatural acts", another evocation of this theory.

Another problem with natural law theory related to the concept of law is that the very status and plausibility of scientific law are now being seriously questioned by scientists and philosophers of science. It has long been held that the physical laws governing nature are somehow absolute, universal, eternal, and unchangeable, like the laws of logic. Just as the equation "$2 + 2 = 4$" is absolutely true for all time and in all places, so has the law of gravity operated and always will operate everywhere in the same way. It was long believed that the laws of physics, like the laws of Moses, were carved in stone, but now this supposed absoluteness and universality of scientific laws are being challenged. Laws are no longer understood as quasi-mythic and abstract forces at work in the world but are simply descriptions of perceived regularities in nature. Physical laws are currently understood as little more than "statistical generalizations". We have come to realize that just because specific events have always occurred in a certain way in the past, it by no means follows that they will or must thus occur in the future. And just because physical laws are known to operate constantly in our part of the universe, it does not mean that they do so everywhere else — the regularities among natural events that we observe in our corner of the world may not occur elsewhere.

Incidentally, the preceding discussion of the concept of scientific law belongs to the philosophy of science, another branch of philosophy related to epistemology, metaphysics, and logic. This is yet another example of how other philosophical disciplines are indispensable to ethics — in this case, how the philosophy of science raises problems for a particular normative ethical theory, namely the theory of natural law.

There is yet another problem with this theory which is a recurrence of a problem we had with the divine command theory. Natural law theory also violates the principle of parsimony by presupposing the existence of God. Let me explain. The only things that can have purposes, having the capacity to frame, implement, and expedite them, are minds. Human minds, of course, can act purposively or intentionally (although behaviorists deny it); however, organisms bereft of minds, intelligence, or consciousness, such as trees, can hardly be said to be capable of acting purposively. The only purposes they can properly be said to have are not their own, but those that we bestow upon them. Thus, trees serve many purposes (as building materials, food, fuel, or recreation), but these are all human purposes. None of them is indigenous to the trees themselves. Again, the photosynthetic production of oxygen, if it is indeed a purpose or function of trees, is not one belonging to trees themselves as they can scarcely be aware of such a thing. Nor is it something that we have conferred upon them. Their usefulness as the lungs of the planet is not a function that we gave them, as is their furnishing lumber for our houses or ornaments for our gardens. So, if the production of oxygen is a tree's natural purpose or function, and it was bestowed by neither itself nor human beings, then such a purpose can only have been bestowed by God. However, this is to presuppose the existence of something doubtful. Thus, to claim that there are purposes in nature that are being realized through natural processes is to presuppose the existence of God who alone is capable of framing and implementing purposes for things which themselves are incapable of doing so. But, as we saw before in our discussion of the divine command theory, the assumption of doubtful entities in order to prove a point is to walk the edge of Ockham's Razor.

What, then, can we say in defense of the theory of natural law as a normative theory of ethics? One of its advantages, which it shares with the divine command theory, is that it puts our moral lives and judgments on a firm footing. What could be firmer or carry more authority, or be a better guide, than nature? What could be more sensible or commendable than living in conformity to nature's laws and, in concert with the rest of the natural order, realizing our highest purposes as human beings? Moreover, moral judgments based on natural law are not merely expressions of our own ephemeral subjectivism or of the artificial conventions of society, but are reflections of something objective, real, and natural.

Second, the teleological view of nature held by natural law theorists may no longer be obsolete. There is currently a new interest, especially on the part of biologists, in reviving teleology — albeit in a much more complex form than that conceived of by classical or medieval philosophers — in order to explain better the behavior of living things. Re-establishing teleology as a viable scientific postulate would obviously boost the prestige and viability of the natural law theory of ethics.

Finally, the theory of natural law is venerable and has proved itself highly adaptable. It was a pillar of the classical ethics of Greece and Rome and survives even today in Christian ethics, especially that inspired by St. Thomas Aquinas.

Kant's ethics

Immanuel Kant (1724–1804) is one of the five or so greatest philosophers, and a polymath. In addition to philosophy, he taught theology, physics, and astronomy. To the latter field he, along with the French mathematician and astronomer, Pierre Simon De Laplace (1749–1827), even made an original contribution, the so-called Kant-Laplace Hypothesis. According to this theory, the universe consists of star-clusters, or galaxies, scattered throughout the abyss of space like islands in a sea. Appropriately enough, this theory is also known as the "island theory" of the universe. Kant made significant contributions to epistemology and metaphysics, and other branches of philosophy, as well as ethics. Moreover, his epistemology, metaphysics, and ethics are of a piece; no one of them can be adequately studied independently of the others. He was an architectonic thinker whose various ideas, concepts, and theories were united in an all-encompassing system. Thus, to isolate any particular area of his philosophy, such as his ethics, and to study it apart from the context of the whole is to do violence to it. With this warning in mind, we shall be so bold as to attempt to summarize (albeit inadequately) his ethical theory so as to give it its due as an important theory and an alternative to the other normative ethical theories under discussion. However, if it piques your interest, there is no substitute for reading for yourself Kant's own books on the subject. Incidentally, this advice applies as well to all the other theories that we discuss; go to the primary texts themselves whenever you have the time or inclination. Kant wrote two major works in moral philosophy which bear the rather forbidding titles (in English translation) of *The Critique of Practical Reason* and *Foundations of the Metaphysics of Morals*. Our summary is based on both of these books.

Kant was awe-struck, as he said, "by the starry heavens above and the moral law within." His being overawed by the firmament would be natural for an astronomer, but it is especially noteworthy that he found the moral law within — our sense of duty — no less sublime than the heavens. And for a shining example of that moral law in action he needed to look no further than his faithful man servant who was loyal and dutiful. What particularly struck Kant was that this man was unlettered, but though his intellect was dim his moral character was brilliant. Kant's moral philosophy is an attempt to explain why the sense of duty, as his servant displayed, is the very essence of morality. Kant's ethical theory involves three basic and closely interrelated elements — freedom, will, and duty — which it will now be our task to extrapolate.

Kant believed that human beings are capable of *autonomy*, or freedom of will, but we are autonomous or free only when we act according to our duty. To understand Kant's conception of moral freedom, we need first to understand its opposite, which is *heteronomy* or the lack of freedom. To act heteronomously is to be governed in our actions by factors or objects external to ourselves. For example, to do what I want, or to act out of my personal desire, is to be controlled by the object wanted or desired. If I am desperately thirsty and water is offered to me, I cannot help but drink it. For that matter, whenever I act from self-interest or pursue pleasure or happiness, I am drawn as to a magnet by those objects which will satisfy my interests. I am, as it were, bound by them, and so unfree. In this way, I am no different from a circus animal who is bound to perform only from the prospect of a reward or the threat of punishment.

By contrast, I can act with no regard to my self-interest, pleasure, happiness, or any other external object; indeed, I can act against them — I can do things I do not want to do. Such is sometimes the case when I act from a sense of duty. My duty may be painful and may even incur disastrous results for me, but I do it anyway. Let us suppose I have made a promise to someone. Something unforeseen has come up which means that keeping that promise is going to be inconvenient; moreover, no serious consequences will occur by my breaking it. Nevertheless, I do keep my promise. Note that by my not weakly succumbing to the temptation of an easy out but instead manfully keeping my promise and meeting my obligation, I escape the control of those external circumstances which threaten to deflect me from my duty. I am thus acting not from any external impulse but wholly from an inner one. Despite the magnetic pull of exterior temptations, I freely choose to heed the still small voice of duty which I hear within me. I am under no compulsion to do so, and I face no penalty for not doing so. At that moment of freely choosing to do my duty, according to Kant, I am a perfectly free or autonomous agent.

Doing our duty is exercising what Kant calls a "good will". A good will is the uniquely human capacity for freely choosing to act from a sense of duty. Kant deems this good will the only thing in the world that is good without qualification or exception — in other words, it is the sole intrinsic good.

But what is our duty? How do we determine whether a particular deed is right or obligatory? How do we come to know what we ought to do? The last question is for Kant the fundamental question of ethics. Kant answers that we can arrive at this moral knowledge simply through the exercise of reason, or taking rational thought. This is something that any human being of normal intelligence is eminently capable of doing. And exercising reason in moral determinations means asking certain questions of, or applying specific criteria to, the action in question. Let us illustrate this procedure by returning to the case of Mark Fuhrman.

He is tempted, say, to plant the bloody glove in order to incriminate Simpson. Simpson, he is convinced, is guilty, and this will be a sure-fire way of putting him behind bars, thereby satisfying the demand of justice and promoting the public safety. However, something gives him pause. He realizes that planting the glove is a form of deception or lying, and he knows that lying is wrong. But why? Kant proposes that he ask this question of himself: Could he, Fuhrman, rationally wish that the principle upon which he is tempted to act, namely, that it is right to deceive or lie for reasons of expediency, would be a principle upon which all persons in similar circumstances should act? Or, putting it another way, suppose that Fuhrman is a World Law-Maker who has the authority of making moral laws which all persons must obey. As such, could Fuhrman rationally legislate the maxim as law that all persons, for reasons of expediency, ought always and everywhere lie? In other words, could Fuhrman, as a rational agent, impose such a universal law as unconditionally binding on all persons? If he can honestly answer "yes", then it is right and perhaps obligatory to plant the glove; however, if the answer to these questions is "no", then it is wrong for him to do so and his duty is to refrain from doing it. Now note that the principle at work here is the principle of *universalizability*, which Kant formulates as follows: "Act only according to that maxim by which you can at the same time will that it should become a universal law."[13] This means, in a nutshell, we should act only from those principles (Kant calls them "maxims") that we could rationally will that all persons in all times and places should obey — in other words, that we could rationally choose to make them universal. Any maxim or principle that can be universalized in this way is either right or our duty; any that cannot is wrong. This is the test of universalizability.

A crucial term in this test is "rationally" — could we *rationally* universalize a maxim or principle of action? It is not a question of whether we would want to do so; we might desire it because we believe that it might serve our self-interest. Personal wants and desires are purely subjective and so cannot be universalized, and they may also be irrational. I may desperately want something that my reason tells me is bad for me. Neither Fuhrman nor anyone else could rationally will that lying and deception, even for the sake of expediency, should be a principle that all people in all times and places should act on. To make lying and deception a moral norm would be to undercut truth; nobody's word thereafter could be taken on anything, and rational discourse would cease. Thus, for Kant, lying and other forms of deception are morally wrong and our duty to avoid.

It might also occur to Fuhrman that his rationale for planting that bloody glove is to clinch the conviction of someone whom he knows to be guilty, and so he rationalizes that planting the glove is justified because it would ensure that justice is done and contribute to the public safety. Simpson, then, who would be convicted on falsified evidence, is to be used as a scapegoat, an expendable pawn, in the cause of justice. But, for Kant, using a human being in this way — however guilty and wretched he may be — makes planting the glove — however beneficial its consequences — morally wrong. Kant lays down as a fundamental moral axiom the following: "Act so that you treat humanity, whether in your own person or in that of another, always as an end and never as a means only."[14] This he calls the *practical imperative*. Let us now clarify this principle and see what Kant means by treating a person as "a means only" as distinct from "an end".

To treat persons as means is to use or manipulate them, either against their will or without their knowledge, in order to realize some end or purpose of which they either are ignorant or did not freely choose as their own — in other words, it is to use them as pawns or steppingstones without their consent. Examples of such manipulation would include a company closing a local plant, thereby putting thousands of their workers out of work, so that it may relocate in a foreign country and profit by the use of cheaper labor; or a sponsor of children's television programs using commercials to entice unwitting children or their parents into buying its products; or a tobacco company using attractive images and other subliminal tricks in their advertising specifically aimed at youngsters in order to lure them into smoking. To manipulate people without their consent or to trick them thus is to deprive them of their freedom and to give them no opportunity of exercising reason or thought about their actions. It is to treat them as if they were little more than brute animals or inanimate objects which are neither free nor rational agents. By contrast, to treat persons as ends in themselves is to give them every opportunity to exercise their unique human endowments of reason and freedom and so to honor them as free and rational agents. Human beings, insists Kant, must be treated "only as beings who must be able to contain in themselves the end of the very same action."[15] This means that humans are beings who have the freedom to choose their own purposes or ends and are competent to frame and implement them. Thus, to treat them as ends is to give them ample scope to exercise their freedom in choosing, and their reason in implementing, their purpose.

Kant puts the highest premium on our God-like attributes of freedom and reason; they are what constitute our "intrinsic worth" or dignity as human beings and make us valuable "above all price". One reason he thinks we have such *intrinsic* value is that all other things have value only because of their relationship to us, to our particular desires, needs, and ends. Thus, science and technology have value solely because they serve our desire to know and our need to control nature, the fine arts have value simply because they delight us, and the planet's various natural resources have value only because they are indispensable to our survival. All things other than persons, then, have merely *extrinsic* value — that is, their value depends on and is derived from something other than themselves. By contrast, our human value is utterly independent of and not derived from anything else. We have value in and of ourselves. A second reason Kant ascribes intrinsic value to us is that of all known creatures we alone are endowed with the capacities to reason and to choose freely. All other animals are determined in their behavior by the blind forces of instinct. Because of this unique endowment, we are competent to discover the moral law, or know our duty, and are free to act upon it, thereby making us the only moral beings in nature. An implication of Kant's idea of human dignity (other than that we should treat one another "always as an end and never as a means only") is that we ought to be beneficent to each other, to "endeavor, so far as we can, to further the ends of others."[16]

In addition to the principle of universalizability, then there is a second principle that Fuhrman might apply to determine whether he ought to plant the glove, namely, Kant's practical imperative. He might ask, "In planting the glove in order to frame Simpson, would I be treating him merely as a means to an end instead of as an end in himself?" If the answer is "yes", then Fuhrman knows he must refrain from doing so.

According to Kant, there is yet a further test Fuhrman might perform, another principle he might evoke, to determine what he ought to do in the case. He might ask, "Suppose the situation were reversed and I was on trial in Simpson's place; would I want a detective to falsify evidence in order to convict me?" Had he raised this question, Fuhrman would have applied Kant's third principle to determine how one ought to act. It is the *principle of reversibility*, which states that in my moral dealings I ought always to treat others only as I would want to be treated by them if I were in their shoes. This principle is nothing other than a reformulation of the Golden Rule, "Do unto others as you would be done by."

As we have seen and illustrated, Kant proposes three distinct principles, tests, or criteria that we might apply to enable us to decide what we ought to do in any given case. The first is the principle of universalizability which stipulates that we should act only on those precepts or maxims that we could rationally desire to have as universal laws; in other words, do only that which we would rationally want everyone to do were they in our circumstances. The second is the practical imperative which states that we should always treat others as ends and never as means; that is, we should treat all persons, because of their rationality and freedom, as beings having inalienable dignity or worth. The third is the principle of reversibility, which insists that we should always treat others as if they were one with ourselves. Although these are three distinct principles, Kant thought them simply three different formulations of one principle, like the different facets of the same diamond or the different colors of the spectrum refracted by a single beam of sunlight. Whether or not they are distinct principles, or merely different versions of the same principle, is an issue in the interpretation of Kant's ethics which need not detain us.

But there is a common thread linking these three principles which is that they equally demand consistency on our part in our moral judgments. Thus, according to the principle of universalizability, we must ascertain what unexceptionable rule we would rationally want everybody to follow and then, to be consistent, we must follow it ourselves. According to the practical imperative, we must treat all persons as being equal in dignity, which means that our conduct towards any individual must be the same or consistent. And according to the principle of reversibility, we must treat each and every person as being one with ourselves; again, there must be consistency between the way we treat ourselves and the way we treat others.

Kant considers his principle of universalizability — such as to act only according to those moral rules or precepts which we could rationally make universal — as fundamental and his other two principles of the practical imperative and of reversibility as simply alternative formulations of the first. He calls the principle of universalizability the *categorical imperative*. To grasp what he means by this, let us contrast it with the so-called *hypothetical imperative*.

Now as their names suggest, they are equally demands, but of quite different kinds; they both involve something one ought to do, but the basis and bindingness of the "ought" are different. Suppose you want to go to law school. I advise you to major in philosophy as an undergraduate as this will hone the sort of skills you will need to apply as a lawyer. Or, let's say you want to bake a cake. I recommend your using a Betty Crocker cake mix as using it will guarantee a successful cake. Finally, suppose you wish to travel safely on a safari. I strongly suggest that you buy a Land Rover for your expedition as it can withstand the impact of a fully charging rhinoceros. In each of these cases, I am telling you what you ought to do in order to get what you desire and to achieve your goal. I am simply recommending certain means to be followed to reach your desired end; however, your taking my advice depends entirely on whether you want to achieve the goal in question. If you do not want to go to law school, or bake a cake, or go on a safari, then you need not take the steps I suggest; you are neither "bound" nor "obliged" to take them. That you ought to do something in order to achieve a goal depends entirely on whether you desire it. If you do not desire it, the "obligation" ceases entirely. The "ought" involved in these cases is the nonmoral ought. Moreover, if you do desire achieving a certain goal but neglect to take the steps necessary to reach it — that is, you neglect to do what you ought in the case — you may be properly criticized as imprudent or foolish but never as immoral or vicious. Your failure to follow the means to your desired end does not qualify as an object of moral censure. Nor is your success in achieving it morally praiseworthy. The "ought" involved in doing what you ought to do to achieve some desired goal, the demand made upon you in the pursuit of some desirable end, is the hypothetical imperative.

By way of contrast, consider the following moral "oughts": "You ought not to commit murder." "You ought not to steal." "You ought to keep your promises." "You ought to tell the truth." The binding force of these imperatives does not depend on any personal goal you may desire to reach; they bind or obligate you independently of who you are or what you want. They are not merely means to other ends but are ends in themselves. They are to be obeyed not for the sake of anything else but solely for their own sake. As examples of maxims or rules which are rationally universalizable, they are unexceptionable, unconditional, and absolute. They are categorical imperatives.

For Kant, the moral worth of an action depends entirely on its motive; only those actions motivated by a sense of duty or impelled by the force of moral obligation can be deemed morally good. Such actions are intrinsically and unqualifiedly good. Actions done from any other motive, such as self-interest, though they may be morally right and obligatory, are morally impure. Thus, suppose that Fuhrman, though tempted, had decided not to tamper with the evidence, but his motive was fear of the unpleasant consequences to himself if he were caught. To act out of fear is to act in one's own self-interest. On the other hand, suppose his sole motive had been his conviction that lying and deception are wrong and that his duty is to act purely disinterestedly. Note that for Kant, unlike the utilitarians, motives count for everything and consequences for nothing in determining the moral value — the rightness or wrongness — of actions.

Why does Kant deem acts done disinterestedly from a sense of duty morally superior to those done for reasons of self-interest? The reason is that to act from a sense of duty or moral obligation is to act autonomously as a truly free agent; whereas, to act from self-interest — whether it be to secure for oneself or others some future pleasure or happiness or avoid some pain or misery — is to act heteronomously as an unfree agent who is determined instead by factors external to oneself. As we saw earlier, our free will and our reason are the very capacities that constitute our human dignity and confer on us our intrinsic worth as persons. Now, when we act heteronomously we do not act freely. It is only when we act autonomously, even against our deep-seated desires, inclinations, and instincts, that we act freely. Only then are we truly in possession of ourselves as dignified beings.

Our critique of Kant's moral theory begins with his own illustration of why we should never lie. Here is Rachels' retelling of the story:[17]

> Imagine that someone is fleeing from a murderer and tells you he is going home to hide. Then the murderer comes along and asks where the first man went. You believe that if you tell the truth, the murderer will find his victim and kill him. What should you do — should you tell the truth or lie?

Rachels calls this "The Case of the Inquiring Murderer". Kant answers unambiguously that you ought to tell the truth because truth telling is a moral absolute determined by the categorical imperative and so allowing for no exceptions whatsoever. His rationale in this case is curious, coming as it does from a deontologist. He explains that if you lie to save the first man's life you assume that the consequence of telling the truth to the murderer will be the first man's death. But it well may be that the intended victim did not go home but, on second thought, decided to keep running. If this is so, then telling the murderer the lie that his intended victim did not go home is to play right into the murderer's hands and endanger the former's life. Kant's advice, then, is because we can never know with certainty the consequences of our actions, we should play it safe by always abiding by the moral law — in this case, do not lie. Here is Kant's explanation in his own words:[18]

> After you have honestly answered the murderer's ques-
> tion as to whether his intended victim is at home, it
> may be that he has slipped out so that he does not
> come in the way of the murderer, and thus that the
> murder may not be committed. But if you had lied and
> said he was not at home when he had really gone out
> without your knowing it, and if the murderer had then
> met him as he went away and murdered him, you
> might justly be accused as the cause of his death. For
> if you had told the truth as far as you knew it, perhaps
> the murderer might have been apprehended by the
> neighbors while he searched the house and thus the
> deed might have been prevented. Therefore, whoever
> tells a lie, however well intentioned he might be, must
> answer for the consequences, however unforeseeable
> they were, and pay the penalty for them. ...To be
> truthful (honest) in all deliberations, therefore, is a
> sacred and absolutely commanding decree of reason,
> limited by no expediency.

Kant's justification for telling the truth to the murderer is not convincing, for four reasons. First, though he stresses the possible bad consequences of lying, Kant ignores completely the equally possible bad consequences of telling the truth. It could just as well have happened that the intended victim did go home, only to be found and killed by the murderer who was tipped off by your telling him the truth about the whereabouts of his victim. Second, though we perhaps can never have certain knowledge of the consequences of any of our actions, we can have highly probable knowledge, which is good enough for guiding our decisions. Let's say that my best friend and I go to a party and he gets drunk. Anticipating this result, I have taken the precaution of "stealing" his car keys to prevent his driving home and risking his own life and the lives of others. In this case, I may not know for certain the exact consequences of his driving home drunk, but I do know that there is a higher probability of harm resulting from his doing so than from my stealing his keys. If I am thinking consequentially, this is sufficient justification for my theft. And, third, Kant, in his justification for telling the truth to the murderer by citing the possible bad consequences of lying, is contradicting his own principle that consequences are irrelevant in determining what we ought to do. In arguing that as a general rule it is better to tell the truth because of the bad consequences of lying, Kant, ironically, sounds very much like a rule-utilitarian. All that is relevant, according to Kant, is whether or not our action conforms to the categorical imperative. He summarily dismissed what he called "the serpent-windings of Utilitarianism."

The problem illustrated by The Case of the Inquiring Murderer is the moral dilemma of our being torn by two equally absolute but conflicting duties or obligations: On the one hand, we have the duty to tell the truth, but on the other we have the equally compelling duty of beneficence or, as Kant elsewhere described it, to "endeavor, so far as we can, to further the ends of others," which at least means to save innocent human lives. If we seek to save the intended victim's life, then we might tell a lie, but if we are preoccupied with telling the truth at all costs, then we risk killing a man. It is a classic case of "damned if I do, damned if I don't." One problem with Kant's theory of the categorical imperative is that it gives us no procedure for resolving conflicts between moral absolutes, as in the case above. Any moral theory like Kant's that puts us in the impossible position of having to violate one moral precept in the very act of honoring another is flawed.

In defense of Kant, Geach has replied to the above criticism by claiming that The Case of the Inquiring Murderer is an extreme and purely hypothetical case which is unlikely to occur in reality. According to Geach, God will not allow such conflicts between absolutes ever to occur. This is what he says:[19]

> "But suppose circumstances are such that observance of one Divine law, say the law against lying, involves breach of some other absolute Divine prohibition?" — If God is rational, he does not command the impossible; if God governs all events by his providence, he can see to it that circumstances in which a man is inculpably faced by a choice between forbidden acts do not occur. Of course such circumstances (with the clause "and there is no way out" written into their description) are consistently describable; but God's providence could ensure that they do not in fact arise. Contrary to what nonbelievers often say, belief in the existence of God does make a difference to what one expects to happen.

However, to appeal to a supernatural providence to assure that we shall never be caught in the dilemma of having to choose between two

equally binding moral absolutes is to violate the principle of parsimony (i.e., to assume the existence of something which is as problematic as the problem to be solved). If you deny or doubt the existence
of God, then you can hardly take comfort in Geach's assurances.
Furthermore, it is inappropriate to make such an appeal to God in
defending Kant. Kant attempted to establish morality on a purely
rational footing quite independent of a belief in God. To appeal to
divine providence and the faith it presupposes, as Geach does, is to go
beyond Kant's requirements for a moral theory which he wanted to
construct within the limits of reason alone. Finally, recent history has
proved Geach wrong. During the Second World War, for example,
Dutch fisherman, while smuggling Jewish refugees over to England,
would be intercepted by German patrol boats. The German captains
would ask their Dutch counterparts what they were carrying on board
and where they were going. Now, God obviously did not prevent the
Dutch captains from being "inculpably faced by a choice between
forbidden acts" — either lying and saving lives or telling the truth and
causing the death of their Jewish passengers.[20]

A more plausible defense of Kant against the charge that his moral
theory may put us in an impossible moral bind has been suggested by
Anscombe. She writes, "It never occurred to him [Kant] that a lie
could be relevantly described as anything but just a lie (such as 'a lie
in such-and-such circumstances'). His rule about universalizable
maxims is useless without stipulations as to what shall count as a
relevant description of an action with a view to constructing a maxim
about it."[21] An act of lying, as in The Case of the Inquiring Murderer
or that of the Dutch sea captains, may result in the saving of lives. To
describe the act of lying in such cases as simply lying and nothing
more is to leave out a crucially relevant part of its description. It is not
merely an act of lying but, more completely and accurately, an act of
lying which will save a human life. We would not rationally will to
universalize as a moral law the principle of lying for the purpose of
defrauding or bearing false witness, but we would rationally will to
universalize as a moral law the principle of lying for the purpose of
saving lives. Thus, Kant's categorical imperative can be salvaged if we
start with an adequate description of the act we propose to perform
and on that basis formulate the maxim to be universalized.

Kant's fundamental error was his supposition that moral rules
had to be absolute or unexceptionable; however, valid exceptions to
maxims or rules can be built into the very descriptions of the acts
covered by them. Thus, though lying is in principle wrong, lying to

save a life constitutes a valid exception to that general rule. Taking a human life is in principle wrong, but killing in self-defense is a valid exception to the rule against killing. We can still universalize these qualified maxims, such as "Lying is wrong unless it is to save a life," or "Killing is wrong except in cases of self-defense." What this means is that if I lie to save a life or kill in self-defense, then I will that everyone else should do so; however, they may lie or kill only in these exceptional circumstances but not in others. In other words, if I break a moral law for some legitimate reason, then according to the categorical imperative, I will that everyone else may break it for exactly the same reason.

One final criticism may be made of Kant's ethics, which has to do with moral motives. For Kant, only those acts performed purely from a sense of duty or moral obligation have any moral worth. Acts performed from any other motive, such as self-interest, are morally worthless. To illustrate clearly what Kant means here, consider the following case. A father is visited at intervals by his two children. His daughter visits him because she loves him; she delights in his company and enjoys nothing more than to be with him. His son, by contrast, does not visit him out of love or enjoyment of his company; in fact, he hates his father but visits him solely from a sense of duty or obligation. Both children do what is right, but the son's action has more moral worth for Kant because he is acting out of a sense of duty alone. But this flies in the face of our moral common sense. Is it not questionable that the son's motive is morally superior to his sister's? Do we not esteem the daughter's motive more highly and would we not rather be visited by someone like her rather than her brother? Kant's motto seems to be, "No pain, no moral gain."

What, then, can be said in defense of Kant's ethical theory? First, it fully honors human dignity by appealing to our rationality and freedom. Second, it shows that the exercise of reason is at the very heart of the moral life inasmuch as to live by the categorical imperative is fundamentally a matter of being consistent in all of our doings. This means that, in the name of consistency, no one is exempt from the moral law and that the constraints and restraints on our conduct are rational. For Kant, the moral life is fundamentally a rational life, and a rational life is pre-eminently a moral life. Third, unlike utilitarianism, Kant's theory preserves the values of justice and of human individuality. Because it strictly forbids the treatment of people as means to ends, there is no question of using people as scapegoats, however expedient. Fourth, Kant's ethics preserves inviolate the autonomy and integrity of the moral order. Egoists and some utilitarians reduce moral values to nothing more than matters of pleasure or pain, happiness or misery. In their reductionism, morality is nothing other than an aspect of human psychology. The moral realm is dissolved in the psychological, but Kant makes no such reduction of moral value to psychological states. For him, moral obligation, in its sometimes opposing what we want to do, or what will give us pleasure or happiness, reveals itself as something utterly distinct from and irreducible to our psychology. Kant does not compromise the majesty of the moral law.

Let me close this section by mentioning that Kant was no armchair moralist. He was concerned with moral practice and thought that the moral law should apply no less to the conduct of nations. In an essay, whose English title is *Towards Perpetual Peace*, he proposed that the nations of Europe should form themselves into a union or league and pledge to settle any dispute or conflict among them not by force of arms but by the impartial arbitration of an international court of justice. Each nation would be bound by the decision of this court. Kant thus anticipated Woodrow Wilson's League of Nations and the United Nations by more than a hundred years. It is no small irony that in 1795, when Kant's essay was published, a young Corsican corporal was steadily rising through the ranks of the army of post-revolutionary France.

Ross' prima facie *ethics*

As we have seen, a problem with Kant's ethics is that it provides no way of resolving conflicts between absolute duties, such as the conflict between the duties of telling the truth and of preserving human life as in The Case of the Inquiring Murderer. In that case, we are caught in the dilemma of necessarily violating one duty in the very act of performing another. David Ross (1877–1940) sought to salvage Kant's deontological ethics by resolving such conflicts. He did so by making a distinction between so-called *prima facie* duties and actual duties. *Prima facie* means literally "on first face" or "apparently so". *Prima facie* duties, like the categorical imperative, are those which, when considered in themselves in the abstract, are unconditional or absolute and incumbent on us to perform, *unless* they conflict with other *prima facie* duties. Thus, telling the truth is a *prima facie* duty which, on face value, we ought always to do; however, *prima facie* duties may come into conflict. In The Case of the Inquiring Murderer, our duty always to tell the truth clashes with our duty always to preserve human life. In such a case, according to Ross, one of the conflicting duties will be more compelling or obligatory than the other, and so this becomes our *actual* duty, the one that we ought to perform. Note that what may be our actual duty in one case may not be so in another. The context of our actions is crucial in determining which of two conflicting *prima facie* duties is our actual duty. Thus, when we are under oath in a court of law, we must tell the truth, even though our testimony may incriminate someone whom we believe to be innocent. Depending on the circumstances, then, an otherwise *prima facie* duty must give way to another.

Ross distinguishes among different kinds of *prima facie* duty. One kind consists of those duties which arise because of something I did earlier. If I made a promise, then I now must keep it. If I signed a contract, then I now must honor it. Ross calls these duties of *fidelity*. Alternatively, if I wronged someone, then I am obligated to compensate that person appropriately. So if I damage your property, I ought to pay you for its repair or replacement. These Ross calls duties of *reparation*. On the other hand, someone else may have done some good to me, which consequently puts me under the obligation of expressing my gratitude in a suitable way. We are all indebted to our families and friends for their myriad acts of love and kindness toward us. Such obligations Ross calls, appropriately, duties of *gratitude*. Note that these duties of fidelity, reparation, and gratitude derive their force from things done, either by ourselves or by others, in the past.

But there are other duties enumerated by Ross which derive their obligatoriness instead from what may likely happen in the future because of our doing them or not. One such forward-looking duty is that of *beneficence*, which is the obligation to maximize, whenever possible, the public good. This, for utilitarians, is the only duty incumbent on us. Then there is the duty of so-called *nonmalfeasance*, which is the obligation we have of not harming other persons or their property. The duty of *justice* requires the equitable distribution of goods based on the relative merits of the recipients. In Ross' words, "The fact or the possibility of a distribution of pleasure or happiness (or of the means thereto) which is not in accordance with the merit of the persons concerned, in such cases there arises a duty to upset or prevent such a distribution."[22] One final duty we have, according to Ross, is that of *self-improvement* with respect to virtue and intelligence. In other words, we have the obligation to develop our moral character, by exercising it in the habitual performance of our various duties, and to acquire knowledge and cultivate wisdom.

Ross claims that *prima facie* duties, though in theory all equally absolute and universally binding when considered in themselves, are not so in cases of conflict between them. Thus, he regards the duty of nonmalfeasance as having more weight than that of beneficence. As he says, "We should not in general consider it justifiable to kill one person in order to keep another alive, or to steal from one in order to give alms to another."[23] As a general rule this may be so, but consider the case of a Robin Hood stealing from those who have enriched themselves fraudulently in order to provide for the poor. Is it as obvious here that nonmalfeasance should weigh against beneficence? The problem is that Ross gives us no clear criteria whereby to determine the degree of obligatoriness, no standards to help us decide which of the two conflicting duties is the more obligatory. This problem is exacerbated in cases where the conflict is between incommensurable duties, such as the backward-looking duty of fidelity and the forward-looking duty of beneficence.

For Ross, determining which duty is more obligatory is a matter of intuition. Thus he thinks that it is self-evidently true that the duty of nonmalfeasance takes precedence over that of beneficence, though it is not so in some cases. However, it can be argued that the only truths that are self-evident are certain truths in mathematics and logic, such as $2 + 2 = 4$. Intuition is a notoriously vague, unreliable, and even hazardous method for establishing truth or determining how we ought to act. Intuition too often reduces to a matter of personal feeling, which is too subjective a criterion for determining what is right. Furthermore, intuitions about exactly the same situation may differ. Thus, my intuition may tell me that Robin Hood ought not to steal from the rich to give to the poor, but yours may tell you that he ought to. Now we have the impossible difficulty of deciding whose intuition is the correct one.

Yet, there is a further difficulty in Ross' theory. How do we know that his list of *prima facie* duties is correct or complete?[24] Note that according to Ross we have a duty of gratitude for good done to us by others, but we have no correlative duty of revenge for bad done to us. But why exclude revenge? Though contrary to our Christian ethos, there are some ethical views that permit and even demand it. In classic plays such as Aeschylus' *Oresteia* trilogy and Shakespeare's *Hamlet*, revenge is represented as a moral imperative. Ross provides no criteria for either including as *prima facie* the duties he does or excluding others which would provide an underlying unity for his list. Again, he might appeal to a dubious kind of intuition as his criterion. Thus, we are left with the suspicion that Ross' list of *prima facie* duties is arbitrary.

Act-deontologism

Unlike the rule-deontologism of the normative ethical theories of divine command, natural law, Kant's categorical imperative, and Ross' *prima facie* ethics, *act-deontological* theories abandon all rules or principles in making moral decisions. Given the etymological definition of "deontological" as "rule-bound", it may seem odd to call these theories "act-deontological" at all; however, because they are decidedly not teleological, they are referred to as deontological theories. As we have seen, a problem with applying moral rules, if absolute, is that they can conflict with one another, but act-deontologists cite other reasons for rejecting any appeal to rules in deciding moral issues. One is that each situation that calls for a moral decision is utterly unique with no similarities to any other such situation. Moral rules are at best abstract generalizations, rigid and often vague, which cannot adequately cover the complexity and subtlety of a particular moral situation. A second reason is that even when we set out to apply rules to a specific case, the rules are not sufficient to determine our course of action. Even with Ross' theory, which allows for more flexibility in the application of rules than Kant's in deciding which of two conflicting *prima facie* duties to perform, we are thrown back upon our intuitions or feelings. There is no criterion, or rule, which can assure us, for example, that the duty of nonmalfeasance is stronger than a duty of beneficence. A third reason that act-deontologists might cite against making moral decisions on the basis of rules is that rules typically admit of exceptions. Thus, if we are confronted with a case which is clearly an exception to any relevant rule, then we need to rely on something other than rules in making our decision. An example of a morally significant case to which none of our conventional moral rules seems applicable, and so can be of little help to us, is that of the possible cloning of human beings.

Now, if rules are of no avail, then what enables us to decide what we ought to do in any particular case? Act-deontologists answer that it is intuition, and hence they are often referred to as *moral intuitionists*. This is how it works. In making a moral decision, we need to have a clear and adequate understanding of our choices and complete knowledge of all the facts bearing on them. Upon attaining that, we shall know intuitively and directly what ought to be done, independently of any chain of reasoning or facts outside of the moral situation immediately before us. The right course of action will automatically reveal itself, and its moral rightness will instantly flash upon our minds. Classic moral intuitionists in the 17th and 18th century, such as Anthony Ashley Cooper, the Third Earl of Shaftesbury (1671–1713), and Francis Hutcheson (1694–1746), supposed that human beings are endowed with a special sense, analogous to the five physical senses, which is uniquely sensitive to moral qualities such as good and bad, right and wrong. Whenever any of these qualities is present in an action, motive, character, or effect, our *moral sense* will detect it. These intuitionists formed a group which became known as the Moral Sense School.[25]

Act-deontologism is vulnerable to many, sometimes obvious, criticisms. One is the difficulty of knowing when we have enough facts in a case to trigger a correct intuition of what is morally right in the circumstances. Related to this is the further difficulty of knowing what counts as a relevant fact in the case. Do the probable consequences of a proposed course of action qualify as relevant facts? If they do, then we may find ourselves slipping away from strictly deontological considerations into teleological ones. Take the McCummings case. Think of what facts Rodriguez needed to know in order to intuit correctly what was morally right for him to do. Among other things, he would need to know the probability of McCummings' harming others and of escaping with impunity if he did not intervene to stop him with deadly force. Moreover, in judging accurately whether Rodriguez did the morally right thing, we would need to know something of his state of mind at the time — what facts did he know, and, if he were ignorant of or misinterpreted any, is he to blame?

Further difficulties have to do with our so-called moral intuitions. What happens if you and I intuit the same moral situation differently? Who is to say that either of us is wrong? And according to act-deontologism, any judgment about which of us is right or wrong is itself the result of just another moral intuition! The point is that this theory makes impossible both the resolution of moral disputes and the critical evaluation of moral positions. Moreover, an attempt to resolve a dispute or evaluate a position by engaging in any kind of logical reasoning, or by appealing to consequences or moral laws, is illegitimate as it means abandoning the act-deontological theory altogether. Hence, according to this theory, the only way I can justify my moral intuitions is simply by repeating them, as an appeal to reasons or evidence in their justification is inadmissible because it is nonintuitive. Finally, nonrational intuitions are not the only means by which to make moral evaluations; it is possible to make them on the basis of rational appeals to consequences or moral laws as do the teleologists and rule-deontologists, respectively.

Another criticism of act-deontologism is directed at the supposed existence of a moral sense, innate in all human beings, which is presumably the source of our moral intuitions. Not only is there no scientific evidence for the existence of this "sixth" sense, but some people seem either to lack or lose it. Shakespeare's *Richard III* is a penetrating and disturbing study of a man who has a formidable intelligence but is bereft of anything like a moral sense or conscience. And, in *Macbeth*, we witness the awful spectacle of a man whose moral sense is slowly blunted and deadened. King Richard and Macbeth are but dramatic epitomes of real enough historical characters.

Act-deontologism can also be criticized for its bypassing all rules in moral decision making, but experience has shown that rules of some sort, however minimal in number and flexible in application, are indispensable in guiding our moral decisions, a lesson acknowledged by rule-utilitarians. Indeed, the work of morally educating our children is unthinkable without referring them to rules for their guidance. Hare has commented as follows:[26]

> To learn to do anything is never to learn to do an individual act; it is always to learn to do acts of a certain kind in a certain kind of situation; and this is to learn a principle ... without principles we could not learn anything whatever from our elders ... every generation would have to start from scratch and teach itself. But ... self-teaching, like all other teaching, is the teaching of principles.

Yet another criticism that can be lodged against act-deontologism is its assumption that every single moral decision or case which confronts us is wholly different from any other — in a word, unique. However, this assumption is unwarranted. Granted, no situation is identical with another, but different situations do have enough characteristics in common to enable us to generalize about them and so make science and other such undertakings possible. Any one of us might point to myriad different moral situations all having in common the characteristic of someone's lying, breaking a promise, or some other moral offense. This alone permits us to make a judgment about them all on the basis of their common characteristic. The civil law recognizes that there is a sufficient number of characteristics shared in common by many different situations to warrant calling one a case of manslaughter and another a case of first-degree murder.

A criticism of act-deontologism related to its denial of significant similarities among moral cases is that, in doing so, it ignores the purport of moral judgments. We saw earlier that any moral judgment, though seemingly a particular judgment about a single case, is implicitly a universal judgment about all such cases. For example, if I judge that it was wrong for Fuhrman to tamper with the evidence, I am not just making a judgment about Fuhrman; I am also making the judgment that it would be just as wrong for anyone else, in Fuhrman's circumstances, to tamper with evidence. In other words, the judgment, "It was wrong for Fuhrman to tamper with the evidence," implies that, "It would be wrong for anyone situated like Fuhrman to tamper with the evidence." However, such universal moral judgments are possible only if there are significant similarities among different moral cases. If not, then any moral judgment can be no more than a particular judgment, and so not a moral judgment at all. For Frankena, "The point involved here is called the Principle of Universalizability: if one judges that X is right or good, then one is committed to judging that anything exactly like X, or like X in relevant respects, is right or good. Otherwise he has no business using these words."[27] Furthermore, moral judgments require reasons for their support, and giving reasons implies universalizability and hence similarities among different moral situations. Suppose, for instance, that I say that Fuhrman was wrong to tamper with the evidence, and give as my reasons that tampering with evidence is a form of lying, and lying is wrong. Now, these are reasons not only against Fuhrman's actions, but also against any similar cases of evidence tampering. And, the moral judgment that "lying is wrong" is a universal judgment that means *all* individual cases of lying are wrong, not just the one involving Fuhrman. However, as we have seen, moral intuitionists cannot even give reasons for their moral judgments beyond saying that they are based on intuitions, thereby denying that their judgments are universalizable. Reasons, though, *can* be given in support of moral judgments.

What, then, might be said in defense of act-deontologism or moral intuitionism? First, intuitionism is indispensable to Ross' ethical theory for it is the only means we have of picking out our actual duty from conflicting *prima facie* duties. And, second, act-deontologists, like Kant, preserve intact the integrity and autonomy of the moral realm. Unlike teleologists, they do not reduce moral qualities such as goodness or rightness to anything other than themselves. The rightness of an action is immediately apparent to a rational mind, and beyond that it cannot be described or explained, nor does it need to be; just as the redness of a red rose is immediately apparent to the eye, with no further description of its redness being necessary.

Assessment of deontological theories

There are, then, fundamentally two kinds of deontological theories of ethics, rule- and act-deontologism. Rule-deontological or formalistic theories are the theories of divine command, natural law, the categorical imperative, and *prima facie* duties. Act-deontological or intuitionist theories include the moral sense theories which enjoyed a vogue in Great Britain during the late 17th and early 18th centuries. Rule-deontologists, as their name suggests, locate the source of moral value in some kind of rule or law. They differ as to its origins and how it is known. For the divine command theorist, the moral law originates in the will of God and is known through revelation or faith. According to the natural law theorist, it is derived from the purposes of nature and found in a knowledge of them. For Kant, it is found within ourselves through reason. And, for Ross, it is discovered through a form of rational intuition. The chief problem with rule-deontologism is that, by conceiving of moral laws as being unconditional and absolute, it has difficulty in resolving conflicts between them. Ross is more successful in their resolution than Kant, but he can only achieve it by resorting to the nonrational and unsystematic method of intuition. By contrast, the most glaring problem for act-deontologism is that, by abandoning moral laws altogether, it leaves us no guidance for our moral decisions other than our vague, unreliable, and subjective intuitions. The principle merits of deontological theories, in contrast to the teleological variety, are that they do not compromise justice, they acknowledge the moral value of motives, and they do not dissolve away moral values by reducing them to such human psychological states as happiness and pleasure.

Notes

1. Brunner, Emile (Olive Wyon, trans.), *The Divine Imperative: A Study in Christian Ethics*, The Westminister Press, Philadelphia, PA, 1947, p. 53.
2. Socrates asks Euthyphro this question: "Is what is holy holy because the gods approve it, or do they approve it because it is holy?" (From Plato,

Euthyphro, in *The Collected Dialogues of Plato*, Hamilton, E. and Cairns, H., Eds., Bollingen Series LXXI, Princeton University Press, 1961, p. 178.)

3. Leibniz, Gottfried W. von (George R. Montgomery, trans.), Discourse on metaphysics, in *Basic Writings*, The Open Court Publishing Co., La Salle, IL, 1968, pp. 4–5.

4. William of Ockham (died in 1349), an English Franciscan philosopher and theologian, who formulated the principle as follows: "*Entia non sunt mulplicanda praeter necessitatem,*" or "Things are not be multiplied beyond necessity." (From Rolbiecki, J.J., Parsimony, law of, in *Dictionary of Philosophy*, 16th ed., rev., Runes, D.D., Ed., Philosophical Library, New York, 1960, p. 226.)

5. "Lastly, those are not at all to be tolerated who deny the being of a God. Promises, covenants, and oaths, which are the bonds of human society, can have no hold upon an atheist." (From Locke, John, A letter concerning toleration, in *Great Books of the Western World*, Vol. 35, Hutchens, R.M., Ed., Encyclopedia Britannica, Chicago, IL, 1952, p. 18.)

6. Euthyphro explains his understanding of how religion differs from morality, to which Socrates agrees: "Well then, Socrates, I think that the part of justice which is religious and holy is the part that has to do with the service of the gods; the remainder is the part of justice that has to do with the service of mankind." (From Plato, Euthyphro, in *The Collected Dialogues of Plato*, Hamilton, E. and Cairns, H., Eds., Bollingen Series LXXI, Princeton University Press, 1961, p. 181.)

7. "In plants too that is produced which is conducive to the end — leaves, for example, grow to provide shade for the fruit. If then it is both by nature and for an end that the swallow makes its nest and the spider its web, and plants grow leaves for the sake of the fruit and send their roots down (not up) for the sake of nourishment, it is plain that this kind of cause is operative in things which come to be and are by nature." (From Aristotle, Physica, in *The Basic Works of Aristotle*, Richard McKeon, R., Ed., Random House, New York, 1941, p. 250.)

8. "It is plain then that nature is a cause, a cause that operates for a purpose." (From Aristotle, Physica, in *The Basic Works of Aristotle*, McKeon, R., Ed., Random House, New York, 1941, p 251.)

9. "For 'contemplation' is the highest form of activity, since the intellect is the highest things in us and objects which come within its range are the highest that can be known." (From Thomson, J.A.K., Ed., *The Ethics of Aristotle*, Penguin Books, Baltimore, MD, 1956, p. 303.)

10. Holmes, Eugene, Xenophanes of Colophone, in *Dictionary of Philosophy*, 16th ed., rev., Runes, D.D., Ed., Philosophical Library, New York, 1960, p. 340.

11. Sir Francis Bacon, who anticipated and enormously influenced the outlook of the Royal Society, thought the study of purposes or "final

causes" had retarded the development of the true sciences of nature and so had no place in them: "For the handling of final causes in physics [i.e., science] has driven away and overthrown the diligent inquiry of physical causes, and made men to stay upon these specious and shadowy causes, without actively pressing the inquiry of those which are really and truly physical; to the great arrest and prejudice of science." (From Bacon, Francis, *De Augmentis Scientiarum III.4: Works,* Vol. IV, p. 363; as cited in Purver, Margery, *The Royal Society: Concept and Creation,* M.I.T. Press, Cambridge, MA, 1967, pp. 26–27.)

12. Winslow, Ola E., *Jonathan Edwards, 1703–1758: A Biography,* Macmillan, New York, 1940, p. 318.

13. Kant, Immanuel (Lewis White Beck, trans.), *Foundations of the Metaphysics of Morals,* Bobbs-Merrill, Indianapolis, IN, 1969, p. 44.

14. Kant, Immanuel (Lewis White Beck, trans.), *Foundations of the Metaphysics of Morals,* Bobbs-Merrill, Indianapolis, IN, 1969, p. 54.

15. Kant, Immanuel (Lewis White Beck, trans.), *Foundations of the Metaphysics of Morals,* Bobbs-Merrill, Indianapolis, IN, 1969, p. 55.

16. Kant, Immanuel (Lewis White Beck, trans.), *Foundations of the Metaphysics of Morals,* Bobbs-Merrill, Indianapolis, IN, 1969, p. 55.

17. Rachels, James, *The Elements of Moral Philosophy,* 2nd ed., McGraw-Hill, New York, 1993, p. 117.

18. Kant, Immanuel (Lewis White Beck, trans.), On a supposed right to lie from altruistic motives, in *Critique of Practical Reason and Other Writings in Moral Philosophy,* University of Chicago Press, Chicago, IL, 1949, p. 348.

19. Geach, Peter T., *God and the Soul,* Routledge and Kegan Paul, London, 1969, p. 128.

20. This third objection to Geach is made by Rachels in *The Elements of Moral Philosophy,* 2nd ed. (McGraw-Hill, New York, 1993, p. 124).

21. Anscombe, Elizabeth, Modern moral philosophy, *Philosophy,* 33, 3, 1958.

22. Ross, (William) D., *The Right and the Good,* Clarendon Press, Oxford, 1973, p. 21.

23. Ross, (William) D., *The Right and the Good,* Clarendon Press, Oxford, 1973, p. 22.

24. I owe this criticism to John Hospers' *Human Conduct: An Introduction to the Problems of Ethics,* Harcourt, Brace & World, New York, 1961, p. 305.

25. A convenient and compact anthology of selections from the works of the moral sense theorists is in Selby-Bigge, L.A., Ed., *British Moralists,* Vol. I, Dover Publications, New York, 1965.

26. Hare, R.M., *The Language of Morals,* Clarendon Press, Oxford, 1952, pp. 60–61.

27. Frankena, William K., *Ethics,* 2nd ed., Prentice-Hall, Englewood Cliffs, NJ, 1973, p. 25.

chapter five

Alternative theories of ethics

> Why that the naked, poor, and mangled peace,
> Dear nurse of arts, plenties, and joyful births,
> Should not in this best garden of the world,
> Our fertile France, put up her lovely visage?
> Alas, she hath from France too long been chased,
> And all her husbandry doth lie on heaps,
> Corrupting in its own fertility.
>
> —Shakespeare *(Henry V)*

The social contract theory

Imagine what it would be like if there were no police, local, state, or federal. Imagine further that there were not even any criminal laws to be enforced, or legislatures to make them, or judges to interpret them. In brief, imagine our human condition if there were no government at all. This is what Thomas Hobbes (1588–1679) invites us to do, and this is the way he describes that condition, or what he calls the *state of nature*, where there would be[1]

> No place for Industry, because the fruit thereof is un-
> certain: and consequently no culture of the Earth; no
> Navigation, nor use of the commodities that may be
> imported by Sea; no commodious Building; no Instru-
> ments of moving, and removing such things as require
> much force; no Knowledge of the face of the Earth; no
> account of Time; no Arts; no Letters; no Society; and
> which is worst of all, continual fear and danger of
> violent death; And the life of man, solitary, poor nasty,
> brutish, and short.

Hobbes further describes this state of nature as follows. First, all human beings would have exactly the same needs, such as clothing, food, shelter, and companionship. Second, the resources for supplying these needs would be finite and in some cases hard to come by. Third, human beings would be essentially equal with respect to their power. Though some individuals would be stronger or weaker than others with respect to their physical and mental power, the weaker would have the opportunity of joining with others and so increasing their strength through sheer numbers. And, fourth, each person could expect only limited altruism from others. In the perilous state of nature, the only real incentive for helping another is that in so doing one would help himself. Indeed, one could ill afford to be too generous (say, in sharing one's limited supply of goods), as in the future he might very well need them all for himself and could hardly depend upon the generosity of others who are in like circumstances.

Little wonder, then, that Hobbes describes human life in the state of nature as being "solitary, poor, nasty, brutish, and short". Because of the scarcity of goods available, each would be locked in an unrelenting conflict with others for his share, and the more rapacious among the strong would inevitably prey on the weak for more than their fair share. Hobbes thus speculates that individuals finding themselves in this onerous state of nature would naturally tend to form themselves into groups for the sake of mutual protection and survival. This is the basis of Hobbes' theory as to the origins, nature, and function of government, and so of the emergence of civil or political society. According to his theory, were we to find ourselves in a state of nature, we would immediately seek to extricate ourselves from the limitations, inconveniences, and dangers of that state. We would come together to make, directly or indirectly, certain rules or laws, to which we would all give our assent and pledge our allegiance. The express purpose of these laws would be understood as the regulation of human conduct in order to protect people's lives and property; to allow maximum flourishing of the various arts, sciences, and industry which enhance human life; and to secure borders against foreign invaders. These laws would be enforced by police and militia, and their infraction would entail appropriate penalties. Certain individual freedoms or rights that we heretofore enjoyed in the state of nature, such as that of retaliation against those who harm us, we willingly relinquish in exchange for the official protection of the state-sanctioned police. They relieve us from the burden of having to protect ourselves, and they can do a better job of it than we.

This collective agreement or compact, bringing us out of the state of nature and intended to preserve our lives and properties, goes by the name of the *social contract*. As in any legal contract, there are at least two parties, each of whom has its responsibilities. In the case of the social contract, these parties are the governed and their governors. Though we now have the responsibility of obeying the laws that we have sanctioned through a legislature, the government has the reciprocal responsibility of honoring its side of the bargain by providing protection. If we, the people, break the law, then we are punished. But, if the government itself fails to protect our lives and property or makes laws contrary to the will of the people, then the original social contract becomes null and void, and the government may be legitimately dissolved, even through violent means if necessary. According to Hobbes' view, then, the origin of civil society or government is the desire to escape the perils and hardships of the state of nature; its nature is that of a mutually agreed-upon contract, freely entered into by the governed and those they appoint as governors; its purpose is to safeguard the lives and property of its citizens and to nurture that civil peace and harmony which is essential to civilized existence.

Among those, other than Hobbes, who have sought to explain the origin, nature, and function of political society through a form of the social contract theory are John Locke (1632–1714) in his *Two Treatises on Government* and Jean Jacques Rousseau (1712–1778) in his *The Social Contract*. The social contract, however, is considerably more than a theory; it has also taken practical form as historical documents such as the *Magna Carta*, the Mayflower Compact, and the U.S. Constitution.

The social contract, however, has been used to explain the origins, nature, and function of morality as well as that of government. It is, therefore, a normative ethical theory as well as a political theory. According to the social contract theory, the laws embedded in moral codes help meet the needs of living in civil society. Conformity to them makes for a happier and more harmonious social existence. Indeed, without them civilized living would be impossible. Conformity to a moral code is very much to my benefit and to everyone else's. The moral prohibitions against murder, theft, and adultery are obviously beneficial to me and all others. Moral laws help cement society; furthermore, according to this theory, it is the social contract, or something like it, that makes morality possible in the first place. As we mentioned earlier, the "red in tooth and claw" environment of the state of nature is scarcely conducive to the cultivation of moral traits such as benevolence, compassion, and justice. There is little incentive to share our goods generously, especially with potential enemies, and so put ourselves at risk. Moreover, justice, at least with respect to the equitable distribution of goods, would have no meaning in such a state where neither the means nor the rationale for an equitable distribution exists. Rousseau gave expression to this view that the social contract creates the social conditions necessary for the exercise of moral traits:[2]

> The passage from the state of nature to the civil state produces a very remarkable change in man, ... Then only, when the voice of duty takes the place of physical impulses and right of appetite, does man, who so far had considered only himself, find that he is forced to act on different principles, and to consult his reason before listening to his inclinations ... his faculties are so stimulated and developed, his ideas so extended, his feelings so ennobled, and his whole soul so uplifted, that, did not the abuses of this new condition often degrade him below that which he left, he would be bound to bless continually the happy moment which took him from it for ever, and, instead of a stupid and unimaginative animal, made him an intelligent being and a man.

The social contract, as a moral theory, is essentially a form of ethical egoism. According to it, I should be moral because it is in my long-term best interest, as well as that of all other persons, to be so. Consequently, it is subject to the same criticisms which we brought against egoism. Thus, like ethical egoism, the social contract reduces morality to mere expediency or prudence. To use Kantian language, hypothetical imperatives have completely replaced the categorical imperative. A moral rule or trait or action is simply one that is conducive to our collective survival by underpinning, strengthening, or enhancing our social life, but there are other criticisms that are specific to the social contract theory itself which we shall now briefly consider.

First, the theory seems to be operating with two distinct conceptions of morality which it fails to acknowledge and clarify. On the one hand, it considers moral rules such as the proscriptions on murder and theft as necessary conditions for the very existence of civil society — without them civil society would not be possible, and we would still be in a state of nature. Yet, on the other hand, it regards a stable social order as being the necessary condition for the emergence and nurture of moral virtues such as altruism and justice. In other words, the social contract theory is maintaining that morality is necessary for producing society, but also that society is necessary for producing morality. This suggests two incompatible theories as to the sources of morality. According to one, morality is independent of society but must be used to constitute it. According to the other theory, morality is dependent on society inasmuch as without it certain moral traits could not flourish.

Second, the social contract theory, like utilitarianism, disallows any distinction between moral obligations and supererogatory acts. A supererogatory act, if you remember, is one that is morally good, but not obligatory, for us to perform. According to the social contract, supererogatory acts, no less than obligations, are morally good only so far as they have some kind of value for us as social beings. Now, social contract theorists might reply that there is a difference between supererogatory acts and moral obligations which they might explain as follows. Obligations, such as keeping one's promises or refraining from murder and theft, are necessary for the emergence and continuance of a social order; however, supererogatory acts such as self-sacrifice are not necessary for civil society, but are one of its moral fruits. To argue this way, though, presupposes the double conception of morality that is already a problem for the theory. Moreover, justice — though it, like altruism, presupposes a social order — is more than a supererogatory option. It is absolutely necessary for maintaining a decent society, which individual acts of self-sacrifice are not. So the social contract theorist, no less than the utilitarian, has no way of accommodating and explaining the moral goodness of supererogation.

Third, the social contract theory may be wrong in thinking that the emergence and exercise of moral virtues such as altruism are possible only in civil society. Some prisoners in the Nazi death camps, who existed in a virtual state of nature where it was every man for himself, were nevertheless capable of heroic acts of self-sacrifice.[3] Contrary to the expectation of a social contract theorist, even a state of nature can foster acts of selfless altruism with no regard to long-term self-interest, something which is inexplicable in the social contract theory.

Finally, the social contract theory has been criticized for assuming the historical existence of a state of nature, an idea largely discredited by modern social science. Apparently, the rudiments of social organization, however primitive, have always existed. The state of nature is nothing more than a convenient fiction or myth with which sociologically and anthropologically unsophisticated philosophers tried to explain the formation of political societies. Though some social contract theorists perhaps did believe in the literal historical existence of a state of nature, the theory does not depend on it. Locke, for example, replies to this criticism by pointing out that the state of nature exists wherever the rule of law is absent — that is, in the absence of a third, judicial party to arbitrate disputes impartially among individuals with the authority and power to enforce such decisions. This means that all nations of the world, though not their citizens, exist in a state of nature.[4] And, wherever a government breaks down and anarchy prevails, there exists a state of nature within a nation among its former citizens. The state of nature, even if nonhistorical, serves perfectly well the ends of the social contract theory as a hypothetical construct; just conceive of the condition of people outside the rule of any kind of civil law and that is the state of nature.

More recently, the social contract theory has been criticized for being too exclusive. Critics have alleged that the only beings capable of entering (tacitly or otherwise) into contracts and honoring them (and liable to punishment for breaching them) are rational beings. Thus, according to this theory, they are also the only beings who, as bearers of moral rights, have moral worth, thereby excluding children, retarded adults, and nonhuman animals who, being less than rational, are incapable of entering into contracts. However, our moral common sense dictates that nonrational beings such as children and subnormal adults are no less deserving of moral consideration than those who are rational. Unfortunately, the social contract theory, because of its contractarian basis, cannot accommodate the moral rights of any other than rational beings.[5] According to it, our moral treatment of nonrational beings is at best supererogatory, but not obligatory.

Though the social contract theory is vulnerable to the above criticisms, it does have some compensatory strengths, to which we shall now turn.[6] One of them is that it provides a firm criterion for deciding what we ought to do and for justifying that decision, which is that it must somehow help preserve or enhance our social life. One of the problems with Ross' theory, if you remember, is deciding between two conflicting but equally *prima facie* duties. Ross' answer is that we use our intuition, but for the social contract theorist, our duty in any given case is that action which bests promotes social peace and prosperity, which of course is in our best long-term interest. This is a second strength of the theory inasmuch as it provides us a compelling rationale and incentive for obeying certain moral rules.

A third strength of the social contract theory, especially for a moral egoist such as Ayn Rand, is that it does not exact from us moral heroism. As the Titanic sank, women and children were automatically placed in the lifeboats first. The men were expected to give way. This was understood to be a moral obligation; however, for the social contract theorist, acts of heroic self-sacrifice are not obligatory but are only supererogatory — one may perform such acts, and it is good that one does so, but no one *must* perform them. The reason for this is that making self-sacrifice obligatory would defeat the whole rationale of the theory — namely, that our being moral serves our own best interest. Demanding that we give up a major portion of our happiness, or our lives, would be contrary to that interest.

A fourth strength of the theory is that it makes irrelevant the metaphysical issue as to whether moral values are objective or subjective. According to the social contract theory, values are based on nothing other than what is necessary for maintaining those social arrangements necessary for preserving an individual's life and property.

Finally, perhaps the greatest strength of this theory is that it provides a moral rationale for acts of civil disobedience. Thus, if the government, whose only reason for existing is to protect me and my property, fails to do just that by denying me, say, some of my rights (which are part of my property), then it has breached the contract that I tacitly made with it; namely, I agree to give up certain of my freedoms that I would have enjoyed in a state of nature and to obey the civil law, in exchange for the state's protection. Now, if the state reneges on this contract, then on the principle of reciprocity I no longer have any obligation to obey the law which is working against my interests. I now have the right — even the duty — to break the law which lacks all moral legitimacy. This is the principle that lay behind Martin Luther King, Jr.'s decision to break deliberately the segregation laws in the American South in the 1960s. Locke supported this right to civil disobedience in his *Two Treatises on Government*, a work informing the American Declaration of Independence and Constitution.[7]

Virtue-based ethics

All of the normative ethical theories that we have dealt with so far are concerned principally with the question of what we ought to do in a given situation. Their concern is with deciding how to act, and to that end they formulate some general principle or rule to guide us in our decision. Thus, utilitarians, such as Bentham and Mill, formulated the principle of utility, and deontologists, such as Kant and Ross, formulated the categorical imperative and the principle of *prima facie* duties, respectively. Because of their overriding preoccupation with principles or rules with which to guide conduct, these ethical theories are known as *deontic* theories. Do not confuse "deontic" with "deontological". Deontological theories have to do primarily with duties and teleological theories with consequences of actions. However, both appeal equally to a high-level or more abstract principle such as the principle of utility or categorical imperative. "Deontic", then, refers to such principles, not to lower-level moral laws or duties.

One of the earliest ethical theories, however, which predates Bentham's and Kant's by over 2000 years, does not take as its principal question, "What ought I do?" Nor is it concerned primarily with deciding among actions and so does not provide us with a general rule or principle to help us decide how to act. This theory instead is concerned most fundamentally with the question of what makes a character good, or what kind of person one should aspire to become. This is the ethical theory of Aristotle (384–322 B.C.E.), and it goes by several different labels. It is known variously as *virtue-based* ethics, because of its emphasis on the cultivation of moral virtues; as *aretaic* ethics (*arete* is the Greek word for excellence), because the virtues it emphasizes are qualities of excellence; as the ethics of *being*, because of its focus on who we are or the state of our soul or character, as opposed to the ethics of "doing" with its focus on action; and as *dispositional* ethics, because of its stress on the inculcation of certain good dispositions or habits which will dispose us to act well, in contrast to decisional ethics, which stresses principles by which to make the right decision. Although this normative ethical theory associated with Aristotle is quite distinct from deontic ethics, it does share certain things in common with it. Thus, no less than egoism and utilitarianism, it is a teleological theory. It is also a deontological theory because of the central place it gives to natural law.

Aristotle did not originate virtue-based ethics (elements of his theory are already to be found in Plato[8]), but it was Aristotle who gave this ethical theory its first full and systematic formulation in his book, *Nicomachean Ethics*. This book takes its name from Nicomacheus, who was Aristotle's son. The book was actually written by a student of Aristotle who reworked his notes based on the master's lectures. Other books in ethics are credited to Aristotle, but this is the most important. Others, such as St. Thomas Aquinas in his *Summa Theologica*, have developed an ethics of virtue inspired by Aristotle's treatment. We shall now give a brief exposition of Aristotle's theory.

Aristotle's ethics is based squarely on his teleological metaphysics. You will remember in our discussion of natural law that Aristotle thought that everything in nature has some natural purpose or end (*telos*) that it is striving to realize. If it succeeds in realizing its end, it is deemed good. Thus, the natural end or function of a bloodhound is to track prey. If it is in the habit of performing this task successfully, then it is a good bloodhound. Now, what enables something to realize its proper end successfully, thus making it a good specimen of its kind, is what Aristotle calls "virtue". Thus, whatever it is that makes a bloodhound a good tracker, and so a good specimen of the breed, is its virtue; similarly, the combination of talent, knowledge, and training that makes a surgeon skilled in his profession, and a good surgeon, is his virtue. Even inanimate things may have a distinctive virtue in this sense. For example, the virtue of a Stradivarius violin consists in the quality of materials and workmanship that went into its making and made possible its unique and beautiful tone. More generally, whatever it is that makes any instrument or tool good for its particular job is its peculiar virtue.

Aristotle refers to this virtue, which enables a thing to perform its function optimally, in two other ways that help to define it further. He refers to it as a thing's particular excellence, and also as a habit, because to exercise a virtue only sporadically is not as good as doing so consistently over the long term. Hence, Aristotle's complete description of virtue, in its generic sense, goes something like this: It is a good habit, or excellence, which enables something to perform its proper function well.[9]

We, like all other organisms, also have a natural end or purpose that we are uniquely equipped to realize. That end is our *final* end, to which all our activities, endeavors, arts, and sciences tend. It is an *intrinsic* good, which means that it is good in an of itself and does not lead to any other good. Finally, this end is *self-sufficient*, which means that attaining this end is, by itself, enough to make life eminently desirable and lacking nothing. Our end or purpose in life, according to Aristotle, is happiness.[10]

How, then, do we achieve happiness? Aristotle answers that we do so by living life according to reason, which means giving full rein to our capacity for rational thought. Human reason, on Aristotle's account, takes two forms: One is so-called scientific reason that seeks to understand the nature of things — what they are and how they work — and expresses itself in the several disciplines of the natural sciences. The particular good it aims at is truth. In attaining a true understanding or knowledge of reality we achieve *theoretical wisdom,* which Aristotle ranks as the supreme *intellectual* virtue. A second form taken by reason is practical or calculative reason which seeks to realize worthwhile goals and acquire those things having real worth. The particular good it aims at is the habit of always desiring the right things. It issues in what Aristotle calls *practical wisdom*, another intellectual virtue, which is the knack of knowing what is truly good and having the savvy to get it. Happiness, then, results from having and exercising the intellectual virtues of theoretical and practical reason. If we manage to get those things worth having, among which, preeminently, are scientific knowledge of the world and metaphysical insight into the nature of God and goodness, then we shall be happy.[11]

The goal of practical wisdom, however, is actually obtaining what is truly good for us, and this involves our developing in ourselves and practicing a certain discipline or regimen. This means, more precisely, cultivating and exercising certain good habits which Aristotle calls the *moral virtues*. As we have already seen, a virtue, generally considered, is what enables something to realize fully its proper end or purpose or to perform its natural function optimally. More specifically, a moral virtue is a character trait, disposition, or habit of ours that enables us to achieve those goals or acquire those goods that are indispensable to our attaining happiness. Such goods that we aim to get are an adequate supply of food and clothing, a comfortable shelter, good health, education, a job, and friends.

Preliminary to giving a more precise definition of Aristotle's moral virtue, and to help us understand better what he means by it, we shall look at two examples of moral virtue and see what makes them so. Temperance is a moral virtue described by Aristotle but familiar enough to us. To better understand what it is, it is best to begin with what it is not. It is not, for example, being in the grip of excessive emotions such as rage or panic or engaging in overindulgent behavior such as overeating or sexual promiscuity. These are instances of the lack of self-control which are identifiable as the vices of emotionalism, gluttony, and lust, respectively. Intemperance, then, may be too little self-control, but it may also be too much, which is illustrated by the incapacity to feel emotions such as anger or fear under appropriate circumstances, the refusal to eat (anorexia nervosa), or excessive prudery in sexual matters. Though these may not technically be vices, they are nonetheless undesirable disorders.

Now, if intemperance is either too little or too much self-control, what then is temperance? For Aristotle, it is neither too much nor too little, but just the right amount, which stands at the midpoint between these two extremes. Thus temperance is feeling just that degree of anger or fear appropriate to its object; it is eating just enough for good nutrition; it is fully enjoying sexual intercourse, but not obsessively to the exclusion of all other activities.

Another example of moral virtue is courage. Again, to understand better what it is, let us consider first what it is not. Obviously it is not cowardice, which is its opposite. Nor is it, for Aristotle, foolhardiness, which is a willingness to take unnecessary risks, or a complete indifference to danger such as playing Russian roulette or using your car in a game of "chicken". Cowardice falls short of the virtue of courage, whereas foolhardiness overshoots the mark. As in the case of temperance, courage represents the midpoint or balance between too little and too much of an inclination or disposition.

Generalizing from these examples of temperance and courage, we can now formulate Aristotle's definition of moral virtue as follows: Moral virtue is the habit of occupying the middle-point between the extremes of dispositions, emotions, or actions. One extreme is a deficiency in what makes for the virtue in question, the other is excess.[12] To convey his understanding of moral virtue, Aristotle uses the mathematical concept of the mean which means that the moral virtue represents the mean between deficiency and excess. Aristotle analyzes not only temperance and courage but any other moral virtue such as justice, prudence, conscientiousness, and cooperativeness as the means between their respective extremes. In actual life, the morally virtuous person is one who habitually feels and acts appropriately in any situation. This person is subject to the appropriate level of emotion, feeling neither too much nor too little, say, of fear, anger, or love; the emotion expended is appropriate to its object, thus this person loves his family more than strangers and his own country more than other countries. His actions will be appropriate to time and place, so when at work he does not play, and when at play he does not work. This person is driven by appropriate motives, thus his conduct towards his family, friends, and neighbors is animated by benevolence and beneficence; whereas, conduct at work towards colleagues and superiors is motivated by loyalty and cooperativeness.

Aristotle's theory of moral virtue as the mean between extremes of emotions and behavior is particularly applicable to the work of police and corrections officers. The appropriateness of their actions and emotions in a variety of traumatic situations on the beat or in prison is essential not only to their moral integrity, but to their professional success and even their very survival, as well. Policing and corrections especially provide ample scope for certain virtues to come into play simultaneously, particularly self-control and courage. For example, the savage beating of Rodney King represents the complete break-down of self-control on the part of the policemen, which brought in its wake bad consequences for some of the officers involved, not to mention far worse for the larger society. At the opposite extreme is the case where police officers, hamstrung by so many bureaucratic regu-lations they fear violating, fail to act decisively and so risk injury to themselves and others. In the McCummings case, whether or not Rodriguez acted appropriately, and so virtuously in the Aristotelian sense, is still a bone of legal if not moral contention.

Aristotle appreciated that the moral virtues cannot be acquired overnight; the virtuous person is a product not of birth but of long and arduous education and training. Becoming virtuous involves (1) an adequate knowledge of the moral virtues and their value, (2) a strong desire to possess them, and (3) the actual practice of them. For Aristotle, it is not enough to know and want the moral virtues, but to actually have them we must also be willing to practice them at every opportunity. Virtues, being habits, are strengthened through deliber-ate and constant practice.[13] And Aristotle wisely advises that the process of inculcating and cultivating moral virtues must begin in childhood, and so is the responsibility of parents and teachers. Inci-dentally, Aristotle points out that if we are able to practice a virtue, then, paradoxically, we already in a sense possess it; however, to become a fully formed habit, it must be vigilantly exercised. Thus, moral education is an indispensable element in Aristotle's aretaic theory of ethics, in contrast to the deontic theories we have so far discussed.

To summarize, we need to practice the moral virtues in order to secure those goods such as employment and shelter that are necessary for survival, as well as goods such as friendship, health, and education that are essential to a full and happy life. Failure in exercising such virtues as self-control, self-discipline, and cooperativeness may mean failure in landing and keeping a job, loss of friends, and increased susceptibility to disease and injury. Moreover, the refusal to be just in our dealings with others may invite ostracism and retaliation by our neighbors or the state. Turning the moral virtues into personal habits is a vital part of practical wisdom which enables us to enjoy what is truly good in life. Finally, the fruit of practical wisdom is facilitating the attainment of philosophical wisdom, that insight into the nature of the world, man, values, and God which is the only gateway to happiness. If by being morally virtuous we achieve a modicum of security, comfort, and health in our lives, then we shall have the leisure necessary for acquiring that knowledge of the world, humanity, goodness, and God which is the crown of our intellectual lives. For Aristotle, our chief end in life is rational contemplation, through which alone we can achieve felicity.

This idea of moral virtue as the mean between deficiency and excess, though given its classic and first systematic formulation by Aristotle, is embedded in Greek thought. On the entrance to Apollo's oracle at Delphi, a shrine sacred to the god of wisdom, music, and healing to which people from all over the ancient world came for counsel and prophecies, there was the inscription "Nothing to excess." This was more than a principle of moral psychology; it was no less than an aesthetic principle which lies behind the great works of art that have come down to us from the Hellenic age. Greek architects and sculptors, for example, routinely built and sculpted according to the principle of the so-called "Golden Mean", a principle of moderation and proportion that could be expressed mathematically as a determinable ratio which, if adhered to, makes for a perfect balance or proportion among the various parts of a building or statue. Artists down to the present have sought to embody in their works the ideal of the golden mean. The Parthenon, the great temple that graces the Acropolis in Athens, and the Lincoln Memorial are architectural embodiments of this ancient ideal.

Aristotle's ethics of virtue has been criticized on several counts. For one thing, it does not provide us with any firm practical rules to guide us in our moral decisions. This, of course, is to be expected from a theory in which a person's character, instead of his moral choices, has the spotlight. On the aretaic theory, if we have made a habit of moral virtue we need not overly worry about deciding what is best to do; we cannot help but make the morally right decision, which will simply be a spontaneous and natural result of our character, as good fruit is the inevitable result of a sound tree. However, as Aristotle fully appreciates, the cultivation of a morally virtuous character takes a long time and painstaking practice. It can only be achieved through a strict regimen of moral education beginning in early childhood, but what about those who have not had the benefit of such an education? What will enable them to act well, as they lack the virtuous character to act virtuously from? Furthermore, children, whose moral characters are still in a fledgling state, will need in the course of their moral training to fall back occasionally on some rules, as a child learning to ride a bike might need to use training wheels until his balance is sufficiently developed. What we said earlier in our critique of act-deontologism about the indispensableness of moral rules in guiding our actions applies equally well here. Finally, even the virtuous, the beneficiaries of a moral education, might sometimes need to have recourse to moral rules. Thus, more than a good character is needed to enable a woman to make the morally right choice in deciding whether to have an abortion or to enable a member of a jury to make that choice in deciding whether to vote for the death penalty in a capital case. In the McCummings case, consider that Rodriguez's character may have embodied such virtues as courage and self-control, which, say, he fully exercised in shooting McCummings. But the question still remains as to whether he did the right thing. This can be answered only by judging his actions according to some standard or principle, whether utilitarian or deontological. Even the Cowardly Lion in *The Wizard of Oz*, after receiving his diploma of courage, cannot safely rely on just that or other virtues but may need to consult rules such as the principle of utility or the categorical imperative to help him choose between two equally courageous courses of action.

Another criticism takes issue with Aristotle's conception of moral virtue as the mean between deficiency and excess. The mean is literally a mathematical concept and, in its form as the "Golden Mean", may be successfully applied as an aesthetic concept in the construction of buildings or the modeling of statues. Aristotle applied it to the human soul as a regulatory principle for human emotions and behavior, thereby making it a psychological and moral concept, as well. Undoubtedly, regulating our lives by this moral mean makes good psychological sense, being conducive, as Aristotle observed, to a successful and happy life. Yet, though living by the moral mean makes for psychological health and contributes to the good (in its natural sense) life, the question may well be asked as to what is specifically *moral* about the moral mean. What is specifically moral about the so-called moral virtues which represent nothing more than a mathematical relation? Psychological health is unquestionably a natural good, but how is it a moral good as well? Aristotle's moral mean, then, seems to be a rule more of prudence and good taste than of ethics. Albert Schweitzer aptly characterized the Aristotelian conception of moral virtue as "an aesthetic of the impulses of the will."[14]

Furthermore, Aristotle's criterion of moral virtue has been criticized for being excessively intellectual. It does not allow for congenital incapacities or pathological conditions. It makes no distinction between moral vices such as malice or cruelty, on the one hand, and pathologies such as anorexia nervosa or alcoholism, on the other. Any emotion or behavior that fails to observe the mean is, for Aristotle, morally vicious. Many people lack specific virtues such as courage, prudence, and temperance, though we still deem them moral. In Genesis, for example, we read of Noah. Noah had a serious drinking problem, and yet he was the only "righteous" man that God could find in the whole world.[15] Moreover, Aristotle's ethics, paradoxically, diminishes the moral virtues. He, unlike Kant, ranked the intellectual virtues, such as philosophical wisdom, above the moral, which for him were simply stepping stones to the contemplative life. This means that those incapable of exercising the intellectual virtues in contemplation, such as the less intelligent or the mentally deficient, can never be completely moral and so fully rational and human beings. For Aristotle — who, incidentally, advocated the killing of mentally impaired or physically deformed children — the retarded must ever be second-class citizens, something, needless to say, which runs counter to our moral common sense. However, some moral philosophers have conceived the highest state of human existence as something other than the exercise of the intellectual virtues in contemplation. Thus, for St. Thomas Aquinas (1225–1274), who also espoused a virtue-based ethics, it was communion or fellowship with God; for F.H. Bradley (1846–1924), an absolute idealist, the highest state was the fullest realization of one's potentialities for good, not just the purely intellectual ones.[16]

Fourth, Aristotle's virtue-based ethics has been open to the criticism that it encourages a self-centered way of life. Rational contemplation of the universe is, for Aristotle, the highest state of human existence, and happiness is humanity's highest end. Moreover, he extols self-sufficiency as a moral virtue: the less dependent we are upon others for our existence and enjoyments, the better off we are. Schweitzer has pointed out that Aristotelian ethics leaves no room for a virtue such as self-sacrificial love.[17] For Schweitzer, the essence of the moral attitude is the willingness to sacrifice oneself in some way for others, like Mother Theresa or Schweitzer himself, who left several brilliant careers as a concert organist, philosopher, and theologian to go as a medical missionary to Lambarene in Africa and heal the sick.[18] Aristotle's eudaemonistic ethics smacks too much of a self-absorbed quest for personal happiness, even though it is based on the exercise of our noblest faculty upon the noblest objects.

Finally, Aristotle has been criticized for presupposing a criterion of moral virtue other than the mean between deficiency and excess, a presupposition that he neither acknowledges nor explains.[19] Consider the following excerpt from his *Nicomachean Ethics:*[20]

> But not every action nor every passion admits of a mean; for some have names that already imply badness, such as spite, shamelessness, envy, and in the case of actions: adultery, theft, murder; for all of these and such like things imply by their names that they are themselves bad, and not the excesses or deficiencies of them. It is not possible, then, ever to be right with regard to them; one must always be wrong.

What he is saying here is that emotions such as envy and actions such as adultery are bad, not because they represent either excess or deficiency, but because they are bad in and of themselves. Thus, envy is not bad because we feel it either too much or too little, and adultery is not bad because we commit either too much or too little of it, but they are bad even if we observe moderation in them. There is no mean between too much or too little, say, of envy or adultery that represents virtue in these cases. Envy and adultery, even in moderation, are vices, period. But, if this is so, a virtuous character is one that not only observes the mean represented by the various virtues but also eschews the vices, which is not a matter of observing any mean. In one place, Aristotle identifies vice with a lack of proportion, represented by deficiency or excess, with respect to certain emotions or actions; however, elsewhere he identifies it with the emotions or actions themselves, such as envy and adultery, respectively. Yet, he does not explain what, precisely, the badness of emotions such as envy, spite, and shamelessness or the badness of actions such as adultery, theft, or murder consists of. Why are these things bad? Cowardice and foolhardiness are bad because they are disproportionate, but Aristotle gives no corresponding explanation of why envy and adultery are bad. Aristotle, then, appeals to two distinct criteria of vice. The one he clearly describes as being disproportion with respect to emotions and actions. The other criterion, however, he neither describes nor even acknowledges; he simply gives examples of it, such as envy and adultery.

Notwithstanding its flaws, an aretaic theory of ethics such as Aristotle's has certain distinct advantages over the deontic theories of Mill and Kant. For one thing, it fully appreciates and explains that being moral requires more than simply a knowledge of certain moral rules and so is in accord with our moral common sense. We sense that there is more to being moral than merely acting mechanically on principle for the principle's sake, whether it be that of utility or the categorical imperative. It is not enough to act morally, to do what is morally right, but we must also *be* moral, which means having morally good motives and habits — in brief, a good moral character — which will dispose us to act rightly.

A second merit of virtue-based ethics is its recognition that knowing what is morally good is not enough to make us so; we must also will to be so.[21] An old adage has it that you can lead a horse to water, but you cannot make him drink. Though we may know what we morally ought to do, we neglect to do it; though we may know what we morally ought not to do, we do it anyway. There is a diremption between our intellect and our will. Thus, we may understand and assent to the principle of utility or the categorical imperative, and resolve to adhere to it in all our actions, but under pressure of a particular moral choice we may simply lack the will to apply that principle. Virtue-based ethics provides a remedy for unwillingness to do what we know we ought to do, which is moral education and conditioning. The hope is that having steeled our wills with good moral habits or virtues, we shall be naturally disposed to do the morally right thing. Moreover, a virtuous person presumably will be more flexible and responsive to the subtle nuances of a complex moral situation than one who is prepared only to apply one or another rigid principle or rule.

Though aretaic ethics has for a long time been ignored in favor of various forms of deontic ethics, it is now commanding increasingly greater interest and respect. Indeed, some contemporary philosophers such as Alastair MacIntyre, Elizabeth Anscombe, and Mortimer Adler think that the tradition of deontic ethics was wrong-minded from the start and is now moribund, and that a revival of virtue-based ethics is the last best hope for moral philosophy. Anscombe, for one, has written:[22]

> The concepts of obligation, and duty — moral obligation and moral duty, that is to say — and of what is morally right and wrong, and of the moral sense of "ought", ought to be jettisoned. ...It would be a great improvement if, instead of "morally wrong", one always named a genus such as "untruthful", "unchaste", "unjust".

The ethics of love

According to the ethics of love, what we ought to do in all situations, and find every opportunity to express, is love, which is our principal moral obligation. This normative ethical theory is associated with Judaism and Christianity, and in the latter it receives its classic and fullest expression. We find the heart of it in Matthew's gospel, where it is written, "Thou shalt love the Lord thy God with all thy heart, and with all thy soul, and with all thy mind." This is the first and great commandment. And the second is like unto it: "Thou shalt love thy neighbor as thyself." On these two commandments hang all of the law and the prophets.[23] Note that in this passage we are enjoined to love both God and our neighbor; however, the love commanded in this passage is not just any kind of love. It is not erotic or sexual love, nor the love of parents for their children or children for their parents, nor love of country or even a generalized benevolence for humanity. All of these loves are based upon and are responses to some endearing or lovable quality in the beloved. Thus, erotic love is based on sexual attractiveness, parental love on biological kinship, and patriotic love on national or cultural affinity — we tend to love those who are like us. The love extolled in Matthew is something utterly distinct from all of these kinds of love, though it need not be incompatible with them, because it is unconditional and boundless. It is unconditional because it does not depend on some likable quality in the beloved; indeed, this love extends even to the unlovable, to our enemies and those who hate us. It is boundless because it must balk at no sacrifice, even the sacrifice of our own lives for others. This love is perfectly exemplified in the life, actions, and sayings of Christ and many of his followers. It is the same love that God is said to have for all of his creatures. This love goes by the name *agape*. Hence, the ethics of love is more accurately know as *agapistic ethics*.[24]

Agapistic ethics may be classified in different ways because of its kinship with other normative ethical theories, but none of these classifications is without its problems. Because of its emphasis on doing good to all others, it has been interpreted by such as A.C. Garnett and Joseph Fletcher as essentially a utilitarian theory. Mill went so far as to declare utilitarianism as the essence of Christian ethics,[25] but the problem with this interpretation is that though we may show our love to others by doing good to them, we can hardly show our love to God (which is the principal part of agapistic ethics) in this way, as, being perfectly self-sufficient, He, the Creator, does not stand in need of any good from us His creatures.[26] Two replies may be made to this criticism. One is that loving our fellow human beings is identical with loving God; that is, in doing good to our neighbor we are necessarily showing love for God. However, there are two problems with this reply. First, if love for neighbor is expressed by doing them good, then love for God must be expressed in the same way. But, as we have seen, it is not clear how we can do God any good. Second, the passage from Matthew, which is the foundation of agapistic ethics, is quite unambiguous in distinguishing love for God from love for neighbor. A second reply is that we can be of use to God. Though He really does not need anything from us, He created us to be co-creators with Him. According to Christian theology, He chose that we should participate with Him in establishing and furthering His kingdom. By doing God's will and thereby pleasing Him, we are doing good to Him.

Agapistic ethics may also be classified as a form of deontological ethics. Thus, St. Thomas Aquinas, Samuel Clark, and Joseph Butler were all ethical agapists, yet they believed that the rule of love is not sufficient for the moral life but must be supplemented by other obligations, such as the duty to be just. For Butler, "Benevolence, and the want of it, singly considered, are in no sort the whole of virtue and vice."[27] St. Thomas combined agapism with natural law, whereas Kierkegaard and Brunner combined it with the divine command theory. There is a problem with this classification, though, which is suggested in the previous paragraph — namely, that love, though our principal duty, is not enough for the moral life but just one of several duties. If this is so, then "agapistic" ethics is a misnomer, as it is fundamentally but a kind of deontological ethics which gives pride of place to the duty of benevolence. And, on the divine command theory, we ought to love God and one another for no other reason than that God commands it. In other words, what is fundamental in this theory is not love but divine fiat. Our obligation to love is simply derived from our duty to obey God. Thus, agapistic ethics is not a theory distinct from deontological ethics but may be collapsed into the theories either of natural law or of divine command.

Agapistic ethics may be best understood as a form of virtue-based or aretaic ethics, though with teleological and deontological elements, because, like the latter, it focuses on a disposition, specifically love or benevolence, which is to be cultivated as a habit. This habit of love is to animate our moral actions, codes, and judgments: It is to motivate our moral actions, determine the moral rules and values we live by, and inform our moral judgments. Benevolence is the disposition that must permeate our whole being and conduct. It is like a fountain whose waters flow through the several channels of our feelings, thoughts, and deeds. However, inasmuch as benevolence is concretely expressed in doing good to all others, agapistic ethics is teleological, and inasmuch as doing good is a moral obligation, it is deontological.

Agapistic ethics can be distinguished into two distinct kinds. One enjoins us, when we have a moral choice to make, to always do, what is most exemplary of love. We must fully comprehend the moral situation as a whole by ascertaining and interpreting all the relevant facts. Moral rules, generalized from past experience, are to be used when needed only as rough rules of thumb, never as hard-and-fast exceptionless laws. In any conflict between them, what we deem to be the most loving act always overrides a moral edict. Martin Luther (1483–1546), the great Reformer, expressed the superiority of the rule of love to the moral law:[28]

> When the law impels one against love, it ceases and should no longer be a law. But where no obstacle is in the way, the keeping of the law is a proof of love, which lies hidden in the heart. Therefore, you have need of the law, that love may be manifested; but if it cannot be kept without injury to the neighbor, God wants us to suspend and ignore the law.

This kind of agapistic ethics has gone by different names such as *act-agapism, situationalism* or *situation ethics,* and *antinomianism.*

Note that act-agapism parallels act-utilitarianism and act-deontologism and so is vulnerable to some of the same criticisms as they. One of them is that act-agapism, because of its rejection of firm rules, provides no clear criterion for determining which of several possible acts is the most benevolent. Benevolent motives are not enough. We must then have recourse to the principle of utility, such as doing what is calculated best to promote the public good, or to revelation. Now, if we must have recourse finally to the principle of utility in deciding what we ought to do, then we are utilitarians. We may be agapists insofar as we are driven by benevolent motives, but utilitarians with respect to making the critical decision as to what actually to do. Agapism, then, has once again collapsed into utilitarianism. On the other hand, if we appeal to revelation, or some passage from scripture, for moral guidance then we are thrown back on the divine command theory — we know what we ought to do because the Bible (God) tells us so. The result is the same: We are forced to abandon agapism for some other ethical theory. And, if we do abandon agapism for either utilitarianism or the divine command theory, then we have to face again all of the problems associated with them.

The lack of clear moral direction in act-agapism is inadvertently illustrated by a hypothetical case given by Fletcher, a contemporary agapist.[29] An intelligence agency asks a young woman to use sex to blackmail an enemy spy. Fletcher thinks she should comply with the request, as having sex in this context would be an expression of her love of country, or patriotism; however, she could object that offering herself as sexual bait denigrates from her dignity as a human being. Following Kant, she might argue that using persons in this way, as a means to an end, is demeaning and so hardly an expression of love to them. What this case illustrates is that two people, both equally motivated by a loving concern for others, might do completely opposite things in exactly the same situation.

The absence of firm moral guidance stemming from act-agapism's antinomianism (i.e., its rejection of rules) is remedied in part by a second kind of agapistic ethics, namely, *rule-agapism*. As its name suggests, this theory focuses on rules rather than acts. It enjoins us always to follow those moral laws which are most exemplary of love when we are confronted by a moral choice. We should look first to the moral rules applicable to a situation of moral choice which will help us make the right decision, rather than to the situation by itself, and see which rule is the most benevolent. Incidentally, rule-agapism is correlated with rule-utilitarianism and rule-deontologism and attempts to overcome the same sort of difficulties with respect to moral direction.

Rule-agapists such as Fletcher, however, are confused about the force of a moral rule or law. Fletcher distinguishes between two kinds of moral rules. *Summary rules* say that, though performing or refraining from some act normally fulfills the requirement of love or benevolence, exceptions may be made. Examples would be stating that telling the truth is normally love fulfilling or that paying your debts is normally love fulfilling. *General rules*, by contrast, insist that performing or refraining from some act always fulfills the requirement of love or benevolence, with no exceptions. Examples would be stating that telling the truth is always love fulfilling or that paying your debts is always love fulfilling. Now, Fletcher rejects *legalism*, which is to live strictly by general rules, as doing so invites the very difficulties which beset Kantian ethics. The inflexibility of general rules fails to do justice to the moral life. Yet, he rejects as well antinomianism, the opposite extreme, for its failure to provide moral guidance. He thus opts for living by summary rules which, presumably, provide just enough moral direction but without rigidity, thus making him a rule agapist. Some of his summary rules are "No unwanted and unintended baby should ever be born" and "Exploiting persons is always wrong." These moral rules, though normally commanding our allegiance, may under special circumstances be suspended in the interest of love. Here, then, are rules which embody love or benevolence but may sometimes come into conflict with the demand of love. But, under what circumstances exactly may they be suspended? What would be an example of an occasion when the application of a summary rule conflicts with the demand of love? Indeed, how is it even possible for a "love-embodying" rule to come into conflict with the interest of love at all? Specifically, when might we rightfully exploit another person? Fletcher provides no answers. He fails to give us any criteria for the morally legitimate suspension of summary rules. This means that in determining the moral legitimacy of suspending a moral rule we are left to the mercy of our intuitions, hence falling back into antinomianism, the very trap that Fletcher sought to avoid.[30]

A major problem with both kinds of agapistic ethics is related to the fact that benevolence cannot stand alone as our sole duty but must be supplemented by other duties such as the duty to be just. The question for the agapist is how the duty to love is related to other duties such as justice. Agapists agree that love is the principal or foundational duty from which all other duties are derived. In other words, if we love properly then presumably we must also be just, courageous, and temperate among other things. Agapists must agree that love is the primary duty and the source of all others in order that their theory may be distinctively agapistic. However, if agapists concede that love is just another duty that we need to cultivate, then their ethical theory is no longer distinguishable from any other deontological theory; it only adds the duty of benevolence.[31] Agapism, then, loses its distinction as being the ethics of love.

How is justice, for example, logically derivable from benevolence? Before we answer this question, we need to have some provisional understanding of justice and benevolence (*agape*). In a subsequent chapter, we shall discuss in some detail the nature of justice, but for now we shall provisionally understand it to involve the equitable distribution of the world's goods; in other words, justice demands that every one of us has an equal opportunity to get what we need to survive and to enjoy life to the fullest. Thus, we acknowledge that every child has a right to publicly supported education; to guarantee any child that right is just, and to deny it is unjust. Benevolence or *agape* is, as we have seen, an unconditional and magnanimous, even risk-taking, love that extends even to one's enemies. It is a disposition or virtue that serves as a motive; think of it as good will. Benevolence is made concrete and practical through beneficence, which is the doing of good to others.

Some such as Emile Brunner think that justice, far from being a logical derivative of love, is unalterable opposed to it. However, Garnett and Fletcher think that justice is implicit in benevolence; that is, to love as we ought is to be just and to act justly. Garnett reminds us that Christ's command is that we love others equally with ourselves, thereby making the duty of love a double one: We are (1) to love others as we love ourselves, and (2) to love them all equally. Love is a good which, if we are just, we bestow equally on all human beings, as they are all equally entitled to it. Failing to do so is injustice.[32] And according to Fletcher, "*Agape* is what is due to all others, justice is nothing other than love working out its problems."[33] In other words, "to give each his due" is but another name for justice.

Frankena does not perceive the relationship between justice and love as being quite so intimate. He analyzes agapistic ethics into three distinct principles. First, there is the duty to love, which is primary and fundamental. He then identifies love with the principle of beneficence, or the willingness to do good to all others. Second, there is the principle of *distributive justice* or equality, which is that all people should get their equal share of those goods necessary for survival and a decent life. And, third, beneficence must be motivated by benevolence; otherwise, agapism is just a utilitarian ethic. Note that agapistic ethics shares with utilitarianism this problem of how to accommodate justice within itself. For utilitarianism, the problem is the reconciliation of justice with utility; whereas, for agapism, it is the derivation of justice from love.

Frankena, however, is quick to point out further problems with agapistic ethics, even after his sympathetic analysis of it. One problem is that love to God is distinct from beneficence, which is a disposition to do good to all other human beings. Our loving God is not doing Him good, as He stands in no need of any benefits from us. We cannot love God in the same way that we love our neighbor. Another problem for agapism is to explain how our love for neighbor is logically derived from our love for God. Fundamental to this theory is the idea that love for God is our primary and basic duty with love for neighbor being a secondary and derivative duty. However, some agapistic theories do attempt to explain their derivation. A third problem for the theory, however, is that it, like the divine command theory, presupposes the existence of God which is open to question. Agapism makes sense only if God exists.

Frankena does propose a solution to the first two problems with agapistic ethics; namely, that to love God is a strictly religious obligation whereas to love our neighbor is a purely moral obligation.[34] In other words, the moral sphere of our lives is something distinct from the religious sphere, though the two are essentially compatible, with the moral sphere perhaps being contained within the religious.[35]

There are some characteristics of agapistic ethics worth noting. First, like the divine command theory, its acceptance depends on a complex system of religious beliefs and experiences. According to agapism, *agape*, together with the demand that we practice this kind of love, first appeared as a special revelation from God as recorded in John's first letter.[36] Second, because *agape* is a love that makes almost impossible demands on us, theologians have traditionally argued that we are incapable of loving God and others in this way. Even moral education and training of the sort Aristotle recommends, though helpful, cannot implant the principle of agapism in our hearts. This can be done only by God through an act of grace. Theologians differ, however, as to how this supernatural grace is bestowed on us. For Roman Catholics, the sacraments administered by the Church are indispensable channels of grace, whereas for Protestants a conversion experience is essential. And, third, because not everyone is a recipient of the grace required for the practice of *agape*, theologians who subscribe to agapistic ethics allow that there are two moral orders. There is the order of secular morality which does not include the duty of unconditional love for others. Then there is the order of religious morality in which that duty is fundamental. Secular morality is all that persons unredeemed by grace are capable of, whereas religious morality is reserved for the redeemed alone. Secular morality, because it lacks the all-important duty of *agape*, is deemed inferior to religious morality. St. Paul acknowledged the existence of a secular moral order distinct from the religious in observing that the Gentiles who lack the law of love nevertheless have the moral law "written in their hearts".[37]

Let us conclude our discussion of the ethics of love with a consideration of some of its merits as a normative ethical theory. Being, as I have argued, fundamentally a type of virtue (aretaic) ethics, it shares all of the merits of that theory. Hence, it understands that being moral means more than the routine application of rules to conduct but having a moral character exemplary of virtue, as well; that a knowledge of moral goodness is not enough to make us moral or act morally, but that we must also will to be and act so; and that a regimen of moral education and practice is indispensable to being moral and acting morally. Furthermore, agapism, with its insistence that we love even those who are hostile to us, is an ethical theory uniquely suited to resolving conflicts among ourselves, which is one of the chief ends of ethics. The universal practice of agapism would certainly make for a more peaceable society. And, finally, agapistic ethics harmonizes with the moral beliefs and values of Christians, who still make up the dominant religion in our society.

Notes

1. Hobbes, Thomas, Leviathan, in *The English Works of Thomas Hobbes*, Molesworth, Sir W., Ed., J. Bohn, London, 1839, pp. 96–97.
2. Rousseau, Jean J. (G.D.H. Cole, trans.), *The Social Contract and Discourses*, Dutton, New York, 1959, pp. 18–19.
3. One such prisoner was the polish priest, Fr. Maximilian Kolbe, who selflessly volunteered to die in the place of a fellow prisoner so that he might live. He was canonized by the Roman Catholic Church.
4. "Tis often asked as a might objection, Where are, or ever were there, any men in such a state of nature? To which it may suffice as an answer at present: That since all princes and rulers of independent governments all through the world are in a state of nature, 'tis plain the world never was, nor ever will be, without numbers of men in that state." (From Locke, John, An essay concerning the true original, extent and end of civil government, in *The English Philosophers From Bacon to Mill*, Burtt, E.A., Ed., The Modern Library, New York, 1939, pp. 408–409.)
5. James Rachels makes this same point with regard to retarded individuals: "Many humans are mentally retarded to such an extent that they cannot participate in the kind of agreements envisioned by The Social Contract Theory. They are certainly capable of suffering, and even of living a kind of rudimentary human life. But they are not sufficiently intelligent to understand the consequences of their actions or to know when they are hurting others, and so we may not rightly hold them responsible for their conduct. …Since they cannot participate in the agreements that, according to the theory, give rise to moral obligations, they are outside the realm of moral consideration. Yet we do think that we have moral obligations toward them. …The Social Contract Theory can explain our duty in the case of normal people but not in the case of retarded people." (From Rachels, James, *The Elements of Moral Philosophy*, 2nd ed., McGraw-Hill, New York, 1993, p. 158.)

6. Some of these strengths have been noted by Rachels, upon whom I have relied for my own discussion. (See Rachels, James, *The Elements of Moral Philosophy*, 2nd ed., McGraw-Hill, New York, 1993, pp. 148–154.)

7. "When any one or more shall take upon them to make laws, whom the people have not appointed so to do, they make laws without authority, which the people are not therefore bound to obey; by which means they come again to be out of subjection, and may constitute to themselves a new legislative, as they think best, being in full liberty to resist the force of those who without authority would impose anything upon them." (From Locke, John, An essay concerning the true original, extent and end of civil government, in *The English Philosophers From Bacon to Mill*, Burtt, E.A., Ed., The Modern Library, New York, 1939, pp. 490–491.)

8. See especially his dialogues, *Republic, Meno,* and *Crito.*

9. A translation of Aristotle's definition of "virtue" in his own words is: "Excellence [virtue] of whatever kind affects that of which it is the excellence in two ways. (1) It produces a good state in it. (2) It enables it to perform its function well." (From Thomson, J.A.K., Ed., *The Ethics of Aristotle*, Penguin Books, Baltimore, MD, 1956, pp. 63–64.)

10. "Happiness then, the end to which all our conscious acts are directed, is found to be something final and self-sufficient." (From Thomson, J.A.K., Ed., *The Ethics of Aristotle*, Penguin Books, Baltimore, MD, 1956, p. 37.) For Aristotle's discussion of happiness as the purpose of human life, see *The Nicomachean Ethics*, Book I, Chapter 7 (Thomson, J.A.K., Ed., *The Ethics of Aristotle*, Penguin Books, Baltimore, MD, 1956, pp. 35–37).

11. For Aristotle's discussion of the intellectual virtues, particularly practical and theoretical wisdom, and their bearing on happiness, see *The Nicomachean Ethics*, Book VI (Thomson, J.A.K., Ed., *The Ethics of Aristotle*, Penguin Books, Baltimore, MD, 1956, pp. 171–192).

12. "We may now define [moral] virtue as a disposition of the soul in which when it has to choose among actions and feelings, it observes the mean relative to us, this being determined by such a rule or principle as would take shape in the mind of a man of sense or practical wisdom. We call it a mean condition as lying between two forms of badness, one being excess and the other deficiency; and also for this reason, that, whereas badness either falls short of or exceeds the right measure in feelings and actions, virtue discovers the mean and deliberately chooses it. Thus, virtue no doubt is a mean." (From Thomson, J.A.K., Ed., *The Ethics of Aristotle*, Penguin Books, Baltimore, MD, 1956, pp. 66–67.) For Aristotle's full discussion of his conception of virtue as a mean between the extremes of excess and deficiency, see Book II, Chapter 6, of *The Nicomachean Ethics*.

13. "Moral goodness, on the other hand, is the child of habit...The moral virtues, then, are produced in us neither by Nature nor against Nature. Nature, indeed, prepares in us the ground for their reception, but their complete formation is the product of habit...so it is a matter of real importance whether our early education confirms us in one set of habits or another." (From Thomson, J.A.K., Ed., *The Ethics of Aristotle,* Penguin Books, Baltimore, MD, 1956, pp. 55–56.)

14. Schweitzer, Albert, *The Philosophy of Civilization*, Prometheus Books, Buffalo, NY, 1987, p. 125.

15. Genesis 6:9, 9:21 (revised standard version).

16. Frankena, William K., *Ethics*, 2nd ed., Prentice-Hall, Englewood Cliffs, NJ, 1973, pp. 86–87.

17. "But in the doctrine of virtue in the Nicomachean Ethics is nothing which could lead the individual to place his life at the service of the community." (From Schweitzer, Albert, *The Philosophy of Civilization,* Prometheus Books, Buffalo, NY, 1987, p. 131.)

18. "But to everyone, in whatever state of life he finds himself, the ethics of reverence for life do this: they force him without cessation to be concerned at heart with all the human destines and all the other life-destinies which are going through their life-course around him, and to give himself, as man, to the man who needs a fellow-man ... they demand from all that they devote a portion of their life to their fellows. ...But one with another we have all to recognize that our existence reaches its true value only when we experience in ourselves something of the truth of the saying: 'He that loseth his life shall find it.'" (From Schweitzer, Albert, *The Philosophy of Civilization*, Prometheus Books, Buffalo, NY, 1987, pp. 322–323.)

19. Schweitzer makes this criticism: "In the chapter on temperance — in the third Book of the Nicomachean Ethics — he has to admit that the theory which makes the ethical a mean between two extremes cannot be completely developed. The love of beauty, he says plainly, however strong it becomes, remains what it is; there can never be any question of excess. He throws out this admission without seeing that he thereby undermines his feeble definition of the ethical as the appropriate relative mean, and, like Socrates and Plato, acknowledges that there can be something which its content allows to be reckoned as good in itself." (From Schweitzer, Albert, *The Philosophy of Civilization,* Prometheus Books, Buffalo, NY, 1987, p. 127.)

20. Thomson, J.A.K., Ed., *The Ethics of Aristotle*, Penguin Books, Baltimore, MD, 1956, p. 67.

21. St. Paul makes this lament: "I can will what is right, but I cannot do it, for I do not do the good I want, but the evil I do not want is what I do." Romans 7:18–19 (revised standard version)

22. Anscombe, Elizabeth, Modern moral philosophy, in *Ethics, Religion and Politics: The Collected Philosophical Papers of G.E.M. Anscombe*, Vol. III, University of Minnesota Press, Minneapolis, 1981 (as quoted in Rachels, James, *The Elements of Moral Philosophy*, 2nd ed., McGraw-Hill, New York, 1993, p. 159).

23. Matthew 22:37–40 (revised standard version).

24. This term for the theory was suggested by Frankena who calls it "agapism". See his *Ethics*, 2nd ed. (Prentice-Hall, Englewood Cliffs, NJ, 1973, p. 56).

25. "In the golden rule of Jesus of Nazareth, we read the complete spirit of the ethics of utility. 'To do as you would be done by,' and 'to love your neighbor as yourself,' constitute the ideal perfection of utilitarian morality." (From Mill, John S., in *Utilitarianism*, Piest, O., Ed., Bobbs-Merrill, Indianapolis, IN, 1957, p. 22.)

26. Socrates makes this very point in connection with how one might benefit the gods of the Greek pantheon: "But tell me, what advantage could come to the gods from the gifts which they receive from us? Everybody sees what they give us. No good that we possess but is given by them. What advantage can they gain by what they get from us? Have we so much the better of them in this commerce that we get all good things from them, and they get nothing from us?" (From Plato, Euthyphro, in *The Collected Dialogues of Plato*, Hamilton, E. and Huntington, C., Eds., Bollingen Series LXXI, Princeton University Press, 1961, p. 184.)

27. As cited in Frankena, William K., *Ethics*, 2nd ed., Prentice-Hall, Englewood Cliffs, NJ, 1973, p. 57.

28. Luther, Martin, The church postil, in *Works*, Linker, J.N., Ed., Luther House, 1905, p. 175.

29. Fletcher, Joseph, *Situation Ethics: The New Morality*, The Westminster Press, Philadelphia, PA, 1966, pp. 163–164.

30. This critique of Fletcher is derived from Manuel Velasquez's *Philosophy: A Text with Readings*, 5th ed. (Wadsworth, Belmont, CA, 1994, pp. 449–450).

31. Parallel to this, if agapistic ethics is conceived of aretaically, rather than deontically, the virtue of love must be primary and basic, otherwise it is just another kind of virtue ethics.

32. Frankena, William K., *Ethics*, 2nd ed., Prentice-Hall, Englewood Cliffs, NJ, 1973, p. 58.

33. Fletcher, Joseph, *Situation Ethics: The New Morality*, The Westminster Press, Philadelphia, PA, 1966, p. 95.

34. For Frankena's discussion of agapistic ethics, see his *Ethics*, 2nd ed. (Prentice-Hall, Englewood Cliffs, NJ, 1973, pp. 56–59).

35. This distinction between the spheres of morality and religion is firmly drawn by Plato: "Well then, Socrates, I think that the part of justice which is religious and is holy is the part that has to do with the service of the gods; the remainder is the part of justice that has to do with the service of mankind." (From From Plato, Euthyphro, in *The Collected Dialogues of Plato*, Hamilton, E. and Huntington, C., Eds., Bollingen Series LXXI, Princeton University Press, 1961, p. 181.)

36. "Beloved, if God so loved us, we also ought to love one another." I John 4:11 (revised standard version)

37. "When Gentiles who have not the law do by nature what the law requires, they are a law to themselves, even though they do not have the law. They show that what the law requires is written on their hearts, while their conscience also bears witness and their conflicting thoughts accuse or perhaps excuse them on that day when, according to my gospel, God judges the secrets of men by Christ Jesus." Romans 2:14–15 (revised standard version)

part three

Metaethical theory

chapter six

Metaethics: the language of ethics

> "Do you mean that you think you can find out the answer to it?" said the March Hare.
>
> "Exactly so," said Alice.
>
> "Then you should say what you mean," the March Hare went on.
>
> "I do," Alice hastily replied; "at least — at least I mean what I say — that's the same thing, you know."
>
> "Not the same thing a bit!" said the Hatter. "Why, you might just as well say that 'I see what I eat' is the same thing as 'I eat what I see!'"
>
> —Lewis Carroll (*Alice's Adventures in Wonderland*)

Normative statements

As we saw in the first chapter, a dominant preoccupation of philosophy — especially of the analytic movement in the 20th century — is the meaning and logic of language. And so it is with problems relating specifically to the clarification of the meaning and the logic of moral discourse that we shall begin.

Consider these statements:

1. Manuel Rodriguez shot Bernard McCummings twice in the back in 1984.
2. Mark Fuhrman planted a bloody glove at Simpson's estate.

These are factual statements: Statement 1 asserts a fact, whereas statement 2 alleges a fact. They are thus examples of descriptive or empirical statements, which affirm what is the case or the way things stand in the world. Such statements are found in forensic reports which seek to establish the facts of a crime. Interpretations of evidence, explanations of how things came about, hypotheses as to the motives of suspects, and social scientific theories which seek to explain criminal behavior are all expressed in descriptive statements.

Consider now these statements:

3. It's *justice* turned upside down.
4. It was the *right* decision.
5. Criminal behavior *should* not be treated as if it were some sort of quasi-legitimate enterprise.

You will note that these statements are not factual — they neither assert nor allege any facts. Instead, they are evaluative: They either evoke a standard or norm (statements 3 and 4) or affirm how things ought to be (statement 5). They are thus examples of prescriptive or normative statements. Such statements can be easily identified because they typically contain normative terms such as "should" or "ought", "good" or "bad", "right or "wrong".

Statements 3 through 5 above are examples of morally prescriptive statements, but not all statements containing normative terms such as "ought", "good", or "right" are morally prescriptive. Take, for example, the following statements:

6. Because of your aptitudes, you *ought* to become a state trooper.
7. You have maintained a *good* record as a prison warden.
8. Dostoevsky's *Crime and Punishment* is a *good* novel.
9. When faced with a fleeing suspect, it is probably *wiser* for a police officer to do nothing, in terms of civil liability.
10. Once he chose to break the law, he was not *entitled* to be compensated by it.
11. Police officers *may not* use deadly force against unarmed fleeing suspects who pose no apparent threat to officers or to the public.

Statement 6 is a recommendation or a piece of advice. If you heed the advice by becoming a state trooper, we might say that you acted prudently or wisely; otherwise, if you neglect to follow it by not joining the state troopers, then we might say you were foolish or imprudent. But in neither case is there a question of your being morally praiseworthy for joining or morally blameworthy for not. By saying "you ought" in this case puts you under no moral obligation whatsoever. It is simply a recommendation that you are morally free to follow or ignore. Similarly, statement 7, although it uses the adjective "good", in no way suggests that your record is worthy of moral approbation. And calling Dostoevsky's novel "good" (statement 8) is far from being a moral evaluation; it is strictly an aesthetic one. Finally, statements 9, 10, and 11 all imply an ought, such as a police officer probably ought to do nothing when faced with a fleeing suspect, law breakers ought not to be compensated by the law, and police officers ought not to use deadly force against unarmed fleeing suspects. Again, the "ought" in these cases does not have the force of a moral obligation; however, unlike the case of statement 6, compliance is not so much a matter of prudence or good sense as it is of legal obligation. Thus, compensating outlaws, stopping a fleeing suspect, or using deadly force against an unarmed suspect would not be merely imprudent — as it might be when you choose not to become a state trooper when you are fully qualified to do so — but would make you legally liable. Your not joining the state troopers would carry with it no legal sanction, but killing an unarmed suspect would. Thus, statements 9 through 11 imply a *legal* ought, as distinct from a *prudential* or *moral* ought.

Statements 6 through 11 show how normative terms such as "good" and "ought" may be used in a nonmoral sense. In describing your record as good, I am using "good" in what might be called its natural sense. It is the same sense in which I use it when I speak of good health, a good job, a good tool, a good car, or a good friend. But in my esteeming *Crime and Punishment* a good novel, I am using "good" in a somewhat different sense. I am implying something about its merits as a work of art. In this case, I am using "good" in its aesthetic sense. Whenever I speak of a work of art or nature as "beautiful" or "sublime", I am using cognates of "aesthetic good". Note, however, that the same object may be described as good in the two senses of aesthetic and natural. Thus, I might say that the *Mona Lisa* is a good painting, and that it would fetch a good price in the art market. The value of the *Mona Lisa*, then, is twofold; it has both aesthetic and economic (natural) value. Furthermore, these values are quite distinct and must be judged independently.

Normative terms such as "good" and "bad", "right" and "wrong", and "ought" and "should" may be used in two fundamentally distinct senses: either moral or nonmoral. Moreover, in their nonmoral sense, they may be used in a natural or an aesthetic sense. And, of course, the normative or prescriptive statements containing these terms may be either morally or nonmorally prescriptive and, if nonmorally so, either naturally or aesthetically prescriptive. In this book, we shall be concerned exclusively with normative terms and statements in their moral sense. Therefore, we shall now turn our attention to *morally* normative or prescriptive statements — or, more succinctly, ethical statements — which bulk large in the language of ethics.

Consider these statements:

12. Thou shalt not kill.
13. Police officers ought not to torture suspects.
14. You should always keep your promises.

These statements, which instruct us as to what we ought, or ought not, to do, can be readily converted into commands, such as do not kill, do not torture, and keep your promises. They are examples of judgments of *moral obligation*, or deontic judgments for short. *Deontic* is derived from the Greek word, *deon*, which means "binding" or "proper". The implication is that we ought to obey the implicit commands of these statements because we are bound by the moral laws or rules they evoke. If we obey these injunctions, our actions are deemed *right*; thus, keeping promises is right to do. If we do not, our actions are deemed *wrong*; thus, to murder is wrong.

Consider now the following statements:

15. Jack the Ripper was an evil man.
16. Sir Robert Peele's motives for creating a police force were good.
17. Harry Callahan displayed good character in refusing to join the vigilante cops.
18. Justice is a good virtue.

These are examples of judgments of *moral value*, or aretaic judgments. *Aretaic* is derived from the Greek word, *arete*, which means "virtue" or "excellence". In such judgments, the adjectives "good" or "bad" and "virtuous" or "vicious" (and their cognates) are terms of either approbation or disapprobation, and they are applied to persons, character-traits, motives, and intentions which are thought to have the qualities denoted by them.[1]

There are, then, two distinct kinds of morally normative or pre-scriptive statements: deontic judgments and aretaic judgments. Note that they are distinct in two ways: (1) with respect to *what* they say, and (2) the *way* they say it. Thus, deontic judgments are preeminently about behavior or conduct, are sometimes in the imperative mood, and are expressed by "ought", "should", or "must"; whereas, aretaic judgments are principally about the sources of behavior (e.g., persons, motives, intentions, and character traits) and are in the indicative mood, being expressed by "is", "are", and other forms of the verb "to be". Incidentally, it is worth noting that aretaic judgments, and deontic judgments in the indicative mood (those using adjectives such as "right" or "wrong"), might be mistaken for descriptive statements. But deontic statements (those using the verbs "should", "ought", "must", or their equivalents) are obviously not descriptive statements. Finally, deontic and aretaic judgments, though they may be about particular things, are universal in purport. Thus, if I say of Fuhrman that he was wrong to plant the bloody glove, I say not only his *particular* act of evidence tampering was wrong, but that *any* act like it is equally wrong. Thus, moral judgments, though in the form of particular statements, are really disguised universal statements.

The meaning of ethical terms

There are two related problems that come up early in even a prelimi-nary discussion of the language of ethics. One has to do with the definition of morally normative terms and the other with the truth of morally normative statements. The meaning of the words in descrip-tive statements do not (at least for ethics) pose any difficulties. "Glove" and "shot", for example, are easily understood. But what about "good" and "right"? When we speak of Harry Callahan's having a good charac-ter, Peele's having good motives, or promise-keeping's being right, what exactly do we mean? What, indeed, are we even looking for? Normative terms such as these are notoriously difficult to define. It took Plato several hundred pages to formulate an adequate definition of "jus-tice" in his *Republic*. The attempt to define such an apparently simple word as "good" has been beset by difficulties and controversy.

Because definition is central to metaethics, it behooves us briefly to consider what a definition is and some forms it takes.[2] A definition has two parts: the *definiendum* and *definiens*. The definiendum is the word to be defined — it is the word we look up in the dictionary to find its meaning. The definiens is the word or words used to clarify or explain the meaning of the definiendum. For example, in the definition, "The word 'triangle' means a plane figure enclosed by three straight lines," the word "triangle" is the definiendum and the phrase "a plane figure enclosed by three straight lines" is the definiens.[3]

There are two types of definitions which moral philosophers make use of. If they are interested in simply reporting the standard meaning or common usage of a normative term, they will use a lexical definition (sometimes called "real" definition) of the sort contained in a dictionary. "The word 'mountain' means a large mass of earth or rock rising to a considerable height above the surrounding country"[4] is an example of a lexical definition inasmuch as it reports what English speakers understand by the term or how they use it. More typically, however, moral philosophers are interested in doing something more than merely reporting the established usage of a word; they want to explain the nature of the thing referred to by the definiendum so as to make the definition useful in fields such as the sciences. The resulting definiens will be in terms of a theory (typically scientific) about the nature of the thing named by the definiendum. Such definitions are called theoretical definitions (sometimes called "analytic" definitions). Examples include: (1) "The word 'acid' means any substance containing hydrogen as a positive radical;"[5] (2) "The word 'good' means being an object of favorable interest (desire);" (3) "The word 'right' means being conducive to harmonious happiness."[6] It should be remembered that though normative terms such as "good" and "right" may elude precise definition, we should not despair of their being meaningful and useful. In the case of such terms, we are better off inquiring into how they are actually used in moral discourse than trying to nail down their exact meanings.[7]

How we define ethical terms such as "good" and "right" will determine how we verify the truth of the ethical statements containing them. If we want to find out whether any descriptive statement is true, the procedure we follow is relatively straightforward. It is essentially one of looking and seeing, for descriptive statements are factual statements, and if the relevant facts can be found, then these statements can be proved true or false. Thus, if I want to determine the truth or falsity of the statement, "Mark Fuhrman tampered with the blood stains," there are certain tests that can be performed and specific evidence collected which will either confirm or disconfirm this statement. Or, if I want to know whether it is really true that Rodriguez shot McCummings, there are facts that can be adduced to prove it. But what possible facts or evidence, what observations or experiment, could ever prove that Rodriguez was either right or wrong in shooting McCummings or that Fuhrman was right or wrong in tampering with the blood stains or planting the bloody glove? What would it take to prove beyond a reasonable doubt that, say, criminal behavior should not be treated as if it were some sort of quasi-legitimate enterprise? The problem with ethical statements is that they are not obviously factual, but evaluative, and their truth cannot be established by the usual canons of scientific inquiry. Such statements are not amenable to being tested by the scientific method. So, how do we ascertain their truth, if they are true in any sense at all? We shall now consider some classic theories as to (1) the meaning of ethical terms, and (2) the way to verify the truth of ethical statements.

Metaethical theories as to the meaning of ethical language may be classified according to whether they are either objectivist or subjectivist, or either naturalistic or nonnaturalistic.[8] Objectivism holds that ethical statements and terms can be true or false, and those that are true are objectively so. They are objectively true because they reflect the way things really are; they are founded upon the "nature of things" as this is revealed either by common or scientific experience, metaphysical speculation, or divine revelation. By contrast, subjectivism affirms that moral statements and terms can be neither true nor false, as they do not assert any facts about how things really are but merely express the psychological states of the speaker or writer. Whereas objectivists locate the meaning of normative language in some objective property belonging to the external world, subjectivists locate it entirely within the human subject.

Metaethical theories may also be classified according to whether they are naturalistic or nonnaturalistic. Naturalism defines ethical terms such as "good" and "right" in nonethical terms. Thus, utilitarianism presupposes naturalism, as it defines "good" as pleasure or happiness and "right" as whatever promotes the pleasure or happiness of all. Pleasure and happiness are not ethical or normative concepts but psychological states belonging to human nature. They are facts in the natural, not the moral, order. Naturalism interprets ethical statements as being in reality factual or empirical statements because they refer to some actual property or quality in the things they describe. So ethical statements such as "Rodriguez's shooting of McCummings was a morally right act," "Fuhrman's tampering with the evidence was a morally wrong act," or "Dirty Harry displayed good character in refusing to join the vigilante police" ascribe the properties of "rightness", "wrongness", and "goodness", respectively, to particular acts and character. These statements ascribe properties to their subjects in the same way as the empirical statements "the sky is blue," "grass is green," or "snakes are cold-blooded" ascribe the properties of blueness, greenness, and cold-bloodedness to their respective subjects. Naturalism maintains that goodness and rightness are real properties which belong to certain acts, characters, motives, and dispositions, just as blueness and greenness are properties belonging to certain physical objects. However, not all naturalistic theories equate goodness and rightness with pleasure or happiness. We shall now consider some of these others, giving a brief exposition of each theory followed by a critique.

Metaphysical moralism

According to another naturalistic theory of metaethics, ethical terms such as "right" and "good" and the ethical statements containing them refer not to natural properties such as pleasure or happiness, which are observable properties of things in the natural order, but to certain metaphysical properties which are not directly observable because they belong to things in another or supernatural order. Frankena calls this theory metaphysical moralism.[9] An example of a metaphysical property is any property or attribute of God.

Before going on, though, it is appropriate to pause and ask what is "naturalistic" about metaphysical moralism? A metaethical theory that explains the meaning of ethical terms and statements in terms of pleasure or happiness is naturalistic because these are natural properties in the sense that they belong to things in nature and are observable. Specifically, they are psychological states belonging to human organisms. We know that human beings seek and value happiness and pleasure and the sorts of things that give them pleasure and make them happy. And we can readily tell whether somebody approves or disapproves of something just by listening to him or observing his body language. However, divine approbation or disapprobation is not a naturalistic property because it belongs to a supernatural Being who, in one sense, exists outside of nature and whose attitudes are neither directly nor indirectly observable as human ones are. We might have more accurately classified metaphysical moralism as a "supernaturalistic" theory of metaethics; however, the unnecessary multiplication of terminology can be confusing. Therefore, metaphysical moralism, though it refers to "supernatural" properties, nevertheless qualifies as a naturalistic theory for no other reason than it defines ethical terms in nonethical terms. Any metaethical theory that does so is naturalistic.

A normative ethical theory which presupposes metaphysical naturalism is the divine command theory. According to it, the meaning of an ethical statement is be found in God's will. Thus, to say that a particular act is right or a particular character, virtue, or motive is good simply means that God approves of it. On the other hand, to say of anything that it is morally wrong or bad means that God disapproves of it.

However, this form of metaphysical moralism which finds the meaning of ethical statements in divine approbation is beset by some problems. Fundamentally, of anything that God approves, we can still rationally ask the question, "But is it right or good?" God's approval is distinct from the moral rightness or goodness of what He approves. God's attitude toward anything is a theological fact; as such, it is distinct from a thing's moral quality. Moreover, God's approving something may be the *cause* of His declaring it right or good, but that is distinct from the actual *meaning* of His declaration. Suppose God declared, "Adultery is wrong." The cause of His declaration is something other than and logically distinct from the meaning of it. Furthermore, this theory obviates any real discussion of moral issues. Suppose, for example, you and I disagree over whether abortion is morally right or wrong. The only way we can settle our disagreement is to consult a divine revelation to find God's attitude towards it or something like it. If we find evidence of His disapproval in that He forbids, condemns, or punishes it, then we may safely conclude that abortion is wrong. Note, however, that we resolved the issue not through rational argumentation, but simply by looking something up in a book.

Lastly, this metaethical theory that equates the meaning of moral terms and statements with God's approbation or disapprobation is liable to the same criticism we made earlier of the normative ethical theory of divine command. It presupposes the existence both of a personal God, who is capable of approving and disapproving, and of a reliable revelation of what He approves and disapproves. Needless to say, these are highly disputable presuppositions.

Ideal observer theory

Suppose now that the meaning of "right" or "good" and the statements containing them are not what God approves of, because His judgment, though impeccably judicious, may be inscrutable — especially on the divine command theory. Suppose rather that the meaning of such normative terms is what a person who is impartial, aware of all the relevant facts, capable of imaginative sympathy and empathy, and psychologically normal would approve. Such a person alone would be eligible to make moral judgments or issue ethical statements, because they would be expressions of qualified approval or disapproval. Thus, if this "ideal observer" pronounced that Rodriguez did right in shooting McCummings then it would be so, and the statement, "Rodriguez did right in shooting McCummings," would mean that the ideal observer approved of it. This is the ideal observer theory which holds that any true ethical statement expresses the approbation or disapprobation of someone with the above qualifications. The ideal observer's requisite state of mind is described by Hospers as "calm, dispassionate, reflective, able to weigh all the evidence pro and con, and able to see both sides of an issue, not blinded by passion and special interest."[10]

But, apart from the possibility of God, does any ideal observer — being ideal — actually exist? Certainly we can point to historical and current examples of men and women — presumably federal judges and Supreme Court justices — who come closer to realizing this ideal than most, but that the ideal is not fully realizable in the human world does not really matter. It is sufficient for the theory that we can take all the mental qualities we think should belong to the ideal observer, hypothesize the existence of this observer, and then imagine what the observer would approve and disapprove of in any given moral situation.

However, this theory is vulnerable to some of the same criticisms as the theory that equated the meaning of ethical terms and statements with divine approval. For one thing, something's being right or good is distinct from its being approved even by an ideal observer. We can still ask of something so approved or of the observer's approval itself, "But is it right?" "Being right" and "being approved by an ideal observer" are two distinct properties that may belong to the same act, such as Rodriguez's shooting McCummings. Conceivably, that act may have one or another of these properties, both together, or neither of them. This suggests that they are not identical as the ideal observer theory claims. Thus, though the phrases "being right" and "being approved by an ideal observer" may refer to exactly the same act, it does not follow that they have the same meaning. By way of illustration, consider the phrases "equilateral triangle" and "equiangular triangle".[11] Both refer to exactly the same thing, namely, a triangle.

And neither the property of being equilateral nor the property of being equiangular can belong to a triangle without the other property as well — all equilateral triangles are necessarily equiangular and vice versa. But this does not imply that "being equilateral" and "being equiangular" mean the same thing; each refers to a separate property and connotes something different. And just because these properties always belong together in every triangle, it does not follow that they are only one property. By the same token, "being right" and "being approved by an ideal observer" may, though not necessarily, refer to the very same act; but this does not imply that they mean the very same thing or that the properties of being right and of being approved by an ideal observer are really the same property but with different names.

A second criticism has to do with the mental state of the ideal observer. One of the qualities he must have to qualify as an ideal observer is that of being psychologically normal. But what does it mean to be "psychologically normal?" Psychiatrists themselves cannot agree. If we say it means any deviation from the norm, then we are begging the question — yes, but what is the norm and why should that be the norm? And why does being normal qualify one to make moral judgments? Why should this person's approval or disapproval of something count for more than that of someone who is abnormal? It just may be that being normal (assuming we know what that is) is not the best qualification for making moral judgments. Old Testament prophets, such as Elijah and Jeremiah or St. John the Baptist in the New Testament, do not strike us as folks just like us, and I doubt they struck their contemporaries that way. Relative to the conventional and accepted attitudes of their day, their attitudes were abnormal. Yet this in no way derogates from the cogency of their moral pronouncements. They were very likely "strange" men blessed with uncanny moral insight. Indeed, it may well be that an element of abnormality is as essential to the makeup of moral genius as it is to other types. William James believed that religious geniuses, who are given to mystical flights and ecstasies, are, by definition, exceptional or abnormal and typically exhibit pathological traits. These people, too often dismissed as religious "fanatics", exemplify for James the purest religious type. They are the ones who found great religions, and whose religious experiences and insights can change the course of history. Indeed, James goes as far as to say that a certain kind of abnormality in the personality is a necessary condition for having such experiences and insights.[12] The psychological oddness of great creative artists has been well documented and has actually become something of a cliché. It may be that the "moral" genius, like the religious and the artistic, may be slightly mad.

One final criticism of the ideal observer theory with respect to the observer's state of mind is in order. Hospers describes that mental state as being "calm, dispassionate, and reflective." Calmness, dispassionateness, and reflectiveness, then, are qualities which, if one has them, make one's approbation or disapprobation morally significant; in other words, they qualify the observer to make correct moral judgments. On the other hand, if these qualities are lacking, then that person is unqualified to be an ideal observer and make moral judgments; rather, the moral judgments, to be correct, must conform to those of the ideal observer. However, if these qualities qualify one to be an ideal observer, then they must be good qualities. And the reason that they are chosen in the first place as qualifications for the ideal observer is that qualities such as calmness and reflectiveness, and the others cited by Hospers, are considered admirable. But to speak of these qualities as good is to beg the question. We are attempting to define "moral goodness" as what would be approved of by an ideal observer. And then we say that to qualify as an ideal observer one must have certain "good" mental qualities. Now the question is, what makes those qualities *good*? Again, we are back to the question of what is meant by "good", the very question with which we began. To answer that "good" means being approved by an ideal observer is to argue in a circle. Thus, "good", at least in its nonmoral sense, must mean something else, but the adherents of the ideal observer theory do not say what that is.

R.B. Perry's theory

Another metaethical theory as to the meaning of ethical terms and statements is presupposed by Ralph Barton Perry's ethics. He defines "good" as "the character which anything derives from being the object of any positive interest." In other words, "Whatever is desired, liked, enjoyed, willed, or hoped for is thereby good."[13] However, it is not just anything in which we have a positive interest which is *really* good. For example, the alcoholic has an interest in getting another drink or the addict in taking a drug. To be genuinely good, the object of one's positive interest must not obstruct or interfere with his other interests but rather complement, support, and fit in harmoniously with them. Alcohol and drugs, though deemed good by the alcoholic and addict, can wreak havoc with the addict's other interests, such as family, job, and overall happiness — in fulfilling the one interest he may forfeit all the rest. By contrast, fulfilling one's interest in either family or job does not impede fulfilling other interests but can actually contribute to them. An object of positive interest to be good must make for a harmony among all of the person's interests wherein the fulfillment of any one of the positive interests is compatible with the fulfillment of all the others.

However, that any of my positive interests makes for a pattern of harmonious interests in my life still does not ensure that it, or my interests as a harmonious whole, is unqualifiably good. Suppose that the dominant interest of my life is safe-cracking, which, far from obstructing, abets my other interests, and my fulfilling all of them in turn helps me fulfill my interest in safe-cracking. All my interests, then, are in harmony and enable me to live a fulfilled and happy life. The problem, however, is my interest in safe-cracking; although it fits in with all my other positive interests, it is definitely at odds with the favorable interests of all other members of society as a whole. To the degree that I fulfill my interest I necessarily prevent others from fulfilling theirs — my stealing from them stops them from enjoying their property, an object of favorable interest to them. To qualify as genuinely good, then, my interests must be such that in seeking to fulfill any of them I help to fulfill the favorable interests of all others, as well. It is not enough that my interests, or any one else's, make for harmony in private life; they must also do so in public life. Consequently, Perry defines "right" as that which is conducive to the "harmonious happiness" of society.[14]

Some criticisms of Perry's theory may already have occurred to you. First, that a majority of people favor an interest — that is, they desire, hope for, or enjoy something — does not mean that it is morally good or right. Of any of the public's interests we may well ask: "But is it right that they should seek to fulfill it? Is the object of positive interest they see to fulfill itself good?" We might give negative answers to these questions. For example, Nazi Germany favored world conquest and the mass extermination of certain races and sought to fulfill these objects of its collective interest. A majority of Germans either shared these national interests or helped to fulfill them; however, far from being good and right, world domination and genocide, and their pursuit, are monstrous evils. Just as an individual may have a dominant interest, such as safe-cracking, which, though it fits in with and even focuses all his other interests, is pernicious, an entire society may have an interest such as genocide which fits in with and focuses all its other public interests. Closer to home, consider the issue of the death penalty or legalized gambling. A majority of citizens may have a positive interest in these practices, but the issue of whether they are morally acceptable remains open.

Second, Perry's criterion of rightness as that which is conducive to the harmonious happiness of society may run afoul of our moral common sense as to what is right and wrong.[15] For example, on Perry's criterion, tax evasion is morally worse than incest as it stands to impede the fulfillment of the public's interests — at least its economic interest — in a way that incest does not; however, this is not the judgment that most of us would be inclined to make.

Aside from the criticisms that have been made so far of the above naturalistic theories of ethics individually, there is an especially damaging one that can be made of them collectively. This criticism has to do with the fact that these theories define ethical terms such as "good" in nonethical terms, like pleasure or happiness as in classic utilitarianism; or some form of approbation, as in the ideal observer or divine command theories; or as an object of positive interest, as in Perry's theory. The problem is this: normative concepts such as good, right, and ought belong to the realm of values, but psychological concepts such as pleasure, happiness, and approbation belong to the realm of facts. Now the empirical realm of facts or nature is quite distinct from the normative realm of values. This distinction is reflected in the language we use in speaking of them. In speaking of facts, we use descriptive or factual statements as to what is the case, but in speaking of values we use evaluative statements as to what ought to be or what is better or worse. Thus, to define the "good" in terms of pleasure, happiness, or approbation is to reduce a value to a fact, which is a conceptual mistake or fallacy much like defining color in terms of sound. G.E. Moore labeled it the naturalistic fallacy.[16] This fallacy covers three faults in the moral reasoning of moral naturalists. One is that they attempt to define the indefinable; "good" refers to a quality of actions or habits that is utterly simple and so cannot be explained in terms of anything else — it can only be intuited. Second, they attempt to reduce two distinct properties to just one of them — for instance, reduce the distinct properties of goodness and of pleasure to just pleasure. A third fault covered by the naturalistic fallacy has to do not with the meaning of normative terms but with inferences in moral arguments, but this we shall defer to in the next chapter.

Moore devised a technique, the so-called open-question technique (which we have already applied above), whereby instances of the naturalistic fallacy may be exposed and the nature of the fallacy clarified. It works this way. Whenever a normative term such as "good" or "right" is defined naturalistically in terms of pleasure, happiness, approbation, or an object of positive interest, it is always meaningful to ask whether the natural property in question is morally good. Thus, if the hedonist defines "good" as pleasure, we then can still legitimately ask, "But is this pleasure good?" This question suggests that, though pleasure, or some other natural property, may itself be good, it does not necessarily exhaust the whole meaning of "good"; there is still something in the concept of good that is distinct from and other than pleasure, thereby making "pleasure" an inadequate term for it.

However, Frankena gives several reasons for thinking that naturalistic theories of ethics have been unfairly accused of committing the naturalistic fallacy. First, to make the accusation stick, their critics need to show why ethical terms cannot be legitimately defined in terms of nonethical ones; otherwise, they are begging the question. For another, a definition, in attempting to clarify a vague term, may sometimes need to leave out of the definiens certain things to which the term applies. For example, take the technical definition of a circle: "a plane, closed figure, all of the points on whose circumference are equidistant from a point within called the center."[17] Now, using the open-question technique, we may legitimately ask whether this is all that there is to a circle or what people usually have in mind or mean when they speak of circles. In other words, our concept of a circle contains more — a visual image such as a wheel, for example — than what is contained in the definiens of this definition. But this does not mean that this definition of a circle is wrong or commits any kind of a fallacy; geometrically considered, a circle is just such a plane, closed figure. By the same token, "good" may very well be definable as pleasure or happiness, but the fact that it excludes something else about good does not mean that the definition itself is fallacious. A second reason urged by Frankena is that normative terms such as "good" or "right" are notoriously difficult to define; hence, it is easy enough to doubt any of their definitions and challenge them with the open-question technique, even though the definitions may be correct. And third, even if a definition of a normative term commits the naturalistic fallacy, it may still be useful.[18] The next metaethical theory avoids the imputation of the naturalistic fallacy.

Nonnaturalism/intuitionism

Another objectivist theory, but an alternative to ethical naturalism, is ethical nonnaturalism or intuitionism.[19] In marked contrast to the former, this theory denies that ethical terms such as "good" can be defined in nonethical terms; in fact, it insists that they are indefinable. Ethical terms refer to utterly simple properties which are nonnatural or nonempirical; they cannot be grasped empirically or through the senses but must be intuited by the mind. Thus, for Moore, "good" refers to such a property; for Henry Sidgwick, "ought" does; and for Ross, both terms do.[20] For moral nonnaturalists, true moral statements are intuitively or self-evidently true, such as the statements that "2 + 2 = 4" or "a triangle is a plane figure enclosed by three straight lines." They neither require nor are susceptible to any sort of logical or empirical proof.

However, moral nonnaturalism or intuitionism is vulnerable to some serious objections. One is that the theory assumes the existence of things which may not exist: thus, it assumes the existence of nonnatural or nonempirical properties of which goodness or rightness are thought to be instances. But even if we do concede their existence, ascribing them to specific actions may be questionable. For example, suppose that I have a debt to pay. I intuit that the act of paying my debt has the property of obligatoriness, and I accept that the statement "Paying a debt is obligatory" is self-evidently true. Now, using the open-question technique, I can meaningfully ask, "Why should I pay my debt?" Hence, this action is not necessarily obligatory. However, Frankena has pointed out that this question is ambiguous: it can mean either "What should my motive be in paying my debt?" or "What justification should I have for paying my debt?" If the question is about justification, then it should read, "Ought I really to pay my debt?" Now, if I believe that I ought to pay my debt, then I must also believe that paying my debt is obligatory — in other words, that action has the nonnatural property of obligatoriness. To deny that is to beg the question of why I should do it in the first place.[21]

Furthermore, intuitionism assumes the existence of a special sort of intuition (a moral sense) whose objects are moral properties. However, the existence of such a moral faculty, which intuitionists think belongs naturally to all people, is highly questionable. For one thing, some people, such as incorrigible criminals, seem to lack it entirely. Shakespeare's *Richard III* is a dramatic study of a man bereft of a moral sense. For another, moral intuitions differ among individuals and cultures. Thus, the moral intuition of Smith declares capital punishment morally wrong, whereas that of Jones declares it morally right; the collective moral intuition of culture X finds female circumcision to be morally acceptable, whereas that of culture Y finds it morally abhorrent. This means that disagreements over moral issues boil down to conflicts among intuitions, but there is no way to resolve such conflicts rationally, or to validate an intuition except by reaffirming it. Moral intuition, then, is an unreliable guide in the moral life.

Finally, intuitionists believe that some moral statements are self-evidently true such as, "Do unto others as you would be done by." However, the self-evident truth of moral statements is not supported by the fact that individuals and whole cultures can disagree over what counts as a moral truth, and that some mathematicians have dismissed the idea of self-evident truth even in mathematics, where we would expect to find its paradigm.[22]

We shall conclude this section on moral objectivism with a pair of criticisms that strike at the root of both moral naturalism and nonnaturalism, namely, their claim to objectivity. Both naturalistic and nonnaturalistic theories find the meaning of normative terms in some objective property, whether natural or nonnatural; thus, utilitarianism, deontologism, and the divine command theory equate the good with some objective fact such as pleasure, the moral law, or divine fiat, respectively. One criticism is that moral naturalists fail to justify their definitions of ethical terms. For example, Perry's definition of "good" as being "the character which anything derives from being the object of any positive interest" is not based on any fact or objective state of affairs, but rather on the moral principle that such maximum fulfillment is indeed morally right. To avoid circularity, this principle itself requires justification, though none can be given. Hence, because their bedrock principles cannot be logically derived from any objective facts or state of affairs, naturalistic theories fail in being objective at all and moral objectivism is rendered implausible.[23]

The second criticism is that some objectivist theories of ethics fail to take into account that moral statements do more than merely assert facts or ascribe properties to things — if they do so at all — but that they also express feelings or attitudes such as approval or disapproval, prescribe or proscribe behavior, or recommend traits of character.[24] Normative statements are not merely empirical or factual statements, but they have, in Hosper's phrase, an "expressive-persuasive character."[25]

Note that this criticism does not apply to more subjectivist naturalistic theories, such as the ideal observer theory or Perry's theory, which interpret moral statements as expressions of approbation or interest. A merit of the metaethical theory we are about to consider is that it takes it start from the expressive-persuasive character of moral discourse.

Emotivism

Emotivism is a subjectivist theory which holds that the function of moral statements is not at all to inform by stating facts, but rather to express emotions or direct behavior. There are two versions of emotivism: the *expressive* and the *evocative*,[26] depending on the specific function it ascribes to moral statements. The expressive version of the theory maintains that moral statements express personal feelings or emotions.[27] Thus, the statement, "Rodriguez's shooting of McCummings was morally right," simply expresses pleasure at or approval of Rodriguez's action, whereas the statement, "Fuhrman's planting the bloody glove at Simpson's estate was morally wrong," simply expresses displeasure at or disapproval of Fuhrman's action. The evocative version maintains instead that moral statement express implicit commands and so aim to influence behavior. Thus, the statement, "Police officers ought not to take bribes," is simply an indirect way of saying "You police officers are commanded not to take bribes." On both versions of the emotive theory, because moral statements do not state or report facts about the world over which they can be mistaken (this not being their function), they can be neither true nor false and so are not cognitively meaningful.

The emotivist theory, in its worthy attempt to simplify and clarify our moral discourse, can be faulted for having a too restrictive conception of ethical language and of failing to do justice to its complexity — its multiple uses and subtleties. It makes the opposite mistake of objectivist theories such as moral naturalism. If the latter give short shrift to the "expressive-persuasive character" of moral language, emotivism does so with respect to its rational and empirical character. Thus, emotivists are correct enough in saying that moral statements are used to express feelings or influence behavior, but not always. I might very well make a moral judgment without consciously expressing, or intending to express, an emotion or attitude. And moral judgments are not always uttered as implicit commands to influence people's conduct, as the evocative version of the emotive theory would have it. For example, if I make a historical moral judgment such as, "It was wrong of Brutus to kill Caesar,"[28] I do more than command, as the implicit command is now redundant.

However, moral statements are used to do more than express or evoke emotions or change attitudes and behavior; they are used to state something. This is no less true of purely emotive language, the primary purpose of which is to express emotion. For example, if I say "Alas!" or "Wow!" I simply express distress or elation, nothing more. But if I say "There is a time bomb in this room set to go off in two minutes!"[29] I not only express and evoke the emotion of fear in order to evacuate the room but state a fact, as well (if, indeed, there is a bomb). By the same token, my saying, "Mark Fuhrman's planting a bloody glove at Simpson's estate was morally wrong," may express my displeasure at Fuhrman's action, but this moral statement also states a fact (i.e., Fuhrman's planting of a bloody glove at Simpson's estate), which, far from being irrelevant or incidental, serves as an objective basis for my emotional response. On the other hand, a moral judgment need not be a factual statement to be meaningful. Ethical judgments, then, have a core meaning which is factual or rational and so are descriptive as well as emotive; as Frankena puts it, "They make or somehow imply a claim to be objectively and rationally justified or valid."[30]

According to emotivism, because moral judgments can be neither true nor false, there is no such thing as moral truth or error. So, if I say "slavery is morally wrong" but you say "slavery is not morally wrong," neither of us is right or wrong; each of us is merely expressing a different feeling — pleasure or displeasure, respectively. This, though, is a deficient view of the significance of moral language and contrary to our moral common sense. It is possible that some moral judgments are true in some sense, or at least more plausible and worthy of our assent than others. To see how this may be, consider a nonmoral normative statement that might be made in the course of a chess game, such as, "Moving your bishop is a better move than moving your rook." The word "better" makes this a normative or prescriptive statement. Now, suppose that by moving your bishop you could checkmate your opponent in three moves, but if you moved your rook you would lose that piece and risk losing your queen. In the context of this chess game, the normative judgment that moving your bishop is a better move than moving your rook is objectively true. By analogy, then, morally normative judgments such as "Mark Fuhrman's planting a bloody glove at Simpson's estate was morally wrong" might be objectively true under the specific conditions in which that action was done.[31] Furthermore, moral judgments may be supported by reasons which can be said to determine their truth or plausibility; a moral judgment is more nearly true than its alternative if it has more and better reasons in its support.[32] Finally, even if a moral statement does nothing more than express an emotion or a command, emotions and commands may result from beliefs that are rationally defensible; hence, moral judgments may be rationally justifiable or not, depending on whether the emotions or commands they express are based on defensible beliefs.[33] Thus, the fear and the implicit command to evacuate expressed in the statement "There is a time bomb in this room set to go off in two minutes!" issue from a rationally defensible belief if there really is a bomb in the room or compelling reasons for believing that there is. Similarly, the moral judgment, "Mark Fuhrman's planting a bloody glove at Simpson's estate was morally wrong," is rationally justifiable if the displeasure it expresses is based on a defensible belief such that lying and deception are morally wrong. Such a belief can at least be defended, for example, on either utilitarian or deontological grounds.

Because, according to emotivism, moral judgments assert nothing with which to agree or disagree, there can be no moral disagreement but only individual expressions of conflicting feelings. Yet, we do disagree, often vehemently, over moral issues and can back up our moral stands with good reasons. The reality of moral debates presupposes that there is more to moral judgments than mere expressions of feeling. Emotivists, though, may concede that there can be legitimate disagreements over moral issues, but these disagreements are not over "ethical facts," which are nonexistent, but rather over nonethical facts. Go back, for example, to the moral judgment, "Mark Fuhrman's planting a bloody glove at Simpson's estate was morally wrong." There is no objective ethical fact to which "moral wrongness" refers; this phrase simply expresses displeasure — it has no other meaning. Hence, there can be no disagreement here with respect to pleasure or displeasure, but only a difference or conflict between these opposed feelings. But there can be many real disagreements over the nonethical facts of the case, such as whether the blood on the glove is Simpson's or not, or whether the glove belonged to Simpson, or whether the glove was found rather than planted. However, once agreement is reached over these nonethical facts, no more disagreement is rationally possible.[34] If we then try to justify our feeling of disgust at Fuhrman's action, all we can do is to give a psychological account of it — reasons why we personally feel this way about Fuhrman's act. However, this does not constitute a moral justification, but a psychological one, and is completely irrelevant to the issue of whether Fuhrman was actually morally wrong in acting as he did. Moral disagreements and disputes, though, seem to be about considerably more than simply a matter of psychological conflicts between feelings.

To this emotivist analysis of moral disagreement, Hospers has the following rejoinder. Though agreement may be reached over the nonethical facts, a difference in feeling towards those facts may still persist.[35] Thus, suppose that Fuhrman's planting the glove is an undisputed fact. I feel displeased at his action, and so express my feeling by declaring it to be morally wrong, but you do not, and so express your feeling by declaring it to be morally right or neutral. Our conflict in feeling does not come from nowhere; it comes from a difference in interpretation of a somehow morally significant fact (i.e., Fuhrman's planting the bloody glove). Consequently, the moral judgment as to the wrongness or rightness of this action involves not only the expression of a feeling but, no less, the assertion of what is deemed to be a morally significant fact — one, moreover, having a rational connection with one's emotional reaction to it.

A further problem with emotivism is that our feelings toward an act are quite distinct from its moral rightness or wrongness. I may take pleasure in capital punishment, but one may still meaningfully ask whether it is morally right, or even whether my pleasure in it is morally right. We can always ask ourselves, "Ought we approve this?" concerning a morally significant act. If ethical judgments did nothing more than express our pleasure or displeasure, it would make no sense to ask such questions — indeed, it would be contradictory. But the fact is such questions can be sensibly asked.

A final problem with emotivism is that it confuses the cause of one's making an ethical statement with the meaning of that statement. If I say, "Rodriguez was right to shoot McCummings," my approval of Rodriguez's act may be the cause of my uttering this statement. But my being pleased with his act is something quite different from the statement's meaning (i.e., "Rodriguez was right to shoot McCummings"). Indeed, the cause of my making the statement may be other than my being pleased with Rodriguez; it might be that I felt pressured to make it, or perhaps this is a line in the script of a play in which I am performing. But whatever the cause of my utterance, its meaning remains the same. Along the same lines, emotivists similarly confuse the intention or effect of a statement with its meaning. Thus, in uttering the statements above about the bomb and the glove, my intention may have been to express an emotion or attempt to change behavior, and the statements may have had their intended effect. However, their intention and effect are quite distinct from their meanings and enable me to distinguish between the two statements. Moreover, their effect depends upon the meaning of the words; emotive techniques such as speaking more loudly or quickly or using demonstrative gestures are not enough to achieve the intended effect. This is especially true of moral judgments, which can be meaningfully uttered without the use of any emotionally charged rhetorical devices.[36]

A variant of emotivism makes the feeling or emotion more universal, so to say that something is right or good simply means "the majority of people like it." However, what the public likes or approves of at any time can change. So, if our moral judgments and values depend upon what most of us like or dislike, then there can be no consistency or stability within the moral institution of life; our moral beliefs and values would be as changeable as the weather. This would make a mockery of moral education and spell the death of ethics as a rational activity. Furthermore, if moral judgments and values mean nothing more than what the general public likes or dislikes, then what is right and good could be subject to a vote. The right and the good is whatever the majority rules them to be. This is a form of the doctrine of "might makes right" — rightness and wrongness are determined solely by the interests of the powerful, in this case the public. But democracy works only in politics, not in science and morality. Scientific truth is independent of what the majority of people think, and so is moral truth. Moreover, the public can be terribly wrong on many moral issues. At one time or another, a majority of citizens have supported slavery, apartheid, child labor, and other moral abominations. And practitioners of civil disobedience such as Henry David Thoreau, Mahatma Gandhi, and Martin Luther King, Jr., who opposed the moral opinion of the majority in the interest of justice, indicate that morality is independent of public opinion. Now, if moral judgments meant nothing more than what the public likes or dislikes, then moral criticism of public attitude and policies, past or present, would be impossible. But such criticism is indeed possible, even rampant, so moral judgments must mean something more than merely expressions of public feelings — even if it is only an expression of my personal feelings.

Alternative theories of meaning

Two further metaethical theories (which lack official labels) as to the meaning of moral terms and statements deserve our consideration. One of them understands moral judgments to be recommendations or prescriptions for conduct.[37] This is similar to the evocative version of the emotive theory, which states that moral judgments are implicit commands. Thus, to say that a duty ought morally be done, that an action is morally right, or that a trait of character is morally good is nothing more than to recommend the doing or cultivation of them. Moral judgments are essentially plans of action or strategies for living. They are universalizable insofar as they are recommendations which it behooves all people to follow, and they are rationally justified by the beneficial consequences which will redound to those who do follow them. Two objections, however, may be made to this theory. First, it begs the question as to the meaning of "beneficial"; this itself is a normative term that requires definition, but not in terms of being recommendable or prescribable. Second, it reduces moral (categorical) imperatives to mere hypothetical imperatives; that is, we ought to do our duty not for its own sake but for prudential reasons.

The second metaethical theory interprets the meaning of moral judgments as the totality of reasons in their support. Thus, whatever reasons might be adduced to support the judgment that Fuhrman ought not to have planted the bloody glove constitute its meaning. But this theory can be criticized for failing to distinguish between a statement and the reasons supporting it. In other words, the conclusion of an argument is distinct from its supporting premises; the meaning of a statement is something other than its justification. A moral statement is not just a restatement of its justification, for then there would be nothing to support it: that is, the support and the supported would be one. Moreover, one may assent to the truth of any of the reasons in its support but deny the truth of the moral statement itself. A moral statement is related to its justification as a legal verdict is related to its evidence.[38]

Summary

To review, metaethical theories are either objectivist or subjectivist and either naturalistic or nonnaturalistic. Objectivists find the meaning of moral language in some fact or property belonging to external reality; subjectivists find it wholly within the psychological states of persons who use such language. Naturalists, who are objectivists, define moral terms and statements in nonethical terms; nonnaturalists (intuitionists), who are also objectivists, define them strictly in ethical terms. A merit of objectivism is that it takes seriously the cognitive purport of moral language, but at the expense of its emotive force. A merit of subjectivism, particularly emotivism, is that it does full justice to the emotive force of moral language, but ignores or dismisses its cognitive significance. Naturalistic theories are open to the charge of committing the naturalistic fallacy. Nonnaturalistic theories escape this charge, but presuppose the existence of "nonnatural" properties, the existence of which is questionable.

Notes

1. Frankena, William K., *Ethics*, 2nd ed., Prentice-Hall, Englewood Cliffs, NJ, 1973, p. 9.
2. The following discussion of definition is derived from Irving M. Copi, *Informal Logic*, Macmillan, New York, 1986, pp. 137–144.
3. Copi, Irving M., *Informal Logic*, Macmillan, New York, 1986, p. 138.
4. Copi, Irving M., *Informal Logic*, Macmillan, New York, 1986, p. 140.
5. Copi, Irving M., *Informal Logic*, Macmillan, New York, 1986, p. 132.
6. Perry, Ralph B., *Realms of Value*, Harvard University Press, Cambridge, MA, 1954, pp. 107, 109.
7. Hospers, John, *Human Conduct: An Introduction to the Problems of Ethics*, Harcourt, Brace & World, New York, 1961, p. 575.
8. The following discussion of metaethics is largely based on Chapter 6 in Frankena's *Ethics*, 2nd ed. (Prentice-Hall, Englewood Cliffs, NJ, 1973) and Chapter 11 in Hospers' *Human Conduct: An Introduction to the Problems of Ethics* (Harcourt, Brace & World, New York, 1961).
9. Frankena, William K., *Ethics*, 2nd ed., Prentice-Hall, Englewood Cliffs, NJ, 1973, p. 98.
10. Hospers, John, *Human Conduct: An Introduction to the Problems of Ethics*, Harcourt, Brace & World, New York, 1961, p. 546.
11. I owe this illustration to Hospers' *Human Conduct: An Introduction to the Problems of Ethics* (Harcourt, Brace & World, New York, 1961, p. 550).
12. "Like many other geniuses who have brought forth fruits effective enough for commemoration in the pages of biography, such religious geniuses have often shown symptoms of nervous instability. Even more perhaps than other kinds of genius, religious leaders have been

subject to abnormal psychical visitations. Invariably they have been creatures of exalted emotional sensibility. Often they have led a discordant inner life, and had melancholy during a part of their career. They have known no measure, been liable to obsessions and fixed ideas; and frequently they have fallen into trances, heard voices, seen visions, and presented all sorts of peculiarities which are ordinarily classed as pathological. Often, moreover, these pathological features in their career have helped to give them their religious authority and influence." (From James, William, *The Varieties of Religious Experience: A Study in Human Nature*, Macmillan, New York, 1961, p. 25.)

13. Perry, Ralph B., *Realms of Value*, Harvard University Press, Cambridge, MA, 1954, p. 101.

14. Perry, Ralph B., *Realms of Value*, Harvard University Press, Cambridge, MA, 1954, p 107.

15. This criticism comes from Perry, Ralph B., *Realms of Value*, Harvard University Press, Cambridge, MA, 1954, p. 553.

16. Moore explains the fallacy as follows: "It may be true that all things which are good are *also* something else, just as it is true that all things which are yellow produce a certain kind of vibration in the light. And it is a fact, that ethics aims at discovering what are those other properties belonging to all things which are good. But far too many philosophers have thought that when they named those other properties they were actually defining good; that these properties, in fact, were simply not 'other,' but absolutely and entirely the same with goodness. This view I propose to call the 'naturalistic fallacy' and of it I shall endeavor to dispose." (From Moore, George E., *Principia Ethica*, Cambridge University Press, Cambridge, 1959, p. 10.)

17. I owe this example to Hospers' *Human Conduct: An Introduction to the Problems of Ethics* (Harcourt, Brace & World, New York, 1961, p. 550).

18. Frankena, William K., *Ethics*, 2nd ed., Prentice-Hall, Englewood Cliffs, NJ, 1973, pp. 99–100.

19. This metaethical theory has been advocated by a host of distinguished moral philosophers: among them are Anthony Ashley Cooper (3rd Earl of Shaftesbury), Francis Hutcheson, Joseph Butler, Henry Sidgwick, G.E. Moore, Hastings Rashdall, H.A. Pritchard, William Ross, E.F. Carritt, Nicolas Hartmann, A.C. Ewing, and possibly Plato.

20. Frankena, William K., *Ethics*, 2nd ed., Prentice-Hall, Englewood Cliffs, NJ, 1973, p. 103.

21. Frankena, William K., *Ethics*, 2nd ed., Prentice-Hall, Englewood Cliffs, NJ, 1973, p. 104.

22. Frankena, William K., *Ethics*, 2nd ed., Prentice-Hall, Englewood Cliffs, NJ, 1973, p. 103.

23. Frankena, William K., *Ethics*, 2nd ed., Prentice-Hall, Englewood Cliffs, NJ, 1973, p. 101.

24. Frankena, William K., *Ethics*, 2nd ed., Prentice-Hall, Englewood Cliffs, NJ, 1973, p. 105.

25. Hospers, John, *Human Conduct: An Introduction to the Problems of Ethics*, Harcourt, Brace & World, New York, 1961, p. 562.

26. I owe this distinct to Hospers' *Human Conduct: An Introduction to the Problems of Ethics* (Harcourt, Brace & World, New York, 1961, p. 560).

27. Hospers, John, *Human Conduct: An Introduction to the Problems of Ethics*, Harcourt, Brace & World, New York, 1961, p. 560. The emotivist theory that "good" is an expression of approval or pleasure may seem superficially similar to Perry's theory that it is "an object of favorable interest" since approval and favorable interest are both psychological states. However, there are two fundamental differences between them. First, Perry locates the good in the object itself which draws our interest or approval, whereas the emotivist locates it in the psychological response to that object, thereby making Perry's theory objectivist. Second, Perry appears to maintain that ethical statements actually *state* something factual (e.g., "these here are *objects* of favorable interest [italics added]"), whereas the emotivist insists that they simply express feelings.

28. I owe this example to Hospers' *Human Conduct: An Introduction to the Problems of Ethics* (Harcourt, Brace & World, New York, 1961, p. 564).

29. I owe this example to Hospers' *Human Conduct: An Introduction to the Problems of Ethics* (Harcourt, Brace & World, New York, 1961, pp. 562–563).

30. Frankena, William K., *Ethics*, 2nd ed., Prentice-Hall, Englewood Cliffs, NJ, 1973, p. 108.

31. I owe this line of thought to Theroux.

32. Rachels, James, *The Elements of Moral Philosophy*, 2nd ed., McGraw-Hill, New York, 1993, p. 40.

33. Frankena, William K., *Ethics*, 2nd ed., Prentice-Hall, Englewood Cliffs, NJ, 1973, p. 107.

34. Hospers, John, *Human Conduct: An Introduction to the Problems of Ethics*, Harcourt, Brace & World, New York, 1961, p. 567.

35. Hospers, John, *Human Conduct: An Introduction to the Problems of Ethics*, Harcourt, Brace & World, New York, 1961, p. 568.

36. Hospers, John, *Human Conduct: An Introduction to the Problems of Ethics*, Harcourt, Brace & World, New York, 1961, p. 563.

37. Hospers, John, *Human Conduct: An Introduction to the Problems of Ethics*, Harcourt, Brace & World, New York, 1961, p. 106.

38. Hospers, John, *Human Conduct: An Introduction to the Problems of Ethics,* Harcourt, Brace & World, New York, 1961, pp. 573–575.

chapter seven

The logic of ethics

Arguments

Logic is concerned with formulating the rules of correct inference and applying them in the evaluation of arguments. Because the identification, classification, and assessment of arguments are the fundamental tasks of philosophy, and so no less of moral philosophy, we need to be clear as to what an argument is. We shall start, then, with the definition and classification of arguments and then go on to the techniques of assessing and identifying them.

An argument, in its logical sense, is a set of statements, one of which, the principal statement or *conclusion*, is supported by the rest, the *premises*. Here is an example:

A
1. All snakes are reptiles.
2. All copperheads are snakes.
3. Therefore, all copperheads are reptiles.

Note that the conclusion (statement 3) follows necessarily from the other two statements (1 and 2). Indeed, if you had been given only the first two statements, you could easily have inferred the third. In this argument, the premises provide optimal support for the conclusion, such that if you accept them then you cannot deny the conclusion without contradiction. Such an argument is called a *valid* argument. An argument is valid if, and only if, assuming the truth of the premises, it is impossible for the conclusion to be false. Alternatively, an argument is valid if, and only if, assuming the truth of the premises, the conclusion must be true. Valid arguments are said to be truth-preserving because the truth of their premises is carried over to, or preserved in, the truth of their conclusions.

But consider now the following argument:

B

1. All jackasses like classical music.
2. I own a jackass named Francis.
3. Therefore, Francis likes classical music.

Here, the premises are obviously false. I do not have a jackass, and it is far from established that jackasses like classical music (more likely, their tastes would run to country/western). But, the argument is nevertheless valid. The reason is that, to be valid, we need only *assume* the truth of the premises; it makes absolutely no difference whether or not they are in fact true. In the case above, if we assume the premises to be true, there is no avoiding the truth of the conclusion. This points up an important distinction, a distinction first made by Aristotle in his *Prior Analytics:* the distinction between the truth of statements and the validity of arguments. A statement's truth depends, at least on one account,[1] upon whether or not what it says corresponds to the way things really stand. By contrast, the validity of arguments has nothing whatever to do with things as they really are. Instead, it has to do with the relationships among the statements in an argument, with whether the conclusion does indeed follow from its premises. In short, validity is concerned exclusively with the *logical form* of arguments and its correctness. Note that, in the interest of precision, arguments are neither true nor false; they are either valid or invalid. Statements, in turn, are neither valid nor invalid, but are either true or false.

Now, though both the above arguments are valid, the premises of argument A, unlike those of argument B, are factually true. We do not merely have to assume their truth. Argument A, therefore, is an example of a *sound* argument. An argument is sound if, and only if, (1) it is valid, and (2) its premises are factually true. Note that to qualify as sound, an argument must first of all be valid. No invalid arguments can be sound. All sound arguments are valid. Validity, then, is a *necessary condition* for an argument to be sound. The highest honor that can be bestowed on an argument is to declare it sound. It is like winning the gold medal at the Olympics. The second highest honor is declaring the argument valid. This is analogous to winning the silver medal. Thus, argument B is valid, but argument A is sound.

Consider this next example:

C
1. All snakes are reptiles.
2. Some reptiles are in the room.
3. Therefore, some snakes are in the room.

There may in fact be some snakes in the room, as snakes are reptiles. Not all reptiles are snakes, however; some are lizards or tortoises. Thus, some or all of the reptiles in the room may be something other than snakes. Just knowing that statements 1 and 2 are true does not guarantee the truth of statement 3. All we are entitled to infer from these premises is that there *may* be snakes in the room — we do not know for sure. In this case, the conclusion does not follow necessarily from the premises, and to suppose that it does is to commit a *fallacy*, or logical mistake. We shall have occasion later on to note other fallacies. One important task of logic is to classify and identify such fallacies so they might be avoided.

A logical fallacy, which is specific to moral reasoning, is the naturalistic fallacy. We encountered this fallacy as it pertains to the definition of normative terms in the previous chapter. We shall now consider how it pertains to inference. The naturalistic fallacy as it occurs in inference, which Hume discovered but did not name as such,[2] is a highly contentious issue in metaethics. It is illustrated in the following argument:

1. You witnessed a crime.
2. Therefore, you ought to report the crime to the police.

From the premise that something *is* actually the case, the inference is made that something else *ought* to be the case. However, a prescriptive statement of obligation (an "ought" statement) cannot be logically inferred from a descriptive statement (an "is" statement). To slide in this way from an "is" to an "ought" is to commit the naturalistic fallacy. Suppose that a mother tells her son that he ought to clean his room. He asks, "Why?" Her reply is, "Because I am your mother." The son might then logically (but not prudently) inquire, "But what does your being my mother have to do with my having an obligation to clean my room?" The way to avoid the naturalistic fallacy is simply to introduce as a second premise a universal prescriptive statement, or general principle, in arguments like the one above. Thus:

1. You witnessed a crime.
2. Anyone who witnesses a crime ought to report it
3. Therefore, you ought to report the crime to the police.

The conclusion, an "ought" statement, can be validly inferred from the two premises, one of which is also an "ought" statement. It is not always easy to recognize arguments, let alone to understand and evaluate them. So here I shall offer some tips on detecting arguments.

How to detect arguments

An important clue that a passage contains an argument is the presence of certain words or phrases that function as indicators. Consider the following:

1. A, *thus* B.
2. A, *therefore* B.
3. A, *hence* B.
4. A, *consequently* B.

The italicized words are examples of conclusion indicators. There are others, but these are the principal ones, and from them you can easily figure out the others. The letters A and B might refer to clauses or sentences. For example:

D
1. All dogs are mammals.
2. Lassie is a dog.
3. *Thus*, Lassie is a mammal.

The clause or sentence following a conclusion indicator (e.g., the "B" in statements 1 through 4, above) is likely to be a conclusion, as in the case here of statement 3. But note, I only said "likely". Not every statement following a conclusion indicator is a conclusion. It might be an *explanandum* (i.e., a statement that has been explained by previous statements), as in this case:

E
1. The jury duly considered the fact that Fuhrman may have tampered with the evidence, together with the report that he made racist remarks.
2. *Consequently*, the jury found Simpson innocent.

Here, again, the statement coming on the heels of a conclusion indicator may be neither a conclusion nor an explanandum. It may be that the writer is simply sloppy, and he introduces a conclusion indicator as a way of bringing an artificial closure to his text. Moreover, conclusion indicators work backwards as well as forwards. The clauses or sentences coming before them are likely to be premises (e.g., the "A" in statements 1 through 4, above). But, again, they will be premises only if the statement coming after the indicator is a conclusion.

Now consider these expressions:

1. *Because of* A, B
2. *Since* A, B
3. *In light of* A, B

The italicized expressions are all examples of premise indicators. There are more, but these are the main ones; the others are easily recognizable from these. Again, the letters A and B might refer to clauses or sentences. In the above example (D), statements 1 and 2 are premises. The same caution applies here as in the case of conclusion indicators. The statements succeeding a premise indicator are likely to be premises, but not necessarily. They may constitute an *explanans*, which is the account given for the occurrence of a particular event (e.g., statement 1 in example E, above). On the other hand, they may have little or nothing to do with supporting the putative conclusion. Conclusion and premise indicators, then, do not guarantee the presence of arguments; they are at best only clues to the existence of arguments and to the identity of the premises and conclusions within an argument.

Many times, however, an argument is presented with neither premise nor conclusion indicators. In these cases, the best thing to do is to ask yourself, "What statement expresses the main point of the passage?" or "What statement do all the other statements in a given passage support or relate to in some way?" The answer will typically be the conclusion. Sometimes arguments are not given in complete form. The technical name for such incomplete arguments is *enthymeme*. A premise or even the conclusion may have been left out. Another name for a missing premise is *assumption*. In such cases, the missing premise or conclusion is implicit in the passage, and your job is to infer it from the statements that are given and to make it explicit. With practice, you should become adept at this task.

Moral reasoning

From arguments in general, we turn now to moral arguments in particular. Here, we shall be concerned with (1) the anatomy of typical moral arguments, (2) the steps to be taken in their evaluation, and (3) the ways they can help us decide what should be done in a moral situation.

A moral argument begins with a question as to what we ought to do in a morally significant situation which, typically, is a dilemma in which our options are momentous. Its aim is to help us make the right (i.e., rational and moral) decision. Take the McCummings case. Rodriguez sees McCummings brutally assault and rob Sandusky and then flee from the scene. Should Rodriguez shoot McCummings? In the heat of the moment, it is very unlikely that Rodriguez (or anyone else for that matter) could have coolly and calmly engaged in anything like moral reasoning to arrive at a decision. But, suppose that the action were performed in slow motion, thus giving Rodriguez time to work out an argument. Consider what kind of creditable argument to justify his course of action could have been constructed in retrospect. The result might have been as follows:

F

1. If a dangerous suspect flees the scene of his crime, it is always right (indeed, obligatory) for a police officer to use deadly force to stop him.
2. McCummings was a dangerous suspect fleeing the scene of his crime.
3. Therefore, it was right for me, a police officer, to use deadly force to stop McCummings.

This moral argument is an example of a practical *syllogism*. A syllogism is an argument containing exactly three statements. It is "practical" insofar as it is designed to guide our conduct. Let us now look more closely at its features. Note that the second premise (statement 2) is a particular descriptive statement that asserts an essential fact. It describes the situation which gives rise to a question of what one should do. Note that the first premise (statement 1) is a general normative statement — although it is perhaps more legally normative than morally, it certainly has moral implications. Its purpose is to help Rodriguez decide what to do. Now, we can make the following generalizations about any moral argument: First, it must contain at least one particular descriptive statement (e.g., statement 2); second, it must contain at least one general normative statement, either deontic or aretaic, which is usually some moral law or principle. Typically, when we are to make a moral decision or judgment, we refer the case to some moral rule which we think covers it, then we decide accordingly. So much for the anatomy of a moral argument. Next, how do we evaluate it?

Our first step is to determine whether or not argument F is valid. If it is not, then we must reject it and start again. However, its premises are such that, if assumed true, then it is impossible for the conclusion to be false. Hence, this argument is valid. (Note that this argument has precisely the same logical form as example A above). But, is it also sound?

It is here that we encounter difficulties. To begin with, consider the second premise (statement 2). Is this statement true? Remember, for the argument to be sound, both its premises must actually be true. The key terms here are "dangerous" and "crime". Was McCummings dangerous? If he were armed and the subway station crowded with passengers, it would be safe to say that he was. But, let us suppose instead that McCummings was unarmed, and that the subway station was empty. His being dangerous would now be more difficult to establish. Now consider the "crime". McCummings is apparently the assailant, but is it not possible that the victim, Sandusky, initially tried to rob McCummings, who was simply acting in self-defense? All that Rodriguez presumably saw was one man's assaulting and robbing another and then running away. His inference that McCummings was the culprit (especially if McCummings were unarmed) could be taken as slim justification indeed for then shooting him. In this case, Rodriguez was taking upon himself the awesome responsibility of being jury, judge, and executioner, far exceeding his duties as a policeman. Now, the only way the truth of the crucial second premise can be established is with additional facts, but if those facts are not forthcoming, then we are left with some doubt about the truthfulness of Rodriguez's interpretation of the situation, which will cause us to question the argument's soundness.

If the difficulty with the second premise is factual, however, the difficulty with the first (statement 1) is of quite another sort. Note that the crucial words in this statement are, again, "dangerous" and "deadly". What do we mean by a "dangerous" suspect? His brandishing a weapon in a threatening way would certainly count as dangerous, even more so if he were doing it in a crowd. But, let us suppose he were fleeing unarmed in an empty station. He is perhaps not dangerous now. How about tomorrow, though, if he succeeds in escaping? Even unarmed men, if they are trained in martial arts, can be as dangerous as armed men. And what about the meaning of "deadly" force? Does the use of deadly force mean with the *intent* to kill, or simply using enough to stop, albeit with the understanding that it might kill? What we need here are clear criteria as to what would be allowed as deadly force.

Yet, there is a third difficulty, this one involving the application of the general rule expressed in statement 1 to the particular case described in statement 2. Is the case of McCummings' flight one that is covered by the rule prescribed in statement 1, or, is the rule in statement 1 applicable to the case in statement 2? The answer to this question depends on how we define the crucial terms in the premises. Properly applying a general rule to a particular case which it is supposed to cover can often be problematic. Take this example:

G
1. All cases of deception and dishonesty are wrong.
2. Mark Fuhrman's (allegedly) tampering with the blood stains was a case of deception.
3. Therefore, Fuhrman's doing this was wrong.

Again, this argument is valid. But, does the general rule (statement 1) actually apply to the case described in statement 2? Is Fuhrman's tampering really a case of deception? Yes, deception is wrong, particularly if it is used merely to further our own personal interest or for malicious purposes. But, perhaps Fuhrman's case is a *bona fide* exception if his action is guaranteed to put a known felon behind bars who would otherwise go free. Freedom of speech might be the general rule, but it does not entitle us to shout "Fire!" in a crowded cinema.

There are, then, three sorts of problems that might be incurred by moral reasoning which can weaken our arguments in justification of courses of action. One involves establishing the truth of the premise that describes a particular case or situation. The second concerns the meanings of the key terms in the premises. And the third has to do with whether the general rule or principle articulated in the normative premise actually applies to the case at hand.

In light of our above analysis of a moral argument and the method of its evaluation, we may lay down the following procedure which might be useful to you when either constructing your own arguments or evaluating those of others:

1. Get the clearest possible picture of the case or situation; be aware and consider all of the relevant facts. Upon these depends the truth of descriptive premise.
2. Make sure that you are as clear as possible about the meaning of the key terms in your premises, especially those in the normative premise.
3. Determine that the rule, principle, or value formulated in your normative premise does indeed apply to the case described in the descriptive premise, or that the case described is covered by the rule in question.
4. Check the argument for validity.
5. Check the argument for soundness.

However, even after proving an argument sound, our task is not yet done. To illustrate what I mean, consider the following statements:

1. All cases of deception and dishonesty are wrong.
2. If a dangerous suspect flees the scene of his crime, it is always right (indeed, obligatory) for a police officer to use deadly force to stop him.
3. Police officers cannot use deadly force against unarmed fleeing suspects who pose no apparent threat to officers or to the public.
4. Shooting an innocent man is morally (not to mention legally) wrong.

These are normative statements which might occur as premises in moral arguments; for example, statements 1 and 2 are premises in argument F and G, above. If they are premises, then they need only be assumed true in order for their arguments to be valid. But, they must in fact be true for their arguments to be sound. How, though, do we establish their truth? As we have seen, establishing the truth of normative or prescriptive statements is notoriously difficult and contentious. No less so is determining which rule, principle, or value to choose when they come into conflict. The moral rules or principles we live by can often collide and so create classic dilemmas for us. Thus, in the McCummings case, there is the conflict between Rodriguez's duty to enforce the law, on the one hand, and his obligation to honor the rights and to safeguard the life even of a criminal suspect, on the other. Fuhrman is caught between his being honest and being loyal to the ideal of justice. Harry must choose between his duty to uphold the principles of civil law and due process and his commitment to the ideal of moral justice.

A particularly egregious example of the head-on collision of moral principles is the one given by Rachels in his *The Elements of Moral Philosophy*:[3]

> Imagine that someone is fleeing from a murderer and tells you he is going home to hide. Then the murderer comes along and asks where the first man went. You believe that if you tell the truth, the murderer will find his victim and kill him. What should you do — should you tell the truth or lie?

Two moral principles are at stake here: (1) always tell the truth, and (2) do not murder. Now, if you conform to the first principle and tell the truth, then you violate the second by being an accomplice to murder. On the other hand, if you conform to the second principle, then you must violate the first one by lying. It is a classic dilemma: In observing either principle, you cannot help violating the other. The only way out of this predicament is to appeal to some higher order principle which will tell you which lower order principle (first or second) should take precedence in this case. Such a higher order principle might be as follows: The principle of the sanctity of human life should override any other principle that might conflict with it. This principle in turn, however, requires justification. Rationally establishing the truth of morally normative statements or demonstrating why they should be observed and resolving any conflict between moral rules or principles are the main tasks of the normative ethical theories we discussed previously.

Oftentimes, a moral decision or judgment cannot be proved logically in a strict sense (i.e., be validly deduced from a set of premises), but it can still be rationally justified. It is justified "if it is or will be agreed to by everyone who takes the moral point of view and who is clearheaded and logical and knows all that is relevant about himself, mankind, and the universe."[4] Socrates proposes the same criterion for justifying moral judgments in his conversation with Crito on the issue of whether it would be morally right for him to escape from prison: "What we ought to consider is not so much what people in general will say about us but how we stand with the expert in right and wrong, the one authority, who represents the actual truth."[5] Socrates' "expert" is the ideal observer whose assent to our moral judgment justifies it. And Mill propounds a similar criterion for justifying aesthetic judgments, which can be applied analogously to moral judgments: "On a question which is the best worth having of two pleasures, or which of two modes of existence is the most grateful to the feelings, apart from its moral attributes and from its consequences, the judgment of those who are qualified by knowledge of both, or, if they differ, that of the majority among them, must be admitted as final."[6]

Notes

1. This is the so-called correspondence theory of truth, according to which the truth of a statement consists in there being a one-to-one correlation between its terms and some matters of fact.

2. "In every system of morality, which I have hitherto met with, I have always remark'd, that the author proceeds for some time in the ordinary way of reasoning, and the being of a God, or makes observations concerning human affairs; when of a sudden I am surprised to find, that instead of the usual copulations of propositions, *is*, and, *is not*, I meet with no proposition that is not connected with an *ought*, or an *ought not*. This change is imperceptible; but is, however, of the last consequence. For as this *ought*, or *ought not*, expresses some new relation or affirmation, 'tis necessary that it should be observed and explained; and at the same time that a reason should be given, for what seems altogether inconceivable, how this new relation can be a deduction from others, which are entirely different from it." (From Hume, David, *A Treatise of Human Nature*, Selby-Bigge, L.A., Ed., Clarendon Press, Oxford, 1967, p. 469.)

3. Rachels, James, *The Elements of Moral Philosophy*, 2nd ed., McGraw-Hill, New York, 1993, p. 117.

4. Frankena, William K., *Ethics*, 2nd ed., Prentice-Hall, Englewood Cliffs, NJ, 1973, p. 112. (Note that this is a form of the ideal observer theory of ethics.)

5. Plato, Crito, in *The Collected Dialogues*, Hamilton, E. and Cairns, H., Eds., Bollingen Series LXXI, Princeton University Press, 1961, p. 33.

6. Mill, John S., in *Utilitarianism*, Piest, O., Ed., The Library of Liberal Arts, Bobbs-Merrill Company, Indianapolis, IN, 1957, p. 15.

chapter eight

Moral relativism

The penal code adhered to by Islamic countries of the Middle East is quite different from the penal codes of America, and infractions of Islamic law are dealt with much more quickly and severely than are infractions of Western secular law. In the nations of Islam, the drinking of alcoholic beverages is strictly forbidden, and their consumption may lead to a public whipping. A woman who commits adultery may be stoned to death. A shoplifter may have a limb chopped off. In some parts of the Third World, torture is considered to be a legitimate tool for interrogations. In ancient India, a woman who brought an insufficient dowry to her marriage or whose husband died before she did could be placed on a pyre and burned alive. In modern India, "bride-burning" is illegal but still common. In the Sudan, female circumcision is traditional, legal, and common. Even today, the slave trade flourishes in some African and Eastern countries.

Under the Constitution of the United States, the penalties we have mentioned here would be considered cruel and unusual punishment and so strictly forbidden. Yet, these penalties, as well as many others, are routinely used in the societies that sanction them as punishment for infractions, some of which our society would not even consider as legitimate criminal offenses. The fact is that legal and social customs differ from society to society. What is legally or morally acceptable in one place may not be so in another. "Morality differs in every society," according to Benedict, "and is a convenient term for socially approved habits."[1] Benedict is saying that a society's moral code is nothing more than an expression of its traditional customs and cultural ways. An

183

individual's moral beliefs and values are internalizations of the norms of the society to which he belongs. This is a reductionist viewpoint that dissolves the entire moral realm to "socially approved habits"; in other words, morality is nothing more than a branch of sociology. So, as customs and cultures change, so do moral values. If this is the case, that any moral code is only the formalized expression of a society's particular customs and ways which are dictated by its current needs, then moral values are specific or relative to particular societies. This is *moral relativism*, which is based on *cultural relativism*, the truism that social customs and traditions differ from culture to culture because of their differing survival needs.

An implication of moral relativism is that there is no such thing as objective moral truths or universally valid moral laws that are binding on all peoples in all places and at all times. According to this view, there is no set of absolute moral values that all people ought to adhere to, their cultural differences notwithstanding. William Graham Sumner, one of America's premier sociologists, said:[2]

> The "right" way is the way which the ancestors used and which has been handed down. The tradition is its own warrant. It is not held subject to verification by experience. The notion of right is in the folkways. It is not outside of them, of independent origin, and brought to them to test them. In the folkways, whatever is, is right. This is because they are traditional, and therefore contain in themselves the authority of the ancestral ghosts. When we come to the folkways we are at the end of our analysis.

Nevertheless, it is almost axiomatic that people persist in the presumption that the moral code sanctioned by their own particular group is uniquely true and all others differing from it are false. This illusion is easily explained. From earliest childhood, people are conditioned to believe in a specific moral code through the combined pressures of education, religion, and popular opinion. This belief is strengthened perhaps by their ignorance of foreign cultures in which they would find values challenging their own. Finally, they are traditionally taught that the origins of their moral code are divine, the accounts being suitably couched in myths and legends. Many of us were taught that the Ten Commandments, the foundation of our moral code, were inscribed by God Himself on tablets of stone and delivered to Moses at Sinai. And, of course, other cultures (Islamic and

Hindu for example) have their own mythic stories about the sacred origins of their own moral codes. Moral relativists point to this psychological fact as further proof of their position. Because these peoples cannot all be right in believing in the absoluteness of their own codes, then they must all be wrong.

The relativist's argument against there being any objective and absolute moral truth boils down to this: Because there are fundamental differences among moral codes, reflecting the cultural differences of the societies from which they arise, there is no absolute and objective moral truth — no moral laws universally binding on all human beings. A code is simply a collection of beliefs which purport to express the truth of things. The relativist is saying that differences among our beliefs imply that there can be no truth about the world. There are others who say that this argument is clearly invalid, that it confuses beliefs with truths.[3] A belief and a truth are two distinct things. Just because my neighbor believes one thing and I believe the opposite does not mean that there are no truths to be found. If the students in a classroom are asked to guess at the temperature outside, their guesses, or beliefs, may all be different, but this does not mean that there is not a truth about the temperature, which can be ascertained with the use of a thermometer. The students' guesses may have run the gamut from right on the money to way off in left field, but there was a truth to be found. By the same token, human beings hold different moral beliefs, some of which may be true and others false. Please note that we are not assuming there is any such thing as moral truth. Whether there is or not is one of the perennial issues in moral philosophy. We are simply claiming that mere differences among moral beliefs do not imply that there is none which is true. Whether or not there is an objective moral truth out there we leave as an open question.

The argument for moral relativism has several objectionable implications. First, it renders impossible the moral criticism or evaluations of the codes, customs, and practices of other cultures.[4] If I find judicial practices such as public caning morally offensive, then, according to relativism, I have no logical grounds for objecting to them. I am free to vent my outrage, but that is all. This is because to condemn these practices legitimately presupposes that there is some objective and absolute moral standard, independent of and transcending any social mores, against which they can be morally evaluated and so condemned. The moral relativists deny the existence of any such standard.

Second, relativism renders impossible the moral critique of the codes and customs of our own culture or society.[5] Suppose you believe that the death penalty is morally intolerable. Since it is legally permitted and has been duly found not to violate the constitutional ban on cruel and unusual punishment, then, under relativism, you can have no logical grounds for morally objecting to it. According to relativism, moral values are determined only by the dictates of society. They are purely social phenomena, and if a particular society has determined that the imposition of the death penalty on murderers is legal and moral, then it is. There is no transcendent moral law, distinct from and superior to the laws and mores of that society, which is violated by the execution of offenders. To condemn the practice morally is to invoke a nonexistent moral standard.

A third objectionable implication of moral relativism, which is related to the two above, is that moral progress is impossible.[6] We have no logical grounds for condemning past customs, laws, mores, and practices while extolling our own. Thus, we cannot legitimately condemn witch hunting, slavery, or child labor, all of which were practices once sanctioned in the United States by the civil, moral, and religious authorities, because they were simply conforming to the collective moral thinking of their day. There is no timeless moral absolute that can be invoked to judge them. Nor can we proudly point to the emancipation of slaves, women's suffrage, children's rights, or civil rights as examples of moral progress. All that has happened is that the social mores have changed, and they are neither better nor worse than those that came before.

Adherence to moral relativism, then, undercuts the grounds of moral criticism and reduces our faith in moral progress to an illusion. These implications are the basis for a further objection to the theory — namely, that it violates the canons of moral common sense and basic human decency to which (as we saw in a previous chapter) a normative ethical theory should conform. Any theory, however sophisticated and impressive, which (for example) permitted the torture of children or lying on principle would not be worth our further consideration. The fact is we do criticize practices such as slavery on moral grounds, and we can do so rationally. We take it to be a right, no less. We would consider anyone who refused to condemn such practices as morally stunted. Indeed, slavery and other such institutions have been eliminated because of the moral outrage they incurred.

Three final criticisms may be made of moral relativism. First, it confuses customs with moral values, which are distinct concepts.[7] A disagreement among customs does not imply a disagreement as to basic values. Thus, the penalty for theft in some Islamic countries is amputation, while in the United States and other Western nations it is a fine or incarceration. However, this difference in the penalties customarily meted out for the same offense should not disguise the fact that Islam and the West, by dint of punishing crime at all, equally honor the principle of justice as a moral value. They differ only in their conceptions and implementations of justice. In some Middle Eastern nations, the penalty for a woman's exposing her face in public is a flogging; in the United States, a woman who exposes her breasts in public may be fined. There is here a definite difference in the customs concerning appropriate dress for women, yet there is a common regard for the value of modesty. Moral relativists tend to be dazzled by the differences among customs and fail to take into account the common core of values they may disguise.

Second, there are certain basic moral principles that seem universal in scope, transcending all difference of culture.[8] Virtually all societies have strictures against lying, theft, and murder, though they may define these practices quite differently. Indeed, the very integrity and viability of a society depend upon its requiring that people tell the truth and respect human life; not doing so would invite anarchy. As an obvious example, if a society's moral code did not sanction truth telling, then the promises represented by contracts would have no weight and could not be trusted. This, in turn, would jeopardize the smooth running of commercial transactions, and a society that did not morally and legally proscribe murder would quickly descend into barbarism.

Third, the moral relativist claims that a society's moral code simply reflects the sum of its experience and needs in a particular place and time. However, a society need not be restricted to just one moral code; multiple, sometimes conflicting, codes may coexist in the same society (as in American society).[9] There are many moral codes operative in the United States today. There are a broadly secular code and a variety of religious codes. Not only does the secular code conflict with the religious variety, but even the moral codes of different religions and religious denominations come into conflict. This accounts for the deep intractable rifts among people on such issues as abortion, capital punishment, and euthanasia. So, if a moral code is simply a formalized expression of a society's habits and traditions reflecting their special survival needs, then how is it possible for the very same society or culture, which is more or less homogeneous, to give rise to multiple and opposed moral codes? At least in the United States, there seems to be no moral consensus reflecting its relative cultural homogeneity.

The relativist, however, may retort that a complex society such as the United States is actually more heterogeneous than homogeneous. It comprises a host of different racial, ethnic, and religious groups which are nothing less than societies in miniature, each of which gives rise to its peculiar moral code. Little wonder, then, with so many subsocieties, there is a plethora of conflicting moral codes; however, there is still a problem for the relativist — how to explain the emergence of that unique individual whose personal moral code is at variance with that of the dominant group to which he belongs? The Old Testament prophets such as Elijah and Jeremiah relentlessly summoned their people to a higher moral standard than they were accustomed to. And such as Henry David Thoreau and Martin Luther King, Jr., committed acts of civil disobedience in the name of a moral law higher than the one generally acknowledged by the societies of their day. If a person's moral code is simply an internalization of the habits and traditions of his society, then how do we explain the origins of moral codes adhered to by exceptional individuals which are contrary to the *ethos* of the larger society to which they belong? If moral relativism were true, the emergence of the idiosyncratic codes of people such as Thoreau or King would be impossible.

Moral relativism, though incorrigibly flawed as a plausible normative ethical theory, does have something to teach us. It serves to remind us indirectly of the very thing it often ignores — namely, the distinction between a culture's customs and its moral values. Foreign customs may strike us as being strange, comical, bizarre, and irrational, but unless they hurt people they are morally neutral. I am free to disapprove or dislike such customs or find them amusing but not to condemn them on moral grounds. Cultural relativism fosters the virtue of tolerance and enables us to overcome our own culturally conditioned prejudices. The Middle Eastern custom of women wearing veils may strike me as quaint, but when I reflect that the veil symbolizes the modesty that I find becoming in both men and women in my own society, then this custom commands my respect. Thus, we may be amused by or even dislike a custom but approve of the value that it expresses.

Cultural and moral relativism are closely associated with the social sciences. Benedict and Sumner, the exponents of the views cited above, were an anthropologist and a sociologist, respectively. Indeed, if social science can be said to have an official ethical stance, then it is moral relativism, which dates to classical antiquity. The earliest relativists were the Sophists, who represented a distinctive movement in Greek philosophy in the 5th century B.C. One of their leaders was Protagoras of Abdera (ca. 410–480 B.C.E.). Though Greeks, they lived in city-states situated on the frontiers and borders shared with non-Hellenic peoples. Thus, Protagoras hailed from Abdera, a town on the western cost of what is now Turkey, but which was then the Persian Empire. Abdera, like many of these Greek colonies, was on the coast and so traded with peoples from all over the Mediterranean world. The Mediterranean Sea was the crossroads of trading routes that extended to all points of the compass — as far east as India and as far west as Spain. Consequently, the Sophists came into close contact with mariners and merchants from cultures other than their own, who brought with them different religious beliefs, social customs, and moral outlooks, as well as material goods to trade. The Sophists came to see that Hellenic culture, with its particular customs, values, and religion, was but one of many and was not necessarily superior to other cultures, only different. Thus, they denied the existence of moral absolutes and espoused a practical ethics that put a high premium on successful living, good citizenship, and personal happiness. As close students of human nature, the Sophists were the founders of social science.

Sophists did not go unopposed. Indeed, they were notorious in the ancient world because of their cynicism and impiety and for their use of considerable logical and rhetorical skills, not to establish truth, but simply to win debates and legal cases. In his comedy, *The Clouds*, the great Athenian playwright of the 5th century B.C.E., Aristophanes, satirized sophists for their "sophistry" — for making the better way appear the worse, and the worse the better.[10] Socrates, a student of the Sophists, who learned his logical and dialectical skills from them and with whom he shared an interest in ethics, utterly rejected their moral relativism in favor of moral absolutism.

Notes

1. Benedict, Ruth, Anthropology and the abnormal, *The Journal of General Psychology*, 10, 59–82, 1934 (as reprinted in Pojman, L.P., Ed., *Moral Philosophy: A Reader*, Hackett Publishing, Indianapolis, IN, 1993, p. 24).
2. Sumner, William G., *Folkways: A Study of the Sociological Importance of Usages, Manners, Customs, Mores, and Morals*, Ginn and Company, Boston, MA, 1940, p. 28.

3. Rachels, James, *The Elements of Moral Philosophy*, 2nd ed., McGraw-Hill, New York, 1993, pp.19–20.

4. Rachels, James, *The Elements of Moral Philosophy*, 2nd ed., McGraw-Hill, New York, 1993, p. 21.

5. Rachels, James, *The Elements of Moral Philosophy*, 2nd ed., McGraw-Hill, New York, 1993, p. 21.

6. Rachels, James, *The Elements of Moral Philosophy*, 2nd ed., McGraw-Hill, New York, 1993, p. 22.

7. Rachels, James, *The Elements of Moral Philosophy*, 2nd ed., McGraw-Hill, New York, 1993, p. 23.

8. Rachels, James, *The Elements of Moral Philosophy*, 2nd ed., McGraw-Hill, New York, 1993, p. 25.

9. Stace, Walter T., *The Concept of Morals*, Macmillan, New York, 1965 (as reprinted in Pojman, L.P., Ed., *Moral Philosophy: A Reader*, Hackett Publishing, Indianapolis, IN, 1993, pp. 31–32).

10. A character personifying sophistry declares: "Now then, I freely admit that among men of learning I am — somewhat pejoratively — dubbed the Sophistic, or Immoral, Logic. And why? Because I first devised a Method for the Subversion of the Established Social Beliefs and the Undermining of Morality. Moreover, this little invention of mine, this knack of taking what might appear to be the worse argument and nonetheless winning my case, has, I might add, proved to be an *extremely* lucrative source of income." (From Aristophanes, *The Clouds*, trans. by William Arrowsmith, The New American Library, New York, 1962, p. 91.)

part four

Topics in the ethics
of criminal justice

chapter nine

Justice

My object all sublime
I shall achieve in time —
To let the punishment fit the crime.

—Gilbert & Sullivan (*The Mikado*)

"For I the Lord love justice, I hate robbery and wrong," thus declares Isaiah, speaking for God.[1] Socrates, in Plato's *Republic*, esteems justice "a thing more precious than much fine gold."[2] Justice is a central value of both Judaism and Hellenism, the two roots of Western civilization, and is a core value of the American ideal. The Pledge of Allegiance, recited daily in many American classrooms, affirms that the United States stands for nothing less than "justice for all". Martin Luther King, Jr., citing the authority of Isaiah, took that pledge at its word.

There are several types of justice. One of them is so-called *distributive* justice, which has to do with the equitable distribution of the world's limited goods among its inhabitants. Under this model, we think it "just" that no one gets more or less than he deserves, or more than he needs to survive, if at someone else's expense. Various theories as to what constitutes a fair distribution have been offered and different criteria of fairness proposed. However, our concern here is not with distributive justice, but with another type, called *retributive* or *punitive* justice.[3] This model of justice is concerned with the punishment of individuals (offenders) who have committed acts that our society deems crimes.

Punishment presents us with a moral problem. On the one hand, we instinctively believe that offenders deserve to be punished for committing criminal offenses. Yet, on the other hand, punishment involves the infliction of pain (physical or psychic, or both), an intrinsic evil at which decency and rationality may recoil. "But all punishment is mischief," declared Bentham, "all punishment in itself is evil."[4] The problem, then, is how can punishment be *morally* permissible or justifiable. This is distinct from its legal justification, which need be nothing more than an appeal to a prudential reason such as public safety — we punish criminals to protect society. In order to justify morally the infliction of punishment, four theories of punitive justice have been advanced: retributive, utilitarian, contractarian, and restitutive. Before examining each of these theories, however, we need to consider a type of justice, which is distinct from either distributive or punitive justice, but which underlies both.

Comparative justice expresses the principle of impartiality. According to Henry Sidgwick (1838–1900), a leading utilitarian, justice is treating similar cases similarly, whereas injustice is treating them dissimilarly. Suppose two drivers who are not disabled park their cars in spaces reserved for the disabled. The signs designating these spaces clearly state that the fine for non-disabled drivers using the parking spaces is $100. Both drivers are caught committing the infractions. One driver gets a ticket, but the other does not. We would pronounce this unjust, as the cases of illegal parking are the same, but the legal consequences are not. Suppose, however, that there are extenuating circumstances in the case of the driver who is not penalized. Let's say he parked illegally because he was rushing an injured person to the hospital emergency room and the disabled slot was the only parking space available. Under these circumstances, we might be satisfied that the disparity was "just". But suppose the driver who got off the hook was the local mayor and he used the disabled slot because he did not want to walk two blocks to his office? Such circumstances would only serve to heighten our sense of injustice in the case. To qualify as extenuating, the circumstances of one case must show a morally or legally relevant difference from those of another case, though just what it is that makes a circumstance relevantly different may not be clear. The demand of *comparative* justice that everyone be treated the same under the law is one of the cardinal principles of our legal system and is fundamental to each of the theories of punitive justice.

Retributive justice

You may have seen movies such as *Die Hard* or *Under Siege*, in which the hero blasts a series of heinous villains. During these films, you may undergo an exquisite feeling of satisfaction, which you might vent by shouting or clapping, when the miscreants get their comeuppance. And, if the villain's demise at the hands of the hero is especially well suited to his offense, we say that he has received his "just desert" or that "poetic justice" has been done. The expressions "just desert" or "poetic justice" encapsulate the theory of *retributive justice*. This concept of punishment as retribution is traditionally known as the principle of *lex talionis,* or the law of retaliation, which is metaphorically expressed in the Old Testament rule of "an eye for an eye, and a tooth for a tooth."[5] This is commonly misunderstood as a sanction for revenge or for extreme and unusual punishment. On the contrary, the original intent of this rule was to ensure that the penalty be as perfectly proportionate to the offense as possible, neither too little nor too much.

Under the retributive theory of justice, punishment is justified simply because it is deserved. F.H. Bradley (1846–1924) gave it classic expression in his *Ethical Studies* (1877):[6]

> Punishment is punishment, only when it is deserved. We pay the penalty because we owe it, and for no other reason; and if punishment is inflicted for any other reason whatever than because it is merited by wrong, it is a gross immorality, a crying injustice, an abominable crime, and not what it pretends to be. We may have regard for whatever considerations we please — our own convenience, the good of society, the benefit of the offender; we are fools, and worse, if we fail to do so. Having once the right to punish, we may modify the punishment according to the useful and the pleasant; but these are external to the matter, they cannot give us a right to punish, and nothing can do that but criminal desert.

Its rationale is that the commission of a crime creates an imbalance in the system of justice, a situation aptly symbolized by one of the scales in a balance being higher than the other scale. Justice demands that the imbalance be rectified, that the scales be balanced once again. This is done when the penalty is properly apportioned to the criminal's desert, or when the punishment fits the crime. A less metaphorical way of putting this justification is as follows. Say a thief steals your car stereo. He now benefits from its possession — he may enjoy listening to it or he may pawn it for money, but you are no longer able to enjoy it and suffer the pain of its loss. The thief, then, by benefiting precisely at your expense, enjoys an unfair advantage over you. When caught and convicted, how should the thief be punished? Not merely by being forced to return your stereo in perfect condition or by paying you its monetary value. Justice demands more. First, you deserve compensation for your suffering and the loss of that enjoyment you would have experienced had you been in possession of it. Second, the thief deserves to be deprived of any benefit or advantage he enjoyed by possessing your property. Obviously, we cannot roll back the clock and erase your suffering and restore your lost enjoyment, nor can we deprive the thief of the benefit or advantage he had in your property. So, according to the retributivist, the most appropriate punishment that would meet both these requirements would be to either fine or jail the thief. You are compensated symbolically insofar as you have the satisfaction of knowing that the thief is going to suffer for his misdeed, and the thief in turn is stripped retroactively of any advantage or benefit he may have reaped from taking your stereo by having to suffer a proportionate loss of his wealth or liberty. This way, says the retributivist, equilibrium of the scales of justice is restored, which is the sole justification for punishment.

Kant's theory of retribution

Kant formulated a classic theory of retributive justice derived from his categorical imperative. He began by laying down two principles: (1) Punishment is demanded by crime, which is its sole moral justification: "Juridical punishment can never be administered merely as a means for promoting another good either with regard to the criminal himself or to civil society, but must in all cases be imposed only because the individual on whom it is inflicted *has committed a crime.*" (2) The punishment must fit the crime (the principle of *proportionate retribution*):[7]

> But what is the mode and measure of punishment which public justice takes as its principle and standard? It is just the principle of equality, by which the pointer of the scale of justice is made to incline no more to the one side than to the other. ...Hence it may be said: "If you slander another you slander yourself; if you steal from another, you steal from yourself; if you strike another, you strike yourself; if you kill another, you kill yourself." This is ... the only principle which ... can definitely assign both the quality and the quantity of a just penalty.

He then goes on to affirm that punishment is an intrinsic moral good. It is an exercise in justice, which is itself an intrinsic good. Legally sanctioned punishment presupposes and honors the dignity of the person being punished. More particularly, it presupposes a being who is rational and free (a person) and so responsible for his actions. We do not, strictly speaking, punish animals or the insane precisely because they lack rationality and genuine freedom and are not responsible for their behavior. We might correct our new puppy for urinating on the carpet by swatting him with a rolled-up newspaper, or control the behavior of a psychotic by incarcerating him in a mental hospital, but we cannot be said to be punishing them. Neither dogs nor the criminally insane are fit subjects for punishment, as they lack the requisite rationality and freedom. Dogs operate by instinct, and the criminally insane are under the control of irrational compulsions. What we are doing in these cases is simply controlling undesirable behaviors. By contrast, we punish sane criminals because, being rational and autonomous, they are fit subjects for punishment, and by punishing them we respect their reason and autonomy. However, their punishment is not morally permissible if its rationale is merely a desire to eliminate or control their undesirable behavior. In that case we would be treating them as a means to an end — the satisfaction of our desire for improved behavior — and not as ends in themselves. For Kant, their punishment is morally permissible only if its sole rationale is their desert as rational and autonomous beings. When we punish persons for no other reason than that they deserve it, we are honoring them as ends in themselves. Criminals deserve to be punished in two respects: First, they deserve punishment because of their crime — their crime deserves a specific penalty. Second, they deserve punishment because they are human beings — their human dignity deserves the right to be punished.

On Kant's account, punishment is justified not only because it is just and honors the dignity of the person being punished, but also because it is demanded by the categorical imperative — specifically, it is implied by the principle of universalizability and reversibility. Let me explain. Suppose that I murder someone. On the principle of universalizability, by killing another person I have implicitly willed it as a universal law that anyone else may commit murder if he so chooses. This "anyone else" includes the state of which I am a citizen; hence, I am allowing others to kill (execute) me in retribution for my crime. Under the principle of reversibility, by murdering another person, I have tacitly expressed my willingness that others treat me the same way — for example, the state may execute me for my crime.

For Kant, retributive punishment is morally permissible because it is the only type of punishment that honors human dignity (i.e., treats human beings as rational and autonomous beings who are morally responsible for their actions, including their offenses). Not to punish criminals retributively is not only unjust but also fundamentally irrational (according to the categorical imperative) and a denial of their dignity. According to Rachels, Kant's understanding of retributive punishment as an essentially rational act that honors human dignity is his unique contribution to the theory of punishment.[8]

Kant notwithstanding, the retributive theory of justice is beset with difficulties. On the principle of proportionate retribution, the punishment must fit the crime. And, though the character from *The Mikado* deems it an "object all sublime" which he is confident that he "shall achieve in time," letting the punishment fit the crime is more easily said than done. Any attempt to do so invites three problems. One is accurately weighing the degree of the offense. Obviously, premeditated homicide weighs more heavily as an offense than does manslaughter. But, once the weight of the offense has been correctly determined, there is a second problem of weighing the degree of the offender's guilt. Thus, a mere accomplice in a crime is less guilty than the principal perpetrator. Third, after weighing the offense and the offender's guilt, there remains the problem of fairly fixing the penalty that must answer to both — the seriousness of the offense and the degree of the perpetrator's guilt. Hence, the punishment must fit the crime in two ways: it must be proportionate to both the offense and the guilt of the offender.

Of the three problems incurred, making the penalty proportional to the crime is perhaps the most perplexing. What constitutes a fit punishment? How do we go about finding it? What criteria should we use in determining its fitness? Two of those criteria are the seriousness of the offense and the depth of the offender's guilt — which themselves are difficult enough to establish. And, even if we can weigh them up satisfactorily, we have the final challenge of coming up with a penalty that will satisfy both. This problem is illustrated in Shakespeare's *The Merchant of Venice*. The terms of the contract between them specify that if Antonio is unable to pay his debt to Shylock at the appointed time, he forfeits a pound of his flesh. Antonio, because of the loss of his wealth at sea, is unable to pay the debt; therefore, the court determines that he must yield up his flesh. As Shylock prepares to cut a literal pound of flesh from Antonio's body, Portia, Antonio's attorney, warns Shylock that the law permits him to take *exactly* a pound of flesh, no more or less. If he takes anything else, such as blood, or an iota more or less than a pound of flesh, then he will be penalized by forfeiting his life:[9]

> Therefore prepare thee to cut off the flesh,/Shed thou no blood, nor cut thou less nor more/But just a pound of flesh: if thou tak'st more/Or less than a just pound, be it but so much/As makes it light or heavy in the substance,/Or the division of the twentieth part/of one poor scruple, nay if the scale do turn/But in the estimation of a hair,/thou diest, and all thy goods are confiscate.

Even assuming that a pound of flesh in lieu of money for a debt is a fit punishment for indebtedness, Shylock's problem is that exacting the penalty is practically impossible.

One formula for ensuring that the punishment fits the crime is found in the *literal* application of the biblical formula of "an eye for an eye, and a tooth for a tooth." Thus, if I deliberately knock out one of your teeth or blind you in one eye or take your life, then I forfeit my own respectively.[10] However, such a procedure, if legally sanctioned, might run afoul of another of our moral values — namely, our repugnance at gratuitous cruelty, lying behind the Eighth Amendment to the Constitution, which forbids the infliction of cruel and unusual punishment, no matter what the offense. Even if we overcame our repugnance of cruel punishment and amended the Constitution to permit it, the law of retaliation is limited in its application. Indeed, an eye may literally be paid for an eye, a tooth for a tooth, and a life for a life, but not all offenses are so easily quantified. How would you literally pay a kidnapper back for a kidnapping, or what if a rich man stole $50 from a poor man? Under a literal application of *lex talionis*, the thief must have exactly the same amount taken from him. But $50 does not have the same value to a rich man as it does to a poor man. The principle of proportionate retribution requires that, whatever proportion of the poor man's wealth was represented by the $50, the proportionate amount should be subtracted from the rich man's wealth. But this expedient means a departure from the literal application of the law of retaliation. So, in cases where the literal application of the law is impossible, how is the principle of proportionate retribution to be observed?

An alternative is illustrated in Nathaniel Hawthorn's novel, *The Scarlet Letter*. Hester Prynne has been found guilty of adultery — a crime that invites no retaliation in kind. The court decides that as punishment Hester must, for the rest of her life, wear the letter "A" embroidered in scarlet thread on the bodice of her dress. The scarlet letter stigmatizes Hester and is an example of *symbolic retribution*. It symbolizes both her moral crime, of which it is a perpetual reminder, and the shame associated with it. The nearest parallel to such symbolic retribution we have in our criminal justice system is publicizing the identities of "deadbeat dads" (those who fail to pay court-ordered child support) and child molesters. Their photographs and identities are made a matter of public record to both shame them and to remind people of their crimes. However, as in the case of the literal enactment of the principle of proportionate retribution, symbolic retribution has limited scope. What if the child molester is not shamed by public knowledge of his crime? Or what, for example, might be a fit form of symbolic retribution for defrauding an insurance company or cheating on your taxes? It might take some juridical ingenuity to think of a punishment that adequately symbolizes the offense.

Given that retribution in either its literal or symbolic forms is not practicable, what form should it take so as to make it more nearly proportionate to the crime? This question was brought home to me when I worked as a substitute teacher in a middle school. The penalty in that school for students' skipping class was suspension. I thought it ironic that the students were being "punished" by being forced to stay out of school, which was what they desired in the first place. In this case, there is no proportionality whatsoever between the punishment and the offense. Another instance of disproportionality between the penalty and the offense is the way cheating is punished in many academic institutions. Students who cheat on examinations or plagiarize papers are typically punished with failing grades. However, the grade of "F" means that the student tried but failed to meet the minimum standards for success in the class. It means the student made an honest effort in the course. Students who cheat do not even try to meet those minimum standards and obviously have not made any honest attempt to pass the course requirements. Cheating is a moral (and sometimes legal) offense comparable to stealing; failing a test because of incompetence or lack of application is neither, though it may be a disappointment to the student or may even indicate laziness and irresponsibility on his part. Thus, assigning an "F" for cheating hardly fits the crime at all: a failing grade only represents a ranking or evaluation of the student's academic ability and says nothing about the offense he has committed. Such cases of disproportionality

— sometimes quite egregious — are to be found in the criminal code. For instance, under some statutes, the physical abuse of children, even that which results in death, is often punished less severely than bank robbery. Drunk drivers who kill may be fined, lose their licenses, be jailed, or be subjected to some combination of these penalties — hardly adequate recompense for the loss of a life.

These cases illustrate the difficulty of fitting the punishment to the crime but also make it clear that the punishment must be proportionate to the offense with respect to both its *kind* and its *degree.* The punishment ought to match both the nature of the crime and the level of its seriousness. Suspending a student for skipping class is clearly disproportionate to the offense, because the nature of the punishment in no way matches the nature of the offense (it might even be viewed as a reward!). On the other hand, 50 hours of detention for skipping a one-hour class would be equally disproportionate, for even though the nature of the punishment reflects the nature of the offense, its degree of severity is all out of proportion to the seriousness of the offense. An exact fit between the punishment and the crime may be impossible to achieve this side of the Last Judgement. One of the appeals of the traditional Christian doctrine concerning heaven and hell is that it gives its followers assurance that justice will be done at last; if not here and now, then most assuredly hereafter. Therefore, according to Christian doctrine, divine justice makes up for the imperfections of human justice, yet we are concerned with the here and now.

Even if a perfect fit between crime and punishment were possible, with the principle of proportionate retribution being consistently implemented, such justice might not always be desirable. Reconsider the case of Rodriguez and McCummings. Suppose McCummings had been successful in his suit against Rodriguez, and the latter was subsequently convicted of using excessive force. Suppose further that the penalty prescribed by law for Rodriguez's offense is that he be incarcerated for a period of 10 years in the state prison and that this penalty was proportionate to the offense. Strict justice, then, would require Rodriguez to go to prison, but suppose now that there are other relevant factors to be weighed in the balance. For instance, lets say that Rodriguez has an unimpeachable record as a police officer, has been decorated for bravery, and has received numerous citations for actions above and beyond the call of duty. He is highly respected by his superiors, his peers, and the community. Moreover, at the time of the shooting, he made a good-faith decision to shoot McCummings based on his reasonable suspicion as an experienced officer that McCummings had a weapon and was an immediate threat to him. Are these not mitigating factors which should decrease his desert of punishment and soften the dictates of justice in the case? Rodriguez vs. McCumming illustrates that in some cases the principle of proportionate retribution — the strict demands of justice and the letter of the law — must be suspended in light of exculpatory circumstances. Thus, the law recognizes that a woman who shoots and kills an intruder in her home deserves a lesser penalty for homicide than does the man who kills his wife for insurance money.

Another example is juvenile offenders, who are generally considered to be less culpable than adult felons by reason of their immaturity. And, of course, those suffering from severe forms of mental illness are often excused from their offenses due to their inability to act rationally.

The necessity of balancing all these various mitigating factors in fairly determining the offender's degree of desert only makes the apportionment of punishment more complicated and more liable to error. It is rather like a juggling feat in which the juggler has to synchronize the throwing of more and more balls of different sizes. It is complicated in three ways: (1) The adjudicator needs to make sure that all the relevant mitigating factors have been unearthed. (2) These factors need to be duly weighed against each other to determine which should weigh more heavily, and why, in reducing the degree of the culprit's desert. (3) Finally, the adjudicator needs to determine by just how much these mitigating factors should decrease the culprit's desert. This may be illustrated in a judge's process of deciding, within the designated legal guidelines, the appropriate sentence for a convicted shoplifter. Relevant mitigating factors in the case might include the offender's age and psychological state of health (suppose the thief was elderly and suffering from Alzheimer's disease). The judge must weigh these factors against each other to determine which one weighs more heavily against the shoplifter's desert. Then he must ascertain to what degree these factors taken together should diminish the shoplifter's desert and sentence.[11]

You may have noticed a serious problem in this business of weighing mitigating factors against each other. We talk of assigning relative weights to mitigating factors, of determining how they proportionally decrease the degrees of desert and punishment, all in order that the principle of proportionate retribution may be strictly observed and that the punishment is proportionate to the offense. The "weighing" of mitigating factors has been likened to the weighing of physical things such as fruits and vegetables on actual scales. The assumption is that the "weight" of mitigating factors can be quantitatively and objectively measured in the same way as the weight of physical things. This is reminiscent of Bentham's hedonic calculus according to which pleasures are measured and ranked quantitatively.[12] The problem is that mitigating factors (such as age, mental competence, intelligence, or intent) are not the same as physical things, and when we speak of their weight we are speaking metaphorically. Literally, mitigating factors are neither heavy nor light, nor even weighable. Consequently, we cannot assign objective and mathematically accurate weights and measures to them. Furthermore, human beings (who do the "weighing") are not strictly objective and may view things differently from each other. And even when we speak of the principle of proportional retribution, which is fundamental to retributive justice, we are again speaking metaphorically. There can be no literal proportionality between an offense and its penalty, since proportionality or proportion is, strictly speaking, a mathematical relation concerning numerical ratios, which the relation between an offense and a penalty is emphatically not. This means that neither the relative weights of mitigating factors nor the proportionality between an offense and its penalty — since these are "weights" and "proportionality" only in a metaphorical sense — can be objectively and precisely calculated.

Now, given that we cannot objectively and precisely determine the degree of relative importance (weight) that should be assigned to various mitigating factors, nor make the punishment perfectly (mathematically) proportional to the crime, then what can we do? How might we go about deciding the relative importance of mitigating factors or fairly apportioning the punishment to the crime, as not all such factors are equally important and punishment must somehow fit the crime? Our only recourse is to intuitions and feelings — we intuit that the old thief's senility is perhaps more exculpatory than his age, although both exculpate to some degree. Or, we feel that 50 hours of detention for skipping a one-hour class is disproportionate to the offense. But, beyond that, we would be hard pressed to explain exactly why. Appeals to intuition or feeling are suspect, especially in light of our earlier discussion of intuitionist theories of normative ethics, like those of the moral sense theorists Shaftesbury and Hutcheson, or of normative ethical theories that are intuitionist in part, like Ross' *prima facie* ethics. We concluded that intuition (or feeling) is neither a reliable nor an entirely rational guide to making moral decisions or judgments.

Even if all mitigating factors could be found and weighed against each other, with the weight of each being accurately determined so that it could be known by how much they should lessen the offender's desert and the severity of his punishment, the enactment of retributive justice might come into conflict with another of our moral values, namely clemency. In other words, the principle of proportionate retribution conflicts with the "quality of mercy". Mercy takes careful note of those factors mitigating desert. It is motivated by a deep concern for the well-being of the offender and so blunts the sharpness of the punishment due. It may even wipe the slate clean by forgiving or pardoning the offender. It is a response to, and properly requires, the miscreant's repentance of his crime and his resolution never to repeat it. Justice is a purely rational process, or at least aspires to be. Mercy brings into play moral sentiments such as compassion, empathy, and sympathy. Of course, there is the problem of deciding under what circumstances mercy should temper justice and to what degree. This is not unlike the problem of properly apportioning the punishment to the crime. This decision is particularly urgent given that mercy is in inverse proportion to justice — any increase in the one entails a corresponding decrease in the other. This means that if we value mercy — which is arguably no less a moral value than justice itself — then we should be prepared to use it to check the course of retributive justice and so make that justice less than perfect. In other words, the principle of proportionate retribution is open to compromise, which is contrary to its very spirit. Yet, few of us would be willing to see the quality of mercy absent from judicial proceedings.

A well-publicized case, which made poignantly clear the tension between the demand of justice and the appeal to mercy, is that of Karla Faye Tucker.[13] On June 13, 1983, Tucker murdered two people in Texas. It was an especially vicious pair of killings in that Tucker repeatedly struck her victims with a pick-axe and afterward boasted of experiencing sexual gratification during the commission of the crimes. Tucker was caught and convicted of murder. During the lengthy appeals process, while Tucker was incarcerated in prison, she converted to Christianity. The apparent authenticity of her conversion was attested to by all that knew her. Not only did her behavior improve markedly, but she seemed to be quite another person, far different from the woman who had been convicted of murder. Her final appeal for clemency was based on the supposition that she was no longer the same person who had slain two people years before. It was also claimed that she was currently engaged in important work within the prison counseling and in other ways helping her fellow inmates. Her appeal failed, even though prominent religious leaders supported it. Karla Faye Tucker was executed in Huntsville, TX, in March of 1998. This case well illustrates that strict observance of the principle of proportional retribution often requires turning a deaf ear to appeals to mercy.

Let us suppose that mitigating factors were either to be ignored entirely or to mitigate desert and punishment appropriately, and that a deaf ear would be consistently turned to mercy so that the principle of proportionate retribution might be observed to the letter. Even under these restrictive circumstances, the enactment of retributive justice would be far from perfect. The whole rationale behind the retributive theory of justice is that the commission of a crime causes an imbalance in, or somehow impairs, the moral institution of life. Justice requires that the balance be restored and that the moral institution be repaired. Let us imagine that retribution may be made proportionate — even perfectly — to the crime in a particular case, but due to the structure of the American judicial system and the autonomy of each of our 50+ state jurisdictions, there is no guarantee that the proportionate retribution enacted in one case will occur in a majority of cases of the same kind, let alone in all cases. Recent legal history is full of cases where the same crime, complete with similar mitigating circumstances, received quite dissimilar penalties. For instance, Jeffery Dahmer was sentenced to life in prison, while Ted Bundy was executed, though both were serial killers. Such disparity between punishments may be even more acute in cases where accomplices in a crime are given lighter or stiffer sentences than its principal perpetrator.

In light of instances of egregiously disparate penalties being paid for the same kind of crime (or even for the same crime), how can we consider that the scales of justice are balanced or that the moral order of things has been restored? To speak of this requires that proportionate retribution be enacted across the board, not just in a few cases. In other words, the principle of proportionate retribution (which requires that the punishment be proportionate to the crime) needs to be joined with the principle of comparative justice (which requires that similar crimes receive similar punishments). To observe the one principle while ignoring the other does not balance the scales of justice; it merely substitutes one imbalance for another. Indeed, enacting proportionate justice in one case but not in other similar cases may bring about a just resolution in the one case while resulting in injustice elsewhere. Observing the principle of proportionate retribution in one case necessitates doing so in all similar cases in the name of comparative justice. To punish two similar crimes (with similar mitigating factors) differently is a breach of comparative justice. Comparative justice, which is a proportion *between* different cases, is something above and distinct from retributive justice, which is a proportion between the offense and the penalty *within* a particular case.

The issue of retributive justice's compromising comparative justice became a matter of some practical urgency in the United States during the 1990s. The death penalty is the paradigm of the law of retaliation, or the principle of proportionate retribution enacted literally. However, since the re-establishment of the death penalty in the United States in 1977, its application, far from being fair and consistent, has been capricious and apparently discriminatory. It has been alleged that minorities are more likely to be executed for capital crimes than are Caucasians. Because of such inequities, Supreme Court Justice Harry A. Blackmun concluded in 1994 that, "The death penalty experiment has failed."[14]

Now, the retributivist's reply to this may be that it is better that retributive justice occur in just some cases, even though it may not increase the amount of comparative justice but may even threaten to decrease it by necessitating that future cases be adjudicated comparatively. A compromise must be accepted, as perfect justice is a theoretical ideal that can only be partially, never fully, realized. But, if the retributivist is willing to compromise comparative justice in the interest of furthering retributive justice, then he should also be willing to compromise retributive justice in the interest of allowing special factors and clemency to mitigate the degree of desert and the severity of punishment.

Two further, related objections might be made to the retributive theory of punishment. One is that retribution, at least the literal form represented by *lex talionis*, only adds to the evil in the world, disguising it as justice.[15] Thus, a murderer commits one evil, but the state, by executing him, is simply repaying his evil with its own. The result is a compound evil, which is the sum of the evil of murder and the evil of execution. It is for this reason that some opponents of the death penalty refer to state-sanctioned executions as judicial murder; however, this objection can be readily answered. Pain is an intrinsic evil, and if only the pain inflicted by retributive punishment is considered, then retribution may be construed as evil. But there is also something else, no less important, to be considered: there is the double *relationship* of the pain inflicted on the offender both to the pain inflicted by him on his victim and to his own guilt and desert. If this double relationship is considered, then the pain may just as well be construed as just and so as something good. Its goodness lies not in the offender's felt suffering, but rather in its retributive quality (i.e., its redressing both the victim's suffering and the offender's desert and guilt). Moreover, the pain inflicted on the offender and the pain the offender inflicted on his victim are different with respect to motive and intention. The purpose of punitive pain is redressing a wrong, which itself is intrinsically good, but the pain suffered by the victim has no such salutary end, being motivated perhaps by greed, cruelty, or malice. Hence, the retributive good of punishment, as represented by the purpose of punitive pain and its complex relationship to the offender's guilt and desert as well as to the victim's suffering, might be said to more than outweigh its intrinsic evil.

Finally, the objection has been made that retribution, though it may euphemistically call itself "retributive justice", is little more than disguised revenge. It is true that in the ancient world, even among the classical Greeks, it was thought proper and even noble for the wronged or their representatives to avenge themselves on malefactors; indeed, failure to do so was deemed cowardly and imprudent. In Shakespeare's *Hamlet*, Hamlet is visited by his father's ghost who enjoins him to "revenge his foul and most unnatural murder."[16] And Aeschylus' *Oresteia*, a dramatic trilogy, is a concentrated and terrifying study of rampant retribution, both human and divine. In these plays, though vengeance is demanded in the name of retributive justice, the retribution itself smacks heavily of revenge. However, even by the 5th century B.C. in Athens, the wisdom of revenge was called into question. Socrates, in Plato's *Crito*, for example, condemns it in no uncertain terms.[17] And the Old Testament, though allowing for retribution when appropriate, condemns revenge on the part of man, as it was a privilege reserved for God alone.[18]

Nevertheless, a distinction can be made between retribution and revenge. First, they differ with respect to their motives. Revenge is typically motivated by strong passions such as anger, hatred, and resentment. Legally sanctioned and enacted retribution, by contrast, is motivated not by irrational feelings but by a rational decision to achieve justice. Its impartiality and rationality are highlighted by the fact that due process must be scrupulously followed to confer legitimacy. Second, vengeance is personal, indicated by the fact that its motives are emotions, which belong uniquely to persons. Retribution is deliberately impersonal. It is enacted by governmental institutions where every attempt is made to ensure objectivity by eliminating personal factors such as bias or prejudice on the part of people involved in the process. Moreover, due process limits the kind and severity of punishments that may be imposed, thus counteracting unduly harsh sentences motivated by anger or hate. Third, vengeance can be unruly and indiscriminately destructive, harming many more than its intended object. Retribution is disciplined and focused and is confined to the offender, excluding from its purview his friends and family.

To review, according to the retributive theory of justice, punishment is morally permissible merely because it is deserved. Its aim is to apportion fairly the punishment to the crime, either literally through the law of retaliation (*lex talionis*), symbolically, or in some other way. Kant formulated a classic version of this theory according to which retribution is entailed by the rationality and dignity of the offender. The problems with the theory are

1. It is difficult to determine exactly the degree of the offender's desert and guilt and to make the punishment proportionate to it.
2. It is difficult, also, to discover all the mitigating factors, together with ascertaining their relative importance and deciding how far, consistent with justice, they should reduce the desert of the offender.
3. Conflicts between justice and mercy must be resolved.
4. The enactment of retributive justice does not ensure an increase in the level of comparative justice but may in fact decrease it.
5. Retribution may seem to increase the amount of evil in the world.
6. Retribution is sometimes uncomfortably close to revenge.

Obstacle 5 and 6 can be surmounted. The other obstacles may seem intractable, but are no more so than the obstacles blocking our acceptance of the utilitarian theory of punitive justice, the theory to which we shall now turn.

Utilitarian justice

The retributive theory of justice looks backwards; it is concerned with punishing past misdeeds. The penalty is owed to a past transgression. The aim of retributive justice is to restore the moral balance, which was lost when the crime was committed. According to Bradley, considerations such as "the good of society" and "the benefit of the offender" may "modify the punishment" but of themselves "cannot give us the right to punish" — that is the prerogative of "criminal desert" alone. However, in sharp contrast to the retributive theory, the theory of utilitarian justice reverses this emphasis; desert now takes second place, and the good of society and the benefit of the offender are of paramount concern. Utilitarian justice looks forward. It is concerned less with redressing past wrongs than it is with actively increasing the amount of public good. According to the utilitarian theory of punitive justice, punishment is morally permissible or justifiable only if it brings about a greater social good, which outweighs or compensates for the evil of the offense. "If it [punishment] ought at all to be admitted," wrote Bentham, "it ought only to be admitted in as far as it promises to exclude some greater evil."[19] Under utilitarian theory, punishment must aim at benefiting both society and the offender. It is thought to benefit the offender through rehabilitation and deterrence, and thereby society by the safety that stems from deterrence.

For utilitarians, a principal objective of punishment is rehabilitating the offender. His incarceration serves not to make him suffer because he deserves it (retributive theory); rather, his confinement enables society to subject him to a disciplined regimen of education, training, and therapy which aims at curtailing his deviant tendencies, improving his character, and so making him a contributing member of society. What utilitarians are really advocating is not so much punishment for crime but treatment for deviant behavior. Their presupposition is that criminal acts stem not from moral defects of character but from psychological disorders for which therapy is more appropriate. Karl Menninger, the eminent psychologist, opined:[20]

> We, the agents of society, must move to end the game
> of tit-for-tat and blow-for-blow in which the offender
> has foolishly and futilely engaged himself and us. We
> are not driven, as he is, to wild and impulsive actions.
> With knowledge comes power, and with power there
> is no need for the frightened vengeance of the old
> penology. In its place should go a quiet, dignified,
> therapeutic program for the rehabilitation of the disor-
> ganized one, if possible, the protection of society dur-
> ing the treatment period, and his guided return to
> useful citizenship, as soon as this can be effected.

Note that Menninger makes no distinction between revenge and retribution and thinks that public safety is secondary to rehabilitation as the aim of punishment. Additionally, utilitarians think that punishment should benefit not only the individual offender by rehabilitating him, but also society by deterring him and potential offenders from committing similar offenses. And even if punishment fails to deter, they argue, it is better for society that the criminal be put away and so be prevented from further harming the public. Public safety, then, is another facet of punishment under the utilitarian theory. Though the utilitarian theory of punishment appears to be eminently humane, practical, and commonsensical, it is problematic with respect to its emphasis on rehabilitation and deterrence and its conception of punishment as therapy.

First of all, there is no guarantee that rehabilitation will work. Indeed, the high recidivist rate among criminals indicates that rehabilitative efforts fail more often than not. Paradoxically, such efforts seem to have the opposite effect: released prisoners leave detention more hardened than when they entered, and prisons are notorious for being schools for crime.[21]

Second, punishment does not necessarily deter. Even the harshest forms of punishment, such as torture or being put to death, fail to deter others from committing similar crimes. In 18th century London, professional pickpockets plied their trade among the crowd that came to watch the mass execution of convicted pickpockets! And studies have indicated that, in modern America, an execution does little to deter people from committing murder.[22] Why? It has been suggested that criminals are impervious to punitive threats and sanctions because their mindset and values are totally at odds with the majority of people who hearken to reason and common sense. According to this view, miscreants are deviant and seriously disordered personalities, a judgment perfectly consistent with the utilitarian theory of punishment. Menninger, in discussing juveniles, said that the delinquent, because of an adverse social environment such as an abusive home or deviant peer group, may...[23]

> ...believe that the chances of winning by undetected cheating are vastly greater than the probabilities of fair treatment and opportunity. He knows about the official threats and the social disapproval of such acts. He knows about the hazards and the risks. But despite all this "knowledge", he becomes involved in waves of discouragement or cupidity or excitement or resentment

> leading to episodes of social offensiveness. ...In some
> instances, the crime is the merest accident or incident
> or impulse, expressed under unbearable stress. More
> often the offender is a persistently perverse, lonely,
> and resentful individual who joins the only group to
> which he is eligible — the outcasts and the anti-social.

In other cases, it is not a bad environment that makes people do bad things; it might well be that they are just bad persons whom threats of direst retribution will never deter. Such a person is Rhoda Penmark, the protagonist in William March's novel, *The Bad Seed*. The story is about a young girl raised in a good home who is a serial killer. It eventually comes out that the child is the granddaughter of a convicted murderess and so cannot help but follow the ill-fated steps of her grandmother. Moreover, there are certain criminals, men and women of apparently high intelligence, who commit crime for its own sake. They are bereft of any moral scruples and conscience and actually derive an aesthetic delight or erotic thrill from committing certain crimes. A historical example of this type of individual would be the Marquis de Sade, the infamous sado-masochist who received sexual pleasure from torturing women and who chronicled his perversions in novels such as *Justine*. Fictional examples include Sherlock Holmes' nemesis, Professor Moriarty; Raskolnikov, in Feodor Dostoevski's *Crime and Punishment*; Hannibal Lecter, in Thomas Harris' *The Silence of the Lambs*; and Richard III, in Shakespeare's play of the same name. In the first scene of that play, Richard delivers a soliloquy to the audience in which he announces his resolve: "And therefore, since I cannot prove a lover/To entertain these fair well-spoken days,/I am determined to prove a villain."[24] He spends the rest of the play living up to these words, brilliantly and brutally dispatching all of his rivals to the crown of England — virtually turning serial murder into an art form, while we the audience watch in awe as Richard gleefully plots and carries out the murders. There are other cases — rare, yet occurring frequently enough to capture our interest and fascination — where people commit crimes for the express purpose of being caught and punished. These masochists look forward to suffering and are scarcely to be deterred by threats of the retribution they crave.

Third, the utilitarian theory of punishment does not ensure justice. As we have seen, one of the weaknesses of utilitarianism is that it may permit — even stipulate — unjust acts. This is especially true in its theory of punishment. There are several facets to this problem with the theory. One is that it cannot justify the punishing of certain crimes deserving of punishment. For example, in the 1980s, a Canadian businessman went to England to confront his wife's lover. He simply wanted to tell the man to stop seeing his wife. The lover refused and even made light of the situation. At this, the Canadian became so enraged that he stabbed the man to death with an ice pick. When he was tried, the Canadian received a comparatively light sentence — a couple of years in a minimum-security prison in the north of England. This is a classic case of a crime of passion, but on what grounds could a utilitarian justifiably punish the man? Not rehabilitation, since the man does not require it; he was a well-educated, immensely success-ful businessman who had never committed a crime in his life prior to the murder — and the likelihood of his ever killing again is virtually nil. Nor deterrence, as he stands in no need of being deterred from something which, given his character, he would never dream of doing again. Furthermore, given the anomalous nature of the crime, it is very unlikely that anyone else of a similar character would be de-terred from doing something they normally would never intention-ally do and would do only in exceptional circumstances such as extreme rage, jealousy, or fear. Obviously, protecting society cannot be justifiable grounds for punishing people who may commit only the one crime in their lives directed at a single specifically targeted victim. Under the utilitarian theory of punishment, if rehabilitation, deter-rence, and public safety are no grounds for punishment, there can be no moral justification for punishing perpetrators of crimes of passion such as the Canadian's. Yet, society cannot allow crimes of passion to be committed with impunity. Though the Canadian killed under exculpatory circumstances, he still deserves punishment. After all, a man did die, and his killer might have exercised some self-control.

There are two further, related ways in which the utilitarian theory of punishment may sanction injustice. For one thing, it may allow excessively cruel punishments in the interest of deterrence. Robert François Damiens, because of his attempt on Louis XV's life in 1757, had a horse tied to each of his limbs, whereupon the horses were lashed into a gallop. One of the horses did not succeed in pulling Damiens' limb from his body, so the executioner had to assist by hacking it off with an axe. To add insult to injury, after he had been "drawn" Damiens was "quartered". While still alive, he was disem-boweled and molten lead was poured on his body.[25] This punishment may have succeeded as a deterrent as there was no subsequent at-tempt ever made to assassinate a French monarch, but we may still scruple the justice of such a punishment whose severity would be all out of proportion to any conceivable crime. There is, however, no reason for a utilitarian to object to such a Draconian punishment if it did, in fact, deter potential assassins.[26]

Another way in which the utilitarian theory might sanction injustice is by conceivably permitting the judicial punishment of innocent persons in the name of deterrence and public safety. A dramatic illustration of this possibility is provided by Nielsen:[27]

> A magistrate is faced with a very real threat from a large and uncontrollable mob demanding a suspect in a crime be turned over to them. Unless the individual is produced, promptly tried, and executed, the mob will take their own bloody revenge on a smaller and quite vulnerable section of the community. ...The judge knows that the real culprit is unknown and that the authorities do not even have a good clue as to who he may be. But he also knows that there is within easy reach a disreputable, thoroughly disliked, and useless man, who, though innocent, could easily be framed so that the mob would be quite convinced that he was guilty and would be pacified if he were promptly executed. Recognizing that he can prevent the occurrence of extensive carnage only by framing some innocent person, the magistrate has him framed, goes through with the mockery of a trial, and has him executed.

The utilitarian theory of punishment sanctions the judicial execution of the innocent scapegoat to ensure the public safety — if the execution is carried out, many hundreds of innocent people will be spared from harm and death. However, this execution would be rankly unjust on any other than utilitarian principles.

Now the rule-utilitarian might respond that though act-utilitarianism sanctions this execution, rule-utilitarianism emphatically does not. He might argue that the judge should under no circumstances consider framing, trying, and executing the scapegoat. Doing so would certainly prevent more immediate and short-term evil consequences for society than not; however, it might very well lead to worse long-term consequences. It would set a dangerous precedent whereby judges might find it expedient to sacrifice innocent victims by exaggerating the social benefits of doing so. Moreover, people would begin to distrust such a judiciary and suppose it corrupt, an attitude that itself might result in further baneful consequences. Thus, "by so framing and then executing such an innocent man, he (the magistrate) would, in the long run, cause still more suffering through the resultant corrupting effect on the institution of justice."[28] The rule-utilitarian would remind us that the social benefits of following the *rule* that innocent scapegoats should never be sacrificed for the common good are, in the long run, greater than those following from any particular *act* of sacrificing an innocent scapegoat.

The act-utilitarian might reply that the execution of the scapegoat is nevertheless morally justified to safeguard the public good. Thus, if the section of the community threatened with retaliation by the mob were large enough — say, the size of New York City — then the rule-utilitarian might be wise to consider this a *bona fide* exception to the rule. The rule-utilitarian might be exaggerating the potential of the scapegoat's execution for setting a bad precedent and corrupting the judicial system, with all of its attendant evil consequences for society. Such a case is purely hypothetical, and were it to occur its frequent recurrence — if at all — would be so unlikely that it would hardly have the chance of impairing the integrity of the judiciary. If the act-utilitarian is successful in his reply, the potential for injustice in implementing the utilitarian theory of punishment remains. Furthermore, the rule-utilitarian, through his condemnation of the sacrifice of innocent scapegoats for the common good, harmonizes with our moral intuitions and still gives as the reason the bad long-term consequences for society of executing an innocent man if that act became the general rule — but not, note, the rank injustice of deliberately putting to death an innocent man. Presumably, if the long-term social benefits of not following that rule were greater than following it, then the magistrate might see his way morally clear to frame, try, and execute the scapegoat. Thus, even rule-utilitarianism fails to relieve the utilitarian theory of punishment of its unjust implications.

Even rule-utilitarians in condemning the sacrifice of an innocent scapegoat for the common good do so for reasons that ignore the considerations of basic justice. This brings us to perhaps the most serious problem with the utilitarian theory of punishment. This theory substitutes the value of utility for that of justice, thereby slighting fairness and the rights of individuals. The most searching criticism of this theory along these lines has come from Kant and other adherents of the retributivist theory of punishment. For Kant, the utilitarian theory, with respect to both its aims of deterrence and rehabilitation, denigrates human dignity. Thus, to punish criminals for the sake of deterring potential criminals is to use them as a means to an end. Even if such punishment is not cruel and unusual, it still has the effect of diminishing a person's humanity, of reducing him to something like a scarecrow to ward off offenders. The latent inhumanity of punishment for the sake of deterrence is made graphically clear in the custom in 18th-century London of sticking the severed heads of notorious criminals on spikes and displaying them on London Bridge.

Kant also believed that rehabilitation had the effect of reducing people to means. To rehabilitate someone against his will is to deprive him of his freedom as a rational being. Even if he gives his consent for rehabilitation, he is nevertheless having his personality remolded in conformity to the rehabilitator's ideal of a well-adjusted person. Rehabilitation may not seem objectionable in the case of miscreants who have committed numerous heinous crimes and are dangerous to the public, but even their forced rehabilitation may raise in us some moral concern. In Anthony Burgess' novel, *A Clockwork Orange*, a vicious teenage thug who takes sadistic delight in bullying, maiming, and killing whoever is unfortunate enough to encounter him is caught by the authorities. He is subjected to an intense and systematic regimen of behavior modification, a scientifically based form of rehabilitation. In one scene, he is forced to watch disturbing images on a screen. To this end, a mechanical device is applied to his eyes which makes it impossible for him to close them. This is a graphic illustration of how an extreme form of rehabilitation violates the autonomy and integrity of a person, even if he is a criminal. The sinister side of therapeutic rehabilitation, particularly the kind with a pretense to science, is illustrated in Ken Kersey's novel, *One Flew Over the Cuckoo's Nest*. This is the tale of a man committed to an insane asylum because of his "deviant" personality. It turns out the protagonist is not deviant, but something of a free spirit who is at least as sane as the psychiatrists in charge of his treatment. He is not a criminal, but this is not relevant as utilitarians reduce punishment to rehabilitation, regarding criminality as nothing other than a kind of mental illness to be treated accordingly. In the novel, the protagonist, in order to be rehabilitated, is lobotomized.

A final problem with the utilitarian theory of punishment is that it diminishes and trivializes the moral dimension of things. It does so in three ways. First, it elevates utility above justice. Both of these are values: Justice is unquestionably a moral value or virtue; utility, though a natural value, is not so obviously a moral one. Second, the utilitarian theory of punishment construes crime as a malady rather than as a moral defect, and assimilates punishment to rehabilitation and therapy, which are appropriate treatments of maladies. This assimilation of crime and punishment to pathology and therapy, respectively, requires some justification.

To review, according to the utilitarian theory, the aim of punishment is rehabilitation and deterrence for the sake of benefiting both the offender and society by making the offender a law-abiding citizen and preventing others like him from committing similar offenses. It tends to conceive of crime as a psychological malady and of punishment as an appropriate therapy for its treatment. Unlike the retributive theory that looks back to the offense as something to be redressed and so restore the good that was lost because of it, the utilitarian theory looks forward to the prospect of bringing about more good by making an example of the offender. His punishment might deter other potential offenders who otherwise might not have been deterred had he not committed the offense and then been punished for it. High rates of recidivism indicate that efforts at rehabilitation are not very successful; an excessive concern for deterrence and public safety may promote injustice by encouraging the infliction of excessively cruel punishments and the punishment of scapegoats. The utilitarian theory provides scant moral justification for the punishment of crimes of passion where rehabilitation and deterrence are irrelevant concerns. More fundamental criticisms of the theory are that it overvalues utility and expedience at the expense of justice and that it diminishes human dignity by using offenders as a means to ends other than themselves. It violates their autonomy and integrity as persons by seeking to reshape their characters forcibly.

Contractarian justice

The contractarian theory of punitive justice is the application of the contract theory of ethics to the issue of punishment. It is based on the idea that justice — as well as other moral concepts such as obligation or duty — depends on a social contract. To escape the state of nature where human life, in Hobbes' memorable description, is "solitary, poor, nasty, brutish and short," people agree to transfer certain of their natural rights (e.g., the right to avenge wrongs done to them by others) to a government. They do so because they understand that the power of the state can better protect them and their property from harm and theft than their own feeble powers can. By being able to depend upon the superior force of the police, citizens are spared the burden and anxiety of constantly looking out for themselves and their possessions. The social contract between people and their government comes to this: The people voluntarily transfer certain of their rights to the civil authority in exchange for its protection. In addition, they agree to obey all the civil laws which are legislated, specifically, to protect their lives and property and, more generally, to ensure the public peace that is indispensable to human happiness and progress. Under contractarian theory, justice consists of nothing other than obeying the law because obedience to the law has been promised in a contract between the citizen and the state. To break the law is to break a promise and to be unjust.

Socrates eloquently illustrates the contractarian viewpoint in Plato's *Crito*. Socrates has been convicted of heresy and has been sentenced to death. As he awaits execution, his friend Crito visits him in prison and urges him to escape. The escape can be easily arranged by Crito and his confederates. Socrates refuses to escape, explaining that he has enjoyed the manifold benefits of living under the laws of Athens. If he did not like them, he had the freedom to leave the city and live elsewhere. But by choosing to stay he tacitly agreed to abide by them, even the law that sentenced him to death. To escape would be not only to act the coward and contradict the spirit of his teachings, but also to renege on the contract that he had implicitly entered into with the state. Socrates, were he seriously to contemplate escaping, imagines being visited by "the laws and constitution of Athens" who attempt to dissuade him:[29]

> If any of you chooses to go to one of our colonies, supposing that he should not be satisfied with us and the state, or to emigrate to any other country, not one of us laws hinders or prevents him from going away wherever he likes, without any loss of property. On the other hand, if any one of you stands his ground when he can see how we administer justice and the rest of our public organization, we hold that by so doing he has in fact undertaken to do anything that we tell him. And we maintain that anyone who disobeys is guilty of doing wrong ... because, after promising obedience, he is neither obeying us nor persuading us to change our decision if we are at fault in any way.

For the social contract theorist, punishment of crime is morally permissible and justified because the offender has broken the social contract. He has reneged on his promise made to obey the law of the land even after enjoying its protection and other benefits. The offender has openly declared war on the society that has nurtured him. He has willingly separated himself from that society and has disqualified himself from its protection. Society now has the right to retaliate against its enemy in order to protect itself and to preserve the contract among its citizens. If the contract may be violated with impunity, then the laws lack teeth and the citizens have little protection. As Hobbes put it, "Covenants, without the Sword, are but words, and of no strength to secure a man at all."[31] By breaking the law, criminals have violated the *principle of reciprocity*, which states that we agree to obey the law, to honor the rights of others and neither to harm them, steal their property, nor curtail their freedom, only on the condition that they reciprocate. If they do not, we are released from the terms of that agreement to meet our obligations towards them, and may retaliate — through the judicial system which represents us — by depriving them of the rights they enjoyed under the civil law such as their freedom and even their lives. Rachels describes the principle of reciprocity which undergirds the contractarian theory of punishment as follows:[31]

> But why is it *permissible* to punish? The answer is that the criminal has violated the fundamental condition of reciprocity: we recognize the rules of social living as limiting what *we* can do only on the condition that others accept the same restrictions on what *they* can do. Therefore, by violating the rules with respect to us, criminals release us from our obligation toward them and leave themselves open to retaliation.

The contractarian theory of justice has something in common with both the retributive and the utilitarian theories. Like the retributive theory, it looks backwards insofar as it finds the moral basis for punishment in a contract that was made and subsequently broken. Like the utilitarian theory, it looks forward insofar as it justifies punishment by appealing to the evil social consequences that would undoubtedly occur were it not inflicted (e.g., there would be no ultimate sanction to compel obedience to the law). The social contract would be weakened, and a plunge into anarchy would be imminent; hence, the contractarian theory has the double merit of honoring equally the principles of justice and utility. It honors justice by stipulating that punishment must be deserved, and it is deserved only upon a violation of the social contract. It no less honors utility by pointing to the public safety and peace that will be preserved by the infliction of punishment. Hospers writes:[32]

> Both of these conditions, then, must be fulfilled. Pun-
> ishment does not conform to justice if it is undeserved,
> and it does not conform to utility if it produces no good
> results. Before we inflict punishment, then, which after
> all is the deliberate infliction of something *intrinsically*
> bad (displeasure) we should be sure that both of these
> conditions are met.

A principal merit of the social contract theory is that it meets both these conditions.

What the contractarian theory shares in common with the retributive and utilitarian theories is the source not only of twoof its merits, but of some of its defects as well. Like the retributive theory, it has the problem of applying the principle of proportionate retribution. For the contractarian, the severity of the punishment is determined by the degree to which the offense weakens the social contract and threatens the order and peace of society. This means that traitors should be punished more severely than even mass murderers, as was the case in Great Britain well into the 18th century. But what exactly is meant by "weakening" the social contract or "threatening" public order and peace? And assuming that one knows what they mean, just how does one go about determining their exact degree?

In one sense, a breach of contract is a breach of contract, and so *any* breach of contract (all contracts operating on the same principle and being but various embodiments of the social contract that is the foundation of society and its institutions) is going to weaken and threaten as much as any other. Thus, a bounced check, nonpayment of a bill, perjury, and acts of high treason would all equally weaken the social contract and threaten public order and peace. For, on the principle of universalizability, if enough people refuse to pay their income tax, the solvency of the federal government and the economic stability of the nation would be seriously at risk. Therefore, because all such breaches of the social contract amount to an attack on the integrity and order of society, then they should all receive equally severe penalties. Of course, punishing a bounced check to the same degree as murder would be egregiously unjust. The social contract theorist could still come back and say that a murderer should be punished more severely than the writer of a bad check because the social consequences of murder are far greater. But were the theorist to say this he would be arguing no longer as a social contract theorist but as a utilitarian.

If the social contract is the foundation of justice, then any breach of it is the essence of injustice. This would include acts of civil disobedience, such as refusing to serve in an army during time of war. However, civil disobedience is typically carried out in the very name of justice, the justice that means conformity to a higher law (variously denominated as moral, natural, or divine). Such was the civil disobedience practiced by Thoreau, who refused to pay the poll tax that financed the Mexican-American War, and by Rosa Parks, who broke a law by refusing to give up her seat to a white man on a crowded bus. Under the social contract theory, which conceives of justice and injustice as nothing but conformity to and violation of the social contract, respectively, there can be no such thing as justice existing outside (much less superior to) the social contract.

To this the social contract theorist might well reply that one of the advantages of the social contract theory of justice is that it explicitly allows for civil disobedience. Thus, if the state constitutionally guarantees its citizens a right, only to withhold it, then the state itself has reneged on its contract with the citizens, thereby voiding the contract. Since a state of nature now exists between them and the government, the citizens are exempt from the terms of the contract and have the right to disobey the civil law, even to the point of rebellion and revolution. The basis of the citizens' right to civil disobedience is the state's breach of contract with them. But, if some citizens find themselves in a state that *constitutionally* denies them rights enjoyed by others, then the state has not reneged on its contract with those citizens, because no contract ever existed. These citizens cannot appeal to a breached contract as the basis of their right to civil disobedience, but may appeal only to a "higher" law. This was the case with slaves in the United States on whom the Constitution had not conferred any rights because their sole legal status was as property. A social contract theorist who makes that concession is admitting that justice stems ultimately not from a social contract, but from a higher law that transcends any social contract and to which all civil statutes issuing from that contract must conform. This raises the issue of the "justice" of a state punishing a citizen for civil disobedience when the law he has disobeyed is itself contrary to a higher, moral law. The social contract theory of punishment, then, as the retributive and utilitarian theories, may sanction injustice inasmuch as the laws stemming from the social contract may be morally corrupt.

Despite its problems, the social contract theory of punitive justice has something further to recommend it. It simplifies the legal code and its enforcement by limiting criminal acts to those that affect the public domain by impairing the integrity, safety, and peace of society.

It provides no rationale for making illegal completely private acts having no obvious impact on society — however distasteful they may be to some. Thus, under the social contract theory, adults' possessing and enjoying pornography within the privacy of their homes or performing consensual sexual acts that might be considered perverted or unnatural may be legally permitted without posing a social threat. The social contract theory also provides a rational basis for excluding children and the mentally deficient from criminal prosecution for their crimes — not for any humanitarian or sentimental reasons, but simply because they cannot be party to any contract, as they are incapable of giving their rational consent to it. If they are unable to enter into a legally binding contract, they cannot be held liable for breaking it. This does not mean that juvenile delinquents and the criminally insane may not be incarcerated for crimes. But, because they are not deemed fully responsible for their crimes by reason of immaturity or irrationality, the aim of their incarceration is not punishment, but rather rehabilitation and public safety.

Of course, we may question this "merit" of the social contract theory in excluding children and the criminal insane from retributive punishment. The 1990s saw an alarming increase in the number of juveniles committing heinous crimes. In response to this trend, some states have amended their penal codes to allow that children who commit serious felonies be punished as adults. Further, the public has never fully accepted the use of the insanity defense in cases of homicide. "Insanity" is a legal term, not a medical one, and the degree to which mental impairment excuses a perpetrator from the legal consequences of committing a capital crime is very much in dispute. Indeed, in some medical and legal circles, the scientific legitimacy of psychiatry as a *bona fide* science has increasingly been called into question.[33]

To review, the social contract theory of punitive justice combines the essential features of both the retributive and utilitarian theories. It finds the desert of punishment in breach of contract and finds value in its social utility. This, together with its providing a clear and rational basis for limiting the criminal code to just those acts which threaten public safety, security, and peace and for excluding children and the insane from criminal prosecution, may be considered a merit of the theory. It shares with both the retributive and utilitarian theories the defect that it might sanction instances of injustice. It has the totalitarian implication that conscientious acts of civil disobedience — even those against an apparently unjust law or a corrupt constitution — are comparable to treason and should be treated accordingly. To solve this problem, it must appeal to a principle of justice (conformity to a higher law), distinct from the social contract, of which it needs to give an account.

Restitutive justice

Like the retributive theory, the last theory of punitive justice we shall take up also looks backwards, though not to the offender and his desert. This theory looks to the victim and his loss or injury. A defect of the other theories is their indifference to the compensation of the victims of crime as an indispensable aspect of justice. The retributive theory, though it seeks to give the perpetrator his just deserts, does not compensate his victim. And the utilitarian and contractarian theories, though they may have the effect of benefiting the victim in a general sort of way by seeking to make society safer through deterrence, do not provide for compensating him specifically. The *restitutive theory of punitive justice* aims at doing just that. It conceives the chief aim of punishment not so much as retributively harming the offender or rehabilitating him or deterring others, but as providing restitution or compensation to his victim. This theory works, in essence, as follows. If I steal your lawnmower, my punishment consists of being forced to restore the machine to you in the condition that I found it and to pay you damages for any anxiety, inconvenience, or loss of enjoyment you suffered by its loss. During the 1990s there has emerged a greater public awareness that the rights of victims of crime deserve respect no less than those of criminals, and pursuant to this end grassroots movements supporting victims' rights have developed.[34] Underlying this is the restitutive theory of justice.

    Like the previous theories we have discussed, the restitutive theory of justice has its problems. One obvious problem is the impossibility of compensating — either at all or adequately — victims of crimes such as homicide, assault, or rape. In the case of homicide, though no restitution could be made to the victim, it could be made to his bereaved relatives; however, this is at best restitution to surrogates, and what form of compensation would be adequate? If money, what price could be placed on a human life? In the case of an assault where the victim lived but suffered permanent serious injury, what restitution would suffice? And what about so-called "victimless crimes"? When the offense is *mala prohibitum* or the victim is an institution instead of a person, who or what gets compensated? An institution can be regarded as a victim only if it is regarded as a surrogate person capable of suffering a loss.[35]

A second problem with the restitutive theory is that it may sanction unjust treatment of the offender. Suppose that I steal some of your property. I am subsequently apprehended and convicted and ordered by the court, as punishment, to restore to you intact and complete all that I took, as well as to pay you damages. Let us suppose further that I have pawned or squandered the property and so have nothing to return to you. If I were wealthy, making monetary restitution to you would not be difficult, but if I am poor it may be impossible for me to repay you. The point is that poor offenders are less able to make restitution to their victims than rich offenders are; consequently, the burden of restitution is heavier for them. It is unfair that the burden of making restitution falls more heavily on the poor than on the wealthy. To avoid this problem in the parity of means between rich and poor, suppose that restitution takes a form other than monetary — say, labor. Consider the case of Michael Fay who, while living in Singapore in 1994, vandalized some cars by spray-painting them. Now imagine that the court, instead of sentencing him to a caning (a form of retributive punishment), had sentenced him to make restitution to the owners by meticulously cleaning their cars and so restoring them to their original condition. This task should not have taxed his physical capacity, as he was a teenager at the time of the offense, but suppose he had been age 70 or had a serious heart condition. The same act of restitution would have been much more physically taxing. Here, again, the burden of restitution, even though it takes a non-monetary form, may not fall equally upon all.

The natural response to such cases of injustice to offenders because the burden of restitution falls unequally on them might be, "If you can't do the time, don't do the crime." This, however, is to invoke the retributive theory of justice, which does not alter the case that, strictly within the terms of the restitutive theory, an unequal burden of restitution is unjust.

A third problem with the restitutive theory is that it fails to distinguish intentional from unintentional wrongs to others, as restitution is equally deserved in both cases. Thus, whether I injure you accidentally or do so deliberately, restitution in some form is morally and legally required of me. The restitution is the same whether or not I am legally or morally to blame for the injury or damage I have caused. In the one case restitution is punitive and in the other it is not, but there is no way of distinguishing between them because restitution made for a malicious wrong is exactly the same as that for an accidental wrong. This issue is related to a fourth problem with restitutive theory. Even if restitution can be made, and fairly borne by the offender, there is still the fact that the only punishment suffered by him is that he must give back what he never had the right to take in the first place. It is true that he may have to compensate his victim further for anxiety, inconvenience, or the loss of enjoyment or benefits incurred by the wrong, but that is not "punishment". Although the offender has paid his debt to the victim, he still deserves to pay a debt to the *wrong* itself. In other words, he deserves some kind of retribution being exacted from him no less than his victim deserves his making restitution. Restitution alone does not make for complete justice.

To review, the restitutive theory of punitive justice holds that the principal purpose of punishment is to make compensation or restitution to the victim of the crime for the wrong done to him. This theory puts a high premium on the rights of victims in a way that the retributive and utilitarian theories do not. There are, however, four major problems with this theory:

1. It does not allow for the punishment of crimes such as rape, assault, and murder, for which adequate compensation or, for that matter, even any kind of compensation is impossible.
2. It allows for the possible unjust treatment of offenders by imposing upon them burdens of restitution that may fall upon them unequally because of disparities of wealth, physical strength, or health.
3. It fails to distinguish between punitive and non-punitive forms of restitution.
4. It provides for the satisfaction of the victim's desert, but not the offender's.

Notes

1. Isaiah 61:8 (revised standard version).
2. Plato, Republic, in *The Collected Dialogues*, Hamilton, E. and Carns, H., Eds., Bollingen Series LXXI, Princeton University Press, 1961, p. 586.
3. For the sake of clarity, I shall reserve the term "retributive" for a kind of punitive justice.
4. Bentham, Jeremy, *An Introduction to the Principles of Morals and Legislation*, Hafner Publishing, Darien, CN, 1948, p. 170.
5. Mt. 5:38 (revised standard version).

6. Bradley, Francis H., *Ethical Studies*, Oxford University Press, London, 1927, pp. 26–27 (as quoted in Hospers, John, *Human Conduct: An Introduction to the Problems of Ethics*, Harcourt, Brace & World, New York, 1961, p. 458).

7. Kant, Immanuel (John Ladd, trans.), *The Metaphysical Elements of Justice*, Bobbs-Merrill, Indianapolis, IN, 1965, pp. 99–107 (as quoted in Rachels, James, *The Elements of Moral Philosophy*, 2nd ed., McGraw-Hill, New York, 1993, p. 134).

8. Rachels, James, *The Elements of Moral Philosophy*, 2nd ed., McGraw-Hill, New York, 1993, p. 135.

9. Shakespeare, William, The merchant of Venice, in *The Complete Works*, Wells, S. and Taylor, G., Eds., Clarendon Press, Oxford, 1986, p. 503.

10. It is very unlikely that the ancient Hebrews intended that their *lex talionis* should be taken literally; rather, it was a metaphoric way of stating the law of proportionate retribution (i.e., the severity of the penalty should neither fall short of nor exceed the seriousness of the offense).

11. A question occurs here: Does the use of mitigating factors to diminish guilt and desert itself make for a more nearly perfect kind of justice, or does it constitute an abrogation or abridgment of justice?

12. Bentham thought that pleasures (and pains) could be quantified according to our experience of their relative intensities and durations, etc. See his *An Introduction to the Principles of Morals and Legislation*, Hafner Publishing, Darien, CN, 1948, pp. 29–32.

13. Pedersen, Daniel, From death row, Karla Faye Tucker speaks, *Newsweek*, Feb. 2, 1998, pp.66–67.

14. Harry A. Blackmun, *Collins v. Collins*, 510 U.S., 114 S. Ct. at 1129–30 (as cited in Hall, Daniel E., *Criminal Procedure and the Constitution*, West Publishing, Albany, NY, 1997, p. 268).

15. Kant makes much of this point.

16. Shakespeare, William, Hamlet, in *The Complete Works*, Wells, S. and Taylor, G., Eds., Clarendon Press, Oxford, 1986, p. 744.

17. According to Socrates, "One ought not to return a wrong or an injury to any person, whatever the provocation is." (From Plato, Crito, in *The Collected Dialogues*, Hamilton, E. and Carns, H., Eds., Bollingen Series LXXI, Princeton University Press, 1961, p. 34.)

18. Moses reports God as saying, "Vengeance is mine, and recompense, for the time when their foot shall slip." (Deuteronomy 32:35, revised standard version)

19. Bentham, Jeremy, *An Introduction to the Principles of Morals and Legislation*, Hafner Publishing, Darien, CN, 1948, p. 170.

20. Menninger, Karl, Verdict guilty — now what?, *Harper's Magazine*, August, 1959, p. 64.

21. Bureau of Justice Statistics, *Annual Report*, U.S. Government Printing Office, Washington, D.C., 1987, p. 70.

22. Forst, B.E., The deterrent effect of capital punishment: a cross-state analysis of the 1960s, *Minnesota Law Review*, 61, 743–767, 1977.

23. Menninger, Karl, Verdict guilty — now what?, *Harper's Magazine*, August, 1959, p. 61.

24. William Shakespeare, Richard III, in *The Complete Works*, Wells, S. and Taylor, G., Eds., Clarendon Press, Oxford, 1986, p. 209.

25. Damiens, Robert-Francois, *Micropaedia, The New Encyclopaedia Britannica*, 15th ed., Vol. III, 1992, pp. 866–867.

26. One can hardly imagine classic utilitarians such as Bentham and Mill sanctioning such a cruel and unusual punishment. They might respond by saying that if a less severe penalty had equal deterrent value, then it should be substituted for the more severe. But suppose any other, lesser penalty did not have the same deterrent value. It seems that, to be consistent, the utilitarian would have to authorize such a harsh punishment; other than rehabilitation, the aim of punishment is deterrence in the interest of the public good.

27. Nielsen, Kai, Against moral conservatism, in *Moral Philosophy: A Reader*, Pojman, L.P., Ed., Hackett Publishing, Indianapolis, IN, 1993, p. 123.

28. Nielsen, Kai, Against moral conservatism, in *Moral Philosophy: A Reader*, Pojman, L.P., Ed., Hackett Publishing, Indianapolis, IN, 1993, p. 123.

29. Plato, Crito, in *The Collected Dialogues*, Hamilton, E. and Carns, H., Eds., Bollingen Series LXXI, Princeton University Press, 1961, p. 37.

30. Hobbes, Thomas, *Leviathan*, Clarendon Press, Oxford, 1958, p. 128.

31. Rachels, James, *The Elements of Moral Philosophy*, 2nd ed., McGraw-Hill, New York, 1993, p. 150.

32. Hospers, John, *Human Conduct: An Introduction to the Problems of Ethics*, Harcourt, Brace & World, New York, 1961, p. 460.

33. Schmalleger, Frank, *Criminal Justice Today: An Introductory Text for the Twenty First Century*, 4th ed., Prentice-Hall, Upper Saddle River, NJ, 1997, pp. 136–140.

34. Doerner, William G. and Lab, Steven P., *Victimology*, Anderson Publishing, Cincinnati, OH, 1995, pp. 14–15.

35. Whether or not non-human beings such as corporations, states, and other institutions should be accorded moral status as "persons" and thereby capable of being wronged — and so eligible for compensation — or of doing wrong — and so liable to prosecution — depends on how one resolves the knotty metaphysical issue of what constitutes a person. According to "metaphysical individualism", only individuals such as human beings taken separately qualify as persons, but according to "metaphysical collectivism", collectivities such as institutions

rate as persons: "Metaphysical individualism says that only individuals are real and that corporations are fictitious mental constructs, consequently only individuals can be responsible for crimes ... metaphysical collectivists ... hold that corporations are as real as individual human beings ... [and] are like living organisms that think, act, and direct the activities of their members and that, consequently, the corporation ... must be held responsible for its criminal acts." (From Velasquez, Manuel, *Philosophy: A Text with Readings*, 5th ed., Wadsworth, Belmont, CA, 1994, p. 230.)

chapter ten

Discretionary justice

> "The laws of this land are not so vulgar, to permit a
> mean fellow to contend with one of your ladyship's
> fortune. We have one sure card, which is to carry him
> before Justice Frolick, who, upon hearing your
> ladyship's name will commit him without any farther
> questions. As for the dirty slut, we shall have nothing
> to do with her: for if we get rid of the fellow, the ugly
> jade will —" ... "Take what measures you please, good
> Mr. Scout," answered the lady, "but I wish you could
> rid the parish of both." ... "Your ladyship is very much
> in the right," answered Scout, "but I am afraid the law
> is a little deficient in giving us any such power of
> prevention; however the Justice will stretch it as far as
> he is able, to oblige your ladyship ... he hath taken
> several poor off our hands that the law would never
> lay hold on." —Henry Fielding (*Joseph Andrews*)

It has been stated that in Chicago it was at one time customary for the
police to give warning tickets to attorneys for traffic violations. In one
locality, the police and courts prevented an anticipated riot by locking
up 90 black youths and posting such excessively high bail that they
could not gain their freedom (an actual case which drew the ire of the
American Civil Liberties Union). A parole board denied parole to an
eligible prisoner but gave no reasons for its denial in contravention of
the Administrative Procedure Act. Its failure to provide reasons for
granting parole might be explained by a pamphlet the board issued in
1964 which states that because the board does not sit together, and

because each member votes separately and privately, it is impossible to ascertain precisely why or why not a particular parole was granted. A prosecutor, through plea-bargaining, reduces one defendant's felony to a misdemeanor, but fails to do so in another case. And a judge with the authority to sentence a convicted felon to 5 years reduces the sentence to a year and then suspends the sentence, even though he knows that another judge would have imposed the prescribed 5-year sentence.[1]

The above cases, both actual and hypothetical, are examples of the exercise of *discretionary justice*, the opportunity for which occurs for a criminal justice professional "whenever the effective limits on his power leave him free to make a choice among possible courses of action or inaction."[2] As these cases illustrate, the prerogative of exercising discretion belongs to all criminal justice professionals, although it is most frequently exercised by those individuals within the professions who actually have the least amount of power and authority. For instance, the police officer on the street has much more discretionary power than does the chief of police.

The anatomy of discretionary justice

The exercise of discretionary justice theoretically follows a procedure that involves (1) finding and assessing the relevant facts of the case, (2) consulting the law that applies to it, and (3) deciding the desirable course of action based on the facts of the situation and the applicable law. It is at the third stage that discretion is most clearly brought into play.[3] But discretion, at some level, may be used by any criminal justice professional at any stage in the criminal justice process. The patrol officer who decides whether or not to pull you over for running a red light may use discretion. It may be used by the detective who decides which investigative leads are to be pursued. It is used by the prosecutor who decides what cases will come to trial and which ones will be dropped. With respect to the law itself, discretion may be necessary in interpreting law and precedent. Finally, it should be noted that failure to make a decision, or postponing it, involves no less discretion than making a positive decision.

The exercise of discretion differs from the legal reasoning associated with case law with respect to the degree of consistency sought. We are all considered to be equal under the law. This ideal of equality requires strict consistency in the treatment of persons who come into contact with the criminal justice system. The quest for consistency involves formulating and following rules and principles with which decision-making is guided. Law and discretion are separated, but more by a zone than by a line. Davis identifies five ways in which legal precedents (rules) may be regarded in decision making. Legal precedents may be "(1) almost always binding, (2) always considered and usually binding, (3) usually considered but seldom binding, (4) occasionally considered but never binding, and (5) almost never considered."[4] The first two ways belong to case law, the last two to discretion, and the third to the zone between law and discretion.

The legal reasoning in case law and the exercise of discretionary justice both have their strengths and weaknesses. Because of its commitment to consistency by honoring precedents, case law minimizes arbitrariness in decisions and helps preserve the principle of comparative justice. However, it is open to the danger of inflexibility and the failure to do justice, in particular cases, because it neglects to take into account their special circumstances or uniqueness. By contrast, discretion has the virtue of flexibility so as to tailor justice to the requirements peculiar to particular cases. Because of its lower regard for consistency, it is vulnerable to arbitrariness and so may violate the principle of comparative justice. "We must remember," Davis admonishes, "that although the inequality caused by inconsistency can mean injustice, excessive rigidity can mean not only injustice but also a failure to make use of better understanding." Ideally, a balance should be sought between conformity to legal precedents in the joint interests of consistency and comparative justice, and the exercise of discretion in the interests of flexibility and individualized justice: "Our sound objective is to locate the optimum degree of binding effect of precedents for each particular subject matter, so that the role of precedents will be in each instance neither too strong nor too weak."[5]

Because justice demands taking into account the special circumstances of each case and so of tailoring the law to them, there must be flexibility in the law's application. Discretionary justice, therefore, is endemic to any judicial system that aspires to being rational and just. Pound states, "In no legal system, however minute and detailed its body of rules, is justice administered wholly by rule and without any recourse to the will of the judge and his personal sense of what should be done to achieve a just result in the case before him. Both elements are to be found in all administration of justice."[6] And Salmond observes, "The total exclusion of judicial discretion by legal principle is impossible in any system. However great is the encroachment of the law, there must remain some residuum of justice which is not according to law — some activities in respect of which the administration of justice cannot be defined or regarded as the enforcement of the law."[7] In the American judicial system, the scope of discretionary power is such that five forms of discretionary power may abrogate criminal laws: "the discretion of the police not to arrest, the discretion of the prosecutor not to prosecute or to trade a lesser charge for a plea of guilty, the discretion of the judge in favor of suspended sentence or probation, the discretion of the parole officer to release, the discretion of the executive to pardon."[8] According to Breitel, "There is more recognizable discretion in the field of criminal control, including that part of its broad sweep which lawyers call 'criminal law', than in any other field in which law regulates conduct."[9] Such is the scope of discretionary power in the vast criminal justice systems of the United States that, Davis remarks, "Perhaps it is not too much to say that the essence of criminal justice lies in the exercise of discretionary power, despite the continuing importance of the jury trial."[10]

Because of its lack of consistency, discretionary justice, as we have seen, may run the risk of arbitrariness and so violate the principle of comparative justice. It may be further compromised by a variety of emotional and other irrational factors, such as the official's accepting a bribe, or succumbing to political favoritism, or showing partiality toward the object of his discretion, or racial and other forms of prejudice. "I think," writes Davis, "the greatest and most frequent injustice occurs at the discretion end of the scale, where rules and principles provide little or no guidance, where emotions of deciding officers may affect what they do, where political or other favoritism may influence decisions, and where the imperfections of human nature are often reflected in the choices made."[11] This risk may be minimized by curtailing and regulating discretion according to certain rules or principles, despite the difficulty of formulating such rules, and of prejudices favoring unregulated discretion and justice based on intuition geared to individual cases. However, these rules themselves may be too vague to be applicable, or may be sufficiently clear to be applicable, or may be so clear and compelling so as to obviate the need for discretion. The trick, according to Davis, is "not merely to choose between rule and discretion but is to find the optimum point on the rule-to-discretion scale."[12] Furthermore, the degree of discretionary power conferred on an official authorized to exercise it depends upon the scope and limits of his authority.

Given the widespread use of discretionary power in the American legal system, it is reasonable to be concerned that a significant portion of decisions involving the use of discretion might be dubious. Three reasons have been proposed for this concern. One is the unfortunate existence of corrupt officials who possess discretionary power. A second reason is conscientious and well-intentioned officials who exceed the scope of their discretionary authority in order to bring about justice or beneficial consequences for the public. A third reason is legislators who acquiesce to or even encourage illegal discretionary actions.[13] Furthermore, discretionary justice, because of the lack of firm guidelines for its administration, has a great potential for injustice and illegality as well as posing numerous moral dilemmas.

We turn next to the discretion exercised by criminal justice personnel in order to examine the various moral issues raised by its exercise. Moral issues with regard to discretion in performing the duties of criminal justice turn on the sometimes conflicting values of justice, mercy, individual rights, and the public good. Thus, safeguarding the public good may violate the civil rights of individuals. Satisfying the legal demand for justice may mean being deaf to reasonable pleas for clemency. Administering retributive justice in one case but not in others may contravene the principle of comparative justice, and doing what is illegal but expedient may be immoral.

We shall use the normative ethical theories formulated earlier to clarify these issues and to point the way to their resolution. The theories most relevant to these tasks are utilitarianism, deontologism, contractarianism, and aretaic ethics. Ethical egoism falls away because it tends to exacerbate rather than help resolve moral conflicts (one of the many problems with this theory), as does moral intuitionism with its stress on intuition or feeling and its odor of subjectivity, which is too much like discretionary justice itself to be of much help in solving the moral problems that it raises. And, for practical purposes, the divine command theory may be assimilated to deontologism because of their common appeal to law, and agapism to aretaic ethics because of their common emphasis on character. Thus, a great divide opens between rule-oriented deontological ethics and results-oriented utilitarianism, and between rule-based deontic ethics and character-based aretaic ethics.

Discretionary justice and the police

On a daily basis, every police officer utilizes discretion to a greater or lesser extent each time he comes into contact with a citizen. The officer on patrol either decides to pull you over for running a stop sign or chooses to ignore the infraction. The detective decides which leads are important to follow up and which leads are trivial. The juvenile officer decides to turn a young vandal over to his parents rather than involve him in the system. All these actions, or failures to act, are examples of the discretionary power exercised by the average police officer. The police, particularly those who work directly with the public, have an enormous amount of discretion at their disposal.

According to legal statute, the police have the *prima facie* duties (using Ross' terminology) to honor the civil rights of citizens and to enforce the laws. What happens when these duties come into conflict? It is the conflict between apparently equally binding duties when meeting one obligation entails breaking another that is the main source of our moral dilemmas and conundrums. This is no less true for police officers. When an officer faces such a dilemma, he may typically carry out his duty to enforce the law. But what if abiding by the letter of the law results in injustice? For instance, an officer on routine patrol spots a motorist driving the wrong way down a one-way street. In accordance with the law, the officer pulls the motorist over to ticket him, but upon approaching the car the officer finds that the motorist and his family are from out of town and visiting the city on a vacation. The driver did not understand the street system, made an accidental wrong turn, and ended up traveling the wrong direction on a one-way street. What should the officer do? If he issues the ticket, he will be abiding by the letter of both the law and his department's policy and procedures manual. But is the ticket just? Remember the motorist committed the violation unintentionally, and no one was hurt by it. In this and many similar situations, officers use discretion to rectify the situation without involving the citizen in the criminal justice system. Here the officer can get the motorist turned in the right direction and can leave him with very positive feelings toward law enforcement in that city. Discretion usually comes into play when the offense is minor and the resolution can be expediently made to the satisfaction of everyone involved. There are exceptions, however, when discretion can be used in extremely unfair ways. In 1967, 200 minority males were indiscriminately arrested and jailed in a major American city. They were not charged with serious offenses, yet they were detained for up to a month because the courts set excessively high bail. This summary rounding up and detention of unpopular segments of the population was unconstitutional, yet it was defended on the grounds that the action prevented race riots. Judge Louis J. Gilberto justified the action by saying, "There is a legal theory that in these unusual circumstances people should be detained until the unrest is over."[14] This decision illustrates the inevitable tension between the individual and society and the perennial issue of whether his private good should be sacrificed for the public good. It also illustrates how discretion, even when the intentions are good, can be misused.

In making such decisions and resolving this issue, utilitarians would look to the social benefits. If wiretapping produced evidence that convicts criminals, then it is justified, even at the expense of the privacy of non-criminals. Rule-utilitarians might oppose such infringements of an individual's rights if they thought that the principle of infringing rights for immediate social benefits, if routinely applied, would have worse, long-term consequences for society. Indiscriminate wiretapping might catch more criminals, but it would give "big brother" too much access to the lives of ordinary citizens. By contrast, deontologists would not be swayed by the social benefits of violating a person's rights, because to do so would diminish his dignity by using him as a means to an end. Agapists, too, would be loathe to violate individual rights, because they regard all persons as sacrosanct, and any disrespect for their rights expresses contempt not only for them but for God, as well. Social contract theorists, on the other hand, are no less concerned with the preservation of society than are utilitarians, yet they share with deontologists a respect for law because the continuance of society depends upon it. However, they might be more solicitous of civil rights than act-utilitarians, for the social contract depends upon them. If the government, through its agencies, deprives citizens of their rights, which that government is pledged to defend, then the citizenry has the right to revolt. Aretaic ethics, being dispositional in character, would have little to say on this matter, as it involves making a decision.

What if a police officer uses discretion to discriminate against racial minorities? It does happen, perhaps more than we care to believe. Davis reported that the principal grievance of ghetto residents was "police practices",[15] and police relations with minorities were "as serious as any problem the police have today."[16] That was in 1967. Consider the riots in Los Angeles after the first Rodney King trial. Are race relations between the police and minority communities really any better today? The Rodney King case has been cited repeatedly as an egregious example of police brutality directed against racial minorities, but it is far from the only modern example. We tend to agree automatically that any degree of discrimination in the enforcement of the law contravenes the fundamental principle of comparative justice, as well as the principles of every ethical theory (with the possible exception of egoism). Yet bias does exist.

"Selective enforcement" is the term used to describe the discretionary power of the police not to enforce the law when its enforcement would be justified. It includes deciding to whom the law will apply, which laws will be enforced and on what occasions they will be enforced:[17]

> When an enforcement agency or officer has discretionary power to do nothing about a case in which enforcement would be clearly justified, the result is a power of selective enforcement. Such power goes to selection of parties against whom the law is enforced and selection of the occasions when the law is enforced. Selective enforcement may also mean selection of the law that will be enforced and of the law that will not be enforced; an officer may enforce one statute fully, never enforce another, and pick and choose in enforcing a third.

The principle of selective enforcement assumes that "justice does not require equal treatment by police, prosecutors, and other enforcement officers of those who are equally deserving of prosecution or of other governmental initiative."[18] Of all the discretionary decisions the police must make, selective enforcement is the one that carries the most momentous consequences, for to arrest a suspect is to set into motion the complex machinery of judicial procedure involving judges, prosecutors, and perhaps eventually corrections personnel, not to mention their own discretionary powers. There are a number of factors that may cause a police officer to refrain from enforcing the law, and some of these factors may have serious implications for the concept of justice.

Ambivalence toward the law

Society does not remain static. Over time, actions once disapproved of by society may gain acceptance, thereby rendering laws forbidding their practice obsolete. The community and its leaders prefer that the law not be enforced pending its repeal. Additionally, while society might still officially frown upon the activity, the laws regulating it have not been enforced for so long that it becomes impossible to carry out the letter of the law.

The status of the offense

The meaning of the law covering an offense may be vague or open to interpretation, or the offense might be a legitimate custom or traditional practice belonging to a particular subculture and enforcing the law might result in community unrest.

Mitigating factors and leniency

In circumstances involving minor offenses, the officer might take mitigating factors into consideration when making a decision about arresting an individual for a crime. For instance, a juvenile vandal might be turned over to his parents rather than consigned to the juvenile justice system.

Expedience

In some cases, officers may use discretion to expedite various criminal justice matters. If an officer catches a minor criminal in a minor crime, he might choose to "look the other way" in exchange for that criminal's providing information regarding the activities of more serious offenders. In other cases, the officer might realize that if he arrests a perpetrator for a minor infraction, then the offender would be released quickly while he (the officer) is required to complete volumes of paperwork.[19]

Law enforcement

Hobbes, along with other social contract theorists, understood law to be essential to civilization and so compelling our obedience. William Pitt, the 18th-century English prime minister, warned, "Where law ends, tyranny begins."[20] Obeying the law, unless it violates a higher moral or natural law, is a moral as well as a legal obligation. Moreover, law enforcement officers and other criminal justice professionals who are entrusted with its enforcement are sworn to enforce the legal code. Thus, for a criminal justice professional not to enforce the law is both illegal and immoral on utilitarian grounds insofar as it invites anarchy and tyranny, and on both deontological and contractarian grounds insofar as it violates one's sacred oath or promise. Deontologists regard keeping a promise as an inviolable moral law or categorical imperative, and contractarians regard it as the mainstay of society. But, an officer would be morally justified (on utilitarian, deontological, and contractarian principles) in deciding not to enforce laws that violated higher moral or natural law. The legal code is not something to be flouted or ignored, but it is not perfect. Apart from possibly contravening moral law, it is inflexible and may be vague; to hearken only to its demands is to invite injustice, disaster, or absurdity. An example of the absurd is a law in England that stipulated that every taxicab carry a bale of hay to feed the horse that pulls it. No police officer in his right mind would enforce this law today, though it may still be unrepealed. There is no way to completely rid the criminal justice system of selective enforcement, and in many instances it is desirable, but since any act of selective enforcement entails a violation of the law by those sworn to uphold it, it requires that officers carefully consider the implications of their decisions.

Whatever the factors influencing the police not to enforce the law, the fact remains that too many of their discretionary decisions are either illegal or quasi-legal in nature: "A most astounding fact about police policy making is that much of it is unauthorized by statute or by ordinance, that some of it is directly contrary to statutes or ordinances, and that the strongest argument for legality rests upon legislative inaction in the fact of long continuing police practices."[21] More seriously, the unbounded discretionary power of the police, when exercised arbitrarily, infringes the principle of comparative justice:[22]

> Policies differ from one patrolman to another, and policies of one patrolman differ from one case to another, in whatever way his idiosyncrasies move him. For instance, a policeman catches one boy in the act, gives him friendly advice, and perhaps drives him home; on another occasion, he catches another boy in the same act, but his mood is different and the boy is arrested, prosecuted, tried, convicted, and sentenced. A policeman makes a deal with a small narcotics peddler, bartering non-enforcement for information, but on another occasion in the same circumstances he arrests a smaller peddler. One policeman arrests for social gambling or for a particular sex offense, another arrests for one and not the other, a third arrests for the other and not for the one, and a fourth for neither, but none of the four administers even-handed justice or has any special incentive to do so.

Davis cites the following three cases of the arbitrary exercise of their discretionary power by the police which are both illegal and unjust:[23]

> For example, the law of Illinois seems entirely clear that gambling is a crime, and that gambling includes

playing "a game of chance or skill for money or other thing of value." ...The statute makes no distinction between commercial gambling and social gambling. But when Chicago police arrested a group of prominent citizens who were playing a friendly game of poker, the superintendent of police announced on the front pages that he was sorry; his policy, he said, was not to arrest for gambling in the absence of a commercial element. What the Illinois legislature had enacted was partly nullified by the police chief. The law for Chicago is not what the legislature enacts; it is what the police chief says to the newspapers.

A 1958 ordinance of the City of Chicago provides: "No pedestrian shall cross a roadway other than in a crosswalk in any business district." A Chicago newspaper reported February 16, 1966: "Chicago Police Supt. Orlando W. Wilson said Tuesday that city policemen will continue to ignore jaywalking. On the basis of a two-month study of cities that enforce jaywalking laws, he explained, his men will leave well enough alone. He said that Chicago's pedestrian death rate is substantially lower than in cities that have had enforcement programs for years." Yet a Chicago ordinance provides: "It shall be the duty of the traffic bureau [within the police department] to make arrests for traffic violations."

Here is an item from the *New York Times* for October 18, 1963: "The police in Port Chester clamp down on professional card gambling when unwritten rules of procedure are violated, not on the basis of laws, testimony before the State Investigation Commission showed yesterday. ...Fred C. Ponty, Chief of Police, gave the commission his view in these words: 'We don't feel if local men are playing cards and there's no money around — we know they probably divide up later — as long as there are no strangers around, we feel we know what's going on and who's there. ...But when 'outsiders' appeared,' he said, 'we don't tolerate it.' "

Discretionary justice and a prosecutor's prerogative

The decision to prosecute a particular criminal case is the sole prerogative of the district attorney. This use of discretion in deciding whether to prosecute or not may be based on a wide variety of factors, not the least of which is the district attorney's chance of winning at trial. Because of the massive overburdening of the criminal courts in this country, only a small percentage of criminal cases actually makes it to the trial phase. Most are disposed of through a plea agreement or through some other administrative remedy (which may include outright dismissal). Prevalent assumptions underlying the prosecutor's use of discretion are that (1) it ought to be exercised, (2) statutory restraints on it may be violated with impunity, (3) it may be exercised secretly without publicizing its rationale or findings, and (4) decisions resulting from its exercise are not subject to judicial review for abuses.[24] Like the police, prosecutors are granted enormous discretionary power which is especially liable to abuse:[25]

> The prosecutor has more control over life, liberty, and reputation than any other person in America. His discretion is tremendous. ...It is in this realm — in which the prosecutor picks some person whom he dislikes or desires to embarrass, or selects some group of unpopular persons and then looks for an offense — that the greatest danger of abuse of prosecuting power lies. It is here that law enforcement becomes personal.

The prosecutor's broad discretionary power is the result of the legal system's taking greater care that justice be ensured at decisions after hearings, rather than at the levels of enforcement and prosecution. The rationale behind this policy is this. It is practically impossible to apprehend, convict, and sentence every criminal because, among other things, there are only so many police. The courts are deluged with cases to be heard, and there is limited space in prisons. Because not all criminals can be brought to justice, it is sufficient that enough are to deter others from crime and that — above all — the innocent are not punished:[26]

> The proper objective of an enforcement program is not the unrealistic one of penalizing all violators but the practical one of penalizing enough violators to induce a satisfactory degree of compliance. Therefore, the prime requirement of justice is not to penalize all violators but is to avoid penalizing the innocent. The conclusion of this line of reasoning usually is justice is done as long as only the guilty are penalized.

The result is the likelihood "that out of a number of cases equally deserving of prosecution, some will be prosecuted and some not, and also that many cases that are prosecuted will be less deserving of prosecution than many others that are not prosecuted."[27]

The primary moral issue in the discretionary justice exercised by prosecutors has been stated by Davis as follows: "If A and B are equally deserving of prosecution, or if A is more deserving of prosecution than B, is a decision to prosecute B but not A unjust?"[28] It would be unjust on the principle of comparative justice if the decision were based solely on the prosecutor's personal antipathy towards B, but not if it were based on some mitigating factor on A's part.

A second issue concerns the viability of the principle that given the practical impossibility of apprehending all those guilty of crimes, justice is served only if enough of the guilty are punished to ensure deterrence, as long as the innocent are not. If expediency is our chief concern, as it would be for a utilitarian, this principle is viable if punishing a sufficient number of the guilty did in fact serve as a deterrent. The principle is logically defective, however, for it confuses the injustice resulting from the unavoidable difficulties of apprehending all criminals with the injustice resulting from the free but flawed deliberations of prosecutors. Prosecutors' failure to make just decisions owing to faulty discretion is not excused by the failure of the police to arrest all criminals, as prosecutors have a choice. "Failures of detection are usually as impersonal as the lightning which hits X and not Y, but unevenness in officers' conscious choices involve the quality of justice the officers are administering."[29] Therefore, not only do prosecutors have a greater opportunity of exercising their discretionary powers more justly than the police have of consistently enforcing the law, but they have the extra responsibility of doing so to compensate for the limitations necessarily imposed on the police in their pursuit of punitive justice.

The principle that only the guilty are to be punished, though not all, might subvert justice by justifying the punishment of A but not B, though both are equally guilty of the same crime, when political or some other kind of extra-judicial pressure is brought to bear on the prosecutor not to prosecute B. Consider the hypothetical case of two drunk drivers, each of whom accidentally kills a person. Both are equally guilty of the same offense. There is a strong case against driver A, who is prosecuted and subsequently convicted and punished. B is not prosecuted due to a technical error which makes the case against him weak, and the prosecutor does not want to waste scarce resources in a trial he might lose. This situation illustrates failure in two forms of justice. First, B's escaping the penalty he deserves is a failure in retributive justice — justice with respect to one individual. Second, A's being penalized, but not B, is a failure in comparative justice — justice in relation to several individuals. Davis notes this failure in comparative justice by observing, "The question of what is justice in any particular case may not be determined by considering only the one case but must be determined in the light of what is done in comparable cases. If equality of treatment is one ingredient of justice, one cannot know whether penalizing B is just without looking at A's case — and C's and D's."[30]

Discretionary justice and sentencing

The discretionary power of judges lies in their interpretation of the administrative rules, which guide conduct within their courts, as well as in the choice of sentences they may impose upon convicted offenders. For many years, the lack of structure in or regulation of that power resulted in widespread disparities in the kinds of sentences imposed by different judges for the same crimes, so much so that "the degree of disparity from one judge to another is widely regarded as a disgrace to the legal system."[31] In 1958, a senate committee published instances of such disparities:[32]

> The Bureau of prisons has advised the committee that an examination of case histories and court statistics indicates that widespread disparities characterize the sentences now imposed by federal judges. During 1957 average sentences to imprisonment for all types of crimes varied from 8.9 months in New Hampshire to 54.6 months in western Oklahoma. The Bureau's study of case histories indicates that the disparities are even more extreme than the statistics reveal. A postal law violator and drug addict ... received a 6-month sentence, while another postal law violator whose crime and background were much less serious received a 3-year sentence. In two similar cases of check forgery, one defendant received a 3-year sentence, while the other received a 24-year sentence. ...Even the proportion of convicted offenders placed on probation for all types of crimes varies widely, ranging from 15.3 percent in western Texas to 68.8 percent in Vermont. ...The existence of wide disparities casts doubt upon the evenhandedness of justice and discourages a respect for the law.

Remedies for such egregious disparities in sentencing were forthcoming, though. In the late 1980s, new sentencing guidelines to regulate the discretion of judges were adopted by the federal government and some states. There aims were stated by Congress as follows:[33]

1. Effectuate the purpose of sentencing (in brief, those purposes are just punishment, incapacitation, and rehabilitation).
2. Provide certainty and fairness in sentencing practices by avoiding unwarranted sentencing disparities among offenders with similar characteristics convicted of similar criminal conduct, while permitting sufficient judicial flexibility to take into account relevant aggravating or mitigating factors.
3. Reflect, to the extent practicable, advancement in knowledge of human behavior as related to the criminal justice process.

Note that these aims embody not only the principle of comparative justice but also the utilitarian and retributive conceptions of punishment. More specifically, in *Furman v. Georgia*, the U.S. Supreme Court endeavored to make the imposition of capital punishment more just by ruling that it "could not be imposed under sentencing procedures that created a substantial risk that it would be inflicted in an arbitrary and capricious manner."[34] Of particular concern was that capital punishment was being imposed in a discriminatory manner, especially against minorities. Justice Marshall expressed this concern by stating that "the burden of capital punishment falls upon the poor, the ignorant, and the underprivileged members of minority groups who are least able to voice their complaints against capital punishment."[35] *Furman v. Georgia* had the effect of invalidating the statutes pertaining to capital punishment of 41 states.

Plea-bargaining

A plea-bargain is "an agreement between the prosecutor and a criminal defendant under which the accused agrees to plead guilty, usually to a lesser offense, in exchange for receiving a lighter sentence than he or she would likely have received had he or she been found guilty after trial on the original charge."[36] The Supreme Court has affirmed that plea-bargaining "is not only an essential part of the process but a highly desirable part."[37] The extent to which plea-bargaining has become an integral part of the American system of criminal justice is indicated by the fact that over 90% of all felony cases resulted in pleas of guilty, most of which result from plea-bargaining.[38]

When a defendant plea-bargains, he waives his constitutional rights of due process: specifically, his right to a trial by jury, his right to be presumed innocent, and his right to be proven guilty beyond a reasonable doubt.[39] Consequently, a decision to plea-bargain ought not to be made lightly. Three conditions must be met to justify the waiving of these rights. One condition is that there be sufficient evidence to support a guilty plea. A second is that the defendant must fully understand what rights are being waived together with the waivers' legal implications.[40] And the third condition is that the defendant must enter into a plea-bargain voluntarily — there must be nary a hint of coercion or undue pressure exerted by the prosecutor.[41]

Although plea-bargaining enjoys the sanction of the law and is virtually indispensable to the smooth running of the judiciary, it is nonetheless morally objectionable. The main objection is that it violates the defendant's rights of due process, particularly the right to be presumed innocent.[42] Furthermore, it actually penalizes those who opt for a jury trial, as they stand to be convicted of a more serious offense and to be punished more severely. At its most fundamental level, plea-bargaining involves playing the values of efficiency and crime control against the values of individual rights and due process. Most seriously, plea-bargaining may tempt defense attorneys and prosecutors to engage in certain morally dubious practices. One such practice is so-called "train justice", where defense attorneys trade off some cases eligible for plea-bargain for others so as to get a better deal on them. A second is overcharging, where prosecutors charge the defendant with either more offenses or offenses of greater seriousness, neither of which actions is warranted by the evidence, in order to give them leverage to bargain down. A third dubious practice is deliberately misleading the defense attorney about the evidence they have against the defendant or the kind of sentence they can obtain for a guilty plea.[43]

Whether or not plea-bargaining is morally objectionable depends on what normative ethical theory one adopts. A utilitarian would see nothing objectionable in plea-bargaining, even in the above-mentioned practices of trading off cases or overcharging defendants, if it furthers the beneficial end of the efficient running of the courts. However, a rule-utilitarian, who is concerned with the long-term consequences of applying certain principles or policies, might take exception if he thought that plea-bargaining might be the first step in a slippery slope leading to abuses of due process, or if prosecutors' cynically exploiting the policy might contribute to the public's disrespect and distrust of the legal system.

The deontologist would find much to object to in plea-bargaining. First, he would object that any violation of a defendant's rights of due process, though legally expedient and even beneficial to the defendant, diminishes his dignity. He would certainly object to the use of defendants and their cases as a means to promoting judicial efficiency, as this involves using persons as other than ends in themselves. And, for the same reason, he would object to the practice of "train justice".

Plea-bargaining, however, is morally objectionable on other than teleological or deontological grounds. It involves a fundamental miscarriage of justice. First, it involves a miscarriage of proportionate justice that requires that punishment fit the crime. When a defendant is able to plead guilty to a lesser charge — assuming that he committed the offense that he was originally charged with — he unjustly escapes the penalty due to his offense. On the other hand, if he pleads guilty to a lesser charge and is sentenced accordingly, but had he gone to trial he would have been acquitted by the jury of the greater charge, then he must unjustly pay the penalty that he might have avoided. In either case, then, the penalty paid by a guilty defendant will not depend on the actual crime he committed. Second, plea-bargaining involves a miscarriage of comparative justice. The penalty guilty defendants receive will depend on whether they plea-bargain or not and, if they do, on the bargaining skills of the defense attorney and the prosecutor; consequently, there can be a wide disparity in the sentences imposed on them.

Notes

1. Davis, Kenneth C., *Discretionary Justice: A Preliminary Inquiry*, Louisiana State University Press, Baton Rouge, 1969, pp. 9–11.

2. Davis, Kenneth C., *Discretionary Justice: A Preliminary Inquiry*, Louisiana State University Press, Baton Rouge, 1969, p. 4. This definition along with my actual and theoretical discussion of discretionary justice is derived from Davis' study.

3. Davis, Kenneth C., *Discretionary Justice: A Preliminary Inquiry*, Louisiana State University Press, Baton Rouge, 1969, p. 4.

4. Davis, Kenneth C., *Discretionary Justice: A Preliminary Inquiry*, Louisiana State University Press, Baton Rouge, 1969, p. 106.

5. Davis, Kenneth C., *Discretionary Justice: A Preliminary Inquiry*, Louisiana State University Press, Baton Rouge, 1969, p. 107.

6. Pound, Dean, *Jurisprudence*, 1959, p. 355 (as quoted in Davis, Kenneth C., *Discretionary Justice: A Preliminary Inquiry*, Louisiana State University Press, Baton Rouge, 1969, p. 17).

7. Williams, Glanville, *Salmond on Jurisprudence*, 11th ed., 1957, p. 44 (cited in Davis, Kenneth C., *Discretionary Justice: A Preliminary Inquiry*, Louisiana State University Press, Baton Rouge, 1969, pp. 17–18).

8. Davis, Kenneth C., *Discretionary Justice: A Preliminary Inquiry*, Louisiana State University Press, Baton Rouge, 1969, p. 18.

9. Breitel, Charles D., Controls in criminal law enforcement, *University of Chicago Law Review*, 27, 427–428, 1960 (quoted in Davis, Kenneth C., *Discretionary Justice: A Preliminary Inquiry*, Louisiana State University Press, Baton Rouge, 1969, p. 18).

10. Davis, Kenneth C., *Discretionary Justice: A Preliminary Inquiry*, Louisiana State University Press, Baton Rouge, 1969, p. 18.

11. Davis, Kenneth C., *Discretionary Justice: A Preliminary Inquiry*, Louisiana State University Press, Baton Rouge, 1969, pp. V, 15.

12. Davis, Kenneth C., *Discretionary Justice: A Preliminary Inquiry*, Louisiana State University Press, Baton Rouge, 1969, p. 12.

13. Davis, Kenneth C., *Discretionary Justice: A Preliminary Inquiry*, Louisiana State University Press, Baton Rouge, 1969, p. 12.

14. Cited in Davis, Kenneth C., *Discretionary Justice: A Preliminary Inquiry*, Louisiana State University Press, Baton Rouge, 1969, p. 13.

15. *Report of the National Advisory Commission on Civil Disorders*, 1968, p. 7 (cited in Davis, Kenneth C., *Discretionary Justice: A Preliminary Inquiry*, Louisiana State University Press, Baton Rouge, 1969, p. 81).

16. President's Commission on Law Enforcement and Administration of Justice, *The Challenge of Crime in a Free Society*, 1967, p. 99 (as cited by Davis, Kenneth C., *Discretionary Justice: A Preliminary Inquiry*, Louisiana State University Press, Baton Rouge, 1969, p. 81).

17. Davis, Kenneth C., *Discretionary Justice: A Preliminary Inquiry*, Louisiana State University Press, Baton Rouge, 1969, p. 163.

18. Davis, Kenneth C., *Discretionary Justice: A Preliminary Inquiry*, Louisiana State University Press, Baton Rouge, 1969, p. 230.

19. This list is paraphrased from Davis, Kenneth C., *Discretionary Justice: A Preliminary Inquiry*, Louisiana State University Press, Baton Rouge, 1969, pp. 81–83.

20. Davis, Kenneth C., *Discretionary Justice: A Preliminary Inquiry*, Louisiana State University Press, Baton Rouge, 1969, p. 3.

21. Davis, Kenneth C., *Discretionary Justice: A Preliminary Inquiry*, Louisiana State University Press, Baton Rouge, 1969, p. 84.

22. Davis, Kenneth C., *Discretionary Justice: A Preliminary Inquiry*, Louisiana State University Press, Baton Rouge, 1969, p. 90.

23. Davis, Kenneth C., *Discretionary Justice: A Preliminary Inquiry*, Louisiana State University Press, Baton Rouge, 1969, pp. 84–86, 90.

24. Davis, Kenneth C., *Discretionary Justice: A Preliminary Inquiry*, Louisiana State University Press, Baton Rouge, 1969, pp. 188–189.

25. Justice Jackson, in *Journal of the American Judicial Society*, 24, 18–19, 1940 (cited in Davis, Kenneth C., *Discretionary Justice: A Preliminary Inquiry*, Louisiana State University Press, Baton Rouge, 1969, p. 190).

26. Davis, Kenneth C., *Discretionary Justice: A Preliminary Inquiry*, Louisiana State University Press, Baton Rouge, 1969, p. 168.

27. Davis, Kenneth C., *Discretionary Justice: A Preliminary Inquiry*, Louisiana State University Press, Baton Rouge, 1969, p. 167.

28. Davis, Kenneth C., *Discretionary Justice: A Preliminary Inquiry*, Louisiana State University Press, Baton Rouge, 1969, p. 167.

29. Davis, Kenneth C., *Discretionary Justice: A Preliminary Inquiry*, Louisiana State University Press, Baton Rouge, 1969, p. 169.

30. Davis, Kenneth C., *Discretionary Justice: A Preliminary Inquiry*, Louisiana State University Press, Baton Rouge, 1969, p. 170.

31. Davis, Kenneth C., *Discretionary Justice: A Preliminary Inquiry*, Louisiana State University Press, Baton Rouge, 1969, p. 133.

32. Senate Reports, No. 2013, 85th Congress (quoted in Davis, Kenneth C., *Discretionary Justice: A Preliminary Inquiry*, Louisiana State University Press, Baton Rouge, 1969, pp. 133–134).

33. U.S.C.A. 991 (b) (cited in Gardner, Thomas J. and Anderson, Terry M., *Criminal Law: Principles and Cases*, 5th ed., West Publishing, St. Paul, MN, 1992, pp. 214–215).

34. 408 U.S. 238, 92 S. Ct. 2726 (cited in Gardner, Thomas J. and Anderson, Terry M., *Criminal Law: Principles and Cases*, 5th ed., West Publishing, St. Paul, MN, 1992, p. 211).

35. 408 U.S. 366, 92 S. Ct. 2791 (cited in Gardner, Thomas J. and Anderson, Terry M., *Criminal Law: Principles and Cases*, 5th ed., West Publishing, St. Paul, MN, 1992, p. 210).

36. Hall, Daniel E., *Criminal Procedure and the Constitution*, West Publishing, Albany, NY, 1997, p. 199.

37. *Santobello v. New York*, 404 U.S. 257, 261 (cited in Hall, Daniel E., *Criminal Procedure and the Constitution*, West Publishing, Albany, NY, 1997, p. 200).

38. Hall, Daniel E., *Criminal Procedure and the Constitution*, West Publishing, Albany, NY, 1997, p. 199.

39. Hall, Daniel E., *Criminal Procedure and the Constitution*, West Publishing, Albany, NY, 1997, p. 200.

40. *Boykim v. Alabama*, 395 U.S. 238 (cited in Hall, Daniel E., *Criminal Procedure and the Constitution*, West Publishing, Albany, NY, 1997, p. 200).

41. Hall, Daniel E., *Criminal Procedure and the Constitution*, West Publishing, Albany, NY, 1997, p. 200.
42. Hall, Daniel E., *Criminal Procedure and the Constitution*, West Publishing, Albany, NY, 1997, p. 201.
43. Pollock, Joycelyn M., *Ethics in Crime and Justice: Dilemmas and Decisions*, 3rd ed., Wadsworth, Belmont, CA, 1998, pp. 227–241.

chapter eleven

Juvenile justice

"I want a boy, and he mustn't be a big un. Lord!" said
Mr. Sikes, reflectively, "If I'd only got that young boy
of Ned, the chimbley-sweeper's! He kept him small on
purpose, and let him out by the job. But the father gets
lagged; and then the Juvenile Delinquent Society comes,
and takes the boy away from a trade where he was
earning money, teaches him to read and write, and in
time makes a 'prentice of him. And so they go on," said
Mr. Sikes, his wrath rising with the recollection of his
wrongs. "So they go on; and, if they'd got money enough
... we shouldn't have half-a-dozen boys left in the
whole trade, in a year or two."

—Charles Dickens *(Oliver Twist)*

Juvenile crime

In the spring of 1998 in Jonesboro, AK, Andrew Golden and Mitchell
Johnson, 11 and 13 years old, respectively, pulled a school fire alarm
and then opened fire on the group of teachers and students who had
gathered outside the building in response to the false alarm.[1] In 1995,
Craig Price of Rhode Island committed the first of four murders at the
age of 13.[2] And, in England in 1996, two 10-year-old boys kidnapped
a toddler at a shopping mall, took him to a deserted railway track, and
there savagely beat him to death.[3] Unfortunately, these are not isolated occurrences. Since the 1970s, there has been an alarming rise in

violent crime committed by juveniles, some as young as age 9.[4] Humes, citing figures from the U.S. Justice Department's Office of Juvenile Justice and Delinquency Prevention's (OJJDP) statistical report for 1994 (based on the calendar year of 1992), reports "a 175 percent increase in juvenile murder rates since the 1970s, with similar boosts in juvenile crime of all kinds. Just in the last five years, violent offenses by children — murder, rape, assault, robbery — have risen 68 percent." He also cites the Justice Department's publication, *Juvenile Offenders and Victims* (May 1995), to the effect that "Juveniles are responsible for one in five violent crimes, one in three burglaries, and nearly half of all arsons and auto thefts."[5] Currie corroborates these findings with his own:[6]

> Indeed, the epidemic of violence that began in the mid-1980s was concentrated among the young, who were both its main instigators and its main victims. Violence among the young has, at this writing, fallen off from its early-1990s peak, but outside of a handful of cities … it remains higher than it was before the sharp percent rises, which brought many cities the worst levels of youth violence in their history. Juvenile arrests for violent crimes fell by 4 percent during 1995, but that followed a 64 percent rise in the previous seven years.

Between 1968 and 1993, the number of murders committed by young people between the ages of 15 and 24 more than doubled. According to the FBI, juveniles committed 13% of all violent crimes cleared by arrest during 1996. Arrests for homicide among juveniles increased 93% from 1988 to 1992. Currie reported in 1991 that, annually, over a million youngsters are committed to juvenile institutions. Between 1985 and 1989, the proportion of the adolescent population confined in juvenile facilities increased by 20%.[7] These statistics indicate a modern trend in which juvenile delinquents pose as great a threat to society as do adult criminals.

    In response to the upswing in juvenile crime and violence, there has been a movement away from the historically solicitous attitude of society toward juvenile criminals. American society has voiced its dissatisfaction with the apparently poor results achieved by the current rehabilitative-based juvenile justice system and has demanded that the system be reformed in the direction of retributive punishment. This "get tough" approach is intended to meet the demands of justice and relieve the suffering of victims, as opposed to promoting the well-being of the delinquent. Other factors amplifying this call to change include the high rates of recidivism, the scant availability of successful rehabilitation programs, and the lack of government funding available for rehabilitative efforts.[8] Thus, in 1985, Alfred Regnery, Administrator of the U.S. Office of Juvenile Justice and Delinquency Prevention, recommended that juvenile justice should stress deterrence, and that the distinction between juvenile and adult criminals should be blurred by leaving the court records of juveniles unsealed.[9] In 1995, the International Association of Chiefs of Police, among others, echoed Regnery's recommendation by declaring that juvenile justice should aim at retribution over rehabilitation.[10]

This call to reform juvenile justice away from rehabilitation and towards retribution and deterrence has been heeded by a number of state legislatures. In 1977, California amended its Welfare and Institutions Code to the effect that juvenile courts should take into account "the protection of the public" in their determinations. In 1978, New York State decreed that proceedings against adolescents between the ages of 13 and 15 be initiated in superior court.[11] In 1995, Texas lowered the age at which juveniles may be tried as adults from 15 to 14, relaxed restrictions on identification procedures for juvenile suspects, made most juvenile hearings public, and opened the way to sentencing delinquents convicted of some felonies to as much as 40 years in prison. In 1995, Minnesota implemented a policy of "extended jurisdiction" whereby delinquents would be sentenced as adults if they failed to meet the conditions of their juvenile sentences; furthermore, these extended jurisdiction trials would be public.[12] The need for rescinding the privileges traditionally accorded to juvenile suspects brought before juvenile courts was dramatically illustrated in the case of the 14-year-old transfer student who stabbed his pregnant teacher to death. The student had a record of violent offenses, but this information was withheld from the administration of his new school because of his right to privacy as a juvenile. Moreover, in the case of *New Jersey v. T.L.O.* a school principal had found marijuana during the search of a student's purse. The student was subsequently found delinquent in juvenile court. The New Jersey Supreme Court ruled that the principal's search was unreasonable and was an infringement of the student's right to privacy.[13]

A more extreme manifestation of the retributive policy towards young criminals may be seen in the trend of transferring jurisdiction of juvenile suspects (in some states as young as 13 years) from juvenile court to superior court where they are adjudicated as adults. Judgments in two such cases were appealed to the Supreme Court (resulting in landmark decisions) which highlight the legal issues surrounding modern juvenile justice. The first relevant case was *Kent v. U.S.* (1966). In 1959, a 14-year-old named Morris Kent, Jr., was charged with several burglaries in the District of Columbia. Kent was tried for the crimes and placed on juvenile probation. He was then released to the custody of his mother. In 1961, Kent was charged with rape and burglary; however, the juvenile court judge ruled that Kent be remanded to superior court for trial, giving no explanation for his ruling. He was convicted of six counts of burglary and robbery and was sentenced from 5 to 15 years in prison for each count. On appeal, Kent argued that he ought to have had a full hearing in juvenile court; as a result, his conviction in superior court was unjust. The Supreme Court agreed. This decision mandated that before the transferal of juveniles to superior court, a minimum level of due process must be observed in juvenile court hearings — specifically, that juveniles be accorded a formal hearing and be represented by an attorney. The second case was *Breed v. Jones* (1975). In 1971, at an adjudicatory hearing in juvenile court, Jones, a robbery suspect, was found delinquent and remanded to superior court for trial. Jones was convicted of first-degree robbery and was sentenced to prison. Jones appealed his conviction on the grounds of double jeopardy, as he had already been adjudicated in juvenile court for the same offense. The Supreme Court concurred. This decision is significant because it limited the conditions under which a transfer from juvenile court to superior court may be made. It specifically stipulated that the transfer of juveniles occur before adjudicatory hearings in juvenile courts are conducted. The Supreme Court's decisions in these cases are more generally significant inasmuch as they affirm that juveniles have the right to the same due process guaranteed to adults.[14]

The rights of the victims of juvenile crimes — specifically, the victims' right to restitution for the wrongs they have suffered — have not been lost in the impulse to reform the system of juvenile justice. On behalf of the victims of juvenile crimes, the OJJDP recently created a victim restitution program for juvenile court. The Restitution, Education, Specialized Training, and Technical Assistance (RESTTA) Program is intended to fulfill this need.[15] Victims rights have become an urgent matter, as a higher proportion of juveniles are being arrested for violent crimes.

The more stringent attitude toward juvenile crime has resulted in more punitive measures being taken not only against juvenile delinquents but also against their parents. Parents of delinquents are increasingly being held legally accountable for their offsprings' actions. Thus, under California's Street Terrorism and Enforcement and Prevention Act, Gloria Williams was indicted after her 15-year-old son was charged with rape. The California Supreme Court unanimously upheld that state's family responsibility law in the case of Williams v. Carcetti.[16] Since 1995, parents in Silverton, OR, may be fined up to $1000 for crimes committed by their children.[17] Since 1995, more than 100 municipalities throughout the nation have enacted, or are considering the enactment of, ordinances like Silverton's.[18] Atlanta passed a municipal ordinance requiring an 11:00 p.m. curfew for juveniles under 17 years of age. The parents of juveniles who violate this curfew may face a $1000 fine. Washington, D.C., followed Atlanta's lead and instituted a similar curfew.[19] The state of Oregon passed a parental responsibility law in 1995 which directed that parents, after a warning, be fined up to $1000 and be required to attend parenting classes if their children are deemed delinquent.[20]

The system of juvenile justice

The criminal justice system in the United States is not a single governmental system. It is, rather, a vast and loosely organized network of systems operating at the federal, state, and local levels which fall under the headings of law enforcement, courts, and corrections. Juvenile court is a branch of the court system and normally operates at the local level. The idea that juvenile offenders should be treated differently from adult criminals emerged in the United States during the first quarter of the 19th century, though its roots may be traced to the Chancery Courts of medieval England. It was believed that children, because of their youth, should not be held in close proximity to adult criminals and that the courts should make every effort to protect and rehabilitate them. Prior to this time, juveniles convicted of offenses were essentially treated the same as adult offenders. In 1824, the Society for the Reformation of Juvenile Delinquents was granted a charter by the New York State Legislature to establish a House of Refuge for abandoned, neglected, and delinquent children in New York City. The first state-operated juvenile institution was opened in Massachusetts in 1847. By 1875, a majority of the remaining states had created similar agencies; in 1899, with its Juvenile Court Act, the Illinois legislature established the first truly separate juvenile court in Cook County. The Illinois law became the model for juvenile court laws nationally. It legally established the distinction between juvenile and superior (criminal) courts and stipulated that the court should serve the juveniles' best interests through rehabilitation rather than retribution.[21] At the federal level, the Juvenile Court Act of 1938 incorporated the main provisions of the Illinois Act, and by 1945 every state in the union had established a juvenile court system.[22]

Notwithstanding the uniformity in juvenile courts required by federal mandate, they enjoy considerable latitude with respect to their jurisdiction, based as it is on state law. Much of this latitude is centered on the age of the offender and the offense he is alleged to have committed. Generally speaking, a juvenile is defined as a person under the age of 18 years, but in some states (e.g., Texas and Illinois) a person 17 years old or younger is considered a juvenile. In North Carolina, New York, and Connecticut, the protective designation of "juvenile" is extended only to those offenders under the age of 16 years. In some states, juvenile courts have *exclusive jurisdiction* over juveniles who commit status offenses such as truancy, but not over those who violate the criminal code. In other states, juvenile courts have *original jurisdiction*, or the sole authority to initiate proceedings against juveniles who have committed either status offenses or criminal violations. In still other states, though, the principle of *concurrent jurisdiction* allows superior courts to initiate proceedings against juvenile offenders who have committed serious felonies. All state governments and the federal government provide for judicial waivers, which permit juveniles suspected of serious felonies to be remanded to superior court. And Delaware, Louisiana, and Nevada permit no juvenile court jurisdiction at all over juveniles charged with first-degree murder.[23]

Some municipalities have instituted alternatives to traditional juvenile court, particularly for minor, non-violent offenses. In Delaware County, PA, "Youth Aid Panels" made up of private citizens who volunteer their time, adjudicate cases involving juvenile delinquents in lieu of a juvenile court.[24] In 1980, Columbus County in Georgia empowered its juvenile court to allow convicted juvenile offenders to appear before a jury of their peers during the disposition phase of their hearing.[25] In 1983, the Junior League of Odessa, TX, instituted a "Teen Court" where all the participants in the hearing process, with the exception of the presiding judge, are selected from the local youth population. The teenage participants have the authority to determine the sentence imposed on the offender; only 2% of the juveniles adjudicated by the Teen Court went on to commit further crimes.[26]

The principal differences between juvenile court and superior court stem from the former's traditional goal of rehabilitation over retribution. Thus, the privacy of juvenile offenders is strictly protected and their dispositions are more often determined and informed by the theories of social science rather than by the strict demands of retributive justice. The principle of discretionary justice is given full play in the adjudication of juvenile cases. Convicted juveniles typically receive probation or short terms of detention rather than lengthy periods of incarceration. With its emphasis on rehabilitation, the juvenile court seeks to meet the distinctive needs of juvenile delinquents while protecting the interests of society. The juvenile court system is designed to accommodate three groups of juveniles: (1) delinquents who violate the criminal code, (2) status offenders who commit such offenses as truancy or running away, (3) dependent children who have no parents or guardians, and (4) abused or neglected children.[27]

Moral concepts and issues in juvenile justice

As perhaps has already occurred to you, the administration of the juvenile court system in the United States presupposes some fundamental moral concepts — especially those relating to justice — that need to be made explicit and examined and raises a welter of moral issues that beg to be resolved. Traditionally, roughly from the passage of the Illinois Act in 1899 to the 1970s, the principal aim of the juvenile court was conceived of as rehabilitation — deterring the delinquent from committing further crimes and returning him to society as a law-abiding and productive citizen. The theory of punitive justice, and the more general moral theory, underpinning this rehabilitative conception of juvenile justice (whether explicitly acknowledged or not) is utilitarianism. A yet more fundamental assumption is the immeasurable value of the child, someone who is worthy of rehabilitation and, because of his essential difference from the adult, especially amenable to it. A political assumption made by this conception is that the state is the patron of all children residing within its bounds, having both the legal and moral authority to act in the child's best interest. *Parens patriae* (literally, "the father of his country") is a legal concept that traces its roots to the Chancery Courts of England in the middle ages. The King was considered to be the father of all of his subjects and through the court, his representative, was entitled to act as the parent of a delinquent child. A problematic implication of this rehabilitative concept of juvenile justice is that the due process expected in proceedings against adult criminals may be suspended in order to promote the best interests of the child. The Supreme Court has sought to balance this due process/child's best interest dilemma through four landmark rulings in prominent juvenile cases.[28]

Since about the 1970s, however, there has been an alarming rise in violent crime and serious felonies committed by juveniles. Public outrage at this increase has prompted lawmakers to re-evaluate the nation's stance on punishing juvenile criminals. The principle aim of the juvenile court today is shifting from rehabilitation to retribution, either for its own sake or as an attempt to deter other juveniles from committing crime, as well as for promoting public safety. Underlying this redefinition of the purpose of the juvenile court is either the retributive theory of punitive justice and some form of deontological ethics or the contractarian theory (again, whether explicitly acknowledged or not). Deeper assumptions are that the child is not essentially distinct from the adult, at least with respect to culpability for misbehavior, and that the state should not overreach its authority by acting as a surrogate parent but instead should fulfill its proper function of protecting society from criminals. An implication of this retributive conception of juvenile justice is that even children are not exempt from the legal requirements (and privileges) of due process. Thus, in the history of the juvenile court in the United States, three distinct theories of punitive justice have been operative (either implicitly or explicitly): the utilitarian, the retributive, and the contractarian, along with the ethical theories they presuppose.

Our above discussion of the administration of the juvenile court system raises weighty legal and moral issues, but we are concerned here only with the latter, as they fall within the scope of the ethical dimension of criminal justice. Legal issues such as whether juvenile defendants may waive their rights under Miranda, though no less important, belong more properly to jurisprudence or the philosophy of law. Now, these specifically moral issues (or issues of justice) can be grouped under eight headings:

1. Purpose of juvenile justice
2. Role of due process
3. Right to privacy
4. Culpability of parents for a juvenile's conduct
5. Relationship of the state to the family
6. Treatment of minority juveniles

7. Disparities in the disposition of juvenile cases
8. Trying juvenile offenders as adults

The first is perhaps the fundamental issue raised by the administra-tion of the juvenile court system — namely, whether rehabilitation or retribution is the proper end of juvenile justice.

The second issue concerns the place of due process in juvenile court. To what degree, if at all, should due process be granted or suspended in juvenile cases, even in the honorable pursuit of the juvenile's best interest? Under the current system, juveniles may be incarcerated for a variety of status offenses (which do not apply to adults) simply because they are under a legal age limit. So, should juveniles be punished for behavior that adults would not be punished for?

The third issue involves privacy. Should a juvenile suspect enjoy a greater or lesser right to privacy than is given to adult suspects? Due process guarantees the adult suspect certain rights, yet the courts have denied some of these rights to juveniles because of their age.

The fourth issue has to do with the responsibility of parents. Should the family bond be used as a method of social control by the state? Is it acceptable that parents are held accountable for the actions of their child, and should they be punished for those actions along with the child or perhaps in his place? The American Civil Liberties Union thinks not; it contends that punishing parents for their children's crimes is egregiously unjust, as it punishes a person for another's offense.[29]

The fifth issue revolves about the power of the state and its limits. How far does the legitimate authority of the state extend? Does it include the prerogative to intervene in households where juveniles receive little or no supervision? What about state interventions in homes where child neglect and abuse are suspected? A controversial case where the federal government intervened in an unorthodox do-mestic arrangement is that of David Koresh and the Branch Davidians. In 1993 in Waco, TX, federal justice officials cited suspected child abuse as a factor in their decision to raid the Branch Davidian com-pound. This action resulted in a firefight in which several federal agents were killed or wounded, an armed siege, and the eventual burning of the compound which killed Koresh and many of his fol-lowers (including the allegedly abused children).[30]

The sixth issue concerns the treatment of minorities in juvenile court. Statistically, minority males make up a disproportionate num-ber of the suspects who appear before juvenile courts. Prothrow-Stith reports, "Approximately one in four African-American males between the ages of 20 and 29 is incarcerated, on probation, or on parole.[31]

The seventh issue involves the disparity in adjudication of juveniles in the United States. The United States has 50 states, the District of Columbia, and several territories within its constitutional bounds. Due to the governmental autonomy granted each of these jurisdictions by the federal constitution, we have over 50 different juvenile justice systems in operation within this country. Thus, there are wide disparities between these systems and the way they operate — differences such as the ages at which juveniles may be tried as adults and in the forms of jurisdiction that may be exercised by juvenile courts (exclusive, original, or concurrent). There are also wide disparities in penalties that may be given to juveniles convicted of crimes. These differences are especially critical in capital cases. In Texas, a 14-year-old may be tried as an adult for first-degree murder and, if convicted, may be executed shortly after his 18th birthday; whereas, in Massachusetts, he may face neither trial as an adult nor execution. The issue raised by such disparities is whether or not they violate the principle of comparative justice that stipulates that similar cases should be treated similarly. In other words, are not juveniles entitled to receive comparable treatment for comparable offenses, or does the American system of government make that impossible?

Finally, the eighth issue is whether juveniles should be tried as adults, or executed for capital crimes. Our resolution of this moral issue depends on how we resolve three more basic metaphysical issues: When does a child become an adult? What are the criteria that a person needs to fulfill in order to qualify as an adult? What are the morally relevant differences between children and adults such that they should be treated differently by the legal system? A resolution of these three metaphysical issues of what constitutes adulthood and its distinction from childhood has a bearing on how we resolve virtually all of the above moral issues; we need now to consider them. Though the resolution of these metaphysical issues would be a baffling and controversial task requiring some knowledge of developmental psychology, it is nevertheless important to clarify them.

What most concerns us are the *morally* relevant differences between adults and children which justify the legal system's treating them differently from adults. In the popular view (which is the one that perhaps informs jurisprudence governing juveniles), to qualify as a morally "mature" adult and thus be held culpable for one's misdeeds a person must be fully "rational" in the Kantian sense, or "morally accountable". Minimally, he must be able to distinguish between right and wrong, understand the differences between them, and be free to act on his moral choices. Infants and toddlers clearly lack full rationality and moral maturity, and so are not held criminally accountable. Recalling Kant, rationality entails and entitles one to liability for punishment. The problem is how to classify children from early pre-puberty (say, age 5) through late adolescence (ages 16 to 18). Are they rationally and morally mature enough to be punished as adults for their criminal offenses, and how do we make this determination? One useful method is Lawrence Kohlberg's stages of moral development.

Kohlberg's stages of moral development

Kohlberg, who has long been preoccupied with the problems of moral psychology and education, has formulated a theory according to which every person moves sequentially through increasingly more sophisticated levels and stages of moral thought to moral maturity. These stages are an invariant sequence through which all people must pass in specific order, though we do so at different rates and might stop (become fixated) at any stage short of the final one. Furthermore, these stages are universal; persons in non-Western cultures as well as Western culture pass through them. Kohlberg derived his theory of the stages of moral development from the work of Jean Piaget, who theorized about the stages of cognitive development in children. Kohlberg built on Piaget's ideas and suggested that moral development depends upon and so parallels cognitive or logical development. In Kohlberg's words, "moral judgment has a characteristic form at a given stage and that this form is parallel to the form of intellectual judgment at a corresponding stage. This implies a *parallelism* or *isomorphism* between the development of the forms of logical and ethical judgment."[32] Thus, Kohlberg has found empirical justification for an insight that dates back to Plato; namely, there is a correlation between cognitive maturity and moral maturity. Kohlberg does make the qualification that intelligence is a necessary, but not sufficient, condition for sound moral judgment and action. As history has shown us, one may be supremely intelligent, yet still be a moral moron.[33]

In his longitudinal studies of children, adolescents, and adults, Kohlberg has discerned three levels of moral development, each level being divided into two stages for a total of six.[34] Each stage presupposes passage through the previous stage and represents an advance over it. The three levels, as indicated by their names, correspond fundamentally to "three different types of relationships between the *self* and *society's rules and expectations*."[35] The description of each stage is a generalization based on interviews with select subjects who were given hypothetical moral dilemmas to resolve. Kohlberg points out that few completely or perfectly exemplify any given stage; thus, typically one may still be partly within a previous stage as he moves into the next or, while occupying a given stage, one may be in the process of moving into the subsequent one.

The first level (level A) is the pre-conventional level. An individual at this level perceives social rules and expectations as being external to himself. Those typically at this level are most juveniles under 9 years, some adolescents, and many juvenile delinquents and adult criminals. The normative ethical theory tacitly held by persons at the pre-conventional level — particularly at the second stage — is moral egoism. Level A contains the first stage of moral development, which is the stage of punishment and obedience. Persons at this stage conceive of moral rightness as obeying rules and authority for the sake of obedience; more specifically, it is refraining from physically hurting other persons or damaging their property. They make no distinction between the moral value of an individual human life and its social or physical value; in their eyes, the more physically strong or more socially prestigious an individual the more value he has. Their motives for doing what is morally right are avoidance of punishment and fear of the superior power of those in authority. Their viewpoint is egocentric; they ignore the interests of others, or fail to consider that these interests may differ from their own. Actions are judged in terms of the physical consequences to themselves, not the psychological interests of others. Finally, they confuse the perspective of authority with their own. Level A also contains the second stage of moral development, or the stage of individual instrumental purpose and exchange. Here, moral rightness is conceived of as pursuing one's own interests and allowing others to do likewise. Fairness is thought of in terms of contracts involving the equal exchange of goods or services. Persons at this stage value human life according to how it satisfies its possessor and others and distinguish between the value of life to one's self and its value to others. Their motive for acting rightly is self-interest, a desire for reward or benefit. They view the prospect of punishment for misdeeds pragmatically and may dismiss feelings of guilt that might result from wrongdoing. Their social perspective is individualistic; they are able to separate their own interests and attitudes from those of others such as those in authority. Finally, their strategy for resolving conflicts of interest is by making informal contracts or deals wherein benefits are exchanged for losses.

The next level up (Level B) is the conventional level, and, as the name suggests, people on this level are preoccupied with conforming to and upholding moral and social rules. The individual identifies himself with, or has internalized, social rules and expectations, especially of those in authority. Most adolescents and adults are at this level. Level B is basically deontological in orientation, although with a utilitarian strain. Within Level B is the third developmental stage, which is the stage of mutual interpersonal expectations, relationships, and conformity. The conception of moral rightness operating here is that of playing one's social role well and living up to others' expectations as to how one should behave. People at this stage are concerned with "being good", which consists of acting from principled motives and out of concern for others. They seek to sustain social relationships by cultivating and practicing the virtues of trust, loyalty, respect, and gratitude. For them, a person's value depends upon others' love for him for himself, not upon his usefulness to them or any pleasure he might give them. In Kantian language, a person is valued as an end in himself, not as a means to an end. Their motive for behaving morally is the approval of others or their own (that approval may be actual or hypothetical). Finally, people at this stage understand themselves to be fundamentally and inextricably bound in relationship with others; the feelings of others and commitments to them take precedence over personal interests. They generally abide by the Golden Rule (Kant's principle of reversibility).

The fourth stage is also located in Level B. This is the stage concerned with maintaining the social system and with conscience maintenance. Here, the morally right is conceived of essentially as the performance of one's duties. Laws must be obeyed unless they conflict with rules of a higher nature. It is the stage of law and order. People at this stage put the highest premium on maintaining the social order and contributing to the common good. For them, human life is sacred; its value is rooted in an objective moral order that transcends any social order. Kohlberg agrees with the sociologist Emile Durkheim (1858–1917) that the fourth stage is the "normal" adult morality for any society.[36] The motives for doing what is morally right at this stage are the perpetuation of the social group, a clear conscience (self respect) from meeting one's obligations, and the dread of dishonor (institutionalized blame) and guilt over harming others. People at this stage are able to distinguish formal dishonor from informal disapproval, and guilt from social disapproval. They adhere to the principle that the same law applies to everybody (Kant's principle of universalizability). Finally, these people understand that it is society that specifies the rules and roles for its members; they evaluate interpersonal relations according to their place within the social system.

Between Level B and Level C, Kohlberg posits the existence of an intermediary level, which he calls Level B/C, or the transitional level. Here, moral choices are understood as personal, subjective, and emotionally based. Moral concepts such as conscience, duty, and moral rightness are regarded as arbitrary and relative. Persons at this stage see themselves as autonomous individuals standing outside of society and making choices independently of loyalties to or contracts with society. They consider themselves free to pick and choose among socially defined obligations according to their tastes, but not to any principle. This transitional level smacks of ethical relativism.

At the pinnacle of moral development is Level C, which is the post-conventional and principled level. At this level of moral development, the individual is capable of disassociating himself from social rules and expectations and lives by freely chosen moral principles which he understands as transcending and undergirding social moral codes. Only a minority of adults ever attain this level of moral development, and then only after reaching psychological and social maturity. Depending on the stage, the normative ethical theories operating on this level are forms of the social contract and natural law theories.

Contained within Level C is the fifth stage, the stage of honoring human rights and the social contract and utility. At this stage, people are, to a degree, moral relativists for whom moral rightness consists of conformity to the moral values indigenous to the particular society or culture of which they are a part. These individuals are moral absolutists to the extent that they consider such rights as the rights to life and liberty as inviolable. For them, the value of human life is intrinsic, and the obligation to respect it is absolute. Their motives for doing what is morally right are respect for the social contract, a concern for the public good, and a desire to maintain their own self-respect as well as the respect of the community. They understand that there are certain moral values that transcend any social order and from which social norms are derived and receive their legitimacy. These persons make a clear distinction between the civil and the moral law, which may be in conflict.

The sixth stage, within Level C, is the stage of universal ethical principles. At this stage, people are moral absolutists with respect to moral values such as justice and respect for human rights and dignity. They consider certain moral laws as universally binding and to which civil laws must conform. They regard human life as sacrosanct because of the intrinsic value of persons and distinguish between moral respect for human beings and legally honoring their rights. They respect persons as ends in themselves and not as means. People who have reached this stage are motivated to do what is morally right from a conviction of the validity of their moral principles and from fear of self-condemnation over betraying them. These individuals differentiate between the respect of the community and their own self-respect. They believe that there is a natural or objective moral law that precedes and grounds the social contract. Individuals who have reached the sixth stage are morally autonomous, in the Kantian sense.[37]

Kohlberg's stages and juvenile justice

Kohlberg's theory of moral development suggests that there are significant morally relevant differences between children and adults that would justify their distinct and separate adjudication. One such difference is that children under 9 years of age, and even some adolescents, are at the pre-conventional level of moral development, the lowest level, whereas most adults and adolescents are at the conventional level, particularly its fourth stage, which is thought normal for adults. Associated with the difference in these levels is that a sense of guilt (moral self-judgment), which depends on the person's internalization of mature moral values, does not emerge until late childhood or pre-adolescence. According to Kohlberg, "projective-test studies indicate that self-critical guilt appears at about the same age as conventional moral judgment."[38] Furthermore, the lower stages of moral judgment are perhaps not authentically moral at all. Echoing Kant, Kohlberg claims that moral judgments, to qualify as such, must be "universal, inclusive, consistent, and grounded on objective, impersonal, or ideal grounds" and goes on to explain:[39]

> When a ten year old at Stage 1 answers the moral question "Should Joe tell on his younger brother?" in terms of the probabilities of Joe getting beaten up by his father and by his brother, he does not answer with a moral judgment that is universal or that has any

> impersonal or ideal grounds. In contrast, Stage 6 state-
> ments not only use moral words but also use them in
> a specifically moral way. ...The individual whose judg-
> ments are at State 6 asks, "Is it morally right?" and
> means by "morally right" something different from
> punishment (Stage 1).

Is it proper, then, that a 9-year-old such as Cameron Kocher — a juvenile murderer arraigned as an adult who, according to Kohlberg's theory, occupied only the pre-conventional level of moral develop-ment and so is incapable either of feeling guilt over his actions or even of making authentically moral judgments — should be tried for mur-der as an adult?

Using Kohlberg's moral stages to distinguish morally between children and adults as the rationale for adjudicating them differently is problematic. For one thing, the theory is controversial; it has re-ceived considerable criticism to which Kohlberg has been obliged to respond by amending his original theory.[40] For another, according to this same theory, adults may occupy the very same moral level as children. Significantly, many adult criminals are found to be on the pre-conventional level, at either the first or second stage of moral development. This means that taking Kohlberg's scheme seriously would require our treating as children criminals who are chronologi-cal adults. This would obviously strike many as being absurd. What-ever the merits of using Kohlberg's theory as the basis for adjudicating children and adults separately, it has important implications for the potential resolution of the moral issues in juvenile justice.

Resolving moral issues in juvenile justice

We have at our disposal three main theories of punitive justice (re-tributive, utilitarian, and contractarian) designed to clarify and re-solve moral issues. We shall now apply them to some of the moral issues surrounding juvenile justice to see how each of these theories might resolve them.

The retributive theory of punishment holds that crime deserves punishment, that a wrong requires rectification. As Bradley put it, "We pay the penalty because we owe it, and for no other reason."[41] Furthermore, the principle of proportionate retribution (a principle of fairness) is fundamental to the theory — the punishment must fit the crime, and the penalty must be as nearly perfectly proportionate to the seriousness of the offense and the degree of the culprit's desert as is humanly possible. As to the purpose of juvenile justice, the retributive theory would, by definition, come down squarely on the side of retribution.

A retributive theory of juvenile justice is vulnerable to the same difficulties besetting the retributive theory in general. In the case of juveniles, their immaturity, their moral malleability or potential to improve, and compassion for their tender years are factors that might mitigate or even exculpate their guilt and the degree of their desert. The principle of proportionate retribution would seem to demand their consideration. Here Kohlberg's theory would be particularly relevant. Knowing that a juvenile offender was at the pre-conventional moral level and lacked the capacities to feel guilt and to make authentic moral judgments would qualify as a mitigating factor. For a Kantian retributivist, in particular, it is crucial that a person qualify for punishment by being fully rational and free. If it can be established that a juvenile, because of his age, is not fully rational, then juridical punishment for his crime is out of the question; the only measures permissible are his rehabilitation or confinement for the protection of society. As we have already seen, judiciously weighing up and balancing these factors in order to arrive at a just penalty is a very tricky business. The alternative, of course, is simply to ignore all such factors and simply determine the fact of guilt and inflict the punishment called for by law. This is not a new idea. In 18th-century England — during the so-called "Age of Enlightenment" — children were hanged alongside adults for crimes such as petty theft. Though such sentences observe the principle of comparative justice, they run afoul of the no less compelling principle of proportionate retribution, not to mention the quality of mercy.

How might other moral issues surrounding juvenile justice be resolved by applying the retributive theory? Punishing parents for the crimes of their offspring would be ruled out; under the retributive theory, only the wrongdoer can pay the penalty for his crime. The American Civil Liberties Union has objected to this practice on the grounds that it in effect punishes people for crimes committed by others. Moreover, it uses the family bond as a means of officially sanctioned social control, which is an instance of using persons as a means to an end other than themselves (i.e., public safety), which a Kantian retributivist would not sanction.[42] The only way, according to the retributivist theory, that parents may be justly punished for their child's offense is if the child, by reason of its young age or a mental deficiency, cannot possibly be held accountable. For example, suppose your 3-year-old son finds your gun and, while playing with it, accidentally shoots and kills his sister. Clearly, in such a case you would be liable, both morally and legally, and for the same reason you would be if your dog attacked and killed your neighbor's child. Finally, the retributivist, from the principle of comparative justice, would undoubtedly find intolerable the disparities in the legal treatment of juvenile offenders, and that minorities make up a disproportionate number of those appearing before juvenile courts.

The utilitarian theory of punishment holds that punishment, to be moral, must bring about some greater public good, which compensates for the evil of the offense as well as of the pain necessitated by the penalty itself. In Bentham's words, punishment "ought to be admitted in as far as it promises to exclude some greater evil."[43] The means by which punishment brings about that public good is by rehabilitating the offender or by deterring both him and others. Thus, a utilitarian theory of juvenile justice would have the twin aims of rehabilitation and deterrence. Yet, the problems endemic to the utilitarian theory of punitive justice in general also apply to the utilitarian theory as applied to juvenile justice.

First of all, rehabilitation of the offender by the state has not proven to be an unqualified success, as indicated by the high recidivist rates of both adult and juvenile criminals. Kohlberg gives a possible explanation of this with respect to juvenile recidivists. His research determined that there was an apparent discrepancy in moral maturity between the correctional institution's officers and its juvenile inmates. Thus, its officers, in their attitudes toward and treatment of their wards, may exhibit a stage of maturity that is actually lower than that of the inmates: "Impressionistic observation suggests that many reform schools have an official level of justice that is a Stage 1 obedience and punishment orientation, while the inmate peer culture has a Stage 2 instrumental exchange orientation. An inmate high in participation in either of these structures is not likely to advance in moral judgment."[44] Indeed, one study found that some inmates actually regressed on the scale of moral maturity while incarcerated by dropping to a lower stage of moral judgment than what they were on when they arrived at the institution.[45]

Kohlberg's insights may give some support to the policy of rehabilitation as it relates specifically to juveniles. His research has shown that, while many juvenile delinquents as well as most children under age 9 are at the pre-conventional level of moral development, they may have a greater potential to move upwards on the moral scale than do adults. Furthermore, as Kohlberg has observed, juvenile inmates are morally affected by the institution in which they are placed, such that juveniles on a higher moral level than that represented by the institution tend to regress to the institutional level. This suggests that if the institutional policy reflected a higher stage of moral development, then the juveniles might move upwards on the moral scale to meet it. The feasibility of rehabilitating juveniles depends on the empirical question of just how much more amenable to change (specifically moral improvement) are juveniles than adults, and this question has yet to be answered in any concrete manner.

A second problem with a theory of utilitarian juvenile justice has to do with its aim of deterrence. History has shown us that harsh penalties do not deter others from committing crimes. The death penalty — the harshest punishment available to us — does not deter homicide. Paradoxically, states that employ capital punishment have higher rates of homicide than do states without the death penalty. Furthermore, the aims of deterrence and rehabilitation may come into conflict. On the one hand, utilitarians want to promote public safety by deterring actual and potential juvenile crime. On the other hand, they want to further the good of both the delinquent and society by rehabilitating him; however, deterrence might be achieved not only independently of rehabilitation, but might even require its suspension. Regnery, for example, proposed substituting retribution for rehabilitation for the sake of greater deterrence.[46] Now suppose that severe retributive sentences did in fact deter. In many Asian and Middle-Eastern countries, severe penalties for crimes are the norm, and these countries apparently do have far less crime than the United States.[47] If America followed these examples and utilized harsh punishments, and as a result the crime rate dropped significantly, the public good would be better served without any effort being made to rehabilitate. The utilitarian, to be consistent, must choose that policy which best promotes the common good, and if that entails exacting cruel penalties that may be disproportionate to the offense, then so be it. There is an ambivalence threading through the utilitarian theory of juvenile justice which, commendably, has a humane concern for the well-being of juveniles as exhibited in its insistence on their rehabilitation; however, it has a greater commitment to promoting the larger good of society which may be better served by severe sentences intended to deter rather than to rehabilitate.

The response of the utilitarian theory to some of the other moral issues of juvenile justice are predictable enough, making due allowance for differences between act- and rule-utilitarians in their resolution of them. Utilitarians quite likely would not be too scrupulous over suspending due process in juvenile court or holding parents legally accountable for their children's criminal acts, as long as such measures advanced the causes of rehabilitation and public safety. As to the discrepancies in adjudicational jurisdiction or the problems with the disproportional representation of minorities within the system (issues of comparative justice), utilitarians would be most concerned with their possible deleterious social consequences.

According to the contractarian theory of punitive justice, crimes are breaches of the social contract, which is the very basis of public order, peace, and prosperity. To commit a crime is to violate a tacit oath to uphold the social order by obeying its laws. Punishment for crimes is warranted by the reneging on an obligation and the need to maintain the social bond, which is essential to public order and the myriad advantages attendant upon it. The theory of the social contract has some important implications for juvenile justice, one of which is that children cannot be properly prosecuted and punished as adults. To be adjudicated as an adult presupposes that one is rational enough to understand what a contract is, what its terms are, and the importance of abiding by it. It also means that one is sufficiently mature to enter into it. Thus, since children cannot legally enter into business deals or contracts (adults must stand proxy for them), they cannot break the social contract to which they cannot be party. Significantly, in the United States, the voting age of 18 years is the same age that in some states persons may be prosecuted as adults for their crimes. Kohlberg's theory of moral development is particularly relevant to the social contract theory because of its insights as to what constitutes an adult stage of moral judgment.

Two objections may be made to this application to juvenile justice of the social contract theory. First of all, there is little analogy between legal contracts and the social contract. The former are entered into explicitly, which means one must read and understand a document and indicate their assent to it in writing. The latter is entered into implicitly. Simply by willingly living in a country and enjoying its benefits, one has tacitly pledged to obey its laws. Second, the social contract is primordial, which means that it is foundational to all other legally binding contracts and is thus inescapable. Just by dint of being born into a society one is involved in the social contract upon which it depends. Thus, children enjoy the benefits and privileges conferred by their society. Some of these benefits they enjoy immediately, such as education, health care, and the protection of the law. Though not yet full citizens, they are virtual citizens who will become fully enfranchised upon reaching their majority or will be allowed to emigrate if they so choose. There are sufficient differences between the social contract and legal contracts such that while children may be disqualified from entering into a legal contract, they may not be disqualified from entering into the social contract. As such, children are thus responsible for complying with the social contract and may be held liable for breaking the laws it sanctions.

The social contract theory has important implications for other issues specific to juvenile justice. Its exclusion of children from adult adjudication implies that juvenile justice has a purpose distinct from the rest of the criminal justice system. And because it excludes children from the social contract, it means that adults need to act on their behalf in matters of law and business. Thus, if children, being barred from the contract, are not liable for their crimes, then their parents or legal guardians must be. The social contract theory, then, could be used to support the prosecution of parents for their children's crimes.

Finally, the restitutive theory of punitive justice, which emphasizes restitution to or compensation for victims of crime, has application to some of the issues of juvenile justice. A restitutive theory of juvenile justice would have neither rehabilitation nor retribution as its principle aim, thereby making the theory especially attractive in light of the failures in rehabilitation and the problem of applying the law of proportionate retribution to non-adults. Under the restitutive theory, juvenile thieves might sell their labor in exchange for money with which to compensate their victims. In cases of victimless crimes, juveniles might be sentenced to perform some type of community service. Working off their offenses in this way would have not only restitutive value, but perhaps rehabilitative and retributive value, as well. A problem with subjecting adult offenders to the demands of restitutive justice is that because of the disparities of age, physical condition, financial status, and health, some are better able to perform the requirements of restitutive justice more easily than are others. This would not typically be a problem with juveniles who, because of their youth, enjoy generally better health and physical conditioning. The advantages of a restitutive theory of juvenile justice are offset by the disadvantage that there may be no adequate restitution for some crimes. How would one repay the victim of a homicide or a rape?

With its emphasis on restitution to victims, the restitutive theory of juvenile justice mutes some of the other issues raised by juvenile justice. Thus, since juveniles are quite capable of working off their offenses, there is no rationale for punishing their parents. Because of the absence of retribution, violations of the principle of comparative justice where juvenile offenders are adjudicated differently in different jurisdictions or where minorities are over-represented in the system are less acute.

In summary, juvenile justice raises a host of moral issues and gives us an opportunity to apply our theories of punitive justice to their clarification and resolution. Traditionally, juvenile justice has aimed at rehabilitation rather than retribution, its assumption being that there are morally relevant differences between juveniles and adults that warrant adjudicating the former differently. More recently, however, in response to the failure of rehabilitative efforts and the increase in violent crime committed by juveniles, juvenile justice has been redirected towards retribution, a course reflected in state legislation throughout the country. Resolutions of the moral issues depend upon resolution of the twin metaphysical issues concerning the criteria of adulthood and the age at which a child meets them. Kohlberg's theory as to the stages of moral development is pertinent to resolving both kinds of issues, especially his finding that a morally relevant difference between children and adults is that children typically occupy a lower moral stage than do adults. All four theories of punitive justice can clarify and go some way to resolving some of the moral issues raised by the administration of juvenile justice, but none does so decisively and satisfactorily. The retributive theory favors punishing juveniles as adults for their crimes, assuming children are rational enough to qualify for judicial punishment, on the grounds of their moral desert and of deterrence. The utilitarian theory favors rehabilitating and deterring juveniles, assuming that the morally relevant differences between them and adults are significant enough to justify their rehabilitation. But the high recidivism rate casts serious doubt on the effectiveness of current rehabilitative efforts. Moreover, the ends of rehabilitation and deterrence may come into conflict. The social contract theory would excuse juveniles from adjudication as adults because they are ineligible to enter into the social contract and therefore not liable for breaking it. Their parents may legitimately punish them, but not the government responsible for upholding the social contract. This theory makes the problematic assumptions that juveniles are ineligible for adjudication as adults, that all moral responsibilities stem from the social contract, and that the social contract is perfectly analogous to conventional legal contracts. Finally, the restitutive theory, though eminently humane and practical, and avoiding the problems specific to the retributive and utilitarian theories, makes justice in the restitutive sense impossible to the victims of crimes for which no restitution may suffice.

Notes

1. Gegax, T. Trent; Adler, Jerry; and Pedersen, Daniel, Schoolyard killers, *Newsweek*, April 6, 1998, pp. 21–26.

2. Schmalleger, Frank, *Criminal Justice Today: An Introductory Text for the 21st Century*, 4th ed., Prentice-Hall, Upper Saddle River, NJ, 1997, p. 531.

3. Liverpool boys back in court, *USA Today*, March 4, 1993, p. 4a.

4. Kenney, John P. et al., *Police Work with Juveniles and the Administration of Juvenile Justice*, 7th ed., Charles C Thomas, Springfield, IL, 1989, p. 17.

5. Humes, Edward, *No Matter How Loud I Shout: A Year in the Life of Juvenile Court*, Pantheon Books, New York, 1991, p. xi.

6. Currie, Elliott, *Crime and Punishment in America*, Henry Holt & Company, New York, 1998, p. 24.

7. Currie, Elliott, *Dope and Trouble: Portraits of Delinquent Youth*, Pantheon Books, New York, 1991, p. xi.

8. Kenney, John P. et al., *Police Work with Juveniles and the Administration of Juvenile Justice*, 7th ed., Charles C Thomas, Springfield, IL, 1989, p. 4.

9. Kenney, John P. et al., *Police Work with Juveniles and the Administration of Juvenile Justice*, 7th ed., Charles C Thomas, Springfield, IL, 1989, p. 4.

10. IACP, *Murder in America: Recommendations from the IACP Murder Summit*, International Association of Chiefs of Police, Alexandra, VA, 1995.

11. Kenney, John P. et al., *Police Work with Juveniles and the Administration of Juvenile Justice*, 7th ed., Charles C Thomas, Springfield, IL, 1989, pp. 17, 18.

12. Schmalleger, Frank, *Criminal Justice Today: An Introductory Text for the 21st Century*, 4th ed., Prentice-Hall, Upper Saddle River, NJ, 1997, p. 531.

13. *New Jersey v. T.L.O.*, 105 S. Ct. 733, 1985.

14. Schmalleger, Frank, *Criminal Justice Today: An Introductory Text for the 21st Century*, 4th ed., Prentice-Hall, Upper Saddle River, NJ, 1997, pp. 544, 547.

15. OJJDP, Introducing RESTTA, *Juvenile Justice Bulletin*, Office of Juvenile Justice and Delinquency Prevention, Washington, D.C., 1985.

16. Now, parents on trial, *Newsweek*, October 2, 1989, pp. 54–55.

17. Schmalleger, Frank, *Criminal Justice Today: An Introductory Text for the 21st Century*, 4th ed., Prentice-Hall, Upper Saddle River, NJ, 1997, p. 540.

18. Glamser, Deeann, Communities seek to stem youth crime, *USA Today*, Feb. 21, 1995, p. 1A.

19. Schmalleger, Frank, *Criminal Justice Today: An Introductory Text for the 21st Century*, 4th ed., Prentice-Hall, Upper Saddle River, NJ, 1997, p. 540.

20. Oregon will punish delinquents' parents, *USA Today*, July 18, 1995, p. 3A.

21. Mennel, Robert M., *Thorns and Thistles: Juvenile Delinquents in the United States 1825–1940*, The University Press of New England, Hanover, NH, 1973, pp. 130–132.

22. Schmalleger, Frank, *Criminal Justice Today: An Introductory Text for the 21st Century*, 4th ed., Prentice-Hall, Upper Saddle River, NJ, 1997, p. 529.

23. A peer jury in the juvenile court, *Crime and Delinquency*, 30(3), 423–438, 1984.

24. Schmalleger, Frank, *Criminal Justice Today: An Introductory Text for the 21st Century*, 4th ed., Prentice-Hall, Upper Saddle River, NJ, 1997, p. 553.

25. A peer jury in the juvenile court, *Crime and Delinquency*, 30(3), 423–438, 1984.

26. In this court teens sit in stern judgment on violators, *Fayetteville Observer-Times* (North Carolina), May 3, 1992, p. 22A.

27. Schmalleger, Frank, *Criminal Justice Today: An Introductory Text for the 21st Century*, 4th ed., Prentice-Hall, Upper Saddle River, NJ, 1997, pp. 529–548.

28. In the case of *In Re Gault* (1967), the U.S. Supreme Court ruled that juveniles have such rights of due process as the right to advanced notice of the charges against them, the right to counsel, the right to address and cross-examine witnesses, the right of protection against self-incrimination, the right to a transcript of the adjudicatory hearing, and the right to appeal. In the case of *In Re Winship* (1970), the Court ruled that at the adjudicatory hearing the case against juveniles must be proved beyond a reasonable doubt. In *McKeiver v. Pennsylvania* (1971), the Court reaffirmed the long-standing opinion that the Constitution did not require jury trials in juvenile court, and *Schall v. Martin* (1984), though allowing that the preventative detention of juveniles was not punitive, did stipulate that juveniles could not be detained unless they were given notice, subject to a fair hearing, and informed

by the judge of the reasons for their detention. (From Schmalleger, Frank, *Criminal Justice Today: An Introductory Text for the 21st Century*, 4th ed., Prentice-Hall, Upper Saddle River, NJ, 1997, pp. 544–547.)

29. Schmalleger, Frank, *Criminal Justice Today: An Introductory Text for the 21st Century*, 4th ed., Prentice-Hall, Upper Saddle River, NJ, 1997, p. 540.

30. Schmalleger, Frank, *Criminal Justice Today: An Introductory Text for the 21st Century*, 4th ed., Prentice-Hall, Upper Saddle River, NJ, 1997, p. 10.

31. Prothrow-Stith, Deborah, with Weissman, Michael, *Deadly Consequences*, Harper Collins, New York, 1991, p. 163.

32. Kohlberg, Lawrence, *Essays on Moral Development*. Vol. 1. *The Philosophy of Moral Development: Moral Stages and the Idea of Justice*, Harper & Row, San Francisco, CA, 1981, pp. 120, 105, 116, 136.

33. Schmalleger, Frank, *Criminal Justice Today: An Introductory Text for the 21st Century*, 4th ed., Prentice-Hall, Upper Saddle River, NJ, 1997, pp. 663–664.

34. The exact number of stages is open to question. Kohlberg himself has suggested that his sixth stage "is perhaps less a statement of an attained psychological reality than the specification of a direction in which, our theory claims, ethical development is moving." He has further entertained the possibility of their being a seventh stage, "a metaphoric post-conventional stage of religious orientation attained after the achievement of principled morality." See Kohlberg, Lawrence, *Essays on Moral Development*. Vol. 1. *The Philosophy of Moral Development: Moral Stages and the Idea of Justice*, Harper & Row, San Francisco, CA, 1981, pp. 100, 307–372.

35. Kohlberg, Lawrence, *Essays on Moral Development*. Vol. II. *The Psychology of Moral Development: The Nature and Validity of Moral Stages*, Harper & Row, San Francisco, CA, 1984, p. 173.

36. Kohlberg, Lawrence, *Essays on Moral Development*. Vol. 1. *The Philosophy of Moral Development: Moral Stages and the Idea of Justice*, Harper & Row, San Francisco, CA, 1981, p. 151.

37. This summary of the stages of moral development is based on Kohlberg's description on pp. 409–412 in his *Essays on Moral Development*, Volume 1.

38. Kohlberg, Lawrence, *Essays on Moral Development*. Vol. II. *The Psychology of Moral Development: The Nature and Validity of Moral Stages*, Harper & Row, San Francisco, CA, 1984, p. 66.

39. Kohlberg, Lawrence, *Essays on Moral Development*. Vol. 1. *The Philosophy of Moral Development: Moral Stages and the Idea of Justice*, Harper & Row, San Francisco, CA, 1981, pp. 170–171.

40. Kohlberg, Lawrence, *Essays on Moral Development.* Vol. II. *The Psychology of Moral Development: The Nature and Validity of Moral Stages,* Harper & Row, San Francisco, CA, 1984, p. 207.

41. Bradley, Francis H., *Ethical Studies,* Oxford University Press, London, 1927, pp. 26–27 (as quoted in Hospers, John, *Human Conduct: An Introduction to the Problems of Ethics,* Harcourt, Brace & World, New York, 1961, p. 458).

42. It should be noted that the family is considered by most sociologists to be the most basic and effective instrument of social control, since within and through our families we first learn (or at least should learn) the difference between right and wrong and those moral values that help socialize us. There is no reason to suppose that Kant would object to this, as parents nurture their children's moral growth (we hope) voluntarily and spontaneously, but there is reason to suppose that he would object to the state's manipulating and exploiting the family bond, with neither the parents' knowledge nor consent, in order to promote the public good — however laudable that end — as this involves using persons as means to ends which they did not explicitly choose.

43. Bentham, Jeremy, *An Introduction to the Principles of Morals and Legislation,* Hafner Publishing, Darien, CN, 1948, p. 170.

44. Kohlberg, Lawrence, *Essays on Moral Development.* Vol. 1. *The Philosophy of Moral Development: Moral Stages and the Idea of Justice,* Harper & Row, San Francisco, CA, 1981, pp. 144–145.

45. Kohlberg, Lawrence, *Essays on Moral Development.* Vol. II. *The Psychology of Moral Development: The Nature and Validity of Moral Stages,* Harper & Row, San Francisco, CA, 1984, p. 61.

46. Kenney, John P. et al., *Police Work with Juveniles and the Administration of Juvenile Justice,* 7th ed., Charles C Thomas, Springfield, IL, 1989, p. 4.

47. Schmalleger, Frank, *Criminal Justice Today: An Introductory Text for the 21st Century,* 4th ed., Prentice-Hall, Upper Saddle River, NJ, 1997, pp. 623–625.

chapter twelve

Corruption

> Leuci prided himself on being a tough cop — they all did — but in the end he proved far less tough than any of the others. Perhaps he had more conscience than they did, or perhaps he merely was more troubled by what all of them were doing. In any case, he was the one who stepped forward, and, in so doing, brought on the ruin of everyone else. It was almost biblical. Like Samson, he first did penance, and then he pulled the temple down. —Robert Daley (*Prince of the City*)

A rookie patrol officer and his veteran partner investigate a break-in at a liquor store. When they arrive at the scene they find several other patrol cars, a broken window, and a ransacked store. The rookie notices that his veteran colleagues are taking a great deal of interest in the remaining liquor. Some of them are taking bottles back to their cars. One veteran hands a couple of bottles to the rookie: "Here, kid, have yourself a party. It's all covered by insurance anyway." The young cop pauses a moment, then takes the liquor to his car.

Several years of hard work in an inner-city precinct have finally paid off for a patrolman; he has been designated Captain's bagman. On the first and 15th of every month, he makes the rounds of the book joints, speakeasies, and numbers writers in the district, collecting protection money. Back at the precinct, the money is divided into shares. The Captain, Lieutenant, and Sergeant get the most, but even for some patrol officers the illegal take exceeds $1000 per month.[1]

There is nothing new about corruption in policing. In 1170, Henry II of England found it necessary to dismiss some corrupt sheriffs. Up until the French Revolution of 1783, the Paris Police were deep into crime. In the 19th century, the Surete of Paris, thinking that thieves would know best how to catch other thieves, recruited them for police work only to find that they reverted to their former habits. In 1845, New York City revamped its police force and gave the authority to appoint officers to elected ward officials. As a result, the police over-looked irregularities in elections and were complicit in crime and kickback schemes with ward officials and criminals. In 1892, the Lxow Commission exposed widespread police involvement in a variety of crimes: extortion, bribery, sales of political office, and irregular enforcement of vice laws. Seventy years later, the Knapp Commission found little had changed except for the addition of the irregular enforcement of drug laws. Scandals have not been confined to the police force in New York City but have embroiled forces in other cities as diverse as Chicago, Denver, Des Moines, Atlanta, Miami, and Los Angeles, and have even included full-scale burglary rings.[2] Reiss' estimate, based on findings from 1966, is that "during any year a substantial minority of all police officers violate the criminal law, a majority misbehave toward citizens in an encounter, and most engage in serious violations of the rules and regulations of the department."[3]

The nature and forms of corruption

Police corruption is essentially the misuse or abuse of duly conferred police power or authority for personal gain:[4]

> Generally, police corruption involves the misuse of official position either to commit or ignore an unauthorized act, which may or may not violate the law. As payment for misusing his position, the officer expects at some point in time to receive something of value but not necessarily money. The payoff may take the form of services, status, influence, prestige, or future favoritism for the officer or someone else.

It can take a variety of forms, depending on how one understands the misuse or abuse of that power. Most broadly understood, police corruption is either internal or external. Internal corruption occurs within a department and involves corrupt interactions among the officers themselves. One example is patrol officers' giving "Christmas money" to their radio dispatchers who can conveniently cover up for officers who go off duty without authorization or decline to respond to calls in dangerous neighborhoods. A second example is officers' distributing or selling drugs among themselves which may then be used to plant on suspects, to reward informers, as evidence in other cases, or for their personal recreation. An actual case of internal corruption occurred in Chicago where police cars still in good condition were sold cheaply to officers, thereby necessitating the purchase of new cars by the police department.[5]

External corruption occurs between members of a police department and civilians and involves corrupt interactions between them. The forms it can take may be ranked on a rough scale that ranges from activities that are unambiguously immoral and illegal (bribery and drug dealing) to those which are not and whose corruptness is questionable (accepting a free cup of coffee or a "cops" discount on a meal).

Unambiguous corruption

Felonies

These include *bona fide* crimes such as theft, selling lawfully confiscated property, drug trafficking, and protecting organized crime and vice operators. It should be noted that they count as forms of police corruption only if the officer uses his power, authority, or professional knowledge and skills to perpetrate them; otherwise, they are simply criminal activities perpetrated by the officer in his civilian capacity.

Shakedown

Shakedown is taking expensive goods for personal use while investigating a burglary or encountering an unlocked door and blaming the loss on thieves.

Prejudice

Prejudice is treating certain groups of people, typically minorities, less justly because they perhaps lack the political clout with which to bring the unjust officer to book.

Extortion

Extortion is demands made by an officer for money, goods, or services in exchange for favors. For example, he may pressure citizens to buy tickets for police functions or convene "street courts" where one can pay a cash bail directly to the arresting officer, without the need of a receipt, in lieu of being issued a traffic ticket.

Misconduct in office

This "refers to any willful malfeasance, misfeasance, or nonfeasance in office and may be considered within the context of police corruption when an officer acts with malice and aforethought to thwart justice."[6] Malfeasance is breaking the law, such as an officer's warning suspects of an imminent police raid. Misfeasance is the sloppy performance of one's duty. Nonfeasance is the omission of one's duty, such as an officer's failing to crack down on known criminal activity in the community. Note that these three forms of official misconduct are corrupt only if they are intentional and motivated by malice or a desire for personal gain; otherwise, they are simply incompetent.

Shopping

Shopping is lifting goods of little worth such as candy, cigarettes, and gum from stores where the door has been accidentally left unlocked after closing.

Selective non-enforcement of the law

This is the exercise of the otherwise legitimate and necessary power of discretion for selfish and personal ends. Whether or not discretion is used corruptly depends, for analytical purposes, on whether or not the officer is pursuing personal benefits. In practice, though, even this may be difficult to judge. An officer who aggressively uses his discretionary powers to get information from numbers runners may eventually arrest higher ups in the operation and thus be doing a good job. But, if he does this solely to win promotion to detective, where he hears that bribe money comes easy, he is abusing his discretion for private gain.

Favoritism

Favoritism is the use of license tabs, window stickers, or courtesy cards to receive immunity from arrests or citations related to traffic offenses.

Chiseling

Chiseling involves such activities as an officer's requesting or demanding price discounts on meals or merchandise.

Ambiguous corruption

Perjury

Perjury is an officer's lying under oath, for such reasons as protecting a fellow officer or ensuring that a defendant who is unquestionably guilty is punished.

Bribery

Bribery involves payment in the form of cash or "gifts" to the officer for past or future illegal services, such as a tip-off to a planned raid.

Violations of regulations

This is unauthorized breaking of departmental rules and occurs most frequently when the rules are unclear or not enforced.

Mooching

Mooching is accepting gifts, tips, and gratuities such as free coffee, meals, liquor, cigarettes, or groceries from merchants who offer the items as an expression of gratitude for services rendered or from the expectation of possible future acts of favoritism towards the donor.[7]

Comparing unambiguous and ambiguous corruption

Though some of these forms of corruption are related, they are nevertheless distinguishable. Thus, in both the shakedown and pre-meditated theft, equally valuable goods may be taken, but they differ with respect to the arrangements and plans made preparatory to them. For instance, a successful burglary requires careful planning and acquiring things such as tools with which to do the job; whereas, shakedowns may be carried out on the spur of the moment with a minimum of preparation. Furthermore, burglaries are more easily proved than shakedowns. The shakedown differs from shopping with respect to the higher value of the goods stolen and the relative ease with which the rightful owner can be established. Finally, bribery differs from mooching inasmuch as the payment or gift has greater value, and the favor expected is certain to be granted and illicit (e.g., officers' being paid to look the other way in cases of organized crime).

The causes of corruption

Explanations of police corruption focus on the individual, the group, or the larger society. In reviewing them, Johnston has concluded that the real cause is to be found in society at large. We shall closely follow his summary here.

The personalistic/individualistic approach

This approach to explaining police corruption blames it on the individual person, finding its cause in a bad moral character composed of certain undesirable traits of personality stemming either from genetic predisposition or molded by the environment.[8] The principal motive behind corruption, according to this view, is the egoistic pursuit of personal gain. A corollary of this approach is the so-called "rotten apple" theory, which maintains that a mere handful of corrupt officers is all that it takes to corrupt an entire police department. One variant of this individualistic approach seeks the cause of corruption in the particular ethnic groups' socioeconomic classes and the educational levels from which police officers are predominantly recruited. Its profile of a typical officer is a white, working-class male with little education. Another variant attributes corruption to the "police personality", which is a function of both the officer's personal background and his professional training and socialization.

Johnston, however, makes several objections to the personalistic theory of police corruption, four of which he directs to the "rotten apple" theory. One is that it is a convenient scapegoat, which diverts administrative attention from the institutional sources of corruption. A second objection is that corruption involves group conformity more than individual deviance; corrupt officers have typical psychological profiles for policemen, and they themselves attribute corruption to learning and socializing on the job. " 'Rotten apples' are not corrupting the rest of the barrel," cautions, Johnston. "If anything, we ought to be looking at the barrel itself." A third objection he makes to the theory is that it has proven nearly impossible to screen out potentially corrupt officers, and even more sophisticated recruitment programs have still not eliminated corruption. A fourth objection is that the corrupting influences of a few do not convincingly explain the systematic and systemic corruption endemic to some police departments. As to the search for the sources of corruption in the ethnic, economic, and social groups from which police are typically recruited, Johnston objects that morally good officers come from precisely the same groups. Moreover, white, "ethnic", working-class males have no monopoly on corruption; well-educated and professional "WASPS" may be no less corrupt than their socially inferior brethren, a fact clearly brought home by the insider-trading scandals of the 1980s. Finally, in regard to attempting to pin the blame for corruption on a so-called "police personality", Johnston rejoins that the very traits making up that personality (e.g., aggressiveness, courage, willingness to follow orders, suspiciousness, and impulsiveness) are desirable and even necessary for effective policing and do not necessarily make for corruption.[9]

The institutional approach

What Johnston calls the "institutional" approach to explaining police corruption blames it on the group, finding its cause in the social dynamics of the group or the nature of the profession itself. Thus, this approach has found the cause in the dynamic of "peer group social-ization", the process whereby the rookie learns values and standards of conduct from his more experienced fellow officers. More specifi-cally, he learns an unofficial code of conduct sanctioning certain kinds of misconduct which is known within police circles as the "code", and he is initiated into the "code of silence" that cloaks it. The rookie is urged not to inform on another officer whom he discovers engaging in unofficially sanctioned misconduct, and he may even have his loyalty tested by his fellow officers who want to determine his will-ingness to "play along". If the rookie breaks this code of silence, he risks ostracism or worse. The rookie is under considerable pressure to keep silent and play along even in the face of conduct which violates his personal moral code, the policies and procedures of his agency, and even the law. Of course, some egregious kinds of misconduct fall beyond even the pale of the "code" and so are not covered by the code of silence. The rookie must learn to distinguish between misconduct that is unofficially acceptable and conduct that is not. The justification for the "code" and its cloak of silence is that it both expresses and fosters loyalty and solidarity within a social group, but, according to one authority, "in practice the code of silence leads to a perversion of ethics and makes corruption possible. It shields the corrupt police officer from exposure and condemns any colleague who would ex-pose him."[10] Corroborating this assessment, Stoddard concludes that the source of police corruption is to be found not in individuals but in the socially derived "code": "Illegal practices of police personnel are socially prescribed and patterned through the informal 'code' rather than being a function of individual aberration or personal inadequa-cies of the policeman himself."[11]

Alternatively, the institutional approach has found the cause of police corruption in the very nature of police work. Policing is an isolated activity; police on the beat work largely outside the ken of their departmental supervisors and of the general public, who might otherwise monitor, correct, and discipline them. Policing necessarily involves the exercise of enormous discretionary power, along with the concomitant potential for its abuse. As we have already discussed in a previous section on discretionary justice, the police cannot avoid exercising discretion in their work, but the use of discretion may be legitimate or illegitimate, depending upon what motivated the officer to use it. A traffic officer who believes a speeder's promise to obey the speed limits in the future and gives only a verbal warning may be acting legitimately. An officer who makes the same decision in exchange for money is not. Police officers are especially susceptible to cynicism and low morale because of their professional experience. Far more so than the average citizen, the police officer deals on a daily basis with the dregs of humanity. Even when they have contact with respectable, relatively honest citizens, it involves some kind of trouble. The cop rarely sees people at their best. These almost daily experiences can shake the officer's faith in human nature. Furthermore, they may see the cause of justice miscarry in the courts through legal loopholes and technicalities, or they may be hobbled in their own departments by bureaucratic incompetence and inefficiency. Consequently, they may be tempted to be less scrupulous in their own professional conduct and come up with rationalizations for their behavior such as: "There is no justice in the world." "Others are getting away with murder, why shouldn't I?" "Why should I be moral when no one else is?"

Finally, endemic to policing are legitimate conflicts over the proper goals of criminal justice and the best ways of achieving those goals:[12]

> The police officer's role in the criminal justice system creates two serious dilemmas. One concerns the means of providing justice, the other the ends. The dilemma of means involves conflict between professional and bureaucratic standards of police conduct. The dilemma of ends is one of differing conceptions of justice itself. The police officer resolves these dilemmas by making informal and unsatisfying compromises on behalf of a system to which he or she may have little commitment.

On one side, there is the officer who prides himself on his technical competence and expertise developed through specialized training and practical experience and who jealously guards his privilege of exercising discretionary and other forms of autonomous judgment. On the other side, there are bureaucratic standards, conformity to which is necessary to the efficient and effective running of any police department. The standards, no less than the officer's skills, knowledge, and independent judgment, are essential to the pursuit of justice. However, the professional aspirations of the individual officer are at loggerheads with the standards imposed by bureaucratic administration. According to Reiss, "*Command organization* threatens professional status because it expects men to follow orders regardless of their judgment. The professional ideal holds that orders are antithetical to the exercise of discretion."[13] This conflict between individual professionalism and administrative bureaucracy is a classic dilemma because the pursuit of justice by one means requires blocking its pursuit by another. Johnston gives a graphic illustration of this dilemma, and how it might force an otherwise morally responsible officer to break the law:[14]

> Consider the case of a narcotics detective who carefully cultivates a set of informants. Relationships here are delicate and based on a number of understandings. The officer may "have something" on the informant and use the threat of arrest to get information. Or she may trade drugs or money for tips and leads. Here is the dilemma: if the officer follows her department's regulations on dealing with informants — which may require her officially to record the informant's name and may prohibit exchanging drugs or money for information — she will quickly find she has no informants. The department also requires her to ring up a certain quota of drug arrests each month, and to get arrests she needs information. What does she do? In most cases she will disregard the regulations — and often break laws — to get information and make arrests. The tension between professionalism and bureaucratization often forces a "good cop" to break the law in order to produce arrests.

Not only is there the conflict within police departments between the ideals of professionalism and bureaucracy over the best means to realizing justice, but there are conflicts between the police and other agencies within the criminal justice system over its proper end — namely, the nature of justice. There is the conflict between the police and both the legislatures and the courts over procedural justice. On the one hand, police often accuse legislators and judges of making impractical and unclear laws which favor criminals but hamper police by holding them to excessively stringent standards of conduct. On the other hand, judges and attorneys are too ready to believe that the police are overly fond of brute force and indifferent to the subtleties of the law and due process. To put it more bluntly, they tend to regard the police as bulls blundering in the judicial china shop. Thus, the Supreme Court's Miranda and Escobedo decisions, which strengthened the rights of the accused, were not popular with the police. Reiss succinctly sums up the difference between the police and the courts over procedural justice as follows: "Matters that the police want defined by rules, the courts want to leave open to discretion. And what the courts want defined by rules, the police want to leave open to discretion.[15]

There is also the conflict between the police and both the legislative and judicial branches of government over substantive justice. The police have complained about the harshness of the law towards vice, embodied in virtually unenforceable criminal statutes, but its leniency towards violent crimes, the perpetrators of which are exonerated on technicalities. The police have also expressed the belief that the courts deal more harshly with the "ordinary guy" than with incorrigible criminals or with wealthy white-collar offenders. And the police are frustrated that suspects they know to be guilty of crimes will go free because of the difficulties of developing sufficient legally admissible evidence to convict them.

These conflicts between the police and other branches of the criminal justice system over the nature of procedural and substantive justice open the way for corruption. Disillusioned with the system, officers might develop cavalier attitudes toward their professional standards of conduct. They might find themselves obliged to break the law, as well as departmental policy, in order to enforce the law. If their departments place a higher premium on the quantity of arrests than on the number of convictions resulting from those arrests, then the officers may be less scrupulous about whether the evidence they collect will stand up in court and so be guilty of misfeasance, or they may even use illicit means to make their arrests and so be guilty of malfeasance, as were the members of New York's Special Investigations Unit when they carried bags of cocaine to pay informers.[16]

The profession of policing invites corruption at the command level as well as among the lower ranks. Supervisors may act vindictively or high-handedly towards officers whom they dislike by assigning them additional duties, giving them unpopular assignments, or conferring or withholding promotions. Supervisors may be subject to political pressures and, consequently, might transfer an officer who is getting too close to exposing some criminal activity that the local political authorities want protected — such as the honest policeman in Boston who was transferred to cemetery duty as his investigations might have proven embarrassing to municipal officials. Or, they may be tempted by prospects of personal gain. For example, there are documented cases of cooperation between police commanders and gambling operators:[17]

> In exchange for money, favors, and occasional political support, police commanders restrained anti-gambling activities. When, for public relations reasons, a raid had to be conducted, commanders would tip off their counterparts in the gambling organizations. That way, important individuals and large sums of money could be protected. Gambling bosses could even put these sporadic raids to disciplinary use by making sure troublesome subordinates would be on the scene to be arrested. This cooperation meant larger profits for gambling operators, extra income for police commanders, and a general reduction in conflict and violence between both.

Finally, departmental administrators and supervisors may be passively complicit in corruption within the ranks of their subordinates. They have usually advanced through the ranks to their positions of authority and so are reluctant to investigate or punish their subordinates' misconduct — and resent the prying of the public into what they consider to be a private "police" affair.

The systemic approach

Now, a problem besetting this institutional theory of police corruption, pointed out by Johnston, is that it fails to fully explain corruption. The institutional police department may very well provide the opportunity and encouragement for corrupt activities such as bribery and extortion, but their initiation often requires contacts and cooperation with the civilian population outside the department. To remedy this defect, Johnston proposes his systemic approach, which looks at the relationship between the police and the wider community. It finds the cause of corruption in moral pluralism. There is within society a diversity of sometimes conflicting moral beliefs and values occurring among groups, institutions, and individuals. An example is the issue of pornography. Some believe that it is a morally neutral enterprise, which should be permitted by law, whereas others believe it is a moral evil that should be outlawed or at least regulated. Similar deep conflicts are found over the issues of abortion, euthanasia, and capital punishment. Occasionally, there is a conflict between the moral values presupposed by the law and those held by individuals. The law may forbid certain sexual acts that it deems "unnatural" and so immoral, but many people routinely practice such acts without moral compunction. Such a conflict gives rise to the familiar protest that government should not legislate morality. Furthermore, the public may have a greater tolerance of so-called "victimless" crimes such as prostitution, gambling, and drug abuse than do governmental officials.

These moral conflicts come to a head in laws intended to curtail vice, such as prostitution, pornography, gambling, and the imbibing of liquor — activities which are innocuous pastimes for some, but heinous sins for others. Vice laws reflect the moral values of only a portion of society. The conflicts are exacerbated by the extreme inconsistency of these laws, and the arbitrary and capricious way in which they are applied:[18]

> "Playing a number" at the drugstore is against the law; buying a state lottery ticket in the same store is not. A person of legal age can walk into any bar in Pennsylvania and buy a six-pack to go, but a Connecticut bartender who sells beer to go can land in jail. In some states, liquor and other vice laws are matters of local or county option, further confusing the matter. For many people and police officers alike, vice laws are a nuisance.

Vice laws have several counterproductive consequences. One is that they do not curtail vice but only make it more profitable. Indeed, vice is a deeply entrenched and powerful multi-billion-dollar industry. A second consequence is that people tend to flout laws which forbid or regulate activities that they do not regard as vices or as harming anyone other than perhaps themselves, and they may be emboldened to do so out of resentment towards those who succeed through legislation in imposing their restrictive moral codes on the whole society. A third consequence is that the police may not be vigilant in enforcing unpopular laws against activities in which people engage voluntarily, and instead choose to exercise their discretion in enforcing them selectively. The police, who are put in the unenviable position of separating supply from demand in transactions involving vice, are especially vulnerable to bribery; those whose business is vice can well afford to pay officers large sums of "protection money" that can be written off as a necessary business expense.

Johnston concludes that the chief culprit in police corruption is neither deviant individuals nor institutional pressures, but rather the conflict of values in society at large. He blames society for imposing contradictory duties on the police which force them into dilemmas from which the only escape is corrupt behavior:[19]

> We have, I think, placed demands upon our police that are contradictory and can never be satisfied. We expect the police to regulate matters of personal morality while respecting the privacy and civil liberties of suspects. We expect them to crack down on clandestine activities while scrupulously obeying regulations on how they may obtain information and gather evidence. We hold them responsible for enforcing myriad regulations dealing with economic enterprise while somehow remaining immune to the pressures and temptation these laws inevitably create. We cannot have things both ways, and one result of these tensions and contradictions is corruption.

The consequences of corruption

Police corruption seems to have advantages as well as disadvantages. Johnston argues, for example, that transactions in vice, wherein the operators pay the police for protection and the consumers can enjoy the services without interference, benefit all concerned and reduce the risk of violent confrontations. In particular, bribes enable police to supplement their meager incomes and permit people to get services they would otherwise forgo (e.g., the restaurateur who receives a police escort to the bank in exchanges for giving them free meals). These transactions also help boost the economy by allowing legal and illegal businesses to flourish together.[20] Finally, the "code" to which recruits are expected to conform, though blamed by Stoddard for corruption, serves as a "right of passage" which serves to socialize recruits into their department and to reinforce its stabilizing hierarchy; fosters solidarity, loyalty, trust, and pride among personnel by sanctioning secret and shared behavior which only they are entitled to enjoy; and helps defuse potential moral conflicts among them.[21]

Others, however, have noted the baneful consequences of corruption. Because the more affluent entrepreneurs of vice can afford to bribe, they stand to have more influence over the police than the majority of citizens who are less affluent or more honest, a situation both unjust and undemocratic. Thus, the latter may receive fewer police services than they are legally entitled to or may be more likely to incur stiffer penalties than those who can afford to pay. Additionally, police corruption creates conditions favorable to criminality. It increases public tolerance for certain crimes and makes them more lucrative. It has the possible ripple effect of fostering crime in places far away from where police pursue their corrupt activities. Corruption takes a heavy toll in neighborhoods (typically in the inner city) where various forms of vice flourish. It subverts efforts in crime control by allowing criminals to buy immunity and protection from arrest and prosecution. Finally, corruption on the part of police officers undermines public trust in, and esteem for, the police force.

Remedies for corruption

The remedy for police corruption and its success depend upon which of the personalistic, institutional, or systematic approaches to the problem is taken. Each, though, will be seen to be flawed, thus the personalistic approach favors better methods of recruiting and screening candidates and improved on-the-job training of recruits. However, Johnston's critique of the individualistic approach casts doubt as to the efficacy of this remedy.

The institutional approach recommends making various changes within the police department. First, departmental inspectors, answerable not to the police chief but solely to the mayor or city manager, might be appointed specifically to ferret out, report, and eliminate corruption, though this measure would predictably be resisted by departments jealous of their autonomy. Second, police officers might be rewarded with extra pay or attractive assignments for outstanding work to reduce their temptations to bribes; however, this expedient has potential for pitfalls. For one thing, it might prove to be expensive. For another, the close observation of an officer's work required for its evaluation would be difficult, as it is mostly performed out of view of his supervisors, and such evaluation might conflict with the officer's discretionary judgment. Further, there is the difficulty of determining who should be rewarded, and the resentment it might incur among officers who fail to qualify for a reward. Also, there is no guarantee that misconduct will not lurk behind the veil of peer-group secrecy. Third, commanders might wholeheartedly commit themselves to rooting out corruption in their departments, though this would mean tightening control over their subordinates and so threaten the latter's professional autonomy and discretionary judgment. Fourth, the tension between the police and the courts might be relaxed if police concentrated not so much on the quantity of arrests, but rather their quality. The courts in turn need to better appreciate the difficulty of enforcing vice laws and to honor police discretion more highly. Finally, laws governing the collection of evidence might be modified, consistent with the constitutional rights of suspects, to spare officers the dilemma of having to break the law in order to enforce it.

The systemic approach recommends making certain political and social changes through legislation and education. One such change might be the elimination of laws forbidding or curtailing crimes such as prostitution, pornography, gambling, and the recreational use of drugs. However, this solution makes the dubious assumption that vices are really harmless, except perhaps to those who indulge in them.[22] Thus, gambling may make victims of families impoverished by it. Drug abuse, by dulling the senses of the abuser, may make him a danger to others at work. Consequently, the decriminalization of certain vices could take a serious though hidden social toll. A second kind of systemic change might be to educate the public and its representatives as to the problems endemic to policing and the socio-economic causes of crime in the hope that more effective and enlightened criminal legislation might be enacted. Such a program might, however, serve only as a panacea and be late in bearing practical fruit. The major flaw in the remedy proposed by the systemic approach, though, is that it scarcely addresses moral pluralism and the conflicts it engenders, which, according to this approach, is the root of police corruption. Any resolution of these deep moral conflicts does not seem to be immediately forthcoming — indeed, they may be firmly entrenched as permanent features of the moral landscape of a democratic society committed so uncompromisingly to individualism.

The flaws in these remedies lend credence to the view that the complete extirpation of police corruption is a utopian dream, the realization of which is not even desirable much less possible. Thus, Johnston recommends that instead of trying to eliminate it we should be seeking to determine which kinds of corruption, and within what limits, might actually prove beneficial:[23]

> Our choices are instead more like cost-benefit calculations; what sorts of social behavior *must* we police, and what can we live with? How much police corruption is tolerable, and how much is too much? Might we not

> actually benefit from certain kinds of police corrup-
> tion, and might there not be situations in which the
> corrupt cop is also the best cop?

Paradoxically, some of the traits in an officer's personality that make
for misconduct are just those that make for his success in policing:[24]

> There came a day when Assistant U.S. Attorney
> Rudolph Giuliani, trying to put together a major nar-
> cotics investigation with new narcotics detectives newly
> assigned to him, realized that they were all inept. ...They
> could not conduct a surveillance without calling in that
> they were lost. They never played hunches.
>
> A great detective, Giuliani thought, should be a man of
> imagination and fearlessness. A man with a sense of
> adventure, a man not limited by procedure. In his new
> detectives, all these qualities were absent, so he asked
> himself almost in despair: Where have all the great
> detectives gone? The answer that came back to him
> was this one: I put them all in jail.

Moral implications

Two sets of moral issues are raised by police corruption: one concerns
the various forms of corruption, and the other its causes and remedies.

The moral evaluation of the forms of corruption

The fundamental question raised by the various forms of corruption
is this: What is it exactly that makes an act corrupt? You perhaps have
noticed how various the forms of corruption are, ranging from apparently innocuous activities such as accepting a free cup of coffee to
serious felony crimes such as drug dealing. All are lumped together
under the rubric of corruption. This suggests two further and related
questions: Are these different activities equally corrupt, or do they
admit of different degrees of corruptness? If the latter, then by what
criteria do we decide its degree? Answering these questions requires
our turning to normative ethical theory, and the answer we get depends upon the particular theory we apply.

Consider now the first question of what makes an act corrupt.
From the above definition of corruption and the various forms it can
take, we can derive three characteristics that an act must have in order
to qualify as corrupt:[25]

1. Fundamentally, it must involve the intentional misuse or abuse of duly conferred police power or authority for personal gain — "the misuse of official position either to commit or ignore an unauthorized act." In other words, the act must be perpetrated by the officer while on duty or facilitated by his expertise and skills in policing. If it is done off duty or without his using the resources of police work, then it is not corrupt but simply a criminal act.
2. The act must be ill intentioned; if not, as in the cases of malfeasance, misfeasance, and nonfeasance, then it is merely an instance of incompetence — it is the "malice and aforethought to thwart justice" that makes them corrupt.
3. The act must be motivated by narrow self-interest — "as payment for misusing his position, the officer expects at some point in time to receive something of value."

Note that this analysis of corruptness exclusively in terms of bad intentions and motives of private self-interest represents a deontological approach to ethics; there is no mention of its bad social effects as contributing to an act's corruptness, which would be the chief concern of the teleologist.

As to the second question of whether these activities listed as corrupt are equally so or display varying degrees of corruptness, a strict deontologist such as Kant would respond that they are equally corrupt inasmuch as they all equally involve either committing or overlooking an unauthorized act, thereby violating the categorical imperative and clouding moral judgment by rank self-interest. The teleologist would look to the harmful impact — in the form of lost property, psychological intimidation, and physical harm — of these acts on others, both the immediate victims and society at large. Because corrupt acts such as drug dealing and theft have more grave social consequences (such as the loss of valuable property) than acts such as mooching and chiseling, they may be ranked according to the seriousness of their effects which would serve as the criterion of their relative degrees of corruptness. Thus, the forms of corruption as listed above are roughly ranked in order of their degree of corruptness from highest to lowest.

The first nine categories of corruption, listed in the Unambiguously Corrupt section, would be unanimously condemned by both the deontologist and the teleologist, though on different grounds, and by all other moral theorists with the possible exception of the moral egoist — but even he might balk at the personal risks involved in committing a felony. Among those who accept that corrupt acts have varying degrees of corruptness, there may be disagreement over whether to condemn or condone those acts listed as being "ambiguously corrupt", particularly with respect to mooching and bribery. We shall now look closely at the controversy over mooching and bribery, two representative types of ambiguously corrupt acts, and the moral theories it presupposes. This will serve as an apt illustration of the sort of moral debate that might be prompted by any of the other types of ambiguously corrupt acts.

The apparently innocuous police practice of mooching, their accepting small gifts and gratuities such as free coffee and meals from grateful merchants, is categorically proscribed by Aubry, who lays it down that the whole duty of a police officer is "enforcement of the law courteously and appropriately at all times without fear or favor, never employing unnecessary force and *never accepting gratuities of any sort.*"[26] The case against mooching can be based on either deontological or teleological considerations. The former are suggested by the statement that, "A public official is *corrupt* if he accepts money or money's worth for doing something that he is under a duty to do anyway, that he is under a duty not to do, or to exercise a legitimate discretion for improper reasons."[27] To condemn mooching thus is to condemn it on grounds that the practice itself or its motive is inherently corrupt. The corruption lies in the officer's receiving compensation for something for which he has already been compensated (which is unjust), or his accepting a bribe for doing something illicit (which is violating both the law and an oath), or for doing something illicit but for personal gain. The case against mooching takes a teleological form if it or its motive is condemned not for its intrinsic wrongness but rather for its undesirable consequences:[28]

> If accepting gratuities from businessmen is condoned, and granting of small favors is considered within a department to be of little or no overall consequence, real harm can result. Eventually, more serious forms of corruption will tend to be unrecognized or overlooked.

In other words, mooching may be in and of itself innocent enough, but it is the first step on the slippery slope to practices that are not. Toleration for mooching will invariably extend to flagrantly immoral and illegal practices. Moreover, the mooching officer puts himself in the debt of the person providing the gratuity and risks having that debt called in: "Persons that give much to others try to get much from them, and persons that get much from others are under pressure to give much to them."[29] Consequently, the officer may find himself obliged to give preferential treatment to those citizens who can pay and perhaps less consideration to others whom he is duty-bound to serve, which is unfair on two counts. A broader and more sinister implication of mooching, then, is the undemocratic circumstance of wealth's dictating justice.

Nevertheless, a convincing case can be made for mooching. It begins with a criticism of the teleological case against it. One reason advanced against mooching is the "slippery slope" argument; if it is condoned, more serious forms of corruption will eventually tend to be unrecognized or overlooked. Note that saying "more serious forms of corruption" begs the question. It already assumes that mooching is corrupt, though to a lesser degree, which is the very point at issue. Moreover, it claims that the condoning of mooching will eventually lead to the condoning of more serious offenses. This argument is similar to one used against the recreational use of marijuana and other "soft" drugs; one puff on a joint will inevitably result in addiction to hard drugs such as cocaine and heroin. Both arguments, however, commit the logical fallacy of the slippery slope. An argument commits this fallacy when its conclusion depends upon the occurrence of a domino effect for which there is scant justification. Here is another example:[30]

> Immediate steps should be taken to outlaw pornography once and for all. The continued manufacture and sale of pornographic material will almost certainly lead to an increase in sex-related crimes such as rape and incest. This in turn will gradually erode the moral fabric of society and result in an increase in crimes of all sorts. Eventually a complete disintegration of law and order will occur, leading in the end to the total collapse of civilization.

The conclusion that civilization will collapse if pornography remains legal does not follow validly from the premises; there are insufficient reasons for believing that this event will occur because of the legalization of pornography. By the same token, it hardly follows that the worst cases of corruption will "eventually" be tolerated and so occur because of the mere toleration of mooching. Note that this fallacy occurs only when the conclusion is said to follow necessarily. That is, when it is claimed that the result of the domino effect *must* happen. This is the case with the examples above: *"Eventually*, more serious forms of corruption will tend to be unrecognized or overlooked. ...*Eventually*, a complete disintegration of law and order will occur." Substituting a less forceful term such as "possibly" for "eventually" and thus suggesting that the events in question may not happen would enable the arguments to escape the slippery slope fallacy. Moreover, the inference that mooching will inexorably lead to the worst forms of corruption is not only logically fallacious but also refuted by the facts. Kania reports, "The New York City Police investigated by the Knapp Commission felt that the slope was not irresistible; they made a sharp distinction between the unacceptably corrupt 'meat eaters' and the acceptably corrupt 'grass eaters'."[31]

Furthermore, a case can be made for mooching on teleological grounds by citing its social benefits. Mooching improves the public's relationship with the police by making it more cohesive. With this in mind, Kania writes, "The police especially and, under certain circumstances, other justice officials should be encouraged to accept freely offered minor gratuities and such gratuities should be perceived as the building blocks of positive social relationships between our police and the public, and not as incipient corrupters."[32] That the ritual of offering and accepting gratuities makes for social cohesiveness is borne out by the findings of the social sciences. On Leach's analysis, "If I give you a present you will feel morally bound to give something back. In economic terms, you are in debt to me, but in communicative terms the sense of reciprocal obligation is an expression of a mutual feeling that we both belong to the same social system."[33] This positive social benefit more than outweighs any possible negative consequences, such as the danger that his accepting a gratuity puts a police officer in the debt of the person offering it and risks the calling in of that debt. Kania found from his own experience in the police force that this fear was ungrounded, as debts typically were not called in. Indeed, an officer's scrupulously refusing gratuities on moral grounds may in fact impair his relationship with the public and even the performance of his duties. Kania provides the following illustration from his personal experience on the beat:[34]

> I had a junior officer assigned to me for training, an
> officer of unquestionably strong moral character who
> accepted the academy creed at face value. He stead-
> fastly refused even the most minor discounts from

restaurateurs, and twice became embroiled in arguments over the matter in my presence. On the second occasion, the argument actually became heated, and the inflexible officer accused the restaurant owner of trying to corrupt the police force. At that point, the officer was verbally evicted from the establishment and told not to return. The argumentative officer was called an "ass-hole" to his face and, in my opinion, had earned the label for his rigid refusal to accept an inconsequential discount. In the few months left of that inflexible but ethical officer's appropriately short, difficult, but uncorrupted police career, he found it necessary to bring a bag lunch and eat in the car while his "corrupted" partners ate at discount in neighborhood eateries. This deviation from the "ethical" behavior of his peers served to provide the businesses of his patrol sector less on-site protection than was provided by the "corrupt" police who continued to accept meal discounts in the spirit which they were offered.

Mooching may also be defended on purely deontological grounds by considering both the spirit in which the gift is given (the giver's perception of the gift and his motives for giving it) and the spirit in which it was received (the receiver's perception of the gift and his motives for receiving it). The spirit in which it is given and received determines both the nature of the gift and either the rightness or wrongness of the transaction. The following are the different perceptions and motives the giver might have, together with the type and moral quality of the gift they determine:[35]

1. Gratitude for and appreciation of police service, which make the gift a *reward* for them
2. A sense of obligation or indebtedness to the police for their services, which makes the gift the *payment of a debt*
3. A desire to foster good relations with the police to ensure the continuation of their beneficial services, which makes the gift a *gratuity*
4. A desire to establish a special relationship with the police in order to get extra services (which may be legal but go beyond the call of duty), which makes the gift an *investment*
5. A desire to procure illegal or morally questionable services from the police, or to stop them from performing their duties, which makes the gift a *bribe*

The following are the different perceptions and motives the recipient may have together with the type and moral quality of the gift they determine:[36]

1. Perception of the gift as a reward given out of gratitude for and appreciation of the recipient's services
2. Perception of the gift as payment of a social debt that the giver believes he owes
3. Perception of the gift as a gratuity with which to foster good relations with the recipient so as to ensure the continuation of his service
4. Perception of the gift as an investment with which to establish a special relationship with the recipient so as to get from him extra services (which may be legal but not among his duties), and an awareness of the debt to the giver which he thereby incurs
5. Perception of the gift as a bribe with which to procure illegal or morally questionable services from the recipient, or to stop him from performing his duties

Bribes are morally wrong because they entail violating the legal and moral codes. Moreover, an officer who knowingly takes a bribe or extorts a gift is culpable in two ways: (1) for breaking the law, and (2) for breaking his oath to uphold the law. Investments are morally wrong for the giver because his motive is to gain an undeserved advantage over other citizens, which is unjust. They are morally wrong for the officer, because he aids and abets the investor in the latter's unjust intent. And the officer compromises his position by putting himself in the debt of an unscrupulous investor. Even if the debts are not called in, or are ignored if they are, the officer has still compromised himself by indebting himself, if only in principle. For Kania, mooching is immoral only if the officer believes his accepting the gift obligates him to give preferential treatment to the givers, as it violates his commitment to give equal treatment to all. This both violates the public trust and promotes injustice:[37]

> If the gift is accepted as a payment for future legal or quasi-legal services, the officer is committing him/ herself to an unspecified obligation that he/she owes to no other citizen. This is a violation of the special trust that exists between the police officer and the general public. If the officer enters into the exchange

> with the perception that he/she does owe a special
> obligation to a single citizen, then that sense of exclu-
> sive obligation is what makes the acceptance unethical.

Mooching that does not entail any such "sense of exclusive obligation" such as rewards, payments, and gratuities (items 1 through 3,
above) is not morally wrong; indeed, it can be argued that it is
morally right. Thus, police officers may have a moral obligation to
accept such gifts. To refuse a gift offered out of gratitude or from a
sense of obligation is to deny its giver the opportunity to express his
gratitude or to discharge his perceived debt. In other words, it is to
frustrate his efforts to be moral and thus to demean him. Moreover,
the officer's refusal to reciprocate the offer of the gift by accepting it
is an affront to their common sociality, to the "mutual feeling that we
both belong to the same social system." Officers arguably have a
moral obligation to nurture good relations with the public. That can
be done by graciously accepting a non-binding gift given in the
proper spirit. Their refusing the gift may be taken as an insult. Officers ought not to offend the public, whose support is needed for
effective policing.

Mooching, then, is a morally ambiguous practice, which is a
central issue in police ethics. Equally good reasons, teleological and
deontological, can be given either to defend or to condemn it. Fundamental to resolving this issue is carefully distinguishing among the
different forms a gift can take as determined by the different motives
and perspectives of its giver and receiver. Both teleological and
deontological reasons may converge in its defense when the gift does
not indebt the receiver to the giver and promises to yield social
benefits (e.g., an officer's accepting a discount on a meal thereby
meeting his obligation to show respect to the restaurateur and honor
their common sociality, as well as enabling him to police more effectively). Mooching is morally wrong only insofar as it causes the
officer to violate his public trust and constrains him to be unjust;
otherwise, it is a benign practice, perhaps even obligatory, sanctioned
by "long-standing and universally tolerated practice".

We turn next to the issue of bribery, which, like mooching, is
morally ambiguous, and the moral theories presupposed in its discussion and resolution. Bribery is not just another representative type
of ambiguously corrupt act but, along with extortion, is the most
pervasive form of corruption in law enforcement and significantly
influences its conduct.[38] As we saw earlier, some (e.g., Johnston)

defend bribery and other forms of corruption on the grounds that it yields social benefits. Bribery compensates poorly paid police, enables citizens to receive service they otherwise would not, and oils the economy. Others oppose it, however, on the grounds that it spawns social ills. Bribery prostitutes justice to base ends, unfairly favors the affluent who can buy their way out of it, encourages criminal behavior, and undermines public trust in and esteem for the police. Defending or opposing bribery in terms of its social consequences presupposes a teleological — more specifically, utilitarian — stance. Resolving the issue of whether bribery is morally acceptable on teleological grounds entails determining whether its socially good effects significantly outweigh its socially bad effects; if they do, then bribery is morally permissible and perhaps even obligatory. If they do not, then bribery is morally wrong. Howard Kahane, a social contract theorist after Hobbes, has advanced the interesting argument — as did Mandeville — that vices generally, not just those associated with the police force, make for social stability. A society composed exclusively of moral saints would inevitably collapse from the weight of its rectitude:[39]

> Speaking of saints and sociopaths brings to mind the point that both, but especially saints, are bound to be rare in any human population. A society composed exclusively, or even on the whole, of one or the other cannot be *evolutionarily stable*. A group composed primarily of saints will be invaded, sooner or later, by those programmed to clever cheating. A society made up chiefly of sinners will fail to hold its own against more diversely populated competing groups.

The consequences either good or bad of bribery are irrelevant to the deontologist who is concerned with motives and moral principles. If an officer's motive for accepting a bribe is personal profit, then he acts heteronomously, to use Kant's terminology. He does not exercise a good will or act autonomously in conformity to the moral law, and so does not act morally. Moreover, if accepting a bribe entails a subversion of justice or a violation of other laws, it is intrinsically wrong for that reason alone. Finally, it is highly doubtful that taking a bribe or extortion is consistent with either agapistic or aretaic ethics, and that a virtuous character, one animated by either benevolence or a felicitous integrity, would issue spontaneously in such conduct.

Moral presuppositions

We turn now to the moral presuppositions in the theories as to the causes of and remedies for corruption. Now, every one of these theories presupposes that the causes of corruption ultimately lie not in the character of the individual person but rather in something external to him and out of his control. Even though the so-called personalistic (individualistic) theory attributes corruption to bad character, it goes on to find the ultimate cause not in the character itself but in those genetic and environmental factors that presumably determine character; in the socio-economic, ethnic, and cultural groups which furnish the majority of police recruits; or in the so-called "police personality" which emerges both from the officer's personal background and his professional training and socialization. The implication of these explanations is that blame attaches not to the individual person but instead to his genes or social environment. The alternative theories of the causes of police corruption, the institutional and systematic, are even more explicit in attributing corruption to the social environment and shifting the blame from the individual to either the institution of policing itself or the larger society. A deeper, metaphysical assumption made by these theories is that the individual person lacks moral autonomy or freedom in making his moral choices but is wholly at the mercy of physical or environmental forces. These presuppositions are reflected in the remedies for corruption proposed by each of the above explanations of it. Each proposes various institutional or social changes, thereby making the group instead of the individual responsible for eliminating corruption. Thus, the personalistic theory favors improved methods of recruiting, screening, and training of recruits; the institutional theory, alterations in the organization of police departments; and the systematic theory, political changes through legislation and changes in social attitudes through public education.

These assumptions that the social environment or genes are to blame for corrupt individuals and that the person lacks moral autonomy or freedom are just that and questionable. Indeed, they represent but one side of deep and perennial issues. If they are false, then the resultant explanations lose their force and the remedies will fail. Furthermore, blaming the group for the corruption of its members begs the question. If it is the group that makes the individual corrupt, then what is it that makes the group corrupt? After all, the group is nothing more than the individuals who compose it. In a similar vein, Edwards argues that the bad example set by others is not sufficient to explain or exculpate the badness of individuals:[40]

> Now concerning this way of accounting for the corrup-
> tion of the world, by the influence of bad example.
> ...'Tis accounting for the thing by the thing itself. It is
> accounting for the corruption of the world by the cor-
> ruption of the world. For, that bad examples are gen-
> eral all over the world to be followed by others, and
> have been so from the beginning, is only an instance, or
> rather a description of that corruption of the world
> which is to be accounted for.

If it is the group that contributes to the individual's corruption, then how do we explain the fact that some individuals, but not others, are *prone* to the corruptive influences of their group? As Edwards puts it, "So that evil example will in no wise account for the corruption of mankind, without supposing a natural proness to sin."[41] Kania's junior officer who steadfastly refused the offered discount on his meals, even against the urgings and insults of the restaurateur, is an example of one who was not prone to corruptive influences.

The personalistic approach further assumes that improving the training of recruits, which would presumably include some moral education, would help eliminate corruption; however, as we saw earlier, increased knowledge and insight are no guarantee that moral improvement will result. Knowing moral theory is quite different from actually being moral and behaving morally. This requires an act of will for which a mere appeal to the intellect is insufficient. To quote the old adage yet again, "You can lead a horse to water, but you cannot make him drink it."

Notes

1. Johnston, Michael, *Political Corruption and Public Policy in America*, Brooks/Cole Publishing, Monterey, CA, 1982, pp. 72–107; reprinted in Close, Daryl and Meier, Nicholas, *Morality in Criminal Justice: An Introduction to Ethics*, Wadsworth, Belmont, CA, 1995, pp. 285–286.
2. Close, Daryl and Meier, Nicholas, *Morality in Criminal Justice: An Introduction to Ethics*, Wadsworth, Belmont, CA, 1995, p. 287.
3. Reiss, Jr., Albert J., *The Police and the Public*, Yale University Press, New Haven, CN, 1971, p. 169.
4. Training key #254: police corruption, in IACP, *Police Chief*, International Association of Chiefs of Police, Alexandria, VA; reprinted in Close, Daryl and Meier, Nicholas, *Morality in Criminal Justice: An Introduction to Ethics*, Wadsworth, Belmont, CA, 1995, p. 276.

5. These examples of police corruption are taken from Johnston, Michael, *Political Corruption and Public Policy in America*, Brooks/Cole Publishing, Monterey, CA, 1982, pp. 72–107; reprinted in Close, Daryl and Meier, Nicholas, *Morality in Criminal Justice: An Introduction to Ethics*, Wadsworth, Belmont, CA, 1995, p. 288.

6. Training key #254: police corruption, in IACP, *Police Chief*, International Association of Chiefs of Police, Alexandria, VA; reprinted in Close, Daryl and Meier, Nicholas, *Morality in Criminal Justice: An Introduction to Ethics*, Wadsworth, Belmont, CA, 1995, p. 276.

7. This list of possible forms of police corruption and their labels is largely derived from Stoddard, Ellwyn R., The informal "code" of police deviancy: a group approach to "blue-coat crime", *Journal of Criminal Law, Criminology and Police Science*, 59(2), 201–213, 1968; reprinted in Close, Daryl and Meier, Nicholas, *Morality in Criminal Justice: An Introduction to Ethics*, Wadsworth, Belmont, CA, 1995, p. 317.

8. Vollmer, August, *The Police and Modern Society*, 1936, pp. 3–4 (cited by Stoddard, Ellwyn R., The informal "code" of police deviancy: a group approach to "blue-coat crime", *Journal of Criminal Law, Criminology and Police Science*, 59(2), 314, 1968).

9. Johnston, Michael, *Political Corruption and Public Policy in America*, Brooks/Cole Publishing, Monterey, CA, 1982, pp. 72–107; reprinted in Close, Daryl and Meier, Nicholas, *Morality in Criminal Justice: An Introduction to Ethics*, Wadsworth, Belmont, CA, 1995, pp. 291, 294.

10. Training key #254: police corruption, in IACP, *Police Chief*, International Association of Chiefs of Police, Alexandria, VA; reprinted in Close, Daryl and Meier, Nicholas, *Morality in Criminal Justice: An Introduction to Ethics*, Wadsworth, Belmont, CA, 1995, p. 278.

11. Stoddard, Ellwyn R., The informal "code" of police deviancy: a group approach to "blue-coat crime", *Journal of Criminal Law, Criminology and Police Science*, 59(2), 313, 1968.

12. Johnston, Michael, *Political Corruption and Public Policy in America*, Brooks/Cole Publishing, Monterey, CA, 1982, pp. 72–107; reprinted in Close, Daryl and Meier, Nicholas, *Morality in Criminal Justice: An Introduction to Ethics*, Wadsworth, Belmont, CA, 1995, pp. 288, 295, 297.

13. Reiss, Jr., Albert J., *The Police and the Public*, Yale University Press, New Haven, CN, 1971, p. 124.

14. Johnston, Michael, *Political Corruption and Public Policy in America*, Brooks/Cole Publishing, Monterey, CA, 1982, pp. 72–107; reprinted in Close, Daryl and Meier, Nicholas, *Morality in Criminal Justice: An Introduction to Ethics*, Wadsworth, Belmont, CA, 1995, p. 298.

15. Reiss, Jr., Albert J., *The Police and the Public*, Yale University Press, New Haven, CN, 1971, p. 132.

16. Johnston, Michael, *Political Corruption and Public Policy in America*, Brooks/Cole Publishing, Monterey, CA, 1982, pp. 72–107; reprinted in Close, Daryl and Meier, Nicholas, *Morality in Criminal Justice: An Introduction to Ethics*, Wadsworth, Belmont, CA, 1995, p. 299.

17. Johnston, Michael, *Political Corruption and Public Policy in America*, Brooks/Cole Publishing, Monterey, CA, 1982, pp. 72–107; reprinted in Close, Daryl and Meier, Nicholas, *Morality in Criminal Justice: An Introduction to Ethics*, Wadsworth, Belmont, CA, 1995, p. 300.

18. Johnston, Michael, *Political Corruption and Public Policy in America*, Brooks/Cole Publishing, Monterey, CA, 1982, pp. 72–107; reprinted in Close, Daryl and Meier, Nicholas, *Morality in Criminal Justice: An Introduction to Ethics*, Wadsworth, Belmont, CA, 1995, p. 302.

19. Johnston, Michael, *Political Corruption and Public Policy in America*, Brooks/Cole Publishing, Monterey, CA, 1982, pp. 72–107; reprinted in Close, Daryl and Meier, Nicholas, *Morality in Criminal Justice: An Introduction to Ethics*, Wadsworth, Belmont, CA, 1995, p. 307.

20. "Corruption benefits all of the direct parties to vice transactions, at least in the short run. The consumer procures his or her gratification, the entrepreneur buys protection, and the police officer makes some money. Corruption also does away with the need for violence or coercion. It is an attractive way of avoiding tasks that could never be accomplished anyway, such as the complete eradication of prostitution or of numbers games ... corruption is well suited to resolving the conflicts inherent in policing a complex society." (See Johnston, Michael, *Political Corruption and Public Policy in America*, Brooks/Cole Publishing, Monterey, CA, 1982, pp. 72–107; reprinted in Close, Daryl and Meier, Nicholas, *Morality in Criminal Justice: An Introduction to Ethics*, Wadsworth, Belmont, CA, 1995, pp. 302–303, 306–307.)

21. Bracey, Dorothy H., A Functional Approach to Police Corruption, Criminal Justice Center Monograph No. 1, The John Jay Press, New York, 1976, p. 8.

22. This raises the ticklish issue of whether we have a moral right to harm ourselves. Laws against suicide implicitly deny it. The issue has recently been brought to the public's attention by the movement promoting so-called "physician-assisted" suicide.

23. Johnston, Michael, *Political Corruption and Public Policy in America*, Brooks/Cole Publishing, Monterey, CA, 1982, pp. 72–107; reprinted in Close, Daryl and Meier, Nicholas, *Morality in Criminal Justice: An Introduction to Ethics*, Wadsworth, Belmont, CA, 1995, p. 307.

24. Daley, Robert, *Prince of the City: The True Story of a Cop Who Knew Too Much*, Houghton Mifflin, Boston, MA, 1978, p. 292.

25. Training key #254: police corruption, in IACP, *Police Chief*, International Association of Chiefs of Police, Alexandria, VA; reprinted in Close, Daryl and Meier, Nicholas, *Morality in Criminal Justice: An Introduction to Ethics*, Wadsworth, Belmont, CA, 1995, p. 276.

26. Aubry, Jr., Arthur, The value of ethics in the police service, *Police*, 12, 41, 1967.

27. McMullan, A theory of corruption, *Soc. Rev.*, 9, 183–184, as cited in Kania, Richard, Should we tell the police to say "yes" to gratuities?, *Criminal Justice Ethics*, 7(2), 37–49, 1988; reprinted in Close, Daryl and Meier, Nicholas, *Morality in Criminal Justice: An Introduction to Ethics*, Wadsworth, Belmont, CA, 1995, p. 327.

28. Training key #254: police corruption, in IACP, *Police Chief*, International Association of Chiefs of Police, Alexandria, VA; reprinted in Close, Daryl and Meier, Nicholas, *Morality in Criminal Justice: An Introduction to Ethics*, Wadsworth, Belmont, CA, 1995, p. 279.

29. Homan, George C., Social behavior as exchange, *American Journal of Sociology*, 63, 606, 1958.

30. Hurley, Patrick J., *A Concise Introduction to Logic*, 5th ed., Wadsworth, Belmont, CA, 1994, p. 142.

31. Kania, Richard, Should we tell the police to say "yes" to gratuities?, *Criminal Justice Ethics*, 7(2), 37–49, 1988; reprinted in Close, Daryl and Meier, Nicholas, *Morality in Criminal Justice: An Introduction to Ethics*, Wadsworth, Belmont, CA, 1995, p. 331.

32. Kania, Richard, Should we tell the police to say "yes" to gratuities?, *Criminal Justice Ethics*, 7(2), 37–49, 1988; reprinted in Close, Daryl and Meier, Nicholas, *Morality in Criminal Justice: An Introduction to Ethics*, Wadsworth, Belmont, CA, 1995, p. 328.

33. Leach, Edmund, *Culture and Communication: The Logic by which Symbols Are Connected*, Cambridge University Press, London, 1976, p. 6.

34. Kania, Richard, Should we tell the police to say "yes" to gratuities?, *Criminal Justice Ethics*, 7(2), 37–49, 1988; reprinted in Close, Daryl and Meier, Nicholas, *Morality in Criminal Justice: An Introduction to Ethics*, Wadsworth, Belmont, CA, 1995, p. 332.

35. Kania, Richard, Should we tell the police to say "yes" to gratuities?, *Criminal Justice Ethics*, 7(2), 37–49, 1988; reprinted in Close, Daryl and Meier, Nicholas, *Morality in Criminal Justice: An Introduction to Ethics*, Wadsworth, Belmont, CA, 1995, pp. 333–334.

36. Kania, Richard, Should we tell the police to say "yes" to gratuities?, *Criminal Justice Ethics*, 7(2), 37–49, 1988; reprinted in Close, Daryl and Meier, Nicholas, *Morality in Criminal Justice: An Introduction to Ethics*, Wadsworth, Belmont, CA, 1995, pp. 334–335.

37. Kania, Richard, Should we tell the police to say "yes" to gratuities?, *Criminal Justice Ethics*, 7(2), 37–49, 1988; reprinted in Close, Daryl and Meier, Nicholas, *Morality in Criminal Justice: An Introduction to Ethics*, Wadsworth, Belmont, CA, 1995, p. 335.

38. Johnston, Michael, *Political Corruption and Public Policy in America*, Brooks/Cole Publishing, Monterey, CA, 1982, pp. 72–107; reprinted in Close, Daryl and Meier, Nicholas, *Morality in Criminal Justice: An Introduction to Ethics*, Wadsworth, Belmont, CA, 1995, p. 290.

39. Kahane, Howard, Sociobiology, egoism and reciprocity, in *Moral Philosophy: A Reader*, Pojman, L.P., Ed., Hackett Publishing, Indianapolis, IN, 1993, p. 71.

40. Edwards, Jonathan, Original sin, in *The Works of Jonathan Edwards*, Holbrook, III, C.A., Ed., Yale University Press, New Haven, CN, 1970, p. 196.

41. Edwards, Jonathan, Original sin, in *The Works of Jonathan Edwards*, Holbrook, III, C.A., Ed., Yale University Press, New Haven, CN, 1970, p. 199.

chapter thirteen

Force

> It is curious that Mill makes very little mention of the police as a danger to liberty. In our day, they are its worst enemy in most civilized countries.
>
> —Bertrand Russell ("John Stuart Mill")

The problem of force in policing

According to Muir,[1] "Coercion is a means of controlling the conduct of others through threats to harm." The capacity to use force or coercion is, for Bittner, the very core of the police role. The police are the only civilian authority empowered to use physical force in situations demanding it. Their unique function is to enforce the law, control crime, and keep the public peace by physical coercion if necessary; however, they are permitted to use force only as a last resort:[2]

> The specific competence of the police is targeted on the handling of all sorts of problems in which force may have to be used to bring an untoward development under control. The police, and the police alone, have the authority to proceed coercively in every conceivable crisis, and they alone have the duty not to retreat in the face of opposition. This competence, I further propose, underlies every kind of police activity all the way from crime control to the care of lost children. But while the possible use of force in accordance with situational needs is uniquely entrusted to the police, the skill involved in policing consists of techniques designed to avoid recourse to it.

The prerogative of using physical force to enforce the law belongs as much to the police as to the military; without it, the law would have no teeth and anarchy would be invited. As Hobbes bluntly put it, "And Covenants, without the Sword, are but Words, and of no strength to secure a man at all."[3] This prerogative invests the police with tremendous power and gives them the opportunity to abuse and misuse it. For this reason, the law strictly circumscribes the exercise of police use of force and limits its use to restraint: "The fundamental maxim of the methodical exercise of coercion by the police is that ... [it] must be restricted to an unavoidable minimum. Above all, force must not be used for any other purpose except to effect restraint."[3] Furthermore, there lurks the danger that police power might be used to serve political interests, or even that the state might use the police to control its citizens and quash political dissent. When in 1829 the British parliament instituted a police force for the Metropolitan District of London, care was taken to ensure that it would be politically neutral in its efforts to enforce the law and keep the peace.[4] To this end, the codes of ethics in effect in many police departments stipulate that police must always operate under, never above, the law.

Even the law's careful circumscription of the essentially coercive role of policing has not prevented our ambivalence towards it. We perceive coercion as a direct threat to our freedom and peace, values central to our democratic ethos. Where coercion begins freedom ends; and yet coercion is necessary for maintaining freedom:[5]

> The police, by the very nature of their function, are an anomaly in a free society. They are invested with a great deal of authority under a system of government in which authority is reluctantly granted and, when granted, sharply curtailed. The specific form of their authority — to arrest, to search, to detain, and to use force — is awesome in the degree to which it can be disruptive of freedom, invasive of privacy, and sudden and direct in its impact upon the individual. ...Yet a democracy is heavily dependent upon its police ... to maintain the degree of order that makes a free society possible. ...The strength of a democracy and the quality of life enjoyed by its citizens are determined in large measure by the ability of the police to discharge their duties.

Coercion is no less necessary for preserving peace. The police are authorized to use coercion to curb the unauthorized coercion by others for selfish and destructive ends. In society, as in nature, the strong prey on the weak who, without the help of the police to make up for their weakness, would have to look to their own defenses. They would all the time have to exercise the greatest vigilance, which would only increase their anxiety and take time from other pursuits, but with no guarantee that their most vigilant efforts in self-defense will be effective. Without the threat of police coercion, as Hobbes grimly and pointedly reminds us,[6]

> Every man is Enemy to every man; the same is conse-
> quent to the time, wherein men live without other
> security, than what their own strength, and their own
> invention shall furnish them withall. In such condition,
> there is. ...no Society; and which is worst of all, con-
> tinual feare and danger of violent death; And the life of
> man, solitary, poore, nasty, brutish, and short.

A show of brute force is incompatible with our prizing of peace and our preference for using peaceful means to sustain it. Beginning early in the last century, the futility of war and the superiority of diplomacy have slowly dawned on the western world, attested to by the Concert of Vienna, the League of Nations, and the United Nations:[7]

> During the past 150 years, the awareness of the moral
> and practical necessity of peace took hold of the minds
> of virtually all people. The advocacy of warfare and
> violence did not disappear entirely, but it grew pro-
> gressively less frank and it keeps losing ground to
> arguments that condemn it.

Today we resort to war reluctantly and only when diplomatic efforts to prevent it are exhausted. This pacific tendency is evident in our domestic affairs as well as in those of the international realm. In democracies, obedience to political authority is not compelled by overt threats of physical force, but is achieved by the voluntary consent and cooperation of the governed. Thus, taxes are collected not by armed tax collectors but by written directives. Power is communicated symbolically, not physically: "The extent to which we have become accustomed to, and take for granted, the indirect ways of authority implementation and peaceful governing is perhaps best illustrated by the fact that the notorious 'knock on the door' that is associated with totalitarian regimes is generally viewed as the supreme political abomination,"[8] nor is the judicial process against criminals still brutal, with the intent of humiliating the offender. The modern court is not an inquisitorial Star Chamber, but a forum for hearing reasoned arguments pro and con. Punishment is no longer corporal, resulting in mutilation and death, but takes the form of incarceration with rehabilitation as typically its end:[9]

> It would seem that the criminal process of today, at least in terms of its official script, seeks to dramatize the possibility of life without violence even under conditions where the imposition of coercive sanctions is the business at hand.

The philosophical justification for peace and the non-violent means of conducting our social, legal, and political affairs is found in Hobbes' theory of the social contract, with its exposure of the terrible perils of the state of nature, and in utilitarianism, with its insight that violence in the long term serves neither one's own, nor society's, best interests.[10]

Ironically, the modern police force, particularly in English-speaking countries, was instituted precisely to preserve freedom and peace and to curb the greatest internal threat to them: the wielding of arbitrary and excessive force, especially for political ends. As such, the police are a uniquely and quintessentially Western institution.[11] Now a philosophical problem emerges here. How can we reconcile our valuing of peace and nonviolent solutions to social problems with empowering the police to use physical force when unavoidable? Two solutions are available to us. The utilitarians would argue that these morally questionable means, by serving socially beneficial ends, are thereby made moral themselves. There is a danger in this solution. A social benefit such as national security might be used by a government to excuse the violation of human rights through the abuse of police power. An alternative solution, which insists that no one is exempt from the rule of law, is provided by the social contract theory. According to it, lawbreakers violate the social contract and so lapse into a state of nature, thus tacitly declaring themselves as public enemies. Consequently, the police are justified in using whatever force is necessary against them to protect society and to preserve the social contract.

Yet, there is some justification for our moral ambivalence towards even the carefully controlled and philosophically defensible use of coercion. Those in positions of power and authority who have the opportunity and responsibility of using force are in danger of compromising their moral integrity. Weber warns:[12]

> "He who lets himself in for politics, that is, for power
> and force as means, contracts with diabolical powers
> and for his action it is *not* true that good can follow
> only from good and evil only from evil, but that often
> the opposite is true."

In other words, he sometimes finds that good ends such as peace and
order can come from evil means such as violence. Anyone who wields
state-authorized power encounters the "ethical paradoxes of coercion" which involve the "irreconcilable conflict" between the "demon
of politics" and the "god of love" — that is, between political neces-
sities and moral demands. To undertake political life naively without
understanding these ethical paradoxes is to invite psychological distress and moral ruin. Apart from ensnaring politicians in moral dilemmas, their burden of power can also corrupt them if they succumb to
the temptation of abusing or misusing that power. "Power tends to
corrupt," observes Lord Acton, "and absolute power corrupts absolutely."[13]

The Dirty Harry problem

The moral ambiguity in the use of force for good ends is epitomized
and brought vividly home in the so-called Dirty Harry problem. Even
if the use of police coercion can be morally justified in the name of the
common good or the social contract, another moral issue immediately
arises as to whether force may be used to extract information from
suspects. This issue is made razor sharp in the film *Magnum Force*, in
which the protagonist, a cop named Harry Callahan, beats information out of a suspected psychopathic killer and kidnapper in an attempt to locate, and thus save the life of, the suspect's latest victim.
The effort proves futile inasmuch as the information is obtained too
late to save the victim's life and, due to the illegal way in which it was
obtained, is inadmissible in court. This is a fictional example of a
larger issue: whether or not the police should use "dirty means" to
achieve their goals, or, more philosophically, whether a socially good
end such as the doing of justice ever justifies immoral or illegal means;
if so, under what circumstances? Torturing or beating confessions out
of suspects, as in the *Magnum Force* case, is an especially egregious
example of the use of dirty means. Less extreme examples, in the case
of stop and frisks, are an officer's falsifying probable cause, making a
false arrest, or fabricating some fraudulent pretext to conduct an
illegal search that might be legitimate in other circumstances. In the

case of interrogation of persons suspected of crimes, examples would be the use of threats or coercion or the manipulation of the Miranda procedure. There is also the administration of "curbside" justice to suspects the police know to be guilty, but whom the courts will likely exonerate for lack of legally admissible evidence. In our discussion below, we shall confine ourselves to the example of applying excessive physical force to extract information; whatever we say about it applies to other examples, as well. This is an old issue, which used to be called "dirty hands" but is now nicknamed the Dirty Harry problem after the character made famous by actor Clint Eastwood. Klockars puts it "at the core of the police role, or at least near to it."[14]

Clarification of the problem

Before considering attempts to resolve it, we need to clarify the issue, beginning with the term describing it. "Dirty" applies to acts which, according to Klockars, are both intrinsically bad, because they violate some moral law, and extrinsically bad, because they threaten the social order. They are dirty on both deontological and teleological grounds:[15]

> "Dirty" here means both "repugnant" in that it offends widely shared standards of human decency and dignity and "dangerous" in that it breaks commonly shared and supported norms, rules, or laws for conduct. To "dirty" acts there must be both a deontologically based face validity of immorality and a consequentialist threat to the prevailing rules for social order.

On this analysis, Harry's treatment of the suspect is doubly bad. Deontologically, it violates the moral and legal principle against the infliction of pain on suspects who are presumed innocent before their conviction; it denigrates human dignity insofar as it uses a person merely as a means to an end, in this case to get information. Teleologically, it sets a dangerous precedent whereby any presumably innocent citizen, even those who are in fact innocent, might be brutalized for the sake of extracting valuable information. Now, what makes this issue particularly onerous is that it puts the one confronting it into a classic dilemma, a case of being "damned if I do or damned if I don't". If an officer in Harry's situation does as Harry did and beats a confession out of a suspect, then he is to be blamed for both the deontological and teleological reasons explained above. On the other hand, if he refrains from brutalizing the suspect and, consequently, his victim dies (in the *Magnum Force* example, suppose that the girl had lived because of the information extracted by Harry but would not have otherwise), then the officer is culpable for the death of an innocent victim. The officer, then, is not in the position of having to choose between a clearly right action and a clearly wrong one, but is in the unenviable position of having to choose between two equally wrong actions, though wrong for different reasons:[16]

> The troublesome issue in the Dirty Harry problem is not whether under some utilitarian calculus a right choice can be made, but that the choice must always be between at least two wrongs. And in choosing to do either wrong, the policeman inevitably taints or tarnishes himself.

Police might apply certain criteria in deciding whether the use of dirty means is legitimate, and which may subsequently be used to justify or rationalize them. One criterion is the assumption that the suspect is guilty, either of the crime under investigation or of some crime in the past. A second is the so-called "Great Guilty Place Assumption" which habitually views certain places and situations as suspicious and assumes that a person found there is guilty of some offense associated with them:[17]

> As a consequence of his job, the policeman is constantly exposed to highly selective samples of his environment. That he comes to read a clump of bushes as a place to hide, a roadside rest as a homosexual "tearoom", a sweet old lady as a robbery looking for a place to happen, or a poor young black as someone willing to oblige her is not a question of a perverse, pessimistic, or racist personality, but of a person whose job requires that he strive to see race, age, sex, and even nature in an ecology of guilt, which can include him if he fails to see it so.

Related to this is a third criterion, the so-called "Not Guilty (This Time) Assumption" which regards most people found in particular areas as not innocent, even though stopping them proves unjustified, and interrogating or searching them turns up nothing. The assumption is that they are guilty of something as yet undetected. A fourth criterion is the belief that the dirty means alone will work in a given situation, which depends on the officer's professional competence and the legitimate and viable options open to him. The more competent the officer in applying legal means, the better his training, and the more resources he has available to him, the less likely he is to employ dirty means unnecessarily. A fifth criterion is the belief that the employment of dirty means will most likely have a good outcome which morally outweighs any bad consequences; however, this belief is at best only probably true, and to support its probable truth some questions must be answered affirmatively. First, can the suspect who is the target of the dirty means provide the information sought? The suspect in *Magnum Force* could. He had confessed to the kidnapping and had previously sent teeth and descriptions of the girl's clothing to the police. Second, will the dirty means prove effective? Harry was justified in believing that the girl was still alive and could be safely rescued. The legitimacy, if any, of using morally questionable means to achieve an unquestionable moral good depends upon how warranted any of these assumptions is.[18]

Resolutions of the problem

Various attempts have been made to resolve the Dirty Harry problem. Three attempts identified by Klockars appeal to three different models of policing — the professional model, the peacekeeping model, and the skilled craft model. These attempts fail, however, because they reduce the officer's choice to something other than a moral choice and so deprive him of his moral autonomy. They also tend to evade the issue entirely. A fourth attempt involves legislation intended to limit police discretion. The four remaining attempts do not resolve the problem so much as morally evaluate the police use of dirty means: one condemns the practice as morally wrong and meriting punishment, whereas the other two seek to excuse it. We turn now to a brief consideration of each of these attempts at a resolution of the Dirty Harry problem and their defects.

Under the professional model, the police force is a sophisticated bureaucratic machine, and its officers are cogs who must obey mechanically the orders and policies of a central administrative authority. Klockars states:[19]

> It envisions a highly trained, technologically sophisti-
> cated police department operating free from political
> interference with a corps of well-educated police respond-
> ing obediently to the policies, orders, and directives of a

> central administrative command ... to use Bittner's phrasing, as ... "cogs in a quasi-military machine who do what they are told out of a mix of fear, loyalty, routine, and detailed specification of duties."

The police department is then a typical bureaucracy, the administrators of which set tasks and expectations for levels of production (e.g., arrest quotas). Its motto is *sine ira et studio* (without anger and partisanship). Officers are expected not to act emotionally, but coolly and rationally to implement departmental policies. Their motives and purposes for performing their duties are to be found wholly within their department.[14]

We are already familiar with the defects in this model with respect to police corruption. One defect is that it pits bureaucratic control against the professional autonomy of the individual police officers and curtails their opportunities for making discretionary judgments, which causes resentment and invites corruption. A second defect of the professional model is that strict administrative control is not always effective in providing satisfactory human services; the public, moreover, tends to react unfavorably to the help — however well intentioned — provided by soulless bureaucracies with their coils of red tape and stultifying insistence on protocol.

The third defect is the most serious for us, as it pertains directly to the resolution of the Dirty Harry problem. The professional model appears to resolve the problem by "replacing the morally compelling ends of punishment and peace with the less human, though by no means un-compelling, ends of bureaucratic performance."[20] In other words, the officer's end in deciding to use dirty means is no longer the moral one of punishing malefactors or preserving the public peace, but the non-moral one of conforming to departmental policy, with perhaps the ulterior motive of keeping and advancing in his job. Thus, Harry's aim and motive in beating the information out of the suspect would have been conformity to an administrative directive. Now, it is plain to see that this is no resolution of the problem at all; if anything, it simply changes the problem. The essence of the Dirty Harry problem is that illegal and morally questionable means are used to realize moral ends. In this resolution, the ends of bureaucratic exigency or personal interest replace moral ends. Now we have a moral problem of another sort, which is the use of immoral means to realize non-moral ends. This is no longer a dilemma where either choice is going to be in some sense wrong and blamed on the individual who perpetrated it, but where the choice to use dirty means to achieve non-moral ends is clearly wrong on either teleological or deontological grounds. As Klockars notes, "This resolution certainly does not imply that dirty means will disappear, only that the motives for their use will be career advancement and promotion."[21] These are non-moral motives from a utilitarian viewpoint, as they do not further the common good, and they are non-moral from a deontological viewpoint, as they are hypothetical and not categorical imperatives. In other words, they are manifestations of prudence, not of the morally good will. Furthermore, if the officer is conditioned to employ without forethought dirty means on command, then he willfully abdicates his moral autonomy. He gives his prerogative of freely exercising his moral choice to the bureaucracy that controls him. Though he may abandon his moral autonomy, he cannot escape moral censure, as many German soldiers attempted to do after the end of World War II by defending their participation in war crimes with the excuse, "We were only following orders."

An alternative to the above professional model of policing is the so-called skilled craft model which envisions the police as well-trained craftsmen who make a moral distinction between "criminal law" and "criminal procedure". Criminal law seeks to control the behavior of wrongdoers, while criminal procedure endeavors to regulate the behavior of the judicial authorities in the exercise of their duties. The suggestion is that what would be unlawful for a citizen to do under the criminal code may be both lawful and necessary for the police officer to do under the aegis of criminal procedure. Skolnick describes policing as a skilled craft by saying:[22]

> The policeman views criminal procedure with the *administrative bias of the craftsman*, a prejudice contradictory to due process of law. ...He sees himself as a craftsman, at his best, a master of his trade. As such, he feels he ought to be free to employ the techniques of his trade, and that the *system* ought to provide regulations contributing to his freedom to improvise, rather than constricting it ... the policeman draws a moral distinction between criminal law and criminal procedure. The distinction is drawn somewhat as follows. The substantive law of crimes is intended to control the behavior of people who willfully injure persons or property, or who engage in behaviors having such a consequence, such as the use of narcotics. Criminal procedure, by contrast, is intended to control authorities, not criminals.

> As such, it does not fall into the same *moral* class of constraint as substantive criminal law. If a policeman were himself to use narcotics, or to steal, or to assault, *outside the line of duty*, much the same standards would be applied to him by other policemen as to the ordinary citizen. When, however, the issue concerns the policeman's freedom to carry out his *duties*, another *moral* realm is entered.

Again, this justification of dirty means in policing by placing it in another moral realm occupied by criminal procedure does not solve the Dirty Harry problem. Like the professional model that merely changes the problem by replacing moral with non-moral ends, the skilled craft model changes it by reclassifying the immoral means as moral. Ironically, the behavior condemned by the criminal law is the very behavior that this model condones under the rubric of criminal procedure. It is a case of fighting fire with fire. Furthermore, the assumption that there are two distinct moral realms (the realm represented by criminal law and the realm represented by criminal procedure) is dubious at best. Grounds must be given for the existence of two distinct moral spheres. It is difficult to justify such a distinction. For one thing, the distinction between criminal law and criminal procedure is a conceptual or legal distinction; it neither is nor implies a moral one. For another, the moral institution of life is monolithic and embraces all other institutions, including the judicial. As we saw in our discussion of moral language, moral judgments (even if they are particular) are essentially universal in their purport. One of the merits of Kant's ethics is his clarifying the principle that nobody under any circumstances is exempt from the moral law. According to the deontologist, torture is torture and intrinsically immoral whether used by a rapist or by a police officer.

A third model of policing, advocated by Bittner, redefines its goals by expanding them beyond simple law enforcement and punishment to include peacekeeping as its primary goal. This model is evident in the recent expansion of police duties to include duties such as mediating neighborhood disputes, organizing crime-stoppers and neighborhood watch groups, public speaking, community policing initiatives, and other tasks which a modern "service"-style police department regularly performs. Correlated with this is the increased variegation of police power to include procedures other than arrest. However, this peacekeeping model comes nowhere near to solving the Dirty Harry problem. At best it is merely a smokescreen that obscures the problem.

Occasions will arise when the service-style police will have to enforce the law forcibly in order to enact retributive justice. Making public peace the principal goal of policing does not make its goals of enforcement and punishment any less necessary. As Klockars puts it, "Bittner leads his readers to conclude that peace is historically, empirically, intellectually, and morally the most compelling unquestionable, and humane end of policing; … [nevertheless] it is certain that individuals or groups will arise who the police … will conclude, on moral if not political or institutional grounds, have 'got it coming'."[23]

A resolution of the Dirty Harry problem has been proposed that is independent of (though compatible with) any of the other models we have discussed. This approach is to pass laws that would permit the police to use some dirty means in those cases where there is no realistic alternative to their use. This resolution resembles that suggested by the professional model inasmuch as they both circumscribe police discretion by taking the decision to use dirty means out of police hands and placing it in the hands of those having authority over the police. The difference is that in the one case police discretion is circumscribed legislatively, whereas in the other it is circumscribed bureaucratically:[24]

> Combating distrust [of the police] requires getting across the rather complicated message that granting the police specific forms of new authority may be the most effective means for reducing abuse of authority which is now theirs; that it is the absence of properly proscribed forms of authority that often impels the police to engage in questionable or outright illegal conduct. Before state legislatures enacted statutes giving unlimited authority to the police to stop and question persons suspected of criminal involvement, police nevertheless stopped and questioned people. It is inconceivable how any police agency could be expected to operate without doing so. But since the basis for their actions was unclear, the police — if they thought a challenge likely — would use the guise of arresting the individual on a minor charge (often without clear evidence) to provide a semblance of legality. Enactment of stopping and questioning statutes eliminated the need for this sham.

But, precisely the same objection can be made to this "legislative" solution to the Dirty Harry problem as was made to the solution based on the professional model: It only relieves the individual police officer of his moral freedom in the case, but not his moral culpability. The moral burden of the problem is simply transferred from the officer's shoulders to the legislators'.

The four remaining attempts to deal with the Dirty Harry problem are simply moral evaluations of those who use dirty means. For Klockars, their use is morally wrong and deserves punishment. They taint the character of their practitioner. His ethical rationale for condemning dirty means is a mixture of aretaic, utilitarian, and deontological principles. His point that dirty means taint the practitioner's character suggests aretaic or virtue-based ethics. His fear — that allowing officers to use dirty means with impunity sets a dangerous precedent which may result in their becoming standard or even desirable procedures — is based on utilitarian considerations. Klockars is appealing to the deontological principle of universalizability when he justifies the punishment of an officer who uses dirty means as a way of ensuring that he "regards his dirty means as dirty by applying the same retributive principles of punishment to his wrongful acts that he is quite willing to apply to others."[25]

Delattre is somewhat ambivalent about police employment of dirty means. He takes a utilitarian tack by warning that one illegal act (such as torturing a suspect) might entail other illegal acts, such as lying and perjury, either to cover up the first or to ensure that the suspect's conviction will not be overturned by the officer's improper procedure. Unlike Klockars, he denies that dirty means are sufficient to damage their practitioner's character. What determines character is virtues, which are well-entrenched habits or dispositions, not isolated acts. As Aristotle puts it, one swallow does not a summer make. Thus, one dirty act does not make a morally bad character; this requires a series of such acts indicative of a deep-set habit to act so:[26]

> If police officials are not tainted by refusing to step onto the slope of illegal action, neither are officials of demonstrated probity necessarily tainted by a last-ditch illegal step. Such an act may be unjustifiable by any unconditional principle, but it also may be excusable. Even if committed without regard to self-interest and at great personal sacrifice, inflicting pain is an undeniably evil act when committed by one who has no right to punish. Although it would constitute a betrayal of the duties of office, it would not necessarily be condemned in any subsequent legal proceeding. An enlightened governor could justifiably pardon the act.

> Still less does it follow that those who commit such acts
> are bad, that their character is besmirched, or that their
> honor is tainted.

On the one hand, Delattre rejects a strict deontological stance by acknowledging that improper acts "may be unjustifiable by an unconditional principle, but also may be excusable," presumably on teleological grounds. Yet, he takes a deontological stance in saying that "inflicting pain is an undeniably evil act when committed by one who has no right to punish." His theoretical framework appears to be aretetaic, given his reference to character and its resistance to contamination from single, isolated transgressions.

Muir, apparently another adherent of virtue-based ethics, makes no deontological presuppositions. He contends that a willingness to use dirty means when unavoidable, if based on knowledge of their utility and counterbalanced by empathy and compassion, is indispensable to the character of a professional or "good" police officer.[27]

> A policeman becomes a good policeman to the extent
> that he develops two virtues. Intellectually, he has to
> grasp the nature of human suffering. Morally, he has to
> resolve the contradiction of achieving just ends with
> coercive means. A patrolman who develops this tragic
> sense and moral equanimity tends to grow in the job,
> increasing in confidence, skill, sensitivity, and aware-
> ness.

The good or professional officer is one whose conscience and compassion remain intact to restrain his use of force. This officer's understanding of the utility of brute force steels him to its use when absolutely necessary, thereby enabling him to do his duty effectively and sparing him any pangs of conscience afterwards. By contrast, a "bad" or unprofessional police officer is one whose tender conscience or surfeit of fellow-feeling incapacitates him when the use of force is unavoidable, thereby making him ineffective, or debilitates him with guilt if he does use it. Alternatively, it may be an officer whose hardened conscience or lack of fellow-feeling makes him overly zealous in employing brutal force with nary a qualm, or makes him cold and calculated in its employment while remaining indifferent to human suffering, as long as the ends justify the means — what Weber called a "really radical 'Machiavellianism'."[28] Note that Muir's stipulation that a good police officer is one who balances the virtues of "tragic sense" and "moral equanimity" (though not Aristotelian virtues) is Aristotelian in spirit. Muir's solution to the Dirty Harry problem is less logical than psychological. He still condones the use of force on utilitarian grounds, which allows that dirty means are justified by worthy ends — the very point at issue — and so begs the question. The problem remains unsolved. Instead, he gives the officer a prescription for living with the problem and not being incapacitated by it in the line of duty.

Kleinig's evaluation of the use of dirty means (or "dirty hands" as he calls it) is deontological. He thinks that, though there may be some genuine moral dilemmas in which whatever the officer does he must do wrong, the examples traditionally given of the Dirty Harry problem do not decisively show that we are morally justified in using dirty means. For one thing, they lack those morally relevant details which, if known, would clearly show that the officer is not necessarily ensnared in a dilemma in which he has no choice but to do wrong, but that he may have a "clean" option at his disposal:[29]

> My own reading of many of the actual cases that are put forward to show that some people sometimes must dirty their hands suggests that when we fill out the details a little more, and look at the options more carefully, the hands look more sweaty than dirty, or more filthy than dirty. And further, that some of the hypothetical examples that are put forward suffer from the lack of detail that we would expect to have in an actual situation, and so we are forcing our moral intuitions in circumstances for which they have not been properly prepared.

"What I am somewhat skeptical of," opines Kleinig, "is whether we can sometimes be said to be 'justified' in making a choice that nevertheless involves us in wrongdoing. It is the willingness to accommodate a certain form of incoherence in moral theory that I find troubling."[23] What worries Kleinig is the attitude of those defending the use of dirty means to achieve good ends that the wrong-doing of others sometimes forces us to do wrong ourselves and exculpates us. "Dirty hands," remarks Stocker, "reminds us of the perhaps archaic view that the immorality of the world can irredeemably stain our acts and lives. They show that not only our own immoralities, but also another's immoralities, can make it impossible to avoid doing what is evil."[31]

All attempts, then, to resolve the Dirty Harry problem fail because they either change or evade the problem or transfer the burden of it to another agent. Each of the four moral evaluations of dirty means examined is inconsistent because it presupposes and confuses different normative ethical theories. Thus, Klockars' view that the use of dirty means taints one's character is an aretaic perspective. His concern that the use of dirty means might lead to their proliferation and their becoming routine is utilitarian. His proposal that the officer who uses dirty means should be punished for precisely the same reason that he uses dirty means to punish suspects (since certain actions are intrinsically wrong whether carried out by civilians or police officers) is deontological. Delattre and Muir are fundamentally committed to virtue-based ethics. Their difference is that Delattre's position still contains utilitarian and deontological elements (e.g., his suggestion of a "slope of illegal action" and of the excusability of dirty acts). Muir's position is aretaic. His sole concern is that the use of dirty means be kept within bounds and occur in the context of the normal use of other, acceptable means. Kleinig maintains his deontological position by noting that those favoring dirty means have not shown decisively that such means are unavoidable because they use artificial examples and minimize the individual's moral autonomy. Of the four moral estimates of dirty means, Muir's appears the most internally consistent.

The following proposal for solving the Dirty Harry problem is less a solution than a dissolution of it. Its basis is that the Dirty Harry problem is not really a problem at all, but instead a pseudo-problem arising from a confusion of ethical theories. Remember that the heart of the problem is the paradoxical use of immoral means to realize moral ends. The means are immoral insofar as they involve the intrinsically wrong acts of torture or lying, but the ends are moral insofar as they promote justice or the common good. However, the very formulation of the problem mixes the incompatible theories of utilitarianism and deontologism, and it is precisely the mixing of these normative ethical theories that generates the problem. Thus, to speak of certain acts such as torture and lying as being intrinsically wrong is to speak deontologically, whereas to speak of the ends as being morally good because of their social benefits is to speak teleologically. Now, for the utilitarian there are no such things as intrinsically right or wrong acts because their moral quality is determined exclusively by their consequences. Acts are only right or wrong extrinsically. Therefore, any act (or rule), so long as it produces as many or more social benefits than an alternative, is deemed morally right. So, to speak of immoral means to realize moral ends is contradictory according to utilitarianism, because means are morally wrong only if they have socially deleterious results. The means cannot possibly be morally wrong if they result in public good. By contrast, for the deontologist, certain acts are either right or wrong intrinsically. The moral quality of the act is completely independent of its consequences. That intrinsically immoral means may lead to morally good results is irrelevant, as these have no bearing on the moral quality of the means. If the means are wrong in and of themselves, their results cannot make them right. The deontologist does not define an end's moral goodness in terms of the greatest pleasure or happiness produced for the greatest number of people, because doing so reduces the means to hypothetical imperatives — not to mention its committing the naturalistic fallacy. Consequently, from a strictly utilitarian or deontological viewpoint, the Dirty Harry problem vanishes. From the point of view of utilitarianism, the moral ends automatically make the dirty means morally right. From the point of view of deontologism, the dirty means are morally wrong regardless of their "moral" ends. The need, then, to reconcile the moral with the immoral is obviated.

Ought the police to use brutality or apply undue physical or psychological pressure to extract information? Should they make a false arrest or concoct some fraudulent excuse for conducting a search in order to administer curbside justice? The answer depends upon the normative ethical theory one adopts. A deontologist would answer "no" because such procedures are intrinsically wrong insofar as they involve harming others unduly, lying, or breaking the law. An adherent or aretaic ethics might answer affirmatively if the use of these procedures were appropriate, minimal, and strictly controlled.

The problem of force in corrections

The use of force in corrections parallels its use in law enforcement. There is the same unease about its employment in correctional institutions as there is on the streets because it is contrary to our commitment to peace and nonviolent solutions to social problems. Yet, there is the same grudging admission that the use of force is inescapable in some circumstances. There are opportunities open to corrections officers (similar to those offered to the police) to misuse and abuse their authority to employ force. The legitimacy of using coercion to keep order and to maintain discipline in correctional institutions is unquestionable;

what is morally illegitimate is to use it to victimize inmates. "Victimization" may be generally defined "as consisting of acts committed by
individuals and groups that go beyond the conditions imposed upon
prisoners by official institutional policy and state laws."[32] In other
words, whether an action victimizes an inmate depends upon whether
the action conforms to published regulations governing the prison in
which the inmate is incarcerated. This definition raises two issues.
One is the difficulty of determining whether a particular coercive
action does in fact conform to the regulations and of distinguishing
coercive acts of victimization from those necessary to protect human
life and health, as well as to maintain institutional order and discipline. Further, an institution's policy concerning coercion might itself
be morally questionable insofar as it sanctions the use of excessive
force in situations where it might be unnecessary. An example might
be the authorization of the use of "goon squads" to break up fights
and subdue unruly inmates. Even though such an action might conform to institutional policy, it would have the effect of victimizing
inmates.

Forms of victimization

Victimization of inmates in a correctional setting may take four forms:
physical, psychological, economic, or social. Physical victimization
might take the form of torture or sexual assault. The following brutal
example of torture occurred in a southern prison:[33]

> In the Tucker telephone, a naked prisoner was strapped
> to a table and electrodes were attached to his big toe
> and his penis. Electrical charges were then sent through
> his body which, in "long distance calls", were timed to
> cease just before he lost consciousness.

In another instance of brutality, again from the south, a juvenile was
the victim:[34]

> In testimony under oath, a 15-year old prisoner ac-
> cused the superintendent of an Arkansas institution of
> kicking and hitting him in the back and stomach while
> another staff member held him on the ground. The
> superintendent did not confirm this allegation, but
> he admitted driving a truck at 40 miles per hour
> with three prisoners draped over the hood and then

jamming on the brakes to catapult them to the ground
as a unique method of punishment.

There is evidence that the victimization of inmates through physical
abuse is more pervasive in juvenile facilities than in adult facilities.
The John Howard Association reported on the Illinois Youth Centers
at St. Charles and Geneva:[35]

Of 46 youths between the ages of 14 and 19 whom they
interviewed at St. Charles, 23 stated that they had been
slapped, kicked, punched, had their arms twisted or
were struck with an object by a staff member. About
half of the youths stated that they had witnessed staff
members committing such acts against other youngsters. Many of the staff members also admitted the use
of extensive corporal punishment, and there were several staff members who were consistently named as
physical abusers of children. One staff member admitted striking youngsters on different occasions with a
stick, a fishing pole and his hands. These situations did
not involve the use of necessary restraint to subdue a
youth that was attacking a staff member or another
youth. Instead, it was a matter of general brutality
when staff members were in bad moods.

Sexual assaults in correctional settings may be one of
three types. One involves the correctional officer himself who, promising rewards or threatening punishment, coerces juveniles to have sexual relations with
him. One youngster who had been sexually abused by
a staff member testified:[28]

He had intercourse with me about every two weeks. I
did not want to do it, but he talked about getting me
out of (here) faster and I wanted to get out because I
have been here a long time. I think the reason I did it
was I just came back from AWOL, and I thought I had
a long time to go so I thought I would get out of here.

Another type of sexual assault involves the officer's vicarious
participation in a sexual exploit. "In one incident a prisoner was
reported as having screamed for over an hour while he was being
gang raped in his cell within hearing distance of a correctional officer
who not only ignored the screams but who laughed at the victim
afterward."[37] Bowker has concluded that though the majority of

corrections officers eschew the various forms of physical victimization, there are enough who do not to ensure its continuation in American prisons:[38]

> Although most correctional officers in most prisons do not engage in any form of brutality and are only concerned with defending themselves against attack, there are enough officers who have values and beliefs that favor brutality and enough incidents that seem to require some sort of a show of force by officers so that there is a steady stream of minor unnecessary or excessive acts of violence in America's prisons, punctuated by occasional acts in which officers go far beyond any reasonable standard of the application of necessary force.

The psychological victimization of inmates leaves no scars and so is invisible, but it is perhaps the more insidious for that very reason. Bowker observed personally the following instance:[39]

> The sergeant placed letters to a prisoner where the prisoner could see them but not reach them, and then claimed that there were no letters for that prisoner. The prisoner became quite agitated as a result and eventually developed considerable paranoia about his mail. In each incident, the officer tormented him throughout the day and then gave him the letters in the evening saying that he had just discovered them. Eventually, the prisoner lost control completely and was cited for a disciplinary infraction, which may well have been the officer's goal in the manipulation.

In other instances, psychological victimization may be so subtle as to elude proof, as in this case of a female inmate with a son in foster care:[40]

> The officer she worked for would wait until she was within hearing distance and then begin a conversation with a second correctional officer about how commonly foster children were mistreated. These discussions went on endlessly, concentrating on subjects such as starvation, corporal punishment, and sexual victimization. The prisoner was not allowed to speak, nor could she report the incidents to the administration. How could

she prove that the officers were deliberately practicing
psychological victimization against her? These inci-
dents, along with the mishandling of a medical condition by the prison physician, almost agitated her enough
to attempt an escape.

Psychological victimization may take the form of compromising a
prisoner by an officer's making public, or threatening to do so, embarrassing facts about the prisoner found in his file. Such psychological
victimization of inmates may lead to nervous breakdowns, self-de-
structive acts, and even suicide.

Inmates may be victimized economically by being exploited in
loan-sharking and contraband operations:[41]

A Tampa newspaper, investigating the homosexual
attack and murder of a 19-year-old prisoner, mentioned
that the prisoners who assaulted the victim were
middlemen for a loan racket run by the officer who was
supervising the area in which the prisoner was raped
and killed. Testimony revealed that the victim had
been subjected to sexual assault before his death as
punishment because the correctional officer believed
that he was "snitching" on him for selling ham from
the kitchen for private profit.

Especially insidious are cases where corrections officers are complicit
with inmates in *sub rosa* contraband but, to appear beyond suspicion,
will conscientiously report unsophisticated prisoners for contraband
violations. "Victimization in this instance consists of enforcing the
regulations that the officer should have been enforcing in a setting in
which the regulations were habitually ignored."[42] Economic exploita-
tion is not always the result of corrupt members of staff, but may be
sanctioned by law and institutional policy. Such is the case in using
prisoners as guinea pigs in drug testing, a practice now forbidden by
federal law, or exploiting their labor by maximizing profits at the
expense of safety, preventing their unionization, or paying substan-
dard wages.

Social victimization involves any form of racial or religious discrimination. Instances of blatantly racial discrimination were observed
by Carroll:[43]

Carroll describes an incident in which kissing between
a prisoner and a visitor, which was officially prohibited

but always permitted for same race couples, resulted
in the abrupt termination of a visit when a black prisoner kissed his white visitor. Carroll also observed
correctional officers admitting white visitors in inmate organizations without searches, but systematically searching visitors to black organizations and
conducting bodily post-visit searches of black prisoners three times as often as similar searches of white
prisoners.

Victimization may also occur when the staff delegates their super-
visory duties to prisoners, who then have the opportunity to abuse
their fellow inmates. According to Bowker, "Testimony in a federal
court alleged that a prisoner in a Texas institution had been set up as
a 'prison enforcer' for which he was rewarded with special privileges
such as a homosexual in his cell to service his sexual needs and the
authority to assault other prisoners at any time in the service of
maintaining institutional order."[44]

Explanations of victimization

Explanations of victimization within correctional facilities mirror explanations of corruption within law enforcement agencies. The constitutional sadism theory mirrors the "rotten apple" theory of police
corruption and blames the victimization of inmates on the flawed
character of individual staff members. Goffman's total institution theory
mirrors the institutional theory of police corruption and attributes
victimization to the structure and dynamics of the correctional institution itself. According to this theory, the maximum-security prison
resembles a totalitarian state. Its staff, whose ties to civilian life are cut,
are fully integrated into the life of the institution which they serve.
The theory suggests that staff members whose integration into institutional life is the more nearly complete would be more prone to
victimizing inmates than those whose integration is less so. There is
little support for this theory based on current research.[45]

Related to the total institution theory is the role theory. The role
theory states that people spontaneously assume the role assigned to
them within the institution. This theory was borne out by the Stanford
prison experiment in which psychologically normal college students
played the roles of guards or inmates in a mock prison setting. The
experiment had to be terminated because the students played their
roles too well, to the detriment of their psychological health:[46]

At the end of six days we had to close down our mock
prison because what we saw was frightening. It was no
longer apparent to most of the subjects (or to us) where
reality ended and the roles began. The majority had
indeed become prisoners or guards, no longer able to
clearly differentiated between role-playing and self.
There were dramatic changes in virtually every aspect
of their behavior, thinking and feeling. In less than a
week the experience of imprisonment undid (tempo-
rarily) a lifetime of learning: human values were suspended, self-concepts were challenged, and the ugliest,
most base, pathological side of human nature surfaced.
We were horrified because we saw some boys (guards)
treat others as if they were despicable animals, taking
pleasure in cruelty, while other boys (prisoners) became servile, dehumanized robots who though only of
escape, of their own individual survival and of their
mounting hatred for the guards.

Roughly a third of the guards tyrannized the inmates, whereas the
remainder did not intervene. Other theories of victimization variously explain it in terms of the staff's fear and distancing of inmates,
a rite of passage for new correctional officers, or the staff code of
silence.[47]

Moral justification of force

The use of force in correctional settings can be morally justified on
either utilitarian or retributive grounds. A utilitarian justification would
show that force is necessary for deterring the misbehavior of inmates
and so maintaining institutional order and discipline. A retributive
justification would indicate that the inmate's crime deserves punishment, which consists of his incarceration and subjection to the coercion that it entails. The moral use of force requires that its use be kept
to a bare minimum and that it be utilized only as a last resort. This is
required of both forms of justification. Thus, the utilitarian insists that
only that degree of force be used sufficient for deterrence and institutional order; excessive or unnecessary force might be counterproductive insofar as it could incite rebellion or be met with resistance,
attitudes hardly conducive to that rehabilitation which utilitarians
seek. The retributivist believes that justice requires that the degree of
force used on inmates be proportional to the offenses they commit in
prison; the use of either excessive or insufficient force is unjust. The

controlled use of force in correctional institutions, then, is morally justified on either teleological or deontological grounds. What is not justified under any circumstances is its excessive or unnecessary use. It is this excessive or unnecessary use of force that constitutes victimization. Victimizing prisoners is morally wrong on teleological grounds because it endangers institutional order and peace and runs contrary to the rehabilitative function of prisons, and it is wrong on deontological grounds because it is patently unjust and derogates the inmate's dignity. Justice Sandra Day O'Connor spoke from a deontological standpoint when she wrote, "When prison officials maliciously use force to cause harm, contemporary standards of decency always are violated."[48]

Even the moral use of force may appear proper when in fact it is rankly immoral. If force is used in cases where nonviolent means would suffice, it might easily be justified as a measure of last resort when in fact it was merely motivated by convenience. The use of excessive and unwarranted force can be readily made to seem to be in conformity with the policy regulating its use. Bowker illustrates this point:[49]

> A mentally ill prisoner was climbing a fence separating two prison yards and was fatally shot in the head by a prison officer who had commanded him to stop. The officer, who was stationed in a tower, probably was unaware of the mental condition of the prisoner and might not have taken that into account in any case. More importantly, he did not need to shoot the prisoner, as going from one prison yard to another does not constitute a risk of escape. Since the prisoner was unarmed, a shot in the leg rather than the head would have been more than sufficient even had he been climbing a fence on the boundary of the prison compound. The warden chose to ignore these arguments and immediately supported the action of the officer, saying that it was appropriate and required by institutional regulations. The local officials outside of the prison also accepted the judgment of the warden and declined prosecution in the case.

Notes

1. Muir, Jr., William K., *Police: Streetcorner Politicians*, The University of Chicago Press, Chicago, IL, 1977, p. 37.

2. Bittner, Egon, *The Functions of the Police in Modern Society: A Review of Background Factors, Current Practices, and Possible Role Models*, Jason Aronson, New York, 1975, pp. XI, 36.

3. Hobbes, Thomas, *Leviathan*, Clarendon Press, Oxford, 1958, p. 128.

4. Bittner, Egon, *The Functions of the Police in Modern Society: A Review of Background Factors, Current Practices, and Possible Role Models*, Jason Aronson, New York, 1975, pp. ix–x, 106.

5. Goldstein, Herman, *Policing a Free Society*, Ballinger Publishing, Cambridge, MA, 1977, p. 1.

6. Hobbes, Thomas, *Leviathan*, Clarendon Press, Oxford, 1958, pp. 96–97.

7. Bittner, Egon, *The Functions of the Police in Modern Society: A Review of Background Factors, Current Practices, and Possible Role Models*, Jason Aronson, New York, 1975, pp. 17–20.

8. Bittner, Egon, *The Functions of the Police in Modern Society: A Review of Background Factors, Current Practices, and Possible Role Models*, Jason Aronson, New York, 1975, pp. 17–20.

9. Bittner, Egon, *The Functions of the Police in Modern Society: A Review of Background Factors, Current Practices, and Possible Role Models*, Jason Aronson, New York, 1975, pp. 17–20.

10. Bittner, Egon, *The Functions of the Police in Modern Society: A Review of Background Factors, Current Practices, and Possible Role Models*, Jason Aronson, New York, 1975, pp. 17–20.

11. Bittner, Egon, *The Functions of the Police in Modern Society: A Review of Background Factors, Current Practices, and Possible Role Models*, Jason Aronson, New York, 1975, p. 21.

12. Weber, Max, Politics as a vocation, in *From Max Weber: Essays in Sociology*, Gerth, H. and Mills, C.W., Eds., Oxford University Press, New York, 1946, p. 123.

13. Quoted in Muir, Jr., William K., *Police: Streetcorner Politicians*, The University of Chicago Press, Chicago, IL, 1977, p. 3.

14. Klockars, Carl B., The Dirty Harry problem, *The Annals of the American Academy of Political and Social Science*, 452(Nov.), 34–35, 43, 1980.

15. Klockars, Carl B., The Dirty Harry problem, *The Annals of the American Academy of Political and Social Science*, 452(Nov.), 36-37, 1980.

16. Klockars, Carl B., The Dirty Harry problem, *The Annals of the American Academy of Political and Social Science*, 452(Nov.), 39, 36, 1980.

17. Klockars, Carl B., The Dirty Harry problem, *The Annals of the American Academy of Political and Social Science*, 452(Nov.), 39, 36, 1980.

18. Klockars, Carl B., The Dirty Harry problem, *The Annals of the American Academy of Political and Social Science*, 452(Nov.), 44, 1980.

19. Klockars, Carl B., The Dirty Harry problem, *The Annals of the American Academy of Political and Social Science*, 452(Nov.), 44, 1980.

20. Klockars, Carl B., The Dirty Harry problem, *The Annals of the American Academy of Political and Social Science*, 452(Nov.), 45, 1980.

21. Klockars, Carl B., The Dirty Harry problem, *The Annals of the American Academy of Political and Social Science*, 452(Nov.), 45, 1980.

22. Skolnick, Jerome, *Justice Without Trial*, 2nd ed., John Wiley & Sons, New York, 1975, pp. 196–197.

23. Klockars, Carl B., The Dirty Harry problem, *The Annals of the American Academy of Political and Social Science*, 452(Nov.), 45-46, 1980. (However, I think Klockars distorts Bittner's conceptions as to the proper role of policing. It is true that he wants to expand it beyond strict law enforcement to include peacekeeping activities; nevertheless, he insists that the capacity and authority to use force is the very core of the police role.)

24. Goldstein, Herman, *Policing a Free Society*, Ballinger Publishing, Cambridge, MA, 1977, p. 72.

25. Klockars, Carl B., The Dirty Harry problem, *The Annals of the American Academy of Political and Social Science*, 452(Nov.), 47, 1980.

26. Delattre, Edwin J., *Character and Cops: Ethics in Policing*, AEI Press, Washington D.C., 1994, p. 211.

27. Muir, Jr., William K., *Police: Streetcorner Politicians*, The University of Chicago Press, Chicago, IL, 1977, pp. 3–4.

28. Weber, Max, Politics as a vocation, in *From Max Weber: Essays in Sociology*, Gerth, H. and Mills, C.W., Eds., Oxford University Press, New York, 1946, p. 123.

29. Kleinig, John, *The Ethics of Policing*, Cambridge University Press, London, 1996, p. 57.

30. Kleinig, John, *The Ethics of Policing*, Cambridge University Press, London, 1996, p. 57.

31. Stocker, Michael A.G., *Plural and Conflicting Values*, Oxford University Press, New York, 1990, p. 22.

32. Bowker, Lee H., *Prison Victimization*, Elsevier, New York, 1980, p. 102.

33. Bowker, Lee H., *Prison Victimization*, Elsevier, New York, 1980, p. 104.

34. Bowker, Lee H., *Prison Victimization*, Elsevier, New York, 1980, p. 104.

35. *Illinois Youth Centers at St. Charles and Geneva*, John Howard Association, Chicago, IL, 1974 (quoted in Bowker, Lee H., *Prison Victimization*, Elsevier, New York, 1980, p. 111).

36. Bartollas, Clemens; Miller, Stuart J.; and Dinitz, Simon, *Juvenile Victimization: The Institutional Paradox*, John Wiley & Sons, New York, 1976, p. 214.

37. Davis, Alan J., Sexual assaults in the Philadelphia prison system and sheriffs' vans, *Trans-Action*, 6, 11, 1968 (quoted in Bowker, Lee H., *Prison Victimization*, Elsevier, New York, 1980, p. 110).

38. Bowker, Lee H., *Prison Victimization*, Elsevier, New York, 1980, p. 107.

39. Bowker, Lee H., *Prison Victimization*, Elsevier, New York, 1980, pp. 113–114.

40. Bowker, Lee H., *Prison Victimization*, Elsevier, New York, 1980, pp. 113–114.

41. Bowker, Lee H., *Prison Victimization*, Elsevier, New York, 1980, pp. 116, 117.

42. Bowker, Lee H., *Prison Victimization*, Elsevier, New York, 1980, pp. 116, 117.

43. Carroll, Leo, *Hacks, Blacks and Cons*, D.C. Heath, Lexington, MA, 1974, pp. 123–124, 127–128 (paraphrased in Bowker, Lee H., *Prison Victimization*, Elsevier, New York, 1980, p. 119).

44. Bowker, Lee H., *Prison Victimization*, Elsevier, New York, 1980, p. 119.

45. Bowker, Lee H., *Prison Victimization*, Elsevier, New York, 1980, pp. 120–121.

46. Zimbardo, Philip, Pathology of imprisonment, *Society*, 9(6), 4, 1972 (quoted in Bowker, Lee H., *Prison Victimization*, Elsevier, New York, 1980, p. 121).

47. Crouch, Ben M., Guard work in transition, in *The Dilemmas of Corrections: Contemporary Readings*, Hass, K.C. and Alpert, G.P., Eds., 3rd ed., Waveland Press, Prospect Heights, IL, 1995, pp. 186–189.

48. *Hudson v. McMillian*, 112 S. Ct. 995, 997, 1992.

49. Bowker, Lee H., *Prison Victimization*, Elsevier, New York, 1980, pp. 107.

Index

Index

A

A Clockwork Orange, 215
A Doctor in Spite of Himself, 42
A Man for All Seasons, 6
Abolitionists, 8
act-agapism, 130, 131
act-deontologism, 103–107, 124
act-utilitarianism, 213, 214, 235
    vs. rule-utilitarianism, 62
ad hoc fallacy, 46–47
advice, 144–145
aesthetics, 18, 19
afterlife, 15, 18, 52
agape, 128, 132, 133, 134. *See also* love, ethics of
agapistic ethics, 35, 36, 37, 128–129, 233, 235. *See also* love, ethics of
    as aretaic ethics, 129–130
    as virtue-based ethics, 129–130
    bribery, and, 298
    kinds of, 130
    natural law, and, 129
    principles of, 133
Age of Enlightenment, 63, 265
altruism, 42, 46, 115
    vs. ethical egoism, 49
altruistic egoism, 64. *See also* utilitarianism
analysis
    critical, 13
    vs. synthesis, 13

Andronicus of Rhodes, 15
animals, moral rights of, 63
anthropology, 11, 12, 16
anthropomorphism, 83
antinomianism, 130, 131
applied ethics, 19, 21–22
appropriateness, 35
Aquinas, St. Thomas, 12, 79, 87, 118, 125, 129
aretaic
    defined, 146
    ethics, 35, 118, 126–127, 233, 235
        bribery, and, 298
        dirty means, and, 317, 320
    judgments, 36, 146, 147
    statement, in moral argument, 177
arguments, 171–174
    definition of, 171
    detecting, 174–175
    evaluation of, 17
    guidelines for evaluating, 179
    incomplete (enthymeme), 175
    logical form of, 172
    sound, 172
    validity of, 171–172, 177, 179
Aristophanes, 189
Aristotle, 7, 12, 15, 16, 25, 26, 54, 55, 56, 72, 80–81, 118–127, 172, 317
assumption, as missing premise, 175